T0291451

A PRACTICAL GUIDE TO MACROECONOMICS

There is an uncomfortably large gulf between academic research and what policy economists use to understand the economy. *A Practical Guide to Macroeconomics* shows how economists at policy institutions approach important real-world questions and explains why existing academic work – theoretical and empirical – has little to offer them. It argues that this disconnect between theory and practice is problematic for policymaking and the economics profession and looks at what's needed to make academic research more relevant for policy. The book also covers topics related to economic measurement and provides a compact overview of U.S. macroeconomic statistics that will help researchers use these data in a better-informed way.

Jeremy B. Rudd has worked as a policy economist for the past thirty years at the Council of Economic Advisers, the U.S. Treasury Department, and the Federal Reserve Board. He was a Deputy Assistant Secretary for economic policy at the Treasury Department in 2007–2008 and 2009–2010.

A Practical Guide to Macroeconomics

JEREMY B. RUDD

CAMBRIDGE
UNIVERSITY PRESS

Shaftesbury Road, Cambridge CB2 8EA, United Kingdom

One Liberty Plaza, 20th Floor, New York, NY 10006, USA

477 Williamstown Road, Port Melbourne, VIC 3207, Australia

314–321, 3rd Floor, Plot 3, Splendor Forum, Jasola District Centre, New Delhi – 110025, India

103 Penang Road, #05–06/07, Visioncrest Commercial, Singapore 238467

Cambridge University Press is part of Cambridge University Press & Assessment, a department of the University of Cambridge.

We share the University's mission to contribute to society through the pursuit of education, learning and research at the highest international levels of excellence.

www.cambridge.org
Information on this title: www.cambridge.org/9781009465786

DOI: 10.1017/9781009465779

First published 2024

A catalogue record for this publication is available from the British Library

A Cataloging-in-Publication data record for this book is available from the Library of Congress

ISBN 978-1-009-46578-6 Hardback
ISBN 978-1-009-46579-3 Paperback

. . . perchè i nostri discorsi hanno a essere sopra un mondo sensibile, e non sopra un mondo di carta.

(. . . our arguments have to be about the world we experience, not about a world made of paper.)

Galileo Galilei
Dialogue Concerning the Two Chief World Systems (1632)

Contents

Figures

Tables

Preface

I decided to write this book when I came to a surprising realization: Very little of the theoretical or empirical research that was being done by mainstream academic macroeconomists was actually all that useful to me in my job as a policy economist.

On the theoretical side, a large fraction of the papers being written seemed to have the goal of showing that something observed in practice could be explained in (received) theory. That's bad science – as Richard Feynman used to point out, you should never use the same data to test a hypothesis that you initially used to come up with it. And it's not clear how such an approach is useful from a practical standpoint unless and until there have been multiple attempts to empirically validate the model's proposed mechanisms (something that rarely if ever seemed to happen).

Other mainstream theoretical works simply came across as pointless exercises in recreational mathematics (in a few degenerate cases, that actually appeared to be the principal goal). In papers like these, a researcher would set themself a question that no one had really asked – like whether it was possible to rigorously demonstrate that a negative shock to aggregate demand could cause a recession – and that was only challenging to answer because of the particular model economy that they insisted on working with. Here too, it was difficult to see what relevance research like this could possibly have for a practitioner.

A third group of models that sought to combine theory and empirics – dynamic stochastic general equilibrium models – also turned out to have surprisingly little to offer in a policy setting. (At my own institution, models like these are mostly employed to provide a veneer of analytical respectability to what are essentially judgmental risk-assessment exercises.) Here, the main problem was that many modellers were starting from ostensibly microfounded specifications of household and firm behavior that had never been all that compelling in the first place. In terms of empirics, modellers who didn't simply rely on calibration would add in as many extensions – and, on occasion, modifications to their "priors" – as were needed to get their models to yield impulse responses that weren't first-order daft. The end result was a mare's nest of incredible identifying assumptions, hard-to-believe transmission mechanisms, and correspondingly hard-to-swallow policy prescriptions.

The situation was equally unsatisfactory as far as pure empirical work was concerned. To give an example from my own subfield, inflation, the papers being written by academic researchers either used data in such an uninformed way as to be effectively worthless or identified "puzzles" using a baseline empirical framework that was two or three decades out of date. More broadly, many empirical papers were of the fullness-of-time variety, with findings that vanished once a couple of data revisions were under the bridge, or after five or ten years were added to the sample period.

For a policy science like economics, a gap between academic and applied work that is this wide is disturbing. As we will see, policy analysts do use vaguely plausible analytical and empirical frameworks in order to forecast and interpret economic developments. But these have obvious limits – for one thing, they tend not to be too helpful when analysts are faced with unusual events or atypical policy actions. Similarly, it's difficult to understand why academic economists would be satisfied generating research that is of such little use to the people producing inputs to policy, or to anyone else who would like to understand how the economy actually works.

The purpose of this book, then, is to provide a critical examination of some of the assumptions and results of mainstream academic macroeconomics from my personal vantage point as a practicing policy economist. The approach I take is to ask whether we can say anything useful – theoretically or empirically – about several important macroeconomic topics, and what that in turn implies for the advice we can give to policymakers. My goal is not to settle any of these questions (they're hard), or to prove that one particular way of doing economics is better than another. Rather, it's to argue that continuing uncritically along the same course is unlikely to yield useful insights into reality, or to produce analysis that can (or should) inform policy. And the book's intended audience is anyone who is as deeply perplexed about these subjects as I am.

This book has another aim as well, which is to familiarize readers with some key features of real-world macro data. Unless they are actually in a policy institution, very few economists ever gain a working acquaintance with topics related to economic measurement – either the analytical framework that underpins how economic aggregates are measured or the way in which the idealized variables of theoretical models can be best mapped into the data series produced by national statistical agencies. While much of the work in this area is properly the domain of specialists, there are many pitfalls associated with using macro data that are easily avoided with only a basic understanding of how these statistics are defined and put together.

Finally, potential readers should be cautioned that the empirical results I discuss only relate to the US economy. That's an unavoidable consequence of my own background as an applied (domestic) macroeconomist in the United States whose own research has only used US economic data. Since these are the data, institutions, and empirical regularities I know the most about (more correctly, they are the only things I know anything at all about), I hope that readers will benefit from whatever understanding I can bring to these topics while also excusing the potential lack of applicability – and narrow chauvinism – that such a focus implies.

1

Introduction: Is Macroeconomics Useful?

Microeconomics is what economists know about. But macroeconomics is what they want to know about. That's what makes it so interesting.
                                    Benjamin Friedman (quoted in Fisher, 1993)

In 1936, in the middle of the worst economic outcome the modern world had ever seen, John Maynard Keynes published a book entitled *The General Theory of Employment, Interest and Money*. The purpose of the book was to try to explain how a market economy could find itself persistently stuck in a situation where, despite ample industrial capacity and willing workers, unemployment and deprivation were widespread. Pretty much no one reads Keynes anymore (especially economists), but the *General Theory* did leave one enduring legacy: It gave rise to macroeconomics as a separate branch of economics, in which the units of study are economic aggregates – things like the overall levels of production, employment, and inflation in an economy.

One other piece of the Keynesian legacy was not so enduring. This was the implicit assumption that in order to explain the behavior of macroeconomic aggregates, it is necessary to use a method of analysis that is distinct from the microeconomic strategy of analyzing the world in terms of optimizing households and firms whose actions are (somehow) coordinated so as to yield an equilibrium in which supply and demand are equal. That disconnect between macroeconomics and microeconomics was viewed by some economists (not all) as a bit of an embarrassment, but it was usually justified on the grounds that pathologies like business cycles and involuntary unemployment simply didn't seem like "equilibrium" phenomena in the microeconomic sense. But, in 1979, Lucas and Sargent published a broadside that argued this latter feature of macroeconomics was wrongheaded

1

and – as far as informing economic policy went – counterproductive.[1] Lucas
and Sargent maintained that macroeconomic phenomena *were* equilibrium
phenomena and could be studied in a Walrasian general equilibrium framework like the one developed by Arrow, Debreu, and others. Today, variants of
the Lucas–Sargent approach permeate mainstream macroeconomic theory,
including "new-Keynesian" economics and other attempts to construct
optimizing, equilibrium models that can produce "Keynesian" results.

   In this chapter, I discuss reasons why the existing general equilibrium
framework of microeconomics isn't suitable for analyzing macroeconomic
questions (or microeconomic questions, for that matter). I also consider the
separate question of whether and to what extent it makes sense to take an
aggregative approach to studying the economy, and the difficulties we face
in choosing to do so.

1.1 Existence versus Stability (and Why the Latter Matters More)

It is one of those ironies of history that almost at the same time that Lucas
and Sargent were laying out their case to macroeconomists, *micro*economic
theorists were starting to have serious doubts about the predictive content
and overall usefulness of general equilibrium theory. The theory's predictive
content had been called into question by a set of papers published between
1973 and 1976 that demonstrated that the assumptions needed to secure the
existence of a Walrasian general equilibrium were not enough to tie down
the aggregate properties of the economy in any meaningful way.[2] In particular, stronger – and therefore special – assumptions were needed to demonstrate that an equilibrium was unique; moreover, no general comparative
statics results could be achieved (it wasn't even possible to unambiguously
demonstrate that increasing the amount of a good in an economy would
lower its price).[3]

---

[1] Like most pieces of agitprop, the Lucas and Sargent paper vastly overstated the deficiencies
   of the old order. And, as in most revolutionary movements, counterrevolutionary activity
   was dealt with harshly – witness Lucas's (1994) choleric reaction to Ball and Mankiw (1994).
[2] The papers were Sonnenschein (1972, 1973), Mantel (1974, 1976), and Debreu (1974). In
   a nutshell, what they showed was that summing individual demands led to an aggregate
   (excess) demand relation that was continuous, didn't exhibit money illusion, and obeyed
   Walras's law – but that was it. Conversely, any function that had these properties could
   actually occur as the excess demand function of an economy.
[3] More recent attempts to salvage general equilibrium theory from the Sonnenschein–
   Mantel–Debreu wreckage have met with little success; see Brown and Matzkin (1996),
   Brown and Shannon (2000), and Nachbar (2002) for some representative examples.

However, there was an even more problematic issue with general equilibrium theory that was starting to become apparent around this time: While the theory could prove that an equilibrium existed, it couldn't show that it would be *stable*, in the sense that mechanisms were present that would return the economy to equilibrium if it happened to be moved away from it, or that would bring the economy to an equilibrium (not necessarily Walrasian) if it didn't start off there. For a macroeconomist, stability seems far more relevant than existence: A basic question in macroeconomics is whether the economy will recover "on its own" after a recession or whether any self-correcting tendencies are too weak to be relied on (or too unreliable to depend on). Without a demonstration of stability and a theory of the out-of-equilibrium processes that deliver it, that question can't be answered with any generality. Relatedly, a belief that the economy will eventually return to a state of full employment as long as prices and wages are given enough time to adjust receives no justification from the existence proofs of general equilibrium theory.

The stability problem has not been solved – and probably never will be – though that fact no longer seems to vex microeconomists overly much. Perhaps the best run at the problem in the context of standard general equilibrium theory was made forty years ago by Fisher (1983), who didn't even find his own (partial) solution all that convincing. The technical problem involves finding a realistic trading process that will act as a Lyapunov function (intuitively, a Lyapunov function is a function that "squeezes" the state of a system toward its equilibrium point; it is used in mathematics to demonstrate the stability of differential equation systems). One reasonably realistic candidate might be a process in which the set of trading opportunities that are perceived as profitable at disequilibrium prices becomes smaller and smaller over time as agents arbitrage them away. The reason Fisher concluded the problem is likely insoluble is that the ability of real-world agents to act on new perceived opportunities for arbitrage – including those that turn out to be incorrect – makes stability impossible to demonstrate without additional strong (and unrealistic) assumptions.

Despite its truly fundamental importance, equilibrium stability receives virtually no attention from microtheorists nowadays. As evidence, Mas-Colell, Whinston, and Green's (1995) exhaustive survey of microeconomic theory devotes only seven of its 980-plus pages to the question of stability (and that mostly to the uninteresting and largely irrelevant concept of so-called tâtonnement stability), but ultimately asserts that the topic is not central to economics (p. 620). That claim is hard to take seriously, though: If you can't show that an economy will converge to a particular equilibrium – and do so relatively rapidly – then it's difficult to argue that such an equilibrium has any real-world relevance, or any claim to priority as an object of study. For instance, comparative statics exercises seem rather pointless if one can't argue that the economy will actually tend to move to its new equilibrium point; likewise, concepts like Friedman's (1968) "natural rate" of unemployment – which is explicitly associated with a Walrasian equilibrium – have no meaningful content.

As Fisher (1983, 2011) also points out, various interesting complications arise once we take the stability problem seriously. Many of these are also extremely relevant to macroeconomics.

- If households and firms find themselves in an economy that is away from equilibrium, they will see that prices can change and will also likely realize that their plans to buy and sell might not come to fruition. Perceived constraints on sales in product and labor markets can, in turn, give rise to Keynesian-style (and decidedly non-Walrasian) underemployment equilibria.[4]

- A claim that the efficiency properties of competitive equilibrium can be enjoyed by instituting "market reforms" is specious, since there's no guarantee that such an equilibrium will actually result (and other bad things could happen along the way).

- Once trading out of equilibrium occurs, phenomena such as path dependence and hysteresis can easily arise. Consider the Edgeworth box diagram in Figure 1.1, which shows a two-person exchange economy with a unique Walrasian equilibrium at point A (given by the intersection of the offer curves ω_1 and ω_2) that is supported by prices P_A from the initial endowment E. Say that prices instead start out at P_B. Points along P_B are not Walrasian equilibria (there is excess demand for the x-axis good and excess supply of the y-axis good). However, mutually beneficial trades are possible, and if they are allowed to do so at the disequilibrium price, then any subsequent equilibrium can easily differ from A – even (especially) if relative prices are restored to P_A.

- Finally, the assumption that markets clear or that any disequilibrium states are resolved quickly enough that the economy will always be at a rational expectations equilibrium is simply that – an assumption.

---

[4] Interestingly, in situations like these Walras's law will only hold in an expectational form – see Fisher (1983, chapter 7).

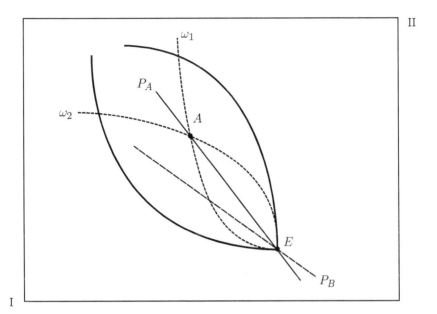

Figure 1.1 Path dependence under disequilibrium trading.

1.2 Microfoundations and Aggregation

If Lucas and Sargent's call to model macroeconomic phenomena using the tools of general equilibrium theory has so little to recommend it, what about their prescription that macroeconomic theory must be grounded in the optimizing behavior of households and firms? Here, again, we quickly run into trouble. Since the 1950s, economists have become increasingly aware that there is no reason to expect that individual-level behavior will show up in any recognizable form in the aggregate unless additional highly restrictive assumptions are made.[5] Worse still, even the simple *time-series* properties of individual-level variables are unlikely to be preserved once the data are aggregated up. And while there do exist ways to deal with this problem – some good, most bad – even the sounder methods are not especially useful from a practical perspective.

Start with one of the bad solutions: the assumption that the overall economy can be described in terms of an "average" household or firm, a so-called *representative agent*. Even today, a remarkable number of macroeconomists

---

[5] Even without being acquainted with this earlier literature, the Sonnenschein–Mantel–Debreu results should give us a hint that such troubles are lurking in the background.

use representative-agent models for both theoretical and empirical research despite there being absolutely no reasonable justification for doing so (a fact that has been well-known for years). As Kirman (1992) details:

- There is no way to formally justify that a combination of individual maximizing agents will itself act like a single maximizer – or, put more starkly, "[t]here is simply no direct relation between individual and collective behavior" (p. 118).
- Using a representative-agent framework to model the effect of a policy change is apt to be misleading: Once a policy setting (or some other feature of the model) is altered, the representative agent can end up responding in a manner that is different to what we would find by aggregating each individual's response to the policy (or other) change. Hence, one thing that makes microfoundations useful in principle – namely, the idea that by explicitly grounding the behavioral responses of the economy's members in optimizing behavior that reflects their "tastes and technology," we can obtain a structural model that is suitable for policy evaluation – is actually absent from representative-agent models.
- In the case of a representative consumer, the "preferences" of the representative agent need not match the preferences of the individuals in the economy, even if each individual happens to prefer the same thing. That is, situations can arise in which the representative agent prefers A to B, even though every individual prefers B to A.

Similarly, on the production side, the conditions needed in order to talk about a "representative firm" (in the sense of an aggregate production relation) are sufficiently stringent that they are unlikely to hold for any economy at any point in time (Fisher, 1993), a point that we will discuss at length in Chapter 4.

In a fundamental sense, it is strange that a macroeconomist would even *want* to entertain the notion of using a representative- or single-agent approach for modelling or estimation purposes. Many of the most interesting decisions in the economy – for example, those pertaining to the choice of how much to produce, hire, consume, and invest – likely reflect behavioral and informational feedbacks that are generated by the myriad interactions that take place among individual agents and groups. As a result, we might expect at least some macroeconomic phenomena to be *emergent*, manifesting behaviors and dynamics that, because they are the result of these interactions, cannot be predicted simply by scaling up or extrapolating the behavior of a single (isolated) agent. Put more simply, we probably aren't going to be able to capture the dynamics of groups of agents very well if we restrict ourselves to considering a single representative agent. And studying the dynamics of groups of agents is pretty much what macroeconomics is all about.

Why, then, does the representative-agent approach continue to pervade macroeconomics? Very likely, some simply don't realize how shaky the justification for this framework actually is, while some others probably don't much care. I also expect that very few people have ever had a paper rejected from a mainstream journal for assuming a representative agent – just as how in the 1970s, no procurement manager ever lost their job for buying IBM. Additionally, these frameworks are very tractable relative to most alternatives. That said, someone of a critical mindset can claim with strong justification that in essentially every context, the predictions that are derived from representative-agent models are at best meaningless and at worst completely misleading. And at a minimum, such models have no claim to being "microfounded" in any serious way.[6]

In recent years, there has been an attempt to move away from a strict representative-agent approach by allowing for some form of heterogeneity among agents (typically consumers). For example, the so-called heterogeneous agent new-Keynesian models try to address a shortcoming associated with the transmission mechanism of monetary policy in standard new-Keynesian models. In the standard model, monetary policy affects the real economy through an intertemporal substitution channel: Changes in real interest rates cause a representative household to either postpone its current consumption or bring forward its future consumption. The problem is that empirical estimates of the sensitivity of consumption to interest rate changes find it to be quite low, which implies that this channel can't really be consistent with monetary policy having a large effect on aggregate demand. The proposed solution involves introducing what amounts to a Keynesian multiplier mechanism by adding households whose consumption is closely tied to their current income; as a result, even a modest response of spending to a change in the return on liquid assets can yield sizeable overall effects on consumption.[7]

---

[6] As a colleague of mine once put it, "I have no problem with microfoundations. But in what way is $\max E_t \sum_{i=0}^{T} \beta^i U(c_{t+i})$ microfounded?"

[7] See Kaplan, Moll, and Violante (2018) for a canonical example. This description omits a number of subtleties associated with these models; we will consider them – along with their shortcomings – in greater detail in Chapter 7.

A second example is provided by Angeletos and Lian (2022), which attempts to explain why shifts in aggregate demand can drive business cycles. In an economy with a representative consumer (and full information), a shock to aggregate demand should not have a "multiplier" effect – that is, an effect on output larger than what is implied by the shock itself – because permanent income is unchanged. In order to generate a larger effect, Angeletos and Lian assume that consumers are imperfectly informed about the state of the aggregate economy, and so misperceive an aggregate demand shock as an idiosyncratic shock to their (permanent) income (the formal setup uses the sort of "islands" economy that Lucas, 1972 employed in order to ensure that individual misperceptions didn't cancel out in the aggregate). The resulting reduction in consumption and aggregate demand induces additional pessimism about permanent income, a further decline in demand, and so on, thereby amplifying the effect of the initial shock.

Although these models do incorporate heterogeneity of a sort, the rationale for doing so has nothing to do with the fact that representative-agent models are theoretically suspect, but rather reflects an attempt to deal with the problems that arise when consumer behavior is modelled using a permanent-income framework with rational expectations. Put differently, approaches like these do highlight the fragility of conclusions derived from representative-agent frameworks, and if one insists on modelling household behavior as the outcome of an intertemporal optimization problem, then modifications like these will be needed in order to obtain halfway plausible results. But these analyses still work within a market-clearing framework where economic fluctuations are essentially equilibrium phenomena. And they still assume agents who solve complicated optimization and information-acquisition problems that are not all that likely to provide realistic descriptions of individual behavior (at least, they have never been shown to do so).[8]

While using representative agents to model the behavior of economic aggregates has no justification and shouldn't be done, we unfortunately don't have workable alternatives that *can* be usefully employed in a practical setting. On the theoretical side, at least two alternatives have been proposed; although both are interesting and explicitly model interactions among heterogeneous agents, neither has found much applicability to policy analysis.

---

[8] We will return to some of these themes in Chapter 3. It also isn't clear that a model that relies on such a contrived setup as an islands economy can seriously be labelled "microfounded" – as Solow (1983) once pointed out, no one has ever discovered such an island (or even found a message in a bottle that came from one). Much the same criticism can be levelled against models that rely on contrivances like Dixit–Stiglitz aggregation.

The first alternative, *agent-based modelling*, constructs model economies with large numbers of heterogenous agents who follow specified behavioral rules (including rules governing how their expectations are formulated) and who interact with each other in different ways and in different venues, such as making transactions in different markets.[9] These model economies are simulated with a computer, and these simulations can generate complex aggregate dynamics despite assuming relatively simple individual-level decision rules.

What has so far limited the applicability of this approach in a policy setting is the difficulty in demonstrating that the models' predictions are robust and that the models themselves faithfully capture some feature of real-world economic dynamics. For the former, there is always a sneaking suspicion that a particular result depends on the specific decision rules agents are assumed to follow (and apparently this is difficult to check in large models – see Dawid and Gatti, 2018, p. 70). For the latter, the fact that a model can generate business cycles or financial crises, or roughly match the dynamics of (or correlations between) macroeconomic aggregates like real GDP or inflation might not be viewed as sufficient validation of the model (though in fairness, it's not clear that any other type of theoretical model is tested more rigorously). Similarly, the fact that these models' principal strength is that they can generate emergent dynamics means almost by definition that it will be difficult to describe and assess the causal mechanisms that are at play in a particular model, and especially how they depend on the way that individual-level behavior and interactions are modelled.

A second theoretical alternative is to take a page from physics – specifically, statistical physics – and model aggregate phenomena in terms of the statistical distributions of outcomes that are generated by large numbers of interacting agents. This approach, which is developed at length by Aoki (1996, 2002) and Aoki and Yoshikawa (2007), is intriguing – there is an intuitive appeal in thinking about a macroeconomic equilibrium as an inherently stochastic object that emerges from the bottom up, rather than as the result of feeding stochastic shocks into a system of (typically linear) equations that supposedly capture the average responses of different classes of agents.[10] However, the methodology has not really caught on. One likely

---

[9] An early example of this sort of approach in a macroeconomic context is described in chapter 9 of Nelson and Winter (1982); see Dawid and Gatti (2018) for a relatively up-to-date overview of some macroeconomic applications of agent-based modelling.

[10] In a preface to Aoki and Yoshikawa (2007), Yoshikawa draws a connection between this approach and Tobin's (1972) conception of a "stochastic macro-equilibrium" in which "random intersectoral shocks keep individual [markets] in diverse states of disequilibrium"

reason is that the mathematics used are unfamiliar to most economists (after all, physics envy doesn't imply physics training). On a deeper level, though, many of the theoretical models derived using this approach are closer to proofs of concept – that is, demonstrations that one can get models of this sort to generate phenomena such as endogenous cyclical movements in aggregate production. Such exercises seem reminiscent of Slutzky's (1937) famous result that moving sums of random variables can yield time series whose fluctuations *look* like business cycles – interesting and suggestive, but hard to know what to make of.[11]

On the empirical side, an approach to modelling the behavior of aggregates in a way that tries to correctly capture the effects of individual heterogeneity involves starting from models that are fit to microlevel data. For example, if we have panel data on household income, expenditures, and other characteristics, we can fit a consumer demand system and allow its parameters to depend on observed household attributes. The resulting estimates can be summed or (equivalently) averaged in order to obtain "correct" aggregate relations. Generally, these relations will be different from what we would get by evaluating the demand system using the aggregates themselves (for example, average income or the fraction of households with a particular attribute): Intuitively, any sort of nonlinearity in the specification, including interactions between household attributes and variables like household income, will drive wedges between the various relations.[12]

In practical terms, the existence of these sorts of issues implies that we will not be able to recover individual-level behavioral relationships using aggregate data; similarly, we should not expect the restrictions on individual behavior that are implied by microtheory to be applicable to an aggregate model, or to be apparent in aggregate data. In fact, it turns out that even the *time-series* properties of individual-level data will not generally carry

---

but "the perpetual flux of particular markets produces fairly definite aggregate outcomes." (The approach is also very appealing to those whose vision of macro theory was shaped by Asimov, 1951.)

[11] A related literature that goes by the name "econophysics" has achieved somewhat wider acceptance. However, most of this work has been focused on describing and understanding the behavior of financial markets – not the broader economy – using tools derived from statistical physics.

[12] To give two trivial examples, the log of an average is not the same as the average of a log, while the presence of a nonzero covariance between a characteristic x and income y means that the average of xy will not equal the average of x times the average of y. See Stoker (1993) and Blundell and Stoker (2007) for useful summaries of the issues involved (the latter reference also includes applications to intertemporal consumption modelling and to models of labor supply).

through to the aggregate level – for example, if household-level behavior implies that variables like consumption and wealth will be cointegrated for each household, it need not be the case that the aggregate analogs of these series will be cointegrated as well.[13] Finally, it seems likely that equations fit to aggregate data will tend to be unstable if the composition of the population changes over time, which is one reason (among many) why we should not expect empirical macroeconomic relationships to work very well over long periods of time.[14]

Being unable to recover individual-level behavior from aggregate data is only an issue, of course, to the extent that we *want* to recover such relations; if we do, then we should probably be looking to microlevel data in the first place. (That said, enough problems attend the use of microlevel data when trying to estimate behavioral relationships that such exercises are often less concerned with theoretical purity than they are with obtaining well-fitting and tractable specifications, especially where capturing the effects of heterogeneity is concerned.) But it is also the case that in nearly every practically relevant application, it will simply not be feasible to correctly aggregate empirical equations that are based on microlevel data: In the United States, the main source of household-level consumption data, the Consumer Expenditure Survey, is not really intended to be used to fit demand systems (instead, its main purpose is to compute weights for the consumer price index); moreover, its data are only available with a considerable lag. There is also no source of readily available, firm-level producer data in the United States that would be suitable for estimating microlevel production relationships.

Where does all this leave us in terms of the sorts of aggregate measures – real GDP and its components, their corresponding price measures, and so on – that are actually produced by US statistical agencies?

In general, the conditions that need to be met in order to ensure that these aggregates will summarize microlevel production and demand relationships in a sensible and well-behaved way turn out to be so stringent that they are almost certainly never met by any real-world economy – and statistical agencies do not approach the problem in this way. Instead, these aggregate series are defined so that they will have certain desirable and intuitively reasonable

---

[13] See Forni and Lippi (1997) for a detailed discussion of this topic.

[14] In addition, we will typically not be able to use estimates from microlevel empirical work in the context of an aggregate model – for example, as a way to "calibrate" a macromodel's parameters (see Browning, Hansen, and Heckman, 1999, for an early discussion of this topic).

"index number" properties.[15] To give one example, price and quantity indexes for total consumption use a formula that ensures that nominal consumption – which, being a value denominated in dollars, is reasonably straightforward to define and compute – will equal the quantity index when it is divided by the price index, and vice versa. While measures like these can be given a tenuous grounding in choice theory, such a grounding will only apply to a single consumer (or a representative agent); once we are dealing with the economy as a whole, any such theoretical justification vanishes.

Similarly, a measure of aggregate production like real GDP shouldn't be interpreted as the output of some economy-spanning firm that uses a neoclassical production technology to make a single homogenous good. Instead, real GDP is better thought of as an index that starts with the change in the total dollar value of the goods and services produced in the United States for final demand and then tries as best it can to remove the portion of this change that is attributable to changes in the individual prices of these goods and services.[16] The resulting quantity index (we hope) provides a reasonable gauge of the change in the overall level of real activity across different points in time that is both useful in its own right and that can be usefully related to other aggregates, such as the unemployment rate or economywide employment. Likewise, aggregate price indexes should allow us to make useful statements regarding the broad direction and magnitude of economywide price changes.

From a purely statistical perspective, using aggregate data can carry one significant advantage: Under certain circumstances, aggregating individual observations will help to reveal common "macrolevel" influences. We can see how this might occur with the following extremely stylized example (which is taken from Forni and Lippi, 1997, chapter 1). Assume that an individual-level variable, x_t^i, is the sum of two components:

$$x_t^i = X_t^i + \xi_t^i. \tag{1.1}$$

Here, X_t^i denotes the effect of macroeconomic shocks, while ξ_t^i is an individual-specific term. (For instance, if x_t^i is an individual's income, X_t^i would reflect the dependence of their income on economywide conditions, while ξ_t^i could be something like a pay raise or a bonus that the individual receives in period t.) These individual-specific shocks are orthogonal across individuals, as well as being orthogonal to any of the "macro" terms.

---

[15] We will consider some of these topics in more detail in Appendix B.
[16] For the sticklers, here "final demand" is meant to include inventory investment.

Purely for illustrative purposes (and to obtain a simple expression), let's assume that for any two individuals i and j, their respective macro terms X_t^i and X_t^j have a constant correlation equal to ρ (the fact that these terms would have *some* correlation isn't too hard to believe – they are related to economywide shocks, after all – though the assumption that this correlation is the same for everyone at every point in time is a rather special one). Let's also normalize things so that the variance of X_t^i is the same for everyone (and equal to 1), and that the macro term explains a fraction R^2 of the variability of x_t^i, which we accomplish by setting the variance of ξ_t^i equal to $(1 - R^2)/R^2$.

Now let's define an aggregate variable X_t (say, total income) as the sum of the individual (income) terms x_t^i:

$$\mathbf{X}_t = \sum_{i=1}^{n} x_t^i = \sum_{i=1}^{n} (X_t^i + \xi_t^i), \tag{1.2}$$

where we assume there are n individuals. Under the various assumptions, the variance of the sum of the macro terms will be $n+n(n-1)\rho$ and the variance of the sum of the individual-level terms will be $n(1 - R^2)/R^2$. Hence, in a sample of n individuals, the fraction of the variance of the *aggregate* variable $\mathbf{X}_t$ that will be explained by the macro term (call this R_n^2) will be

$$R_n^2 = \frac{1 + (n - 1)\rho}{(n - 1)\rho + (1/R^2)}. \tag{1.3}$$

What this means is that even if the macro term explains very little of the variability of the individual variables x_t^i – say, $R^2 = 0.01$ – and even if the macro effects are not very correlated across individuals (say $\rho = 0.01$), we won't need to aggregate over too many individuals in order to have the macro term explain a reasonably large fraction of the aggregate variable (for this example, 10,000 individuals would yield an R_n^2 equal to 0.50).

It's important not to make too much of this result – for various reasons, including the unrealistic nature of the example, things are unlikely to be quite this neat in the real world.[17] And, of course, none of this solves the basic problem that aggregate variables will not typically behave as individual-level variables writ large. But the example does hold out some hope that an atheoretical, basically empirical approach might end up

---

[17] In particular, the effective population size n is not always large, as many aggregate statistics are based on surveys with limited sample sizes. In addition, sampling variability can interact with some commonly used index number formulas in a way that prevents it from washing out at the aggregate level.

capturing informative common movements in the aggregate data that we can associate with macroeconomic shocks.[18]

1.3 Toward a Practical Macroeconomics

The issues raised in this chapter have two implications for the role that microeconomics should play in macroeconomics, neither of which is very constructive.

- First, the lack of any convincing theoretical demonstration of the stability of a Walrasian general equilibrium implies that a market-clearing general equilibrium is neither a relevant nor an interesting object of study, especially when we want to consider dynamic responses of the economy (such as those that occur over the course of a business cycle).
- Second, it is extremely unlikely that the aggregate data that we actually have access to will reflect recognizable theoretical or empirical microeconomic relations. As a result, the type of microfounded model that dominates mainstream macroeconomic thinking will provide no useful predictions about macroeconomic processes or outcomes, and no useful guidance regarding what sorts of empirical macroeconomic relationships are likely to be well-specified or stable over time.

Put more plainly, there is no especially good reason to use microeconomic theory to explain or predict the changes in economic aggregates that we actually observe, or even as a framework for modelling macroeconomic phenomena: Mainstream microeconomic theory simply isn't up to the task, even if we are willing to suspend disbelief and entertain the notion that people's behavior in the economic realm can be well described with the tools of that theory.

---

[18] This notion would seem to be inconsistent with Gabaix (2011), who argues that the distribution of firms is so fat-tailed that idiosyncratic productivity shocks among a small number of large firms account for a large fraction of macroeconomic fluctuations. However, the productivity shocks Gabaix measures are actually sales shocks, and many of the specific examples he gives reflect changes in demand, not firms' ability to produce more or less efficiently. And even for big firms, demand (and therefore sales) will be determined by a large number of agents, some of whom will be in other countries. In addition, using (net) sales ignores inventory investment, which – as we'll see in Chapter 3 – appears to be a major contributor to business cycles and which is (if not imported) part of *some* firm's output. (Also of note is that Gabaix's key theoretical derivation, which he uses to justify his empirical approach, assumes competitive conditions even though his focus is on extremely large firms in what are no doubt highly concentrated industries.)

What, then, might be a practical alternative? The empirical approach that we will consider in much of this book involves treating macroeconomic aggregates *on their own terms*, in the hopes of discerning relationships among these variables – essentially, statistical regularities or stylized facts – that are reasonably robust and well-specified in a time-series sense. We will then attempt to come up with plausible interpretations for these empirical relationships (as well as assessing how well mainstream macroeconomic theory is able to do so).

There are pitfalls, of course, in taking such an approach. When you stop to think about it, it seems hard to believe that *any* sort of empirical macroeconomic regularity would exist in an economy as geographically spread out and complex as ours, let alone one that could be used for forecasting or to predict the likely consequences of a policy change. And as we will see, many of these relations are in fact unstable over time or are able to explain a relatively small fraction of the variability we observe in the data.[19] Moreover, the evidence for a particular explanation or interpretation of an empirical finding will rarely be dispositive, which means that a large number of warning labels will need to be affixed to such an explanation if its purpose is to inform policy.

Unavoidably, therefore, an undertaking of this sort will be more art than (pseudo-)science. But even though macroeconomics probably never will be a science – we have too few relevant observations with which to permit sensible inductive reasoning, and no agreed-on standard of evidence with which to assess proposed hypotheses – it does share the four goals of any science; namely, explanation, understanding, prediction, and control. And because our society contains policy institutions that seek to affect macroeconomic outcomes in a deliberate way, we need to try to achieve these four goals as best we can.

1.4 Digression: Does Aggregation Save *Micro*economics?

The Sonnenschein–Mantel–Debreu theorems demonstrate that the structure that is given to individual-level behavior by standard assumptions about consumer preferences is largely washed away by aggregation. But can aggregation itself yield properties that would allow certain key microeconomic

---

[19] One important practical use of a statistical macroeconomic model is to identify when residuals are starting to emerge, as these can indicate that a consequential change in the economic environment is starting to take place.

propositions to hold? In a remarkable attack on the problem, Hildenbrand (1993) argues that the answer to this question is a qualified "yes."[20]

Hildenbrand asks what features of average behavior and of the data would permit us to claim that the "law of market demand" – very loosely, the notion that prices and demand move in opposite directions – will hold.[21] We can see the intuition behind Hildenbrand's argument as follows.[22]

Start from the Marshallian demand functions $x(p, y)$, where y is income. Taking the derivative with respect to the price vector and adding and subtracting the term $D_y xx'$ (the prime denotes a transpose) yields:

$$D_p x(p, y) = D_p x(p, y) + D_y xx' - D_y xx'. \tag{1.4}$$

Note that the first two terms give the Slutsky matrix. If we take the average of this equation over all consumers and assume that the average Slutsky matrix is negative semidefinite, then the law of market demand will hold if we can show (empirically) that $D_y xx'$ is positive definite on average.

The average value of xx' can be thought of as a measure of dispersion or "spread," since the average of the outer product of the demand vectors will equal the variance of the outer product plus the outer products of the mean demands. What Hildenbrand examines empirically is whether this spread is an increasing function of income; he does so by using household expenditure surveys to compute various measures of dispersion for different pairs of commodities at different income levels. He concludes that there is evidence for increasing spread in the data, which suggests that the law of market demand might well be an aggregate property of the data.

Why is this answer only a *qualified* yes? Several issues are associated with Hildenbrand's analysis, including the use of broad commodity aggregates like "housing," "food," and "transport" (which can only be justified under relatively strict assumptions), as well as a blurred distinction between income and expenditure (which puts the negative semidefiniteness of the Slutsky matrix on shakier ground, as income can be saved rather than spent). In addition, the experiment that would actually need to be done in order to assess the sign of $D_y xx'$ would involve giving each consumer slightly more

---

[20] A very distant relative of Hildenbrand's argument appears in Hicks (1956, VII.7).
[21] Strictly, the law of market demand states that the vector of price changes and the vector of quantity changes "point" in opposite directions; that is, for two different price vectors p and q, aggregate demand $F(\cdot)$ satisfies $(p - q) \cdot (F(p) - F(q)) < 0$. This property in turn ensures the uniqueness of a Walrasian equilibrium.
[22] This discussion is taken from Lewbel (1994).

income and then seeing whether the average spread of their demands rose; because that is not possible to do, Hildenbrand instead looks at demands for households with higher or lower income levels. (He calls the assumption that the two experiments would yield similar results "metonymy.") Finally – and most importantly – even if we accept Hildenbrand's conclusion regarding market demand, it still has nothing to say about Fisher's stability question. So while shifting our focus to the behavior of aggregates isn't quite enough to restore one's faith in the relevance of general equilibrium theory, it does at least let us assert with mild conviction that market demand curves slope down – at least in a dark room from a distance.

2

Trends and Cycles, Shocks and Stability

Alas! I knew how it would end: I've mixed the cycle with the trend,
And fear that, growing daily skinnier, I have at length become non-linear.
I scarcely now, a pallid ghost, can tell ex-ante *from* ex-post*:*
My thoughts are sadly inelastic, my acts incurably stochastic.

D. H. Robertson (1955)

Measures of the level of real activity have two primary characteristics: Over time, they trend upward, but on occasion they swing noticeably, declining before eventually recovering and then continuing more or less along an upward march. These fluctuations are called business cycles, and they have occupied the attention of economists at least since the early nineteenth century.

In the United States the "dating" of business cycle peaks and troughs – and hence of recessions and expansions – is handled by the private National Bureau of Economic Research (NBER), where a committee within the NBER study a number of monthly indicators of real activity in order to identify turning points in the series. Because the NBER wait until such turning points are clearly discernable, the announcement of these dates typically comes well after a turning point is reached. The indicators currently used by the NBER to date business cycles are real personal consumption, total industrial production, real personal income less (government) transfers, real wholesale and retail trade sales, and two measures of employment (of late, income and nonfarm payroll employment have tended to receive the most weight). The rationale for using a number of indicators reflects the NBER's definition of a recession, which is a significant downturn in real activity that is spread throughout the entire economy and that therefore manifests itself across a

18

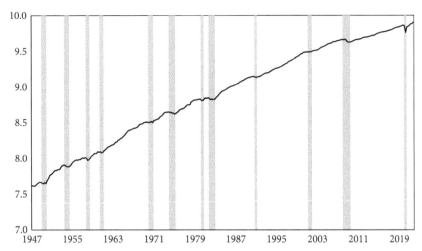

Figure 2.1 Natural log of real GDP. (Shaded bars denote recessions as defined by the NBER.)

broad set of aggregate measures of employment, output, and spending.[1] For reference, Figure 2.1 plots the log of real GDP together with the periods the NBER have identified as recessions (the gray regions).

By contrast, economists often seek a more statistically informed definition of the business cycle. One important reason is that the NBER dates do not identify the "recovery" phase of the business cycle, in which activity is retracing the losses incurred during the recession and has not yet settled back to a more normal rate of advance. A second reason is that the trend itself is of independent interest, so we would like to be able to extract and study that component of real activity as well. And a third reason is that most time-series modelling requires series to be stationary, which requires some way of dealing with the nonstationary ("trend") component.[2]

Like most topics in economics, there is essentially no consensus about the nature of business cycles, why they happen, or even how best to measure them. In this chapter and Chapter 3, we will take a look at some of the more plausible answers to these questions.

---

[1] Hence, the conventional definition of a recession as two back-to-back quarters of declining GDP is not used by the NBER. The NBER also use quarterly values of their cyclical indicators (along with real GDP and real gross domestic income) to identify the *quarter* of a turning point; on rare occasions, the month of the turning point won't fall in the quarter that the NBER identify as a turning point.

[2] See Watson (1986). Note that a trend in this context is just the nonstationary portion – for example, even though it can't rise or fall without limit, the unemployment rate can still be nonstationary and have a "trend" if its long-run mean is different over different periods.

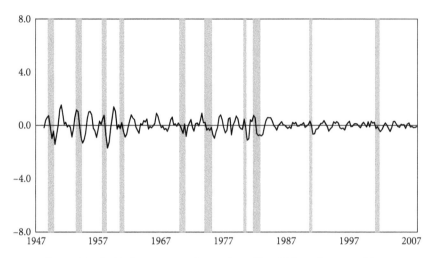

Figure 2.2 Cyclical component from a Beveridge–Nelson decomposition.

2.1 Measuring Trend and Cycle

For the sake of argument, let's assume that it makes sense to decompose a measure of real activity – say the log of real GDP, y_t – into a trend component τ_t and a cyclical component c_t, so that $y_t = \tau_t + c_t$. If we assume that the trend component follows a random walk with drift μ and that in the absence of any additional shocks cyclical fluctuations would eventually die away and real activity would return to its (stochastic) trend, then a reasonable estimate of the trend is given by

$$\tau_t = \lim_{n \to \infty} E_t y_{t+n} - n\mu \equiv \tau_t^{BN}. \qquad (2.1)$$

This is the Beveridge–Nelson (1981) trend. Implicitly, it requires y_t to be I(1) (in particular, we don't want the drift term μ to change). Other than that, though, a decomposition like this is in principle consistent with various alternative views regarding the sources of business cycles. To estimate the Beveridge–Nelson trend, all we need is a forecasting model for y_t; after that, we can define the cycle as $y_t - \tau_t^{BN}$. One straightforward way to model y_t is as an ARIMA(p,1,q) process; if we do so, the cycle that we obtain looks like the solid line in Figure 2.2.[3]

For some economists, results like those in Figure 2.2 were rather baffling. Taken at face value, these results imply that the "cycle" is close to nonexistent,

---

[3] The specific model used here is an ARIMA(2,1,2) fit over the period 1947:Q4 to 2007:Q4; this choice of endpoint means that the estimates are not influenced by the 2007–2009 recession.

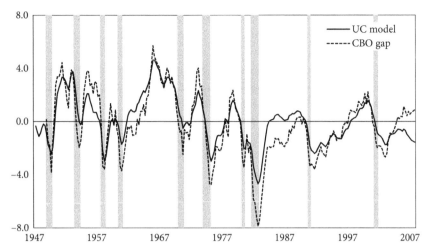

Figure 2.3 Cyclical component from an unobserved components model and CBO's output gap estimate.

and that movements in the "trend" account for most of the observed variation in output; in fact, many of the ordinary fluctuations of the cyclical component are as large as what occur during NBER-designated recessions. Moreover, alternative statistical detrending procedures that modelled τ_t and c_t as unobserved components (using a Kalman filter to back them out) found estimates of the cyclical component that were similar to the solid line in Figure 2.3 and so were both larger and more persistent than the Beveridge–Nelson cycle; such estimates also looked more like the kinds of output gap measures produced by the Congressional Budget Office (the dashed line in Figure 2.3) and other policy institutions.[4]

One reconciliation of these results was provided by Morley, Nelson, and Zivot (2003). These authors noted that a reasonably general trend–cycle decomposition could be written as

$$y_t = \tau_t + c_t$$
$$\tau_t = \mu + \tau_{t-1} + \eta_t$$
$$\phi_p(L)c_t = \theta_q(L)\varepsilon_t, \tag{2.2}$$

with the cycle explicitly modelled as an ARMA(p, q), and where the time-t innovations to the trend and cycle were allowed to be correlated. It turns out

---

[4] The Congressional Budget Office, or CBO, currently maintain an estimate of potential GDP that is intended to measure the level of production that would take place under full-employment conditions; the deviation of actual output from potential is referred to as an output gap. (We will look at this approach to measuring trend output in Chapter 4.)

that what we assume about this correlation is key. Unobserved components models of the sort used to generate Figure 2.3 typically assumed that the trend and cycle innovations had *no* correlation, which reflected the notion that the trend component was determined by the supply side of the economy while business cycles were largely the result of shocks to aggregate demand. But this assumption was not actually tested.

To make things concrete, let's assume that we fit an unobserved components model in which the cycle follows an AR(2) process (so $p = 2$ and $q = 0$) and where the correlation between η_t and ε_t (call it $\rho_{\eta\varepsilon}$) is restricted to be zero. (This is the same model that was used to generate the solid line in Figure 2.3.) In general, when $p = 2$ and $q = 0$ in model 2.2, it is possible to show that y_t will follow an ARIMA(2,1,2) process. However, imposing $\rho_{\eta\varepsilon} = 0$ restricts the coefficients in this process in ways that turn out to be rejected by the data. Specifically, if we allow $\rho_{\eta\varepsilon}$ to be an estimated parameter, we find that it is *negative* (with a value on the order of –0.9), and that the resulting unobserved components model generates a measure of the cycle that looks like Figure 2.2.[5] Equivalently, if we fit y_t using an *unrestricted* ARIMA(2,1,2) process and then use it to compute the Beveridge–Nelson decomposition for y_t – as was done to produce the solid line in Figure 2.2 – we obtain an estimate of the cycle that is identical to what we get from the unobserved components model with $\rho_{\eta\varepsilon}$ freely estimated.

Why does any of this matter? Well, if the trend and cycle innovations for a series like real GDP are strongly negatively correlated, it provides support for the hypothesis that real shocks are the dominant driving force behind economic fluctuations. As Morley, Nelson, and Zivot (2003) point out, a positive real shock – say a technological innovation – will shift up the long-run path of output in the period that it hits, leaving actual output to catch up from below. Hence, if real shocks dominate, positive shocks to the trend will be associated with negative shocks to the cyclical portion of the series, and vice versa. By contrast, shocks that have a transitory effect on output – a shift to an expansionary monetary policy stance, say – will only affect the cyclical component. So if these sorts of shocks were a major driver of output fluctuations, we would find that the correlation between the trend and cycle components is close to zero.

Before we reach such a strong conclusion, though, it is useful to consider some extensions to the original Beveridge–Nelson approach. In order to apply this particular trend–cycle decomposition, we need to have a

---

[5] It is possible to show that we will be able to estimate $\rho_{\eta\varepsilon}$ if the ARMA process for c_t has $p \geq q + 2$, which is satisfied here (see Morley, Nelson, and Zivot, 2003, pp. 236–237).

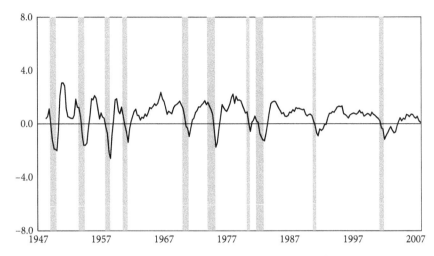

Figure 2.4 Cyclical component from a VAR-based Beveridge–Nelson decomposition.

good forecasting model for output growth (recall Equation 2.1). Moreover, as Evans and Reichlin (1994) point out, the Beveridge–Nelson cycle is essentially the forecastable "momentum" of the series, which means that the share of the observed fluctuations in output that we attribute to the cycle is closely related to how well we can forecast output growth.

To illustrate this point, note that the Beveridge–Nelson definition of the trend naturally carries over to a VAR context (instead of using an ARIMA model to predict a single series, we can use a VAR to predict a group of series). To keep things parsimonious, then, let's consider a two-variable VAR in real GDP and employment (we use employment because it is another measure of real activity that varies over the business cycle in a way that might be informative about output). The resulting "cycle" for real GDP is plotted in Figure 2.4; it's clearly evident that this measure of the cycle is smoother and more persistent than the cycle from the univariate model in Figure 2.2 (it also lines up better with the NBER dates), though its amplitude is not especially large.[6]

A second extension to the original Beveridge–Nelson procedure focuses on the trend component itself. Again, the reason that we end up with a cyclical component like the one in Figure 2.2 is that the decomposition attributes

---

[6] Employment is nonfarm payroll employment from the BLS establishment survey. Both output and employment enter the VAR as log-differences; the VAR has four lags and is estimated from 1948:Q2 to 2007:Q4.

such a large portion of the observed movement in output to changes in the trend. Put differently, because the estimated cyclical component is so small (and continues to be so even after 2007 – not shown), the univariate decomposition implies a trend estimate that follows actual GDP extremely closely, including over most of the 2007–2009 recession and subsequent sluggish recovery.[7] But Kamber, Morley, and Wong (2018) argue that we might view it as *a priori* implausible that the Beveridge–Nelson decomposition implies such large variability in the trend. To give a flavor of their argument, assume that we use an AR(p) model to forecast output growth Δy_t,

$$\Delta y_t = \mu + \sum_{i=1}^{p} \phi_i \Delta y_{t-i} + \varepsilon_t, \qquad (2.3)$$

and note that the time-t change in the estimated Beveridge–Nelson trend from a unit ε_t shock will be equal to $1/(1 - \phi_1 - \phi_2 - \cdots - \phi_p)$, as this is the eventual increase in the *level* of y relative to the level that would obtain absent a shock. If we denote this term as ψ, then the ratio of the variance of a trend shock to the variance of the forecast error ε will equal ψ^2. Hence, if the sum of the AR coefficients is on the order of 0.3 (which isn't too unreasonable in US data), then this ratio – which can be thought of as a signal-to-noise ratio – will be around 2. What that implies, then, is that trend shocks are considerably more variable than the one-quarter-ahead forecast error for (log) real GDP.

Beyond the fact that it generates an output gap that looks silly, why might we view such a high signal-to-noise ratio with suspicion? After all, lag selection procedures generally suggest that an AR(1) or AR(2) model fits output growth reasonably well, and "silly" is ultimately in the eye of the beholder. What Kamber, Morley, and Wong argue, however, is that certain types of processes for output growth – such as an MA process with a near-unit root – will not be well captured by a finite-order AR process, while the parameters of richer ARMA-type models can be poorly tied down in finite samples. They therefore develop a "Beveridge–Nelson filter" that allows one to impose a low signal-to-noise ratio as a (dogmatic) prior, and also to control

---

[7] Extending the estimation period through 2019:Q4 for the unobserved components model (2.2) with uncorrelated trend and cycle causes it to break down completely: If the post-2007 data are included in the sample, the model estimates that output is 5 percent above trend, on average, for most of the sample period before plunging 5 percent below trend in the wake of the 2007–2009 recession. Here, the model's constant average trend growth rate implies that the trend rises too slowly over much of the sample and too quickly toward the end of the sample.

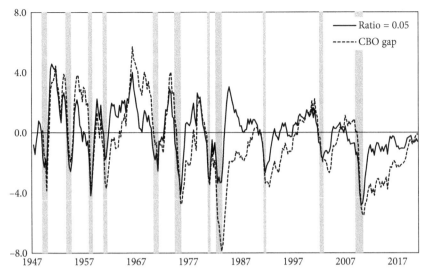

Figure 2.5 Cyclical component from Kamber–Morley–Wong Beveridge–Nelson filter (with signal-to-noise ratio fixed at 0.05) together with CBO's output gap estimate.

for possible trend breaks. Figure 2.5 plots the cyclical component obtained using their baseline filter specification with the signal-to-noise ratio fixed at 0.05 (a relatively small value).[8] The cycle is reasonably well correlated with the CBO output gap (also plotted in the figure through 2019:Q4), though some important differences are apparent (namely, the estimated depth of the 1981–1982 recession and the speeds of recovery from the 1990–1991 and 2007–2009 recessions).

We have now reached the point where we've been able to coax a respectable business cycle out of the Beveridge–Nelson decomposition, though to do so we have needed to venture uncomfortably close to the realm of vulgar curve fitting.[9] Why is this accomplishment worth celebrating? Well, from either a time series or an economic perspective, this definition of the trend (or long-run mean) is extremely intuitive and compelling – so much so that it's not easy to come up with other sensible definitions. In economic terms, the concept seems very close to an equilibrium notion – in other words, the value that a variable would return to once any adjustment mechanisms

---

[8] Kamber, Morley, and Wong (2018) propose an automatic selection procedure, which in this case yields a signal-to-noise ratio of 0.24; using this value instead yields results that are very similar to those shown in Figure 2.5.

[9] That job is better left to the Hodrick–Prescott filter, which we discuss in Section 2.2.

or other frictions have fully played through (and taking into account any persistent effects on the equilibrium itself). Empirically, the method dovetails well with the standard techniques and approaches of time-series analysis, while using a stochastic trend to model the persistent movement in an economic aggregate seems much more defensible than any sort of deterministic alternative. On the other hand, in order to obtain a time-series gap measure that roughly resembles the CBO's output gap, we have needed to drastically reduce the variability of the trend component. That fact raises two questions: First, are statistical detrending procedures like the ones just considered actually useful; and second, why should we view the CBO measure as an appropriate benchmark?

Taking the second question first, the magnitude and persistence of the CBO gap lines up well with another important cyclical indicator, the unemployment rate, and that fact alone is a strong argument in its favor.[10] Regarding the broader usefulness of statistical detrending procedures, the answer is "it depends." Many time series approaches to trend–cycle decomposition, especially the univariate ones, do seem to allow the trend to respond too much to persistent movements in the actual series (we'll see some other examples soon).[11] Ultimately, though, which approach you prefer will probably depend strongly on your priors. Those who believe that the productive capacity of the economy is an important determinant of actual output and is itself subject to large quarter-to-quarter fluctuations (say because of productivity, efficiency, or utilization shocks) will be comfortable with the idea that the trend is highly variable and the cycle relatively small. By contrast, those who think that full-employment output evolves more slowly (say because it is determined by things like growth in the labor force and other additions to existing productive capacity) and that business cycles largely reflect demand-driven departures from full employment will be less likely to accept a procedure that places all of the action in the trend.

If we do continue to confine ourselves to purely statistical methods for measuring the business cycle, there is one other approach to isolating the trend and cyclical components of a time series that is worth thinking about. The fact that we refer to the idea of a business *cycle* calls to mind something that has a more or less regular periodicity. While we wouldn't want to

---

[10] An exception is the 2007–2009 recession, where the peak-to-trough drop in the output gap implied by the CBO measure seems somewhat less pronounced than the corresponding rise in the unemployment rate when compared with what happened in previous recessions.

[11] That said, some sort of statistical detrending procedure is often used one way or another in more-structural approaches to measuring the economy's supply side.

take this idea literally – earlier writers on business cycles referred to them as "recurrent but not periodic" – from 1945 to 2019 the NBER's dating implies that postwar US business cycles have ranged from six quarters to twelve years in duration, with most lasting less than ten years.[12] As a way of measuring the business cycle, therefore, we can apply a particular type of statistical filter (known as a bandpass filter) that takes a series and extracts the portion of its fluctuations that is attributable to cycles with periodicities that fall in this range.[13] The reason we might want to do something like this is that macroeconomic aggregates typically manifest relatively small spectral peaks at business-cycle frequencies; using a suitable filter can throw these cyclical movements into sharper relief. (In an important sense, this is why we seek to detrend a series in the first place.)

For this particular application therefore, we want a filter that "passes through" cycles with periods longer than (say) two years and shorter than (say) twelve years. The problem of how to approximate such a filter as a weighted moving average with a finite number of terms has been worked out by several authors – including Baxter and King (1999) and Christiano and Fitzgerald (2003) – under different approximation criteria. Figure 2.6 plots the results obtained by applying the Baxter–King bandpass filter to log real GDP (times 100) and the unemployment rate, using a window width of 81 quarters – so ten years on either side – and cutoffs equal to two and twelve years.[14] A clear contemporaneous correlation between the series is apparent (the correlation coefficient is –0.91), reflecting the tendency of these series to move closely together (but in opposite directions) over the business cycle.[15]

---

[12] The quote comes from Burns and Mitchell (1946). In their definition of a business cycle, Burns and Mitchell identified the duration of a business cycle as "more than one year to ten or twelve years," but prior to the Great Depression, Mitchell (1927) had used "three to about six or seven years." For the postwar United States (and at the time of this writing), if we define cycles on a trough-to-trough basis, their duration ranges from 2.3 to 10.8 years; on a peak-to-peak basis, the range is 1.5 to 12.2 years.

[13] We know from time-series analysis that we can express a variable as the weighted sum of periodic (cosine and sine) functions with different frequencies (or, equivalently, periods) – very intuitively, the idea is similar to a Taylor expansion, which uses a weighted sum of polynomials to approximate a function.

[14] A filter like this is a two-sided moving average. Using a wider window increases the filter's ability to pass through only the desired frequencies but means that more data are lost from the beginning and end of the sample. One way to deal with this problem is to "pad" the sample with additional observations in the form of forecasts and backcasts from a time-series model; in the figures, the filter is applied to the series starting in 1959:Q1 and ending in 2007:Q4, so only actual data are used.

[15] This phenomenon is related to an empirical regularity called Okun's law, which we will return to in Chapter 5.

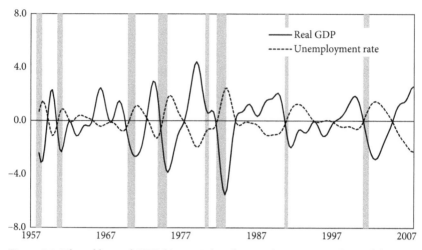

Figure 2.6 Filtered log real GDP (times 100) and unemployment rate obtained from the Baxter–King bandpass filter with cutoffs equal to two and twelve years (window width is 81 quarters).

One problem with an approach like this one is that it is probably too dogmatic regarding the periodicity of "the" business cycle. If we invoke the Burns and Mitchell definition (or use more recent NBER dates) to set the filter cutoffs, we are already buying into that definition of a cyclical contraction or expansion and forcing our filtered series to conform to it. As a check of this definition as it pertains to the comovement of real GDP and the unemployment rate, we can use the cross-spectrum to estimate pairwise coherences for these variables.[16] Figure 2.7 plots the coherence between log-differenced real GDP and the change in the unemployment rate over the 1959 to 2019 period; the x-axis of the chart is given as fractions of π, so the leftmost hill between 0.07 and 0.23 implies a large pairwise coherence at periods between 2.1 and 7.2 years, with a steep dropoff at around 9 years.[17] That's somewhat shorter than the average business cycle duration implied by the NBER dates (and used in the bandpass filter) – and the range is narrower as well – though given the imprecision surrounding estimates of the cross-spectrum, especially at lower frequencies, the correspondence isn't too bad.

---

[16] The coherence between two variables tells us how much of the variation in a series at a particular frequency can be explained by another series.

[17] The period (in quarters) is given by $2/f$, where f is the fraction of π given on the x-axis. (To compute the periods cited in the text, I used values of f expressed to more decimal places than are reported here.)

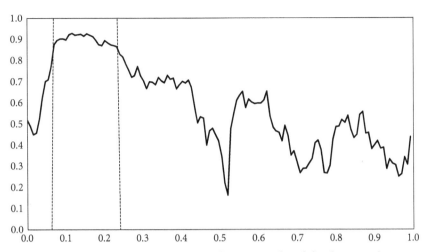

Figure 2.7 Estimated coherence between real GDP growth and the change in the unemployment rate. Values along the x-axis are fractions of π; vertical lines are at 0.07 and 0.23.

Another, related issue that arises with statistical filters can be seen from Figure 2.8, which plots the actual unemployment rate against its "low-pass" or "trend" component (that is, the component that reflects cycles with periods greater than twelve years). There is a distinct dip in the trend series over the first part of the 1960s as the reduction in the actual unemployment rate is interpreted by the filter as being too persistent to be a cyclical phenomenon (an interpretation that is difficult to square with the history of this period). Likewise, at the end of the sample the low-pass component is pulled up by the large and persistent rise in the unemployment rate that resulted from the 2007–2009 recession.

This last result highlights a deeper question, which is whether it is entirely sensible to treat cyclical and trend movements as largely separate phenomena. Even if we think that cyclical fluctuations are mostly demand-driven (as opposed to being the result of supply-side shocks), it is still the case that the demand and supply sides are likely to be linked over periods longer than a business cycle but shorter than the "long run" – for instance, as an investment boom translates into an increase in the economy's productive capacity, or as a prolonged slump causes workers to be persistently "scarred" as their skills atrophy and their connection to the labor force weakens. Conversely, we can imagine that certain types of supply-side disturbances (an oil price shock, say) could contribute to a recession by reducing aggregate demand. With only a dozen postwar business cycles at our disposal, each of which

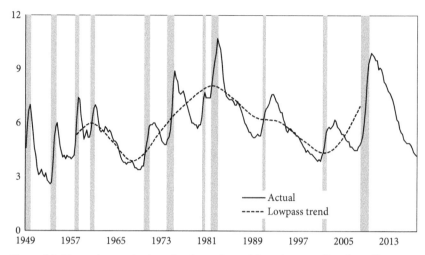

Figure 2.8 Unemployment rate and estimated trend from lowpass filter (cutoff is twelve years).

had its own specific features and causes, it is probably too much to expect that we can pin down the characteristics of "the" business cycle well enough to calibrate the parameters of a bandpass filter, or to use any purely statistical procedure to cleanly separate trends and cycles.[18]

2.2 Digression: "Why You Should Never Use the Hodrick–Prescott Filter"

An alternative method for detrending a time series that was popularized by Hodrick and Prescott (1997) involves fitting a smooth trend component through the series.[19] Specifically, for a series y_t Hodrick and Prescott suggested setting the trend component τ_t to minimize the following criterion,

$$\min \left\{ \sum_{t=1}^{T} \left(y_t - \tau_t \right)^2 + \lambda \sum_{t=1}^{T} (\Delta \tau_t - \Delta \tau_{t-1})^2 \right\}. \tag{2.4}$$

[18] Related issues have been discussed in the literature. For example, Murray (2003) shows that in a model like (2.2), a bandpass filter does not fully exclude the trend component from the measured cycle and so can overstate or understate the importance of cyclical dynamics at the assumed business-cycle frequencies. Murray argues that this problem arises whenever a nonstationary trend is present; however, the appendix to Trimbur and McElroy (2022) shows that the actual issue is that a stochastic trend contains frequency components that extend into the intermediate, "cyclical" portions of the spectrum and that are therefore passed through by a bandpass filter.

[19] Hodrick and Prescott had initially proposed their method in a 1981 working paper.

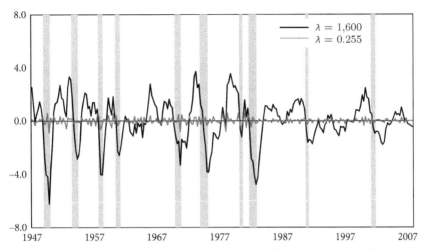

Figure 2.9 Cyclical component from Hodrick–Prescott filter with $\lambda =1{,}600$ (black line) and freely estimated $\lambda =0.255$ (gray line).

If we assume that y_t is in logarithms, then Equation (2.4) expresses a trade-off between keeping the trend as close as possible to the actual series while also keeping the growth rate of the trend smooth. The parameter λ governs this trade-off: When λ is zero, then the trend will be equal to y_t itself so as to minimize the first part of the criterion; as λ becomes very large, then the goal is to have the growth rate of the trend be nearly constant (in the limit where $\lambda \to \infty$, $\Delta\tau_t$ becomes a constant and the trend is a straight line). In most applications (and following Hodrick and Prescott's suggestion), λ is set equal to 1,600 in quarterly data; Figure 2.9 shows the resulting cyclical component when the filter is applied to 100 times the log of real GDP from 1947:Q1 to 2007:Q4.

It turns out that an exact closed-form solution to the minimization problem (2.4) can be computed for a specified λ; the solution is a matrix equation that implies that τ_t will be a linear function of all of the values of y. However, as Hodrick and Prescott pointed out, an alternative way to compute τ_t involves fitting a Kalman smoother to the following state-space representation,

$$y_t = \tau_t + c_t$$
$$\tau_t = 2\tau_{t-1} - \tau_{t-2} + v_t, \tag{2.5}$$

where c_t denotes the cyclical component, c_t and v_t are mutually uncorrelated white noise, and λ equals to the ratio of their variances, $\lambda = \sigma_c^2/\sigma_v^2$.

As Hamilton (2018) demonstrates, either method will yield the same value of τ_t so long as the same value of λ is used and a diffuse prior is used for the initial state in the Kalman smoother.[20]

From this description, we can intuitively discern two potential problems with the Hodrick–Prescott filter.[21] First, the fact that a high degree of smoothing (a large value of λ) will cause the trend to be nearly linear hints that we could easily run into trouble, as linearly detrending a random walk is a recipe for generating spurious dynamics. (As Hamilton also demonstrates, the Hodrick–Prescott filter does in fact induce spurious dynamics even for the smaller values of λ that are typically used, with additional distortions introduced at the end of the sample.) More importantly, we might be suspicious that an estimation procedure that assumes the cyclical component is white noise (recall the state-space representation given by the system 2.5) would yield cycles that look like those in Figure 2.9, which are relatively smooth and persistent. The reason is that we are imposing a value of λ that is wildly at odds with what we obtain from freely estimating it; for example, fitting the system (2.5) by maximum likelihood yields $\sigma_c^2 = 0.125$ and $\sigma_\nu^2 = 0.491$. That implies a value of λ equal to 0.255 (not 1,600), a trend component that is essentially identical to the series itself, and the nonexistent cyclical component shown in Figure 2.9.

Hamilton (2018) also proposes a different way to isolate the cyclical component of a nonstationary time series that does not share the various problems associated with the Hodrick–Prescott filter (the method bears a passing relationship to the Beveridge–Nelson decomposition). Whatever one thinks about Hamilton's suggested alternative, though, one thing is clear: Anyone who shows you empirical results that use the Hodrick–Prescott filter is basically just wasting your time.

2.3 Shocks and Their Propagation

If we are willing to accept that business cycles represent large and persistent swings in real activity relative to a reasonably smooth trend, a natural next question is how to think about them – and especially recessions – in economic terms. In particular, we would like to be able to explain why it is that most business cycles tend to exhibit three "phases" or states, with sharp contractions in real activity (recessions) followed first by a period of rapid

---

[20] Note that we can normalize σ_ν^2 to be unity and set $\sigma_c^2 = \lambda$.

[21] These are discussed formally and in broader terms by Hamilton (2018); unsurprisingly, Hodrick (2020) strongly disagrees with Hamilton's conclusions.

recovery and then by a return to a period of more moderate growth (the expansion state that the US economy typically finds itself in).

Since the 1930s, the dominant paradigm for thinking about macroeconomic fluctuations is one where erratic shocks or "impulses" feed through a stable propagation mechanism with a determinate (single) equilibrium.[22] The idea is that we can model the macroeconomy as a system of dynamic equations; this system (the *propagation mechanism*) summarizes how macro aggregates are related to each other, and is ultimately related to the assumed behavioral responses, technological constraints, and policy reaction functions that link together groups of agents in the economy. Shocks or impulses that arise from outside the system give rise to dynamic responses as the system is first moved away from equilibrium and then returns to it. (Of course, a continuous stream of these shocks will ensure that the system is never actually in equilibrium – or at least won't be in equilibrium for very long.)

In order to explain business cycles in these terms, though, we essentially have to argue that recessions reflect large negative shocks while recoveries represent the dynamic path that the economy follows as the effects of a recessionary shock play out. This view certainly has its adherents; Temin (1989), for example, even goes so far as to explain the Great Depression in these terms.[23] And more generally, this is how many real business cycle (RBC) and new-Keynesian models "explain" downturns. In the former, shocks to productivity or other real-side variables drive fluctuations in activity; the propagation mechanism reflects market-clearing responses to these real shocks.[24] New-Keynesian models assume a slightly different propagation mechanism (market clearing under the assumption of nominal rigidities), but estimated versions of these models typically rely on shocks to household discount

---

[22] This conception was developed by Frisch (1933) in an extremely influential paper. Frisch interpreted business cycles as resulting from repeated random shocks hitting a propagation mechanism that itself generated damped cycles, and claimed that a simple calibrated model could give rise to cycles with periods roughly equal to those observed at the time. However, as Zambelli (2007) points out, Frisch's solution is incomplete and there actually aren't any cycles in his model (the system simply returns monotonically toward its equilibrium state). Zambelli speculates that the development of macroeconomic theory might have taken a somewhat different course had this fact been known by Frisch's contemporaries.

[23] Temin explicitly eschews the explanation that the Great Depression reflected some sort of inherent instability in the economy. Instead, he argues that a very large shock – the First World War – changed elements of the world economic order in such a way that maintaining the prewar policy regime (the gold standard) required overly deflationary fiscal and monetary policies that were maintained for too long.

[24] One reason why RBC modellers favor the univariate Beveridge–Nelson characterization of the business cycle is that it leaves very little cycle to actually be explained through this mechanism.

factors, investment-specific technological change, or wedges between the central bank's policy rate and the interest rate that enters spending decisions in order to generate large cyclical swings. (None of these shocks is observed; rather, they are inferred from the model's inability to fit the data.)

One reason to be skeptical of the "big negative shock" interpretation of recessions is that it seems to require that these shocks would all be one-sided; that is, we do not tend to see large *positive* exogenous shocks that sharply push up real activity – like a "negative recession" – when the economy is in its typical expansionary state. (Of course, it isn't impossible that the distribution of shocks to the economy has a long left tail, but then we would want to be able to explain or model the source of this skewness.) Another reason to be skeptical of this way of looking at recessions is that it assumes the propagation mechanism itself doesn't change as a result of the shock. The amplitude of most recessions and speed with which they occur suggest that they might involve something more than just the economy's typical continuous response to a shock; instead, recessions seem closer to a regime change, in which something happens to induce a discontinuous or nonlinear shift into a separate recession state. In other words, the propagation dynamics that result in a recession seem to be fundamentally different to those that prevail under ordinary circumstances.[25]

We can get a hint that something like this might be going on by considering a statistical model that explicitly permits such a regime change to take place. In 1989, Hamilton proposed describing the dynamics of a measure of real activity (say real GDP growth, Δy_t) with a Markov switching model:

$$\phi_p(L)\Delta y_t = \mu(s_t) + \varepsilon_t$$
$$\mu(s_t) = \mu_0 + \mu_1 s_t, \tag{2.6}$$

where s_t is an indicator variable that equals zero or one. The idea is that the economy transitions between two regimes; in either regime, Δy_t follows an AR process, but the unconditional mean of the process is allowed to be different across regimes. The transition *between* regimes is then assumed to be governed by a Markov process with fixed transition probabilities,

$$\Pr[s_t = 1 \mid s_t = 1] = p; \quad \Pr[s_t = 0 \mid s_t = 0] = q. \tag{2.7}$$

---

[25] Note that a trend–cycle decomposition that is based on a model like Equation (2.2) implicitly assumes that cycles are symmetric since a single ARMA process is used to model the cyclical component.

Hamilton originally wanted to use this approach to model a trend break in real GDP growth (specifically, the post-1970s productivity slowdown). However, when he fit the model to US real GDP, he obtained estimated probabilities for being in one of the states that looked very similar to the NBER recession bars shown in Figure 2.1. Hamilton realized that the model was capturing a switch into a *recession state*, with a reduction in mean GDP growth that goes away after the economy returns to a nonrecession state. In other words, recessions appeared to involve a discrete change in the process for output growth, which in this simple model *is* the propagation mechanism for shocks.[26]

We can get a flavor of Hamilton's results with a slightly different model that – like the NBER – uses several measures of real activity in order to pin down cyclical turning points.[27] Roughly, the idea is to model the behavior of the NBER's main cyclical indicators (nonfarm payrolls, real manufacturing and trade sales, industrial production, and real personal income less transfers, all of which are available monthly) as being driven by a common factor whose mean growth rate changes when the economy enters a recession state. Figure 2.10 plots the estimated probability that the economy was in a recession at a specified date; these probabilities line up tolerably well with the NBER's dating. The model's transition probabilities imply that we should expect the economy to be in a recession 10 percent of the time, with the average duration of a recession equal to 7.3 months and the average duration of an expansion equal to 67 months. For reference, the NBER's dating implies that the US economy has spent 13 percent of the time in a recession over the 1959–2019 period, with a mean recession duration of just under a year and a mean expansion duration of seventy-eight months.[28]

---

[26] An old piece of folk wisdom among macroeconomic forecasters holds that the best way to forecast real activity over the next couple of years is to determine whether a recession is in the offing. If a recession does seem likely, then you should project a downturn roughly in line with average postwar experience; otherwise, assume growth will continue at its current average pace. Hamilton's switching model shows why this approach tended to work reasonably well in practice (so long as you were good at calling a recession).

[27] The model is described in chapter 10 of Kim and Nelson (1999) and is fit over the period January 1959 to December 2019.

[28] The model's estimated transition probabilities are $p = 0.985$ and $q = 0.863$, where state zero is defined to be the recession state (these are the posterior medians). With a Markov process, the average fraction of time that the economy spends in a given state equals $x/(2 - p - q)$, with $x = 1 - p$ for a recession and $x = 1 - q$ for an expansion; once a given state is entered, its expected duration in months is given by $1/(1 - y)$, with $y = q$ for a recession and $y = p$ for an expansion.

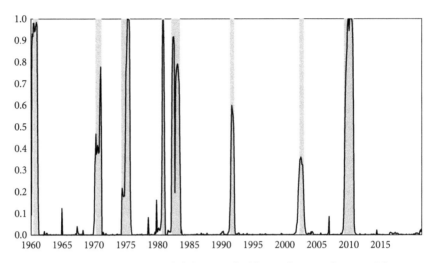

Figure 2.10   Recession probabilities implied by Markov switching model.

Taken literally, the assumption that contractions and expansions evolve according to a Markov process implies that duration dependence is not a feature of the business cycle: No matter how long an expansion has lasted, the probability of entering a recession is always the same (and vice versa). There have been a host of studies that attempt to explicitly test whether duration dependence characterizes recessions or expansions; in general, the results are inconclusive. That probably shouldn't be too surprising: Once again, we only have a dozen data points (postwar recessions) that we can look at, and the proximate causes of these recessions include such disparate events as financial crises, oil shocks, pandemics, and deliberately contractionary monetary policy. It seems unlikely then that duration dependence would be a *structural* feature of the business cycle, and while it is certainly possible that imbalances could build up over long expansions that would make a recession more likely, or that policy responses might become more aggressive in a prolonged slump, these kinds of mechanisms are better studied on their own rather than as "average" properties of cyclical fluctuations.

Empirical models like these capture one sort of asymmetry in the business cycle by allowing real activity to have different underlying dynamics in and out of recessions: In Hamilton's model and its variants, a recession reflects an intercept shift, so a recovery represents the restoration of a normal rate of trend growth. However, we might instead prefer a description of the business cycle that permits the expansion phase of the business cycle to have two distinct pieces: a relatively rapid recovery of activity that occurs once a recession ends; and a slower, trend rate of advance that takes hold after the recovery is complete (and that represents the economy's usual expansion state).[29] Following section 5.6 of Kim and Nelson (1999), we can describe such a model as follows:

$$y_t = \tau_t + x_t$$

$$\phi_p(L)x_t = \gamma s_t + \varepsilon_t$$

$$\tau_t = \mu_{t-1} + \tau_{t-1} + \eta_t$$

$$\mu_t = \mu_{t-1} + v_t, \tag{2.8}$$

where y_t is the logarithm of real GDP; ε_t, η_t, and v_t are uncorrelated innovations; and s_t is a one–zero indicator that follows a Markov process.

This model is similar to the unobserved components model (Equation 2.2) that was used earlier to implement a trend–cycle decomposition, but with two notable differences. First, the rate of trend growth μ_t is allowed to vary (it is modelled as a driftless random walk rather than as a constant). Second, the cyclical component is modelled as an AR process together with a shift term that follows a Markov process. In addition, if we assume that $\sigma_\varepsilon = 0$, then the level of real activity that prevails during the expansion phase will be more like a "normal" or "ceiling" level, rather than a statistical trend for which fluctuations on either side of the trend net out to zero over long enough periods. (We will return to this notion when we discuss the productive potential of an economy in Chapter 4.) Estimates of the cyclical component x_t from this model are shown in Figure 2.11. The model reveals some evidence of asymmetry; the results also indicate that output remained below trend throughout the entire 1970s, which could reflect the model's difficulty in disentangling the post-1965 slowdown in trend output growth from the relatively large and frequent recessions seen over this period. The relatively slow recoveries that followed the 1990–1991 and 2001 recessions are also captured by the model; similarly, output appears to take somewhat longer to recover from the 2007–2009 recession compared with the equally deep Volcker recessions of 1980–1982, even though the model's estimate of trend output (not shown) slows noticeably in the wake of the financial crisis.

The various Markov switching models that we have been looking at represent simple statistical characterizations, not deep structural models of the

---

[29] This three-phase characterization of the business cycle is known as the "plucking" model of recessions (after Milton Friedman) or the "Joe Palooka" model (after Alan Blinder); as originally described, it tried to capture the idea that deeper recessions tended to be followed by correspondingly stronger recoveries.

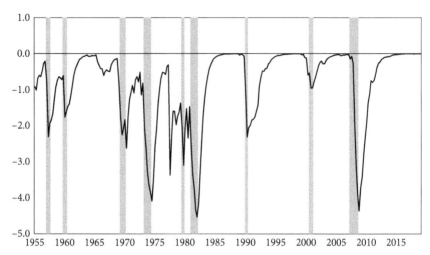

Figure 2.11 Deviations of log real GDP from trend implied by a "plucking" model of recessions.

business cycle. For example, including the pandemic period causes a model like the one used for Figure 2.10 to completely break down: Because the pandemic recession was so deep and rapid compared to previous recessions, the model doesn't identify any prior periods as belonging to a recession state. (Hamilton's original model broke down much earlier – around the late 1980s – likely reflecting both a change in the amplitude of business cycles and slower trend growth.) It is also very likely that the dynamics of a recovery are themselves determined by the *nature* of the shock that causes a recession – for example, the financial crisis almost certainly affected the economy in a way that made the recovery from the 2007–2009 recession more protracted.[30] All that said, switching models like these do strongly suggest that a recession is something more than just the simple propagation of an especially large shock, and instead involves a discontinuous shift in household and firm behavior following a shock. If so, then the idea that business cycles can be modelled as market-clearing equilibrium phenomena seems even harder to entertain.

---

[30] That observation hints that Lucas's (1977) hypothesis that "business cycles are all alike" might be wrong in an important sense, and – in the case of the slow recovery that followed the financial crisis – further suggests that the response of fiscal and monetary policy might be an important determinant of how a recovery plays out.

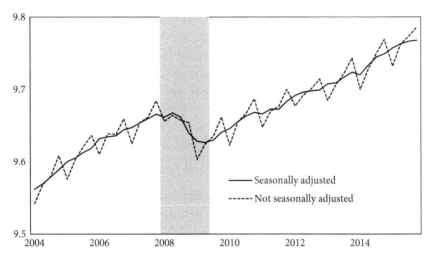

Figure 2.12 Seasonally adjusted and unadjusted log real GDP.

2.4 What Seasonal Cycles Suggest about Business Cycles

It seems that certain events (or combinations of events) are able to tip the economy into a recession state, while others aren't. What other evidence can we bring to bear regarding what's needed to induce an economic downturn?

One suggestive clue is given by Figure 2.12, which plots the logarithm of seasonally adjusted and not seasonally adjusted real GDP. Every year, the United States enters into a deep downturn in the first quarter, followed by a gradual recovery over the remainder of the year. These swings largely reflect consumption patterns associated with the winter holidays, and they are extremely large: On average, the peak-to-trough decline implied by the seasonal cycle (about 4 percent for the period shown) is as large as the *entire* decline in output that occurred during the 2007–2009 recession.[31]

The magnitude of seasonal cycles implies that the realization of a large shock is not by itself sufficient to push the economy into a recession state. The reason, of course, that seasonal swings don't result in actual recessions is that they are largely predictable; they represent anticipated shocks that, while very large, don't cause households and firms to significantly revise

---

[31] As a technical aside, not seasonally adjusted GDP doesn't actually exist: Published GDP is produced using seasonally adjusted source data, while not seasonally adjusted GDP is put together separately by replacing these source data with their seasonally unadjusted counterparts. However, the effects of seasonality are similarly pronounced in other seasonally unadjusted measures of real activity.

their assessment of the current and prospective state of the economy, and that can also be planned for well in advance.[32] In this sense, then, the economy appears to be conditionally stable in the face of certain types of disturbances; namely, those that are not too far out of line with past experience and current anticipations. But whether it is stable more broadly – that is, whether there are natural corrective forces that lead the economy to recover in the wake of *any* shock – remains an open question.[33]

2.5 Recessions and Stability

As an empirical fact, the US economy has recovered from every postwar recession (though some recoveries have been noticeably slower than others). It's far from clear, however, why this would be. In periods where demand is depressed because output is low, and output is low because demand is, it seems as though the economy could easily get "stuck" in a low-activity state. And in theoretical terms, the fact that microtheorists have been unable to come up with a mechanism that would tend to push a model economy toward its (Walrasian) equilibrium also – and correctly – suggests that macroeconomists would have trouble coming up with a convincing theoretical description of what causes the economy to recover following a recession, let alone what would bring it back to a state of full employment.

In early Keynesian analysis, there were various "traps" the economy could find itself in, and no tendency for the economy to right itself absent active policy intervention.[34] This reflected Keynes's vision of the nature of the business cycle, in which a demand multiplier magnified the effects of swings in business investment and investment was assumed to be largely determined by the sentiment of businesspeople (and so largely exogenous). One of the earliest attempts to demonstrate that there *would* be self-correcting tendencies came from Pigou (1943), and was the centerpiece of Patinkin's (1965) analysis; the mechanism these authors had in mind was one where the disinflationary effects of a slump would cause real money balances (or real wealth more generally) to increase, thereby stimulating consumption.[35]

---

[32] This is not a new observation: Burns and Mitchell (1946, chapter 3) used it as a justification for seasonally adjusting economic aggregates before trying to analyze the business cycle.

[33] Seasonal cycles have been used to try to gain other insights into the nature of the business cycle, though not completely convincingly; see Miron and Beaulieu (1996) and the book-length treatment by Miron (1996) for two somewhat dated contributions.

[34] Keynes did allow that depreciation of the capital stock and liquidation of inventories would, under normal conditions, help to stimulate a recovery (Keynes 1936, pp. 317–318).

[35] If these references seem old, it's because they are – stability is as neglected a topic in macro as it is in micro.

From an empirical and theoretical standpoint, the "Pigou–Patinkin" effect is unlikely to be an effective way to end a recession (or stabilize the economy). Empirically, wealth effects on consumption are too weak; and in the case of real balances, most of the money in the economy is generated by bank lending (and so is likely to move with real activity). Given those two facts, the decline in prices needed to appreciably boost consumption would be so large as to cause widespread bankruptcies among producers if labor costs were unchanged (thus reducing wealth), and would also put many households in distress if wages declined too and households had any sort of previously contracted debt obligations.[36]

Moreover, from the standpoint of general equilibrium theory Patinkin's "solution" to the stability problem turns out to be deficient. As Grandmont (1983) has shown, the real balance effect might be too weak *even in theory* to stabilize the economy. What is then needed is for agents' expectations regarding future prices and interest rates to respond in the "right" way (for some agents, not at all) to current prices – a condition that is highly implausible. Grandmont concludes that in a monetary economy, "… full price flexibility may not lead to market clearing after all … [because] there may not exist a set of prices and interest rates that would equate Walrasian demands and supplies."

We can get a flavor of this argument with the following simple example.[37] Consider an exchange economy with two periods and with individual endowments e_t, consumption c_t, prices p_t, and initial money holdings $\overline{m}$. A consumer therefore faces the following intertemporal budget constraint:

$$p_1 c_1 + p_2 c_2 \leq p_1 e_1 + p_2 e_2 + \overline{m}, \tag{2.9}$$

which is given as the line going through the points $\alpha\,\beta\,\gamma$ in Figure 2.13; the consumer's preferences are given by a utility function $u(c_1, c_2)$. Now assume that consumers expect future prices to be higher than current prices such that the price ratio p_2/p_1 exceeds the marginal rate of substitution at the endowment point α, as shown in panel A. If all consumers have these expectations, there will be pervasive excess demand in the market – everyone will want to consume more than their initial endowment e_1. Likewise, if we assume that consumers expect future prices to decline, a situation like the one in panel B can arise, where there is pervasive excess supply. Let's focus on the excess supply case. If p_1 declines in response to the excess supply,

---

[36] See Kalecki (1944).
[37] This discussion is taken from section 1.4 of Grandmont (1983).

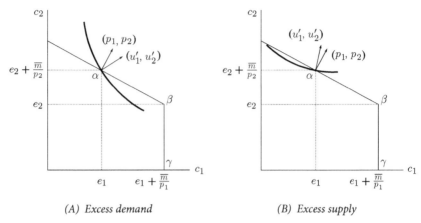

(A) Excess demand   (B) Excess supply

Figure 2.13 An example where the real-balance effect is too weak and price flexibility fails to deliver market clearing.

it will shift out line $\beta \gamma$; what happens to $\alpha \beta$ depends on how consumers' expectations of p_2 change in response. For example, if the decline in the price level is assumed to be permanent, then the *relative* price p_2/p_1 is unchanged and so $\alpha \beta$ shifts out in a parallel fashion. In this case, the real balance effect can be too weak to equilibrate the market.[38]

The preceding example makes it clear that price flexibility does not guarantee market clearing or a return to full employment. The following example and discussion, which is taken from Bénassy (1982, chapter 10), demonstrates how the presence of intertemporal decisionmaking can cause other sorts of problems. Consider the simplest possible setup: one firm, one consumer, and two periods. The consumer's utility function is given by

$$U(c_1, c_2, m_2) = (\alpha - \delta) \ln c_1 + (\alpha + \delta) \ln c_2 + \beta m_2 \qquad (2.10)$$

(putting the consumer's terminal money holding in their utility function is a trick to ensure the existence of a well-defined price level, and assuming $\delta > 0$ implies that the consumer wants to save in period 1). Production q is related to labor l by $q = F(l)$, and labor in both periods is in fixed supply and equal to $\bar{l}$. The firm can store any unsold output in inventory, and remits all profits to the consumer. Finally, there is a fixed money stock $\bar{m}$.

---

[38] This is immediately apparent for homothetic preferences; more generally, if the marginal rate of substitution along the vertical line at e_1 is bounded below by a positive value ε, then if $p_2/p_1 < \varepsilon$, no Walrasian equilibrium can exist for any value of the current price system p_1.

Full employment in this economy implies that the firm produces $\bar{q} = F(\bar{l})$ in both periods; the Walrasian price and real wage are also the same in both periods and given by

$$p^* = \frac{\alpha \overline{m}}{\beta \bar{q}} \quad \text{and} \quad w^*/p^* = F'(\bar{l}). \tag{2.11}$$

However, even if the prevailing price and real wage are both equal to these values, it is very unlikely that a full-employment equilibrium will result. The reason is that demand in the two periods is

$$c_1 = \left(1 - \frac{\delta}{\alpha}\right)\bar{q} \quad \text{and} \quad c_2 = \left(1 + \frac{\delta}{\alpha}\right)\bar{q}, \tag{2.12}$$

which implies that the firm will need to produce $\bar{q}$ in period 1 and store $(\delta/\alpha)\bar{q}$ in inventories in (correct) anticipation that higher demand will materialize in period 2. Put differently, the firm will need to respond to a level of demand in period 1 that is less than its output by purposely accumulating inventories to meet higher demand next period, which is the same as saying that the firm must forecast that demand will exceed the full-employment level of output in the second period despite its having fallen short in the first period. Since the firm receives no signal from the future to tell it that demand will be higher next period, it is more likely to just cut production next period under the assumption that demand in period 2 will be similar to demand in period 1. And all this occurs despite prices and wages being at their "correct" intertemporal (Walrasian) values.

There is actually a strong case to be made that sticky wages or prices are largely irrelevant to business cycles. (As we will see in Chapter 6, though, sticky prices probably *are* needed to explain certain features of the inflation process.) In particular, there are other reasons that don't involve price maladjustment that can explain why workers and firms might be off their Walrasian supply and demand curves and why markets might fail to clear.[39] Similarly, the lack of any proof of stability even for the idealized Walrasian system suggests that an economy might not immediately return to full employment even when the shocks that pushed it into a recession have

---

[39] Examples include pervasive uncertainty; imperfect information and incomplete markets; the presence of nonallocative prices or institutions that favor quantity adjustments over price adjustments (see Bewley, 1999 for some evidence from the labor market); and the price system's broader inability to coordinate the actions of workers, producers, and consumers over nontrivial lengths of time.

abated (at least, no one has ever come up with a convincing description of how this would happen, or why it's bound to occur in a market economy).

We might at least expect that the eventual adjustment of wages and prices in a new-Keynesian model would move economic activity back to its normal level. That also turns out to be not quite right. In many versions of these models, the monetary authority determines the economy's inflation rate and output gap through its choice of policy targets; the policy feedback rule then serves as a regulating mechanism to bring the economy toward these targets (assuming the nominal policy rate does not have to fall below zero to do so). In empirical implementations (such as Smets and Wouters, 2007), this process is helped along because recessions are "explained" in terms of fancifully labelled residuals that are themselves assumed to be stationary; hence, over history much of what brings the model out of a recession simply involves having these "structural" shocks die out or reverse themselves.

The slow recovery from the 2007–2009 recession, which contrasted with the rapid recoveries seen after previous deep recessions, renewed interest in microfounded optimizing models involving multiple equilibria. In these models, the economy can find itself stuck in a (locally stable) low-activity equilibrium that can only be exited through a policy intervention (such as a fiscal stimulus that pushes the economy back to a high-activity equilibrium) or an exogenous shift in expectations. Although models of this sort are intriguing, the specific mechanisms that are used tend to be either too contrived to take seriously or generate counterfactual predictions. For example, early work in this vein by Diamond (1982) assumes that production and consumption can be modelled as a search equilibrium, which doesn't seem like the best way to capture the insight that these activities invariably involve separate parties and so can be difficult to coordinate. Later work by Farmer (2010) uses a model with labor-market search to derive "Keynesian" conclusions about slumps; however, the model also predicts countercyclical real wages (p. 41) and – if the monetary authority respects the Taylor principle – an *upward*-sloping relation between wage growth and unemployment (p. 162).[40]

---

[40] Farmer does provide an interesting extension in the form of a "beliefs function" whereby self-fulfilling expectations influence aggregate demand through their effect on the value of capital and hence household wealth. (The model needs a wealth-based channel because it relies on a permanent-income framework.) While the notion that the public's beliefs can influence the level of activity probably has some truth to it, Farmer's conclusion that the Federal Reserve should target stock prices is harder to take seriously.

So what does cause a recession to end, and is an exit from a recession inevitable? The short answer is that nobody really knows. At best, we might plausibly argue that longer-run expectations about income and demand might help to anchor spending and production and contribute to a revival of "animal spirits" among consumers and producers; in addition, policy stimulus (especially when earlier policy actions were themselves a contributor to the recession) likely plays some role in fostering a recovery as well. But anyone who had read the *General Theory* could have probably told you that much.

3

Determinants of Aggregate Spending and Saving

He solemnly conjured me ... to observe that if a man had twenty pounds a year for his income, and spent nineteen pounds nineteen shillings and sixpence, he would be happy, but that if he spent twenty pounds one he would be miserable.
Charles Dickens (1867, chapter 11)

From a policy perspective, the two most important properties of a component of aggregate spending are its response to changes in real income or real activity, and its response to changes in financial conditions. When a spending component is tied to real activity, it will contribute to Keynesian-style multiplier dynamics that can amplify the effect of *autonomous* shocks to spending – that is, changes in spending that are themselves unrelated to income or activity. And if a component of aggregate demand responds to financial conditions, then it provides a way for monetary policy to influence spending and output. In this chapter, we will review various theoretical and empirical descriptions of several broad categories of spending. We will see that although received theory fails to provide compelling empirical descriptions of how the components of aggregate demand are determined, it is still possible to make some sensible empirical statements about a few of them.

3.1 Personal Consumption

These days, the point of departure for essentially all theoretical discussions of household consumption is some variant of the permanent income hypothesis. In its basic form (derived from the intertemporal optimization problem faced by an infinitely lived representative consumer), this *intertemporal optimization* framework implies a consumption function along the lines of

$$c_t = \frac{r}{1+r}A_t + \frac{r}{1+r}E_t \sum_{i=0}^{\infty} \frac{y_{t+i}^l}{(1+r)^i}, \qquad (3.1)$$

where r denotes the return on the consumer's stock of financial wealth A, and y^l denotes the consumer's labor income. (All variables are expressed in real terms.) The ingredients needed to obtain this equation are a subjective discount rate equal to the market rate of interest and quadratic utility; these imply that consumption follows a martingale process such that $E_t c_{t+1} = c_t$. The usual interpretation of this model is that the household consumes the "annuity value" of its financial and human wealth; for a real return (or subjective discount rate) on the order of $r = 5$ percent per year, the model therefore predicts a marginal propensity to consume (MPC) out of a temporary increase in income that is roughly the same magnitude as r (with a similarly sized MPC out of financial wealth).[1]

In its aggregate form, Equation (3.1) fails virtually every empirical test that has ever been thrown at it. Moreover, the Euler equation that characterizes the consumer's optimal intertemporal decision does a remarkably poor job as an asset-pricing model, even when preferences are characterized by more general utility functions. Empirically, consumption appears to respond to *predictable* income changes, which shouldn't be the case if consumers have already taken these changes into account in setting their optimal consumption level. In addition, the response of consumption to an anticipated income change is relatively large: For the fifty-seven studies using US macrodata that Havranek and Sokolova (2020) consider in their meta-analysis, the mean estimated response is 0.39 with a median estimate of 0.35.[2] This particular shortcoming of the basic model is known as the *excess sensitivity* puzzle; a related problem, known as *excess smoothness*, follows from the model's prediction that a permanent increase in labor income should feed through one-for-one into consumption. Since labor income growth tends to be positively autocorrelated in US data, a one-dollar innovation to income will permanently change the *level* of income by more than a dollar. That in turn implies that consumption should be more volatile than income, which is also at odds with the empirical evidence.[3]

---

[1] The definition of the annuity value as $r/(1 + r)$ instead of simply r reflects a timing convention that is almost universal in this literature.

[2] These values were computed from the replication files for Havranek and Sokolova (2020).

[3] There are numerous subtleties regarding these issues that I am breezing past here. For those who are interested, Deaton (1992) remains the best (and most readable) single introduction to the empirics of the canonical permanent income model, though it's now a bit long in the tooth.

It is also worth noting that the model described by Equation (3.1) differs in an important respect from Milton Friedman's own conception of the permanent income hypothesis (as amended). Although Friedman (1957, chapter 2) had used Irving Fisher's (1907) two-period intertemporal substitution example to argue that the market rate of interest could be one of the arguments of the consumption function, he did not ground his model in a complete optimizing framework. More importantly, Friedman did not view consumers' subjective discount rate as equivalent to a market interest rate. In a paper published several years after his book, Friedman (1963) stated that a subjective rate of time preference of 33 percent was reasonable and in line with the empirical evidence presented in his book. If so, near-term income changes will receive a large weight in permanent income and will therefore have a correspondingly large effect on consumption.[4]

For the version of the basic model summarized by Equation (3.1), it is possible to explain away the excess smoothness and excess sensitivity puzzles in terms of aggregation, though the resulting solution is a bit contrived and hinges on what variables are available to consumers (and when) – see Forni and Lippi (1997, section 13.6). But a more sophisticated version of the consumer's intertemporal optimization problem can also yield a consumption function that is closer in line with the empirical evidence. The key extension is to assume that marginal utility is a nonlinear (specifically, convex) function of consumption, which relaxes the linearity assumption that follows from using a quadratic utility function. If households' labor income is uncertain, convex marginal utility induces a precautionary saving motive, in the sense that the consumer will consume less (save more) than they would if they faced a certain income stream. Intuitively, if we consider the Euler equation for the consumer's intertemporal choice problem and allow the market rate to differ from the subjective rate of time preference ρ:

$$u'(c_t) = E_t \left(\frac{1+r}{1+\rho} \, u'(c_{t+1}) \right), \tag{3.2}$$

we see that higher expected future marginal utility $u'(c_{t+1})$ induces the consumer to reduce current consumption so as to raise today's marginal utility.

---

[4] Using Friedman's timing conventions, the MPC out of a temporary increase in income received at the start of the year would be exactly 0.33. Friedman was perfectly happy with a value like this – which seems large to anyone steeped in the modern version of the model (Equation 3.1) – because a motivation for his study was to show that the Keynesian expenditure multiplier was not much larger than one (and, hence, that the economy had more inherent stability than Keynes gave it credit for). See Friedman (1957, pp. 236–238).

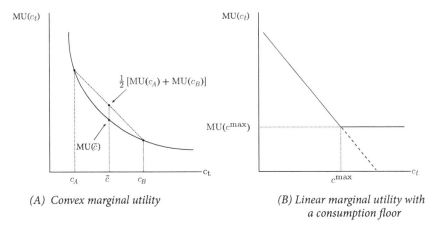

(A) Convex marginal utility

(B) Linear marginal utility with a consumption floor

Figure 3.1 Uncertainty induces a precautionary saving motive if marginal utility is convex (panel A) or if marginal utility is linear and there is a consumption "floor" (panel B).

This increase in expected marginal utility results when income (and so consumption) is uncertain, as can be seen from panel A of Figure 3.1: Here, if consumption levels c_A and c_B are equally likely, expected marginal utility will be greater than it would if the mean consumption value $\bar{c}$ were received with certainty. Formally, something similar can arise even under quadratic utility if a restriction is present that prevents consumption from rising above a certain level. A natural source of such a restriction is a borrowing constraint or possibility of a zero-income event such as unemployment, which ensures that consumption can go no higher than a level $c^{\max}$ (determined, say, by readily available liquid assets). As shown in panel B, even if marginal utility is linear, the presence of the consumption ceiling "convexifies" the marginal utility function that consumers actually face (likewise, if marginal utility is convex, the consumption ceiling makes it more so).[5]

When models like these are fully solved, they give rise to a concave consumption function of the sort shown in Figure 3.2 for a broad class of utility functions (see Carroll and Kimball, 1996).[6] The figure gives consumption as a function of "cash-on-hand" – essentially labor income plus (liquid)

---

[5] Unsurprisingly, things can get more complicated when multiple constraints are involved; see Carroll et al. (2021).

[6] In addition, the model requires consumers to be sufficiently impatient, which holds their precautionary saving motive in check. (Technically, the requirement on the consumer's discount rate, which also involves expected income growth, the market rate of return, and the consumer's intertemporal elasticity of consumption, ensures that a contraction mapping

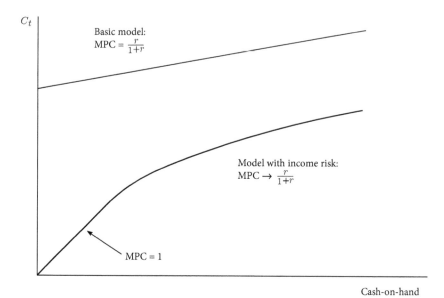

Figure 3.2 Consumption as a function of cash-on-hand. The straight line gives the consumption function that obtains in the basic model; the concave consumption function reflects a precautionary saving motive.

wealth – with both variables assumed to be scaled by the level of permanent income. As is evident from the figure, when cash-on-hand is low, the MPC is close to one; when it is high, consumers behave more like the consumers in the basic model with an MPC of around $r/(1 + r)$. (In addition, the introduction of income uncertainty raises the MPC for any level of cash-on-hand.) Better still, simulations of the model for a large number of consumers using realistic assumptions about the labor income process can yield average MPCs on the order of 0.3 or more (see table 1 of Carroll, 2001). Finally, empirical work finds some support for the model's basic prediction that MPCs should be lower for high-liquidity households.[7]

So why not just use this sort of model and get on with it? Unfortunately, as Allen and Carroll (2001) point out, deriving the optimal solution implied by the model requires computational abilities that are far beyond what human beings are capable of. Moreover, they argue that even an approximate

---

    exists that allows the policy function to be iterated back to a convergent solution – see Deaton, 1991.)

[7] For an interesting recent example, see Ganong et al. (2020), who find that the presence of racial and ethnic wealth gaps drives differences in MPCs across demographic groups.

solution or a simple rule of thumb is unlikely to be uncovered by trial and error: Because the only way to evaluate a consumption rule is to live with it for a number of years – possibly a large number of years – even an approximate solution will be nearly impossible to uncover over the course of a single lifetime.[8] More pithily, the authors point out that if it were possible to identify nearly optimal rules with just a small amount of trial and error, it would represent a dramatic advance in how dynamic optimization problems under uncertainty could be solved. None of this reinforces our faith in the predictive power or usefulness of the standard theoretical models of consumption.

It is fair to conclude, then, that we lack a reasonable aggregate model of consumption that is grounded in intertemporally optimizing behavior: Either the models are rejected empirically or they are so unrealistic that they provide no useful guidance as to how actual consumers would behave. Worse still, the profession's insistence on describing consumption in this manner has seriously impeded the development of theoretical macromodels that are halfway sensible, let alone useable for policy. For example, models of monetary policy transmission end up putting the burden on intertemporal substitution, and so need to assume unrealistically large responses of consumption to changes in real rates so as to generate nontrivial responses of aggregate demand (and labor supply) to policy shocks. Likewise, models of the business cycle need to rely on exogenous shocks to households' discount factors to produce reasonable cyclical fluctuations and lean on other modelling tricks to generate nontrivial propagation dynamics. As an example of the latter, we have the model of "confidence-led recessions" developed by Angeletos and Lian (2022) that was mentioned in Chapter 1. The model assumes full intertemporal optimization by households, which implies weak propagation of aggregate demand shocks: Everyone is a permanent-income consumer, and in this particular model, aggregate demand shocks do not affect permanent income. In order to get plausible propagation dynamics, the model has to assume an extremely contrived "informational friction" that causes consumers to *perceive* an aggregate demand shock as a shock to their permanent income. But the only reason

---

[8] Marglin (2008) makes a related critique, noting that choosing a lifetime consumption plan by comparing the utility from current and future consumption is fundamentally different from the standard consumer choice problem, which involves decisions such as whether to buy a tin of pears or a tin of peaches given their relative price (and for which the consumer likely has enough experience to choose optimally).

that these questionable assumptions are needed is because the point of departure is a deficient model of consumer behavior.[9]

A second, wider-reaching example is given by the so-called heterogeneous-agent models (for instance, Kaplan and Violante, 2018 or Kaplan and Violante, 2022). The goal of these models is to generate stronger propagation dynamics through a higher average MPC; to achieve it, they use an intertemporal choice model with income uncertainty that generates a concave consumption function and specify a wealth distribution that ensures that a large fraction of spending is accounted for by households on the steeper portion of the consumption function. These households can be wealthy in terms of overall assets; so long as much of their wealth is tied up in illiquid assets, though, they will have low cash-on-hand. (Since the consumption, income, and wealth variables are expressed relative to permanent income, wealthy households with few liquid assets can still account for a large portion of aggregate consumption.) Once again, though, the foundation of these models is an optimization problem that is intractable for ordinary persons – no matter how rational they are – and that cannot be well approximated by a simple heuristic process or rule of thumb.[10]

Without a reasonable theoretical description of consumption – and without the data needed to carefully deal with aggregation biases – all that we are left with to guide the specification of an empirical model is our pre-existing intuition that real consumer spending likely depends on real posttax income, and possibly real wealth. To get a rough idea of what the data have to say, we can fit an equation like

$$\Delta \ln c_t = \beta_0 + B_c(L)\Delta \ln c_{t-1} + B_y(L)\Delta \ln y_t^d + B_W(L)\Delta \ln W_t, \quad (3.3)$$

in which growth in total real personal consumption expenditures (PCE), $\Delta \ln c_t$, is related to its own lags, real disposable personal income growth $\Delta \ln y_t^d$, and the growth of real household net worth $\Delta \ln W_t$ (all variables are expressed as annual rates by multiplying them by 400). Note that unlike specifications that are intended to line up conceptually with an optimizing model, Equation (3.3) uses total consumption (not nondurables and services), disposable personal income (not posttax labor income),

---

[9] Despite incorporating a form of heterogeneity, a model like this actually boils down to a sort of representative-agent model (Angeletos and Lian, 2022, prop. 5) because the idiosyncratic shocks are independent and drawn from a common distribution (see Aoki and Yoshikawa, 2012 for a discussion of this issue).

[10] When used to analyze monetary policy, the models have a further deficiency: As we'll see in Chapter 7, in these models the predicted response of real activity following a monetary policy shock hinges on the response of the fiscal authority (it can also depend on how firms distribute their profits).

Table 3.1 *Correlates of quarterly real consumption growth*

	Lags	1987:Q1–2019:Q4		1977:Q1–2007:Q4	
		OLS	IV	OLS	IV
Disposable income	0 to 1	0.250	0.399	0.345	0.492
		(0.072)	(0.139)	(0.112)	(0.252)
Long run		0.375	0.529	0.430	0.567
Net worth	1 to 2	0.106	0.104	0.137	0.128
		(0.026)	(0.027)	(0.048)	(0.051)
Long run		0.160	0.139	0.171	0.147
Consumption	1 to 3	0.334	0.247	0.199	0.133
		(0.109)	(0.132)	(0.134)	(0.169)
F-statistic*			32.6		16.5

* From first-stage regression. Standard errors in parentheses.

and a net worth measure that includes households' stocks of consumer durables (though omitting durables from the net worth measure makes little difference). The price index for total personal consumption expenditures is used to deflate all nominal variables.

The first column of Table 3.1 gives the coefficient sums that obtain from fitting Equation (3.3) over the period 1987:Q1 to 2019:Q4, along with the implied long-run effects. (The long-run effects give the eventual effect on the log-level of consumption from a one-time temporary increase in the growth of income or wealth or the eventual effect on consumption *growth* from a permanent change in income or wealth growth; they are computed by dividing the relevant coefficient sum by $1 - B_c(1)$.) Since we have no interest in testing the martingale prediction of the optimizing permanent income model, we have no reason to omit contemporaneous income growth from the specification. We might be concerned, though, that income will be correlated with the model's residual if a shock to consumption raises income through its within-quarter effect on aggregate demand. There aren't many good instruments that we can use for income growth – lagged income growth is too weak, while measures of real activity suffer from the same issue that income does.[11] One possible choice is to use a real hourly compensation measure, on the grounds that it should be relatively invariant to an increase

---

[11] See Staiger and Stock (1997) for an overview of some of the problems that can arise from using weak instruments.

in total labor compensation that results from an increase in hours worked; the measure used here as an instrument is the log difference of the Productivity and Costs measure of hourly compensation for the business sector deflated by the PCE price index. As the second column indicates, these estimates are quite similar to the OLS results – though note that the direction of the apparent bias doesn't conform to the channel suggested above.[12]

This is an extremely unsophisticated model, and we might be concerned about the stability of its coefficients, especially for wealth. Over time, financial innovations such as credit cards have made it easier for households to borrow, while other innovations (such as home equity lines of credit) have made previously illiquid assets somewhat more liquid. In addition, the massive decline in household net worth during the 2007–2009 recession represents an influential outlier that might drive the coefficient on this term (likewise, most of the variation in income and consumption growth occurs during recessions). More generally, it is always a good idea to try reestimating an empirical model over various sample periods: We wouldn't expect the behavior of aggregate variables to remain the same over long spans of time – for one thing, we typically have no good way to correct for slow-moving demographic effects or changes in the distribution of income or wealth – while one or more influential outliers can have an outsized effect on parameter estimates even in "long" time series. (One corollary to this point is that in empirical macroeconomics, more data aren't always better.) As a check, therefore, the next two columns report results from stopping the estimation in 2007:Q4 (so just prior to the financial crisis), with 1997:Q1 used as the starting point (to keep the sample size similar); in this particular case, the estimates hold up reasonably well.

Taken together, these results suggest an income elasticity of around 0.4 to 0.5 – in line with the estimates from the excess sensitivity literature – with a wealth elasticity on the order of 0.1 or so. Note that these coefficients are elasticities, not MPCs. Since consumption is close to income (the saving rate is generally below 10 percent over this period), the coefficient on income will be similar to an MPC. But the consumption–wealth ratio is much smaller (it has also declined over time, starting at 18.5 percent in 1977 and moving

---

[12] The F-statistics from the first-stage regressions, shown at the bottom of the table, are respectable enough. For connoisseurs of these things, the Cragg–Donald minimum eigenvalue statistic is 27.9 for the first period and 14.5 for the second period – the latter admittedly a bit thin (see Stock and Yogo, 2005). Note also that in cases where heteroscedasticity or serial correlation (or both) is present, the first-stage F-statistics typically need to be a lot higher (see Montiel Olea and Pflueger, 2013).

below 13 percent by 2019), and so the corresponding MPC out of wealth is on the order of 2 cents on the dollar or less.[13]

What about a role for interest rates? It turns out that the real federal funds rate, defined as the nominal rate less the average three-year change in core PCE prices, receives the correct (negative) sign when the model is estimated over 1977–2007 (which does not contain periods where the zero lower bound was in play). However, the semielasticity is small (on the order of –0.2) and does little to improve the model's fit in dynamic simulations; most likely, the variable is simply proxying for the state of general economic conditions. Other measures of the real rate using either the ten-year Treasury yield or the BBB corporate bond rate fail to enter and typically receive positive coefficients.[14] In direct tests of the Euler equation for consumption using aggregate data, Ascari et al. (2021) find no role for the real federal funds rate, but some evidence that stock market returns matter. It seems equally plausible, however, that the dependence of consumption growth on stock returns simply captures the sort of wealth effect that appears in the simple empirical model. In any case, a channel from net worth to consumption provides some scope for monetary policy actions to influence consumer spending even without an intertemporal substitution channel, as we'll discuss further in Chapter 7.[15]

The positive coefficient sums on lagged consumption growth boost the long-run elasticity of income (and wealth) relative to its simple coefficient sum. However, these positive values partly reflect the use of quarterly average data. If consumption is actually determined at a higher frequency (say monthly), then quarterly average changes will tend to manifest first-order autocorrelation even if the higher frequency (monthly) changes are themselves white noise.[16] This would be a particular problem if we were concerned about expectations and information sets – for instance, if we were trying to use lagged variables to instrument for a time $t - 1$ expectation, we would not be able to use the first lag of a quarterly average change as an instrument.

---

[13] See Carroll et al. (2011) for a more nuanced description of empirical wealth effects.

[14] Of course, nominal interest income, which accounted for roughly 9 percent of total personal income from 2010 to 2019, tends to rise and fall with interest rates.

[15] This is not to argue that all forms of consumer spending are insensitive to interest rates – for example, motor vehicle purchases are often financed by loans and depend on credit availability and households' expected ability to make interest payments. That's not quite the same thing as an interest-rate effect mediated through an Euler equation, though.

[16] See Section E.2 of the Appendix for a discussion. (Note that changes in a variable like net worth, which is an end-of-period stock, won't suffer from this problem.)

Table 3.2 *Correlates of monthly real consumption growth*

	Lags	1987:M1– 2019:M12	1977:M1– 2007:M12
Consumption	1 to 2	−0.393	−0.449
		(0.083)	(0.084)
S&P 500*	1	0.067	0.064
		(0.015)	(0.022)
Long run		0.048	0.044
Disposable income	3 to 12	0.394	0.558
		(0.133)	(0.188)
Long run		0.283	0.385

*Twelve-month log difference. Standard errors in parentheses.

It's therefore worth checking how the estimated elasticities change if we use monthly data. These data exist for consumption and personal income, though it is important to be aware of their shortcomings. When the Bureau of Economic Analysis (BEA) construct the national accounts, they often have to use indicators to interpolate higher-frequency series. For example, reasonably good data on services consumption are available quarterly (in the form of the Quarterly Services Survey), but to "fill in" real *monthly* values of these series the BEA might use an indicator such as employment in a particular service industry. Moreover, even when more direct monthly source data are available, their quality might not be as good as their lower-frequency counterparts. And the same is also true for many income components.[17] With that caveat in mind, Table 3.2 gives results from regressions of monthly real consumption growth on two of its lags and lags 3 to 12 of real disposable income growth. (Omitting lags 0 to 2 ensures that no income variable will fall in the same quarter as the monthly dependent variable and removes the need to use instrumental variables.) Since net worth is only available quarterly, the wealth proxy is the twelve-month log difference of the S&P 500 index in real terms (using the PCE price index), lagged one month. Lagged consumption enters negatively (a pattern that is also evident in the deflated monthly retail sales data), while the long-run income elasticities range from 0.3 to 0.4 – lower, but not too different from the quarterly estimates.

---

[17] This issue is not confined to monthly data. The best data that BEA have come from the quinquennial censuses of business; these are used to "benchmark" the national accounts every five years and to compute new input–output tables. But for annual and quarterly series, indicator series of varying degrees of reliability and coverage are used.

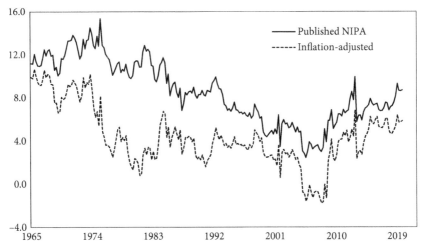

Figure 3.3 Correcting for the portion of nominal interest income that is compensation for inflation implies a very different contour for the saving rate over the past half-century.

3.2 Digression: The Inflation-Adjusted Saving Rate

As measured by the National Income and Product Accounts (NIPAs), the US personal saving rate declined more or less steadily from the mid-1970s until the eve of the financial crisis (see the solid black line in Figure 3.3). Writing in the 1990s, Laibson (1997, section IV.E.) argued that this development could be explained theoretically by financial innovations after the late 1970s that made it easier for consumers to access "instantaneous credit" through credit cards and (since the mid-1980s) to borrow against the equity in their homes.[18] The timing of the decline in the saving rate certainly appears to support Laibson's conjecture. However, one other thing that changed after the early 1980s was that price inflation moved persistently lower. And changes in inflation can seriously bias NIPA measures of personal saving and income.

One way to see how is by thinking about the accounting definition of saving. Budget constraints and accounting identities are defined in nominal terms, though they can be converted to real relationships through suitable

---

[18] Laibson used an intertemporal consumer choice model with hyperbolic discounting. Under hyperbolic discounting, consumers are more impatient over short horizons than over long horizons; the resulting dynamic inconsistency in preferences makes them seek out illiquid assets as a way of committing their future impatient selves to saving.

deflation. Let tildes denote nominal variables, and let i be the nominal interest rate. Nominal saving $\tilde{s}$ is defined as:

$$\tilde{s} = \frac{i}{1+i}\tilde{A} + \tilde{y}^l - \tilde{c}, \qquad (3.4)$$

where $\frac{i}{1+i}\tilde{A}$ is nominal asset income and $\tilde{y}^l$ is nominal labor income, so their sum is total personal income (ignore taxes for now). If we want to write this in real terms, we can deflate by the price level p:

$$\frac{\tilde{s}}{p} = \frac{i}{1+i}\frac{\tilde{A}}{p} + \frac{\tilde{y}^l}{p} - \frac{\tilde{c}}{p} = \frac{i}{1+i}A + y^l - c. \qquad (3.5)$$

The problem is that real saving should be defined using *real* asset income, which is $\frac{r}{1+r}A$, not $\frac{i}{1+i}A$. (Again, we're using the mildly baffling timing convention mentioned in footnote 1.) By the definition of the real interest rate:

$$\frac{r}{1+r} = \frac{\frac{(1+i)}{(1+\pi)}-1}{\frac{(1+i)}{(1+\pi)}} = \frac{i-\pi}{1+i} = \frac{1+i-(1+\pi)}{1+i} = \frac{i-\pi}{1+i}, \qquad (3.6)$$

which means that expression 3.5 overstates the true real saving rate by an amount $\frac{\pi}{(1+i)}A$.

The adjustments needed for the NIPA saving rate are slightly more complicated, but the same principle is at work.[19] The NIPA definition of flow saving $\tilde{S}^N$ is:

$$\tilde{S}^N = \frac{\tilde{Y}^d - \tilde{C} - \tilde{I}}{\tilde{Y}^d}, \qquad (3.7)$$

where $\tilde{Y}^d$ is nominal disposable income (personal income less taxes) and $\tilde{I}$ is nominal *nonmortgage* interest outlays made by consumers.[20] Write nominal interest outlays as $i_t\tilde{L}_t$ (where L stands for "liabilities"), denote consumers' nominal interest-bearing financial wealth by $\tilde{W}_t$, denote their other (non-interest) income as $\tilde{Y}_t^{oth}$, and let τ stand for the tax rate. Then NIPA nominal saving can be written as

$$\tilde{S}^N = (1-\tau)i_t\tilde{W}_t + (1-\tau)\tilde{Y}_t^{oth} - i_t\tilde{L}_t - \tilde{C}_t, \qquad (3.8)$$

[19] See Jump (1980) for a detailed discussion.
[20] These interest outlays don't include mortgage interest payments because the NIPAs consider mortgage interest payments to be a charge against personal rental income. (Personal transfer payments to government and the rest of the world are also included in outlays, but they aren't relevant here.)

which can be converted to real saving by dividing each term by the PCE price index,

$$S^N = (1 - \tau)i_t W_t + (1 - \tau)Y_t^{oth} - i_t L_t - C_t. \tag{3.9}$$

This last expression is not how an economist would define real saving, however, as that should involve *real* interest income:

$$S_t^H = r_t^{at} W_t + (1 - \tau)Y_t^{oth} - i_t L_t - C_t, \tag{3.10}$$

where the real after-tax interest rate, r_t^{at}, is equal to $(1 - \tau)i_t - \pi_t$ (π_t is the rate of consumer price inflation). This concept is sometimes referred to as a "Hicksian" measure – hence the H superscript – as a similar notion was discussed by J. R. Hicks in chapter XIV of *Value and Capital* (1946). Comparing these two expressions, it is apparent that if an increase in inflation takes place, the resulting increase in the NIPA real saving concept will be too large by an amount $\Delta \pi_t W_t$, because the NIPA measure does not take into account that a portion of nominal interest payments is simply compensation for inflation.

Similarly, the NIPA definition of real disposable income is:

$$(1 - \tau)i_t W_t + (1 - \tau)Y_t^{oth}, \tag{3.11}$$

while the Hicksian measure is

$$r_t^{at} W_t + (1 - \tau)Y_t^{oth} - i_t L_t. \tag{3.12}$$

Hence, an increase in inflation that feeds into nominal interest rates will cause the NIPA measure to rise too much (relative to the correct real measure) by an amount $\Delta \pi_t (W_t + L_t)$ (the L_t term is there because $i \approx r + \pi$).

In order to bring the NIPA saving rate (saving as a share of disposable income) into alignment with the Hicksian concept, we therefore need to reduce NIPA saving S^N by an amount equal to the inflation rate times households' holdings of interest-bearing assets. We also need to deduct this from NIPA disposable personal income, along with an amount equal to the inflation rate times households' nonmortgage interest-bearing liabilities. (We are being loose here about the difference between expected and actual inflation; in the calculation, we will use the average rate of inflation over the preceding three years as a proxy for the inflation rate that enters into nominal interest rates.) We can get estimates of these assets and liabilities from the Financial Accounts of the United States (formerly the Flow-of-Funds Accounts), which contain detailed balance sheet data for the household sector.[21] When we make these adjustments, we get the inflation-adjusted saving rate that is given by the dashed line in Figure 3.3. Evidently, once we take into account how inflation can distort measured income and saving, we find that the decline in the personal saving rate was actually concentrated in the high-inflation period of the 1970s, with the saving rate nearly trendless thereafter (the slightly higher average rate in the decade after the 2007–2009 recession likely reflects a combination of increased precautionary saving and households' desire to restore their net worth following the financial crisis).

This exercise gives a hint of how difficult it can be to map theoretical concepts into real-world data. For another example, see Palumbo, Rudd, and Whelan (2006), who found that several empirical consumption papers from the 1980s and 1990s took a cavalier approach to deflation and measurement that unfortunately affected their results.

3.3 Private Fixed Investment

Like consumption, the empirical models used to explain and forecast aggregate investment spending have only a tenuous connection to theory, in part because measured quantities often don't line up well with their theoretical counterparts, but also because the predictions of most theories – including as to what variables "should" matter for investment – don't receive much empirical support.[22] In addition, theoretical models of investment generally fail to deal sensibly with the sorts of issues that surround the construction of measures of the aggregate capital stock or the characterization of aggregate production, which makes them suspect on conceptual grounds and unappealing as empirical guides.[23]

Since we need to start somewhere, let's begin with the so-called *flexible accelerator model* of Kiyotaki and West (1996).[24] In this model, the business sector of the economy is assumed to collectively minimize the following loss

---

[21] The calculation of W includes the nonequity portions of holdings in assets like mutual funds; interest-bearing liabilities L are defined as consumer credit plus loans.

[22] See Caballero (1999) for an early survey, and Kothari, Lewellen, and Warner (2014) for a detailed empirical evaluation of various potential correlates with investment. In firm-level data (and with a little bit of work) it is possible to find a greater role for interest rates or a cost-of-capital measure – see Gilchrist and Zakrajšek (2007) and Frank and Shen (2016) – but apparently these relations don't show up strongly in aggregate data.

[23] We will return to this second point in some detail in Chapter 4.

[24] The goal of a model like this one is to induce a partial-adjustment process for the capital stock; the basic idea dates back at least to Goodwin (1948).

function (all variables are in logs):

$$L_t = E_t \left[\sum_{i=0}^{\infty} \theta^i \left\{ (k_{t+i} - k_{t+i}^*)^2 + \alpha (k_{t+i} - k_{t+i-1})^2 \right\} \right], \qquad (3.13)$$

where the first quadratic term captures the loss associated with having the actual capital stock k_t be different from its optimum value k_t^*, and where the second quadratic term represents an "adjustment cost" that is incurred from changing the capital stock.[25] The parameter α gives the relative importance of these two sources of loss; θ denotes a discount factor. Equation (3.13) can be solved to yield:

$$k_t = \lambda k_{t-1} + \frac{\lambda}{\alpha} E_t \left[\sum_{i=0}^{\infty} (\theta \lambda)^i k_{t+i}^* \right], \qquad (3.14)$$

where $\lambda < 1$ is a root of the lag polynomial associated with the difference equation that is implied by the model's first-order condition.

If the business sector's output is characterized by a Cobb–Douglas production function with capital elasticity β, then the log of the optimal capital stock is given as:

$$k^* = y_t - u_t, \qquad (3.15)$$

where y_t is the log of output and u_t is the log cost of capital (we are ignoring the $\ln \beta$ term).[26] If we further assume that the first differences of these variables follow simple *AR* processes (and so can be used to generate future expected values), we can write the following equation for the growth of the capital stock,

$$\Delta k_t = \lambda \Delta k_{t-1} + A(L) \Delta y_t + B(L) \Delta u_t. \qquad (3.16)$$

We need another step to obtain an investment equation, though. For a rate of depreciation δ_t, the accumulation equation for capital

$$\Delta K_{t+1} = I_{t+1} - \delta_{t+1} K_t \qquad (3.17)$$

---

[25] Adjustment cost functions for capital or investment are an *ad hoc* device to yield smooth responses of these variables; they cannot be identified from empirical investment equations. Even so, adjustment costs are sometimes taken so seriously in theoretical models that they are subtracted from the model's concept of final output (as if they were an actual charge against production).

[26] If we were using a CES production function of the form $y = (aK^\sigma + bL^\sigma)^{(1/\sigma)}$, then u in Equation (3.15) would be multiplied by $1/(1 - \sigma)$.

implies that the growth rate of the capital stock is given by

$$\Delta k_{t+1} = \frac{I_{t+1}}{K_t} - \delta_{t+1} \qquad (3.18)$$

(note that capital is defined as an end-of-period stock, and investment and depreciation are flows over the period). In principle, therefore, we could estimate Equation (3.16) and use the predicted value of Δk_{t+1} and the known value of K_t to back out the level of I_{t+1} (assuming we knew – or could predict – the time-$t+1$ depreciation rate).

It's here that we run into two complications. First, because of the way that the data are estimated, Equation (3.17) doesn't actually hold at the aggregate level. In US data, real capital stocks are constructed at the level of individual assets (for example, metalworking machines), and it is only at this disaggregated level that Equation (3.17) holds in real terms.[27]

The second issue is more subtle. For the model to make sense, the value of k that we are comparing to k^* needs to be a measure of the "productive" capital stock; that is, the level of the capital stock that is combined with other inputs to generate a flow of output and profits. But the BEA data that are typically used to fit models like these don't measure this concept – instead, they are intended to capture a "wealth stock" of undepreciated past acquisitions of capital goods. In particular, the depreciation rate used by the BEA to compute an individual asset stock is not intended to measure the evolution of the asset's flow of productive services; hence, the aggregate of these stocks won't match the overall productive stock. (For that reason, the Bureau of Labor Statistics take a different approach to measuring productive capital stocks in their multifactor productivity calculations; these productive stocks are then weighted by estimated rental rates to generate a measure of capital inputs.)

A related issue is that the "investment rate" I_t/K_{t-1}, which is also often used in empirical investment work, will be essentially meaningless. The ratios of chained real aggregates have no sensible interpretation, as they are simply the ratio of two index numbers. In addition, because we are not in a one-good world, a given amount of real investment in time-t doesn't have to add to each individual stock in a balanced way – that is, the composition of time-t investment needn't be – and probably won't be – the same as the

---

[27] Even this isn't strictly true, since investment flows for some assets are built up from more detailed pieces that can have different price deflators. (See Bureau of Economic Analysis, 2003 for a detailed description of the BEA's procedure for estimating stocks of capital goods.)

composition of the time $(t - 1)$ capital stock (productive or otherwise). If we instead compute the investment rate using nominal measures, we face a similar problem. To construct the current-dollar (nominal) capital stock, the BEA basically "reflate" the components of the real stock using the relevant price indexes for investment (in a rough sense, this gives a replacement-cost measure of the current stock, so long as we think that the price data fully capture all intervening quality changes). Since the shares of individual investment components can differ from their corresponding weights in the nominal capital stock, changes in the investment–capital ratio can occur that are purely driven by price changes.[28]

(If all that weren't enough, the capital stock data are annual, which is another minor drawback if we'd like to make a quarterly investment forecast – or have a decent number of degrees of freedom in the model.)

However, even if we don't want to use a model of capital stock growth to generate an investment forecast, it is still instructive to see what happens when we fit Equation (3.16) to the data. Here we need to be careful about an econometric issue: Most relevant output measures, such as real output for the business sector, will themselves include the domestic production of capital goods (the rest of investment demand will be met from imports of capital goods or drawdowns of capital goods inventories); as a result, the output term will be correlated with the equation's residual. Rather than looking for a suitable instrument for y_t (which is complicated by the fact that we are using annual-average data for investment), we can instead use an output series that strips out investment spending from total GDP. The cost-of-capital variable is then defined using the standard Hall–Jorgenson formula, based on the triple-B corporate bond yield. Finally, we consider two sample periods, one that starts in 1967 (so that we have a reasonable number of observations to fit the model), and one that starts in 1987 (which is likely to be more relevant to today). Both samples end in 2019.

Panel I of Table 3.3 gives the results for total business fixed assets.[29] In either sample period, output growth is an important correlate with fixed asset growth; in addition, since fixed asset growth is relatively persistent

---

[28] Note too that Equation (3.17) doesn't even hold in nominal terms, in the sense that nominal investment plus nominal depreciation will not sum to the change in the nominal stock. The reason is that real stocks are reflated using end-of-year prices while real investment and depreciation flows are reflated using annual average prices – see Bureau of Economic Analysis (2003), p. M-10.

[29] The model includes two lags of real fixed asset growth, lags zero to two of real output growth, and lags zero to one of the cost-of-capital measure. Growth rates are defined as log differences times 100.

Table 3.3 *Correlates of growth in real business fixed assets*

	1967–2019	1987–2019
I. Total business fixed assets		
Output growth	0.129	0.208
	(0.048)	(0.056)
Long-run effect	0.600	0.616
Cost of capital	0.012	0.006
	(0.007)	(0.011)
II. Equipment		
Output growth	0.248	0.280
	(0.100)	(0.130)
Long-run effect	1.186	1.067
Cost of capital	−0.022	−0.038
	(0.013)	(0.017)
Long-run effect	−0.104	−0.146
III. Intellectual property		
Output growth	0.156	0.221
	(0.051)	(0.077)
Long-run effect	0.606	0.691
Cost of capital	0.037	0.042
	(0.033)	(0.049)
IV. Structures		
Output growth	0.116	0.163
	(0.022)	(0.030)
Long-run effect	0.860	0.580
Cost of capital	0.001	0.001
	(0.002)	(0.001)

Note: Annual data; standard errors in parentheses.

(the sum of its lags is 0.79), the long-run elasticity of output is even larger. But the cost-of-capital term fails to enter and has a positive sign rather than the negative sign predicted by theory.

Total business fixed assets encompass an extremely heterogeneous mix of capital goods, and different sorts of capital goods could respond differently to output growth or to changes in the cost of capital. In the United States, there are three broad classes of business fixed investment: equipment, structures, and intellectual property products. (The third category covers things like movies, software, and research and development; the reason BEA consider these to be capital goods is that they involve up-front investments that are intended to provide streams of revenue in future periods.) Panels II through IV of the table repeat the estimation exercise for each of these categories (in each case, the output variable is defined as total GDP, excluding the component of investment whose stock is on the left-hand side of the regression, and the cost-of-capital term is modified to reflect the particular asset type). Once again, output growth figures prominently as a correlate with fixed asset growth, particularly for equipment. Equipment is also the only category that appears to depend negatively on the cost of capital, though this result turns out to be sensitive to whether the financial crisis period is excluded from the sample.

Now let's try modelling investment itself. The usual empirical approach relates aggregate investment (usually the ratio of investment to the capital stock) to a measure of Tobin's q that is derived either from the market value of equities or from some measure of the cost of capital and firms' cash flow or profits.[30] As was already noted, models like these don't fit very well, and using the investment–capital ratio in empirical work is questionable. The approach that we'll take instead is to try to model real investment growth using the same output and cost-of-capital terms that were used for the fixed-asset regressions.

Panels I and II of Table 3.4 present the coefficient sums from the models for total business fixed investment growth and equipment investment growth (both models include two own lags and one lag of output growth and the growth of a cost-of-capital term). Once again, lagged output growth is an important correlate in both models. The cost-of-capital term also enters – and with a negative sign; as the final column of the table indicates, though, this result is not robust to stopping the estimation period in 2007.

As an alternative to the cost of capital, we can look at the spread between triple-B bond yields and the ten-year Treasury yield. Gilchrist and Zakrajšek (2012) find that credit spreads help forecast economic activity and investment, and the increase in corporate-sector risk that is summarized in the spread could have an important influence on investment in a way that's not captured by the cost of capital.[31] Adding the change in the spread signif-

---

[30] Tobin's q is the ratio of the market value of an investment to its replacement value (see also Keynes, 1936, p. 151). Models that use the cost of capital and cash flow often build on Abel and Blanchard (1986), which uses VARs to generate expectations of future discount factors and future marginal profits on capital.

[31] Risk premia also appear to be something that a central bank can influence through policy (see Chapter 7).

Table 3.4 *Correlates of growth in real business fixed investment*

	Coefficient sums			Robust?
I. Total				
Output growth	0.747	0.398	0.427	
	(0.239)	(0.241)	(0.236)	
Long-run effect	1.861	1.095	1.171	
Cost-of-capital growth	−0.074	0.024		No
	(0.035)	(0.041)		
Long-run effect	−0.184	—		
Change in BBB spread		−7.386	−6.747	Yes
		(1.798)	(1.449)	
Long-run effect		—	−18.492	
II. Equipment				
Output growth	1.576	1.005	1.070	
	(0.411)	(0.402)	(0.391)	
Long-run effect	2.748	1.798	1.894	
Cost-of-capital growth	−0.149	0.055		No
	(0.078)	(0.085)		
Long-run effect	−0.260	—		
Change in BBB spread		−12.775	−11.820	Yes
		(2.787)	(2.367)	
Long-run effect		—	−21.013	
III. Structures excluding drilling and mining				
Output growth		2.348		
		(0.757)		
Long-run effect		3.778		

Note: Estimation period is 1987:Q1 to 2019:Q4. "Robust" indicates whether a variable continues to enter the model if estimation ends in 2007:Q4. Standard errors in parentheses.

icantly reduces the importance of the cost-of-capital term (note that the spread is measured in percentage points) and also reduces the importance of output growth (likely because the spread is itself a highly cyclical variable). In addition, the spread continues to enter even if the estimation period ends in 2007.[32]

---

[32] One caveat is that Kothari, Lewellen, and Warner (2014) find little evidence that changes in spreads – including the specific measures used by Gilchrist and Zakrajšek (2012) – are able

3.3 Private Fixed Investment

Table 3.5 *Correlates of growth in additional investment components*

	Coefficient sums			Robust?
IV. Drilling and mining structures				
Real natural gas price*		0.155 (0.044)		
Real oil price (WTI)*		0.559 (0.081)		
Change in BBB spread		−22.168 (8.653)		No
V. Intellectual property				
Output growth	0.712 (0.269)	0.653 (0.265)	0.621 (0.255)	
Long-run effect	1.245	1.146	1.097	
Cost-of-capital growth	−0.128 (0.057)	−0.032 (0.070)		No
Long-run effect	−0.223	—		
Change in BBB spread		−3.554 (1.539)	−3.972 (1.233)	No
Long-run effect		—	−7.014	
VI. Residential				
Output growth		2.407 (0.693)		
Long-run effect		4.690		
Change in mortgage rates		−18.950 (3.307)		Yes
Long-run effect		−36.920		

Note: Estimation period is 1987:Q1 to 2019:Q4. "Robust" indicates whether a variable continues to enter the model if estimation ends in 2007:Q4. Standard errors in parentheses. *Annualized log difference.

Panel III of the table reports results for investment in structures excluding drilling and mining (the reason for omitting these will be clear in a moment). Here, neither the cost of capital nor the spread term appears to matter, though once again lagged output growth seems to.

to forecast aggregate corporate investment over the 1952–2010 period once other correlates are included. However, they do find a role for GDP growth (and profit growth).

Next, panels IV and V of Table 3.5 consider the remaining components of business fixed investment. Growth in drilling and mining investment (think oil wells and fracking rigs) does not seem to be correlated with output growth; as shown, though, it is related to changes in real natural gas and oil prices (here, the GDP price index is used to compute real prices). There is also a correlation with the triple-B spread, though it doesn't survive excluding the latter portion of the sample. The correlation of this component with oil and gas prices raises an interesting question regarding House and Shapiro's (2008) claim that 2002 and 2003 bonus depreciation provisions had a large effect on qualified investment. As is evident from their table 3A, an important portion of the response that they find is for investment goods with a tax depreciation rate of 0.20, which is the tax depreciation rate for petroleum and natural gas and mining investment. Real drilling and mining investment did enjoy a steady boom over this period, rising nearly 45 percent from 2002:Q1 to 2006:Q4. But the increase was likely less related to bonus depreciation than to the 180 percent increase in crude oil prices and 160 percent increase in natural gas prices that occurred at the same time.[33] Finally, the only robust correlation for intellectual property investment (panel V) seems to be with output growth; most likely, this reflects the fact that things like R&D spending depend on cyclical variables like profits, while software spending is tied to other highly cyclical components of investment like information processing equipment.

The last panel of the table reports results for residential investment growth.[34] Although residential investment is treated as a component of fixed investment in the national accounts, it probably straddles the line between being a consumption good and a type of financial asset: The production and purchase of a home yields a good that provides a stream of consumption services (as does any durable consumer good), while owning a home represents an important component of net worth. Both output and changes in mortgage rates have a large influence on residential spending;

---

[33] Zwick and Mahon (2017) find a response similar to House and Shapiro; however, the imputed value for the total effect of the policy that they compute ($73.6 billion per year) is only 5 percent of total business fixed investment in 2001–2004. An interesting feature of this episode is that many firms with qualified investments failed to take advantage of bonus depreciation over this period, possibly because state and local governments did not change their tax codes in line with the federal tax change and also because many firms had contemporaneous losses or loss carryforwards (see Knittel, 2005, 2007; also Kitchen and Knittel, 2011).

[34] Note that residential investment includes brokers' commissions, which means that sales of *existing* homes can contribute to GDP.

the effect of mortgage rates likely also reflects the effect that they have on house prices or housing affordability.[35]

3.4 Digression: Why Don't Interest Rates Matter for Investment?

Textbook descriptions of aggregate demand determination emphasize the effect that changes in (real) interest rates have on business investment; likewise, investment spending is commonly viewed as a component of aggregate demand that is particularly responsive to changes in the stance of monetary policy. The cost-of-capital terms used for the investment models discussed above are highly correlated with changes in interest rates (for total business fixed investment, the simple correlation is on the order of 0.95), but these cost-of-capital terms seem unimportant for essentially all types of investment (which is in line with the findings in Kothari, Lewellen, and Warner, 2014).

There are several explanations for why interest rates don't matter (much) for aggregate business investment. First, firms typically have significant amounts of retained earnings and large liquid asset holdings that can be used to finance their capital expenditures out of pocket. For example, from 2010 to 2019 retained corporate profits averaged about a third of *total* business fixed investment, while nonfinancial corporate firms' holdings of liquid assets (broadly defined) were equal to about one-and-a-half years' worth of total investment. Second, credit could be rationed in a way that does not show up in a market interest rate; if so, that would still let monetary policy affect the economy, but through credit quantity and spreads rather than the interest rate per se (Stiglitz and Greenwald, 2003). Of course, it might also just be hard to disentangle the independent role of interest rates with a simple time-series model: Over a business cycle, pretty much everything moves together, so once the cycle is controlled for with a measure of output growth there might not be too much left to explain. On the other hand, there are other correlates that do seem to matter for aggregate capital spending, so if interest rates are themselves an important determinant of investment – and hence an important contributor to the business cycle – it seems as though their influence would show up more strongly than it does.

There are other reasons to think that interest rate movements have little to no effect on firms' capital spending. The discount or "hurdle" rates that firms

---

[35] In the model, industrial production for final products, which excludes construction and business supplies, is used as an instrument for real GDP excluding residential investment (the first-stage F-statistic is 69.6).

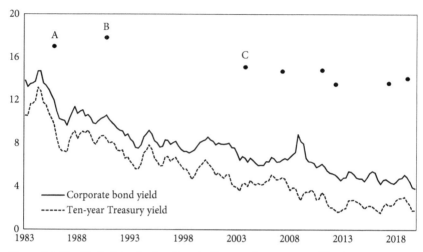

Figure 3.4 The black dots give hurdle rates from various surveys of businesses.
A: Summers (1987); B: Poterba and Summers (1995); C: Jagannathan et al. (2016).
Remaining hurdle rates come from the Duke/CFO magazine Global Business Outlook
survey (various dates).

use to assess a potential investment project are much higher than corporate
bond yields (or firms' self-reported weighted cost of capital) and appear
largely invariant to long-term trends in interest rates. Figure 3.4 updates a
chart from Sharpe and Suarez (2021) that shows nominal hurdle rates from
various surveys (the solid black dots), together with the ten-year Treasury
yield and the yield on investment-grade corporate debt. Over a thirty-five-
year period, the average hurdle rates reported by businesspeople decline
3 percentage points on net, compared with a net decline in interest rates
that is roughly three times larger. It is also worth pointing out that for at least
eighty years, businesspeople have been telling any economist who bothers
to ask that interest rates don't figure much in their capital expenditure decisions. Various surveys from the 1930s-on consistently found that interest
rates were "widely disregarded in business capital planning" (Brockie and
Grey, 1956, p. 667).[36] Lest the reader think that these results are artifacts
of a benighted era in which economic theorists weren't teaching at business schools, a twenty-first-century study by Sharpe and Suarez (2021) finds
exactly the same thing, and for many of the same reasons given in the earlier
studies.

[36] See also Meade and Andrews (1938), Ebersole (1938), and de Chazeau (1954).

These facts and the results discussed earlier suggest that except for residential investment, explanations of how monetary policy influences aggregate demand probably shouldn't lean too hard on an interest-rate channel, either through interest rates' effect on consumption timing or on businesses' cost of capital.

3.5 Inventory Investment

Table 3.6 gives the peak-to-trough change in real GDP and real final sales for each postwar recession, along with the *contributions* of final sales and the change in private inventories (inventory investment) to the change in GDP. The importance of inventories in these cyclical swings is remarkable, with swings in inventory investment accounting for half or more of the overall change in GDP. Of course, that doesn't mean that swings in inventory investment are *causing* these recessions, but it does highlight that during most recessions, production is cut back more rapidly than final sales.

The theoretical literature provides almost no useful insights into inventory behavior. About the only consensus is that production-smoothing or cost-smoothing models of inventories can't explain why production is more variable than sales, or why inventories are procyclical (though some rearguard actions can be found – see Lai, 1991 and Luo et al., 2021). But since most theoretical models try to explain the same set of three or four

Table 3.6 *GDP, final sales, and inventory investment in recessions*

Recession date	GDP change*	Final sales change*	Final sales contrib.**	Inventory contrib.**
1948–1949	−1.5	2.0	1.5	−3.1
1953–1954	−2.4	−0.9	−1.0	−1.4
1957–1958	−3.0	−1.9	−1.8	−1.2
1960–1961	−0.1	0.8	0.8	−1.0
1969–1970	−0.2	0.7	0.7	−0.9
1973–1975	−3.1	−1.0	−1.0	−2.3
1980	−2.2	−0.7	−0.7	−1.6
1981–1982	−2.5	0.0	0.0	−2.5
1990–1991	−1.4	−0.8	−0.8	−0.6
2001	0.5	1.0	1.0	−0.5
2007–2009	−3.8	−2.3	−2.3	−1.6
2020	−9.6	−8.2	−8.1	−1.2

* Percent. ** Percentage points. Detail may not sum to total because of rounding.

stylized facts, it is difficult to judge among them. Nor do the models have much predictive content: Using essentially the same framework, Khan and Thomas (2007) conclude that inventories do *not* amplify aggregate fluctuations, while Wang, Wen, and Xu (2014) reach exactly the opposite conclusion. So there is little to draw on to inform an empirical model or interpretation of observed inventory dynamics.

In the simplest form of dinosaur Keynesianism, the main role of inventories is to bring production and aggregate expenditures into alignment. When there is an autonomous shift in aggregate expenditure, firms find that their inventories are accumulating or decumulating at their current rate of production and adjust their output accordingly until stocks and the rate of inventory investment return to some desired level. (In the case of service-producing firms, who have no inventories of final products, output simply responds to changes in demand.) That is really just a short-run mechanism – it implies that inventories and sales should be negatively correlated over short periods of time (which there is some evidence for – see Wen, 2005).[37] But over longer periods of time inventories and sales tend to co-move, which is another way of seeing why production is more variable than sales.

It is also unclear what aggregate indicators can be used to model inventory investment. If the inventory–sales ratio were mean-reverting (or even stationary), then a vector error-correction system could be contemplated. As Figure 3.5 indicates, however, there is little evidence that either the nominal or real inventory–sales ratio behaves this way.[38] The obvious difference between the two ratios also complicates things. As was mentioned in the discussion of fixed investment, the ratio of two chain-weighted quantities is generally meaningless, and it's preferable to look at nominal ratios. But the composition of inventories is very different from the composition of final sales; in particular, inventories include stocks of raw materials, which means that swings in oil and other commodity prices can cause the nominal inventory–sales ratio to move in ways that aren't necessarily informative about the level of firms' stocks.

One thing that can be established about inventory investment, however, is that it carries essentially no information about future GDP changes. First, if we regress real GDP growth on the lagged contributions of inventory investment and final sales, we find no role for the inventory contributions (see the

---

[37] It is also the case that an upward or downward move in inventory investment is often partly unwound in the following quarter.

[38] The ratios are defined as nonfarm private inventories relative to final sales of goods and structures, where goods sales include wholesale and retail margins.

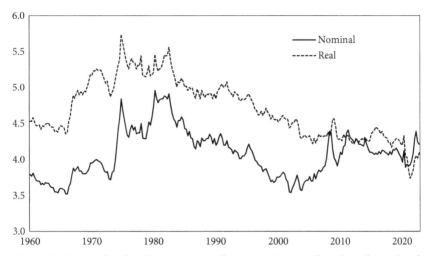

Figure 3.5 Nominal and real inventory-to-sales ratios. Units are "number of months of supply at current sales rate."

first panel of Table 3.7). Similarly, lagged final sales growth contains more information about current GDP growth than does lagged GDP growth itself (panel II).

In fact, we can do even better if we restrict our attention to a subset of final sales called private domestic final purchases (PDFP), which also excludes government and exports (so it is equal to consumption plus private fixed investment). Within a year, government purchases can be noisy inasmuch as they largely reflect variations in the timing of purchases (in other words, the level of government purchases is set for a given fiscal year, and any monthly or quarterly variation tends to reflect faster or slower rates of payout of the total amount); they're also largely determined by factors unrelated to the ones that determine private spending. Similarly, export demand mostly reflects developments unrelated to the state of the US economy. As a result, PDFP growth provides a better signal about the "momentum" or underlying strength of aggregate demand, which is why its lags do even better in forecasting current GDP growth (panel III).

3.6 Digression: Production, Inventories, and Self-Organizing Criticality in the Economy

We noted previously that the pattern shown in Table 3.6 indicates that production tends to decline by more than final demand during recessions. Very

Table 3.7 *Ability to predict real GDP growth*

	Lags	1987– 2007	1987– 2019
I. Contributions to GDP growth			
Inventory investment	1 to 2	0.059 (0.245)	0.106 (0.206)
Final sales	1 to 2	0.571 (0.145)	0.638 (0.109)
II. Final sales			
Lagged final sales growth	1 to 2	0.502 (0.265)	0.523 (0.233)
Lagged GDP growth	1 to 2	0.070 (0.242)	0.112 (0.205)
$\bar{R}^2$		0.13	0.20
III. Private domestic final purchases (PDFP)			
Lagged PDFP growth	1 to 2	0.572 (0.169)	0.652 (0.148)
Lagged GDP growth	1 to 2	−0.143 (0.215)	−0.203 (0.186)
$\bar{R}^2$		0.23	0.31

Standard errors in parentheses.

likely, part of the reason is that aggregate expenditure moves much less than one-for-one with output and income. But to the extent that recessions are led by declines in final demand, the relatively large change in output that results suggests that such an adverse shock to demand is being transmitted fairly widely across producers.

Bak et al. (1993) generate a model in which input–output interactions among producers and nonconvexities in production and inventory holding costs can cause small changes in final demand to have outsized effects on production.[39] The analogy is to a sandpile: When a sandpile forms, it "self organizes" into a critical state in which one additional grain of sand can

---

[39] Scheinkman and Woodford (1994) contains most of the same points (albeit in an easier-to-find journal). Note that the mechanism in Bak et al. is very different from the one in Gabaix (2011), which argues that the distribution of firms is sufficiently fat-tailed that idiosyncratic shocks to large firms account for a large portion of aggregate fluctuations.

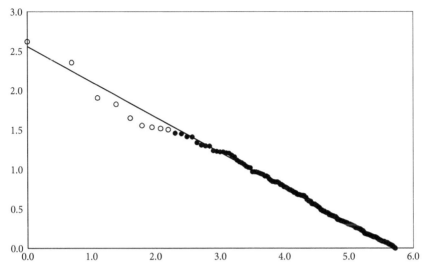

Figure 3.6 Plot of $\ln(1 + |c|)$ against log of rank of $|c|$, where $|c|$ is the absolute value of the contribution of inventory investment to real GDP growth (quarterly rate). Open circles give observations of $|c|$ greater than or equal to 6 percentage points at an annual rate. Straight line gives best linear fit to the solid circles.

cause sand "avalanches" of various sizes.[40] In the Bak et al. model, these avalanches represent production cascades that are set off by small changes in final demand. In fact, in the limiting (large-economy) case of their model aggregate final sales are constant because the law of large numbers smooths out idiosyncratic demand changes; even so, aggregate production changes can be large.

The Bak et al. model is far too abstract to bring to the data. However, in a system where self-organizing criticality is present, events will tend to be distributed according to a power law. Take the size of an event to be equal to $1 + |c_t|$, where $|c_t|$ is the absolute value of every quarterly contribution of inventory investment to real GDP growth over 1947–2022, and rank them from largest to smallest. Figure 3.6, which plots $\ln(1 + |c_t|)$ (essentially $|c_t|$) against the logarithm of its rank, does show the presence of a nearly linear relation; such log-log linearity is what a power law would imply.

Should we take this as evidence of self-organizing criticality in the economy? Probably not. Power laws can exist for many reasons, and their presence is necessary but not sufficient for self-organizing criticality to be

---

[40] There is some question whether actual sand behaves this way – see Jaeger, Liu, and Nagel (1989).

present. (We might also question whether the relationship shown in the figure is actually a power law.) In economic terms, the Bak et al. model is really more about production *increases* than production cuts – there are no negative cascades or uphill avalanches taking place. But the model does try to answer an important question, which is why fluctuations in economic activity that aren't caused by policy actions should ever be seen on a macroeconomic scale. Because the economy is composed of numerous individuals, we might expect that most variations in demand or production would cancel each other out. For that reason, conventional models generate macroeconomic phenomena by assuming *aggregate* shocks that affect every individual – for example, to production ("technology" shocks) or to preferences ("discount factor" shocks). But an aggregate shock of that sort implicitly assumes that there is widespread synchronization of individual-level shocks, which seems *a priori* unlikely. At a minimum, then, the shocks in these conventional models are unrealistic, even if we don't believe that macroeconomic fluctuations spontaneously arise as outcomes of a critical system.

3.7 Exports and Imports

Empirical trade equations have changed little since the 1970s: Export volumes are typically modelled as a function of the real exchange rate and foreign real GDP (with country weights that reflect US export shares), while import volumes are related to US activity and the exchange rate. The dependence of imports on US GDP attenuates the effect that a rise in output has on aggregate spending through an income leakage to the rest of the world; the dependence of both pieces of the trade balance on the real exchange rate provides another channel through which monetary policy can affect aggregate demand.

Table 3.8 presents results from some relatively standard empirical models of trade volumes.[41] Exports and imports are broken out into goods and services (the measure of goods imports excludes oil), and the real exchange rate and foreign GDP weights are adjusted accordingly for each equation.[42] Finally, the estimation period runs from 1987:Q1 to 2007:Q4; the starting

---

[41] It used to be common to see empirical trade models specified in (log) levels, with relatively long lag structures that were modelled as polynomial distributed lags (PDLs). However, every variable in these equations is clearly nonstationary, and PDLs are no longer *comme il faut*; the models shown here are therefore specified in log differences.

[42] The import equations include lagged US real GDP growth, which is instrumented using lagged industrial production growth.

Table 3.8 *Correlates of quarterly trade volume growth*

	Export growth		Import growth	
	Goods	Services	Goods	Services
Output growth	3.225	3.452	1.685	1.704
	(0.555)	(0.808)	(0.717)	(0.895)
Long run	3.225	2.339	2.401	1.239
Real exch. rate growth	−0.394	−0.529	0.248	0.322
	(0.164)	(0.223)	(0.079)	(0.141)
Long run	−0.394	−0.359	0.353	0.234
F-statistic*			25.7	44.7

* From first-stage regression. Standard errors in parentheses. Output growth is foreign GDP for exports and US GDP for imports.

date is set so as to omit most of the large spike in the real exchange rate that occurred in the first half of the 1980s, while the ending date stops just before the global financial crisis, which saw an outsized decline in goods imports.[43] The various coefficients have intuitive signs, with a real dollar appreciation pushing down export volumes and boosting import volumes.

3.8 Putting It All Together

The purpose of this chapter has not been to derive dispositive empirical descriptions of the various categories of aggregate spending – only reasonably robust ones. The ultimate goal is to give an idea of what components of spending appear to respond to financial conditions and real activity, and what some of the orders of magnitude are for the relevant elasticities.

Table 3.9 summarizes the estimates of the output elasticities for each major category and also gives the share of nominal spending that each component represents (these shares are averages over 2015 to 2019). In total, the output elasticity of aggregate demand or (loosely) the "marginal propensity to spend" comes in at about 0.3, which in turn implies an expenditure multiplier (assuming financial conditions are held constant) of about 1.4.[44] In Chapter 8 we'll consider how this value relates to other

[43] The main effect of including the post-2007 period is to cause the exchange rate term in the goods import equation to vanish.
[44] The calculation assumes that a 1 percent increase in real GDP raises real disposable personal income by 0.58 percent. This latter estimate is obtained by relating the compensation

Table 3.9 *GDP elasticities of spending components*

Share of GDP	Component	GDP elasticity
0.677	Personal consumption*	0.26
0.058	Business equipment	1.8
0.045	Intellectual property	1.1
0.025	Structures excl. drilling and mining	3.8
0.038	Residential investment	4.7
−0.112	Nonoil goods imports	2.4
−0.028	Services imports	1.2
	Total (weighted sum)	0.30

* Assumes an income elasticity of consumption of 0.45 and a GDP-to-disposable-income elasticity of 0.58.

empirical estimates – as we'll see, it's not too unreasonable – and will also discuss what might cause the multiplier to be smaller or larger than this value.

As far as the response of aggregate demand to monetary policy is concerned, the most directly interest-sensitive component is residential investment, with an important runner-up being the dependence of consumer spending on net worth. In addition, the central bank can influence net exports through the real exchange rate, at least temporarily. By contrast, business fixed investment growth seems largely unresponsive to changes in interest rates, except inasmuch as risk premia are affected by policy moves – and to the extent that we believe the empirical coefficients on the corporate bond spread.

bill to real GDP, and scaling the resulting value to account for the share of compensation in personal income and the effect of taxes. (No other components of personal income are assumed to respond to GDP.)

4

Production Functions and Growth Accounting

Sicut canis qui revertitur ad vomitum suum,
sic inprudens qui iterat stultitiam suam.

Proverbs 26:11

In Chapter 2, we looked at two different concepts of trend output. The first was essentially a statistical trend, where actual output moved above and below the trend such that deviations from the trend (roughly) averaged out to zero over time. The second concept was exemplified by the measure used to compute the CBO output gap. In this case, the trend concept was intended to capture a high-utilization or full-employment level of activity that we call *potential* output.[1] Actual output sometimes moves above potential – potential is not an absolute ceiling – but most of the time, output is below or close to its potential level when the economy enters a recession or is recovering from one.

In this chapter, we will examine some of the issues associated with estimating potential output, and the related question of how to describe output growth in the US economy. Along the way, we'll become acquainted with some important questions that have never been settled – because they can't be – and that are now brushed aside rather than actively engaged with.[2]

---

[1] Regular estimates of potential output for the United States began with the 1962 *Economic Report of the President*; the methodology was described by Okun (1962). However, the first use of the term "potential" appears to have been in 1954, in a staff publication for the 83rd Congress's Joint Committee on the Economic Report titled "Potential Economic Growth of the United States during the Next Decade." (By 1960, the staff of the Joint Economic Committee were using a production function to estimate potential – see Knowles, 1960 – which might have been the result of having Paul H. Douglas as the committee's chair.)

[2] We will ignore other topics related to growth theory because they lack any practical relevance: To first order, there is basically nothing short of effectively dealing with the

Table 4.1 *Average growth in per-capita GDP (percent)*

20-year intervals		25-year intervals		
1871–1890	2.2	1871–1895	1.9	
1891–1910	1.4	1896–1920	1.4	
1911–1929	1.7	1921–1945	3.3	⎫
1929–1948	2.6	1946–1970	1.5	⎬ 2.4
1949–1968	2.5	1971–1995	2.0	⎭
1969–1988	2.1	1996–2019	1.5	
1989–2007	1.9			
2007–2019	0.9			

Note: Average log-difference of annual data.

4.1 US Output Growth over Time

Before we start, it's interesting to look at how US output growth has changed over time, especially after World War II. Annual NIPA data begin in 1929, and we can push the sample further back in time using increasingly less reliable historical estimates.[3] One of the easiest ways to describe the data is to consider average growth rates (here, log-differences) for per-capita real GDP over various non-overlapping intervals, as is done in Table 4.1. The first column of the table uses 20-year periods, with a bit of fiddling to end one of the intervals just before the Great Depression and another right before the 2007–2009 recession (the final interval ends in 2019). The second column uses 25-year intervals, with another combined average computed for the 50-year interval, 1921–1970; this latter calculation provides a way to assess average growth in a manner that is least affected by the Great Depression and the swings in GDP that took place immediately after the Second World War. These statistics have two interesting features. First, as is evident from the table, there is a slowdown in growth after the 1960s followed by a second decline in the most-recent period. Second, if we regress per-capita GDP growth on dummy variables that are computed for each of these periods, we find that these various growth rates are not statistically different from each other (mostly because the underlying data are so volatile on a year-to-year basis).

---

climate emergency that policy can do to influence the long-run growth rate of an economy like ours.

[3] These are taken from Carter et al. (2006, table Ca11); they are reasonable for estimating average growth rates over longish periods, but that's probably as far as they should be pushed.

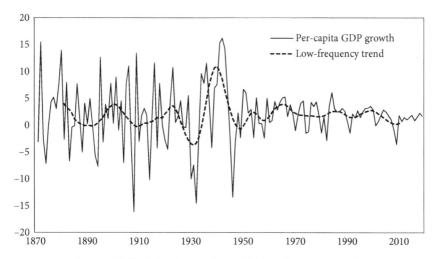

Figure 4.1 Real GDP per capita and its low-frequency trend.

Another way to examine US output growth is to use a lowpass filter like the one discussed in Chapter 2. Because the data are annual, we modify the cutoff to be 12 years and use a 21-year window width (so 10 years on either side). The resulting low-frequency trend for per-capita GDP growth is plotted along with the series itself in Figure 4.1. This figure shows why it's difficult to find much evidence of a statistically significant change in trend growth: With the exception of the depression and war period, the trend merely seems less stable in the first part of the series, not noticeably higher or lower. And the year-to-year volatility in the data shows why even a sample mean taken over a 25-year interval can have a large standard error.[4]

One thing that is difficult to discern from these charts is any imprint of the post-1960s productivity slowdown. That impression is confirmed if we fit a linear spline to log per-capita real GDP that allows for breaks in 1974:Q1 and in 2000:Q1 (Figure 4.2); a post-1973 "kink" is close to invisible, and the estimates imply a slowdown of only 0.3 percentage point after that date.[5]

---

[4] A significant reduction in the volatility of output growth from the prewar to the postwar period is clearly evident from the figure. Romer (1989) argues that the decline is spurious and the result of an overreliance on commodity output to impute changes in total output; see Rhode and Sutch (2006) for a judicious discussion of Romer's argument together with other researchers' counterarguments.

[5] This exercise is intended to be illustrative only; fitting a linear trend to an obviously nonstationary series is somewhat suspect, and the breakpoints are chosen without the benefit of any formal statistical tests.

Table 4.2. *Labor productivity growth (percent)*

1949–1968	2.8
1969–1988	1.7
1989–2007	2.3
2008–2019	1.4

Note: Nonfarm business sector; quarterly data.

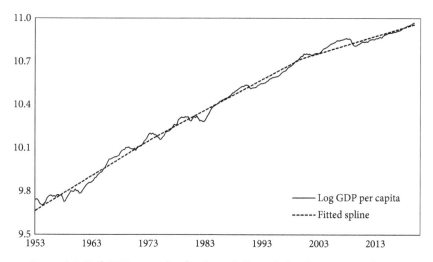

Figure 4.2 Real GDP per capita; fitted trend allows for breaks in 1974 and 2000.

However, we do see a more pronounced downshift in growth after 1999 that amounts to almost a full percentage point. If we instead focus on growth in nonfarm output per hour – Figure 4.3 – we see a distinct decline in the low-pass trend after 1965 or so, and this visual impression is confirmed by Table 4.2, which computes average productivity growth rates over various intervals.[6] Even though quarterly productivity growth is extremely volatile, we find that these growth rates are (just) statistically different from each other, and also that the growth rates for the first two periods are different.

The productivity slowdown had a smaller effect on output growth or output growth per capita both because the baby-boom cohorts came of (working) age and because the labor force participation rate for women rose sharply. (The total labor force rose by 51 percent from 1960 to 1979; of this

---

[6] At the time, this slowdown was noticed and fretted over almost as soon as it got underway – see Perry (1971) and Nordhaus (1972).

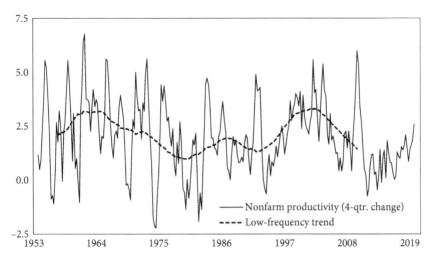

Figure 4.3 Nonfarm output per hour (labor productivity) and its low-frequency trend.

increase, 41 percentage points is attributable to an increase in the working-age population, and 10 percentage points reflects the rise in the participation rate for women, which more than offset a decline in the participation rate for men.) These additional workers muted the effect that the slowdown in productivity had on total output.[7] The break in productivity growth therefore also shows up in a measure of real GDP *per worker* (see Figure 4.4, which repeats the spline exercise from Figure 4.2 on this series), as well as in the series' low-frequency trend (Figure 4.5).[8]

Given what it can obscure, why do economists look at output per capita in the first place? The main reason seems to be that it provides a rough measure of welfare; in addition, population statistics are easier to find for many countries than employment data (especially if a country has a large informal sector) and a continuous series is more likely to be available over long stretches of time. There is also the fact that population growth and workforce

---

[7] While it's tempting to view the influx of women into the workforce as an endogenous response intended to offset the effect of slower productivity and real wage growth on total household earnings, the reasons were likely much more complicated (for example, increased use of birth control, a rise in the number of single-parent households as divorce became more acceptable, higher levels of educational attainment among women, and other changes in social norms). See Goldin (2006).

[8] GDP per worker is defined using data from the NIPAs on full-time equivalent employees (FTEs) and self-employed persons, where a person in the latter category is treated as one FTE. (These data are only available as annual series.)

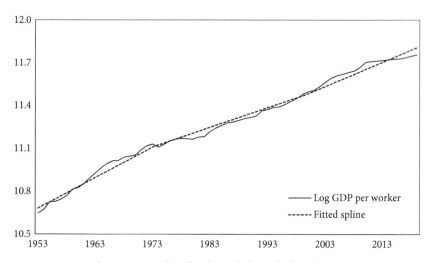

Figure 4.4 Real GDP per worker; fitted trend allows for breaks in 1974 and 2000.

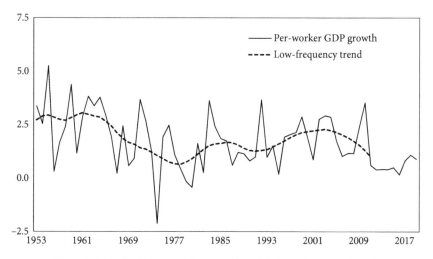

Figure 4.5 Real GDP per worker growth and its low-frequency trend.

growth are often not carefully distinguished in many growth models, even though the distinction can sometimes matter – as we've just seen.

4.2 Growth Accounting and Potential Output

The way that potential output is usually estimated and forecasted involves extracting and then extrapolating trends in labor inputs (hours worked) and labor productivity (output per hour). In order to better reveal these trends, changes in labor inputs are typically decomposed into contributions from population growth, long-run changes in labor force participation, the workweek, and the employment rate (equivalently, one minus the unemployment rate); labor productivity, by contrast, is broken down into contributions from capital accumulation and total factor productivity (TFP). Like potential itself, these trends are intended to be "normal" or benchmark levels that would prevail in a state of full employment and full utilization of resources, not an average level that a given series fluctuates around.

The analytical justification for thinking about potential in this manner comes from viewing the economy as being separable into distinct demand and supply sides. That distinction isn't absolute – demand conditions can affect the supply side of the economy (say by influencing labor force participation or firms' desired investment), while supply conditions can affect demand (say by inducing a policy response to deal with inflation, or by determining how much and what kind of income is generated from production). But the basic assumption is that at any point in time there is a level of productive capacity in the economy whose rate of utilization depends on the overall state of demand.

In order to estimate potential, we need a way to measure the contributions of various inputs and other factors to production; this will tell us how much output can be produced when those inputs are fully utilized, and will hopefully let us uncover any slow-moving trends in the contributions of these inputs to production. Here theory can provide some guidance – though as we'll see, the conditions under which standard theory will be relevant are unlikely to be met by any real-world economy (at least not for any significant length of time).

The theoretical basis for growth accounting was worked out pretty comprehensively by Hulten (1978); it's worth spending a little time on Hulten's main results.[9] We first consider a model of production in which producers use "primary" inputs (like labor) together with the outputs of other producers (intermediate goods) in order to produce final output. Following Samuelson (1966a), we write the production possibilities frontier (PPF) for the economy as:

$$F(L, Y, t) = 0, \tag{4.1}$$

where L is a vector of m primary inputs with price vector w and Y is a vector of n real final demands with price vector p. Under the assumption that equation (4.1) is homogenous of degree zero:

---

[9] The following discussion draws heavily from that paper.

$$\sum_{j=1}^{m} \frac{\partial F}{\partial L_j} L_j + \sum_{i=1}^{n} \frac{\partial F}{\partial Y_i} Y_i, \tag{4.2}$$

and the further assumption that we are always in a competitive equilibrium (with good 1 the arbitrarily chosen numeraire):

$$\begin{aligned} \frac{\partial F}{\partial L_j} &= \frac{w_j}{p_1} \quad (j = 1, \ldots, m), \\[1em] -\frac{\partial F}{\partial Y_i} &= \frac{p_i}{p_1} \quad (i = 2, \ldots, n), \end{aligned} \tag{4.3}$$

then the time derivative of the PPF,

$$\sum_{j=1}^{m} \frac{\partial F}{\partial L_j} \dot{L}_j + \sum_{i=1}^{n} \frac{\partial F}{\partial Y_i} \dot{Y}_i + \dot{F}, \tag{4.4}$$

can be written as

$$\frac{\sum_{j=1}^{m} w_j L_j \left(\frac{\dot{L}}{L}\right)_j}{\sum_{j=1}^{m} w_j L_j} - \frac{\sum_{i=1}^{n} p_i Y_i \left(\frac{\dot{Y}}{Y}\right)_i}{\sum_{i=1}^{n} p_i Y_i} + \frac{\dot{F}}{\sum_{i=1}^{n} p_i Y_i} = 0. \tag{4.5}$$

The last term on the left side of Equation (4.5) is a measure of aggregate productivity change – it is the "pure" change in F in terms of final output. We see that we can express it as

$$\frac{\dot{F}}{\sum_{i=1}^{n} p_i Y_i} = \frac{\sum_{i=1}^{n} p_i Y_i \left(\frac{\dot{Y}}{Y}\right)_i}{\sum_{i=1}^{n} p_i Y_i} - \frac{\sum_{j=1}^{m} w_j L_j \left(\frac{\dot{L}}{L}\right)_j}{\sum_{j=1}^{m} w_j L_j}. \tag{4.6}$$

The expression on the right of the equality is a Divisia index of final demand less a Divisia index of primary input. So we can compute a measure of productivity growth as the share-weighted growth in final outputs less the (factor) share-weighted growth in inputs, and where everything is in principle observable.[10]

Hulten's main result concerns how sector-level production functions are related to the aggregate measure. Assume that the gross output of each sector i can be described with a constant-returns-to-scale production function,

$$Q_i = F^i(X^i, L^i, t) \quad i = 1, \ldots, n \tag{4.7}$$

---

[10] This is the basis for defining total factor productivity growth (TFP) as output growth less growth in an index of total factor input; TFP as defined here is also known as the Solow residual.

with $X^i \equiv (X_{1i}, \ldots, X_{ni})$ and $L^i \equiv (L_{1i}, \ldots, L_{mi})$. Competitive product and factor markets imply

$$\frac{\partial Q_i}{\partial X_{ji}} = \frac{p_j}{p_i}, \quad \frac{\partial Q_i}{\partial L_{ki}} = \frac{w_k}{p_i}, \tag{4.8}$$

which in turn means that the log derivative of (4.7) with respect to time can be written as

$$\frac{\dot{F}^i}{F^i} = \frac{\dot{Q}_i}{Q_i} - \sum_{j=1}^{n} \frac{p_j X_{ji}}{p_i Q_i} \frac{\dot{X}_{ji}}{X_{ji}} - \sum_{k=1}^{m} \frac{w_k L_{ki}}{p_i Q_i} \frac{\dot{L}_{ki}}{L_{ki}} \quad i = 1, \ldots, n. \tag{4.9}$$

If product and factor markets clear,

$$Q_i = Y_i + \sum_{i=1}^{n} X_{ij} \quad i = 1, \ldots, n, \tag{4.10}$$

$$L_j = L_{j1} + \cdots + L_{jn} \quad j = 1, \ldots, m, \tag{4.11}$$

then we can take the log derivative of these and substitute them, along with (4.9), into (4.6) to obtain that aggregate technological change is equal to

$$\sum_{i=1}^{n} \frac{p_i Q_i}{\sum_{i=1}^{n} p_i Y_i} \frac{\dot{F}^i}{F^i}. \tag{4.12}$$

This result has received a surprising amount of attention; it validates an aggregation procedure that was first suggested by Evsey Domar in the 1960s. What it means is that we can combine sectoral productivity growth rates using a "Domar weight" that equals the value of the sector's gross output relative to nominal GDP. The sum of these weights is greater than one, because Q_i equals the sector's production of intermediate goods as well as final output. Intuitively, this magnification of a sector's productivity change occurs because the improvement in a sector's efficiency affects both its final output as well as its production of intermediates. Other sectors that use those intermediates therefore benefit as well and produce more output, so the effect is like a productivity multiplier.

Now, a more common way to approach the measurement of total factor productivity is to work with value-added output rather than gross output – GDP, for example, is an economywide measure of value added – and to express everything in terms of primary inputs (no intermediate inputs). That can be done, but it requires the production function to take the following separable form:

$$Q_i = F^i(\gamma(L_{i1}, \ldots L_{im}); X_{i1}, \ldots X_{in}), \tag{4.13}$$

in which case $\gamma(\cdot)$ can be viewed as a measure of value added. As Sims (1969) and others have pointed out, this is an extremely restrictive assumption: Although it allows value added to be computed as real gross output less real intermediate input (a procedure known as "double deflation"), it is only legitimate when technological progress augments value added only (as opposed to also augmenting intermediate inputs).[11] When productivity analysis or growth accounting is done in practical settings, it takes either the value-added form (typically at an economywide level) or the gross-output form (at the level of individual industries or industry sectors); the latter is often referred to as a KLEMS approach, where gross output is modelled in terms of capital (K), labor (L), energy (E), other materials (M), and services purchased in the course of production (S).

Ignoring for the moment whether it even makes sense to talk about production functions and input (or output) aggregates in this manner, the preceding derivations highlight a key assumption that underpins most growth accounting exercises; namely, that the relevant output elasticities are tied to observed factor prices. That in turn requires ancillary assumptions like competitive factor markets (that is, firms need to be price takers in these markets) and the ability to costlessly adjust inputs (otherwise, we need to worry about shadow prices being out of alignment with observed factor prices).[12] Relatedly, we need everything to be in equilibrium, with product and factor markets clearing and firms' having correctly anticipated current production and input levels. (These issues were once actively worried about – in 1986, the *Journal of Econometrics* devoted an entire issue to them.) As a corollary, if we wanted to estimate full-employment or capacity output, we'd need to know what (true) factor prices would be in a state of full employment, which is essentially impossible to figure out.

But the real problem with this approach – a problem that basically sinks the idea of growth accounting as well as that of potential output estimation – is that well-defined production functions and factor aggregates are extremely unlikely to exist at the sectoral level, let alone for the economy as a whole. We look at why next.

---

[11] The BEA use double deflation to compute value added in their industry accounts; see Strassner et al. (2005, p. 34).

[12] Basu and Fernald (2001) consider ways to deal with a few other problems associated with growth accounting, such as the presence of imperfect competition in product markets and variable factor utilization within a firm or industry.

4.3 Production Functions and Factor Aggregates

Virtually all macromodels that incorporate production describe output determination in terms of a value-added production function with capital, labor, and a measure of factor productivity as inputs.[13] Such a conception of production also underpins most empirical attempts at growth accounting and measuring potential output that aren't purely statistical in nature: For example, CBO's estimate of (nonfarm) potential output uses a Cobb–Douglas production function to combine estimates of potential labor inputs, productive capital, and trend TFP.[14]

The fact that this is the dominant framework for thinking about output determination is rather unfortunate, however, since it has been known since at least the 1970s that there is no theoretical or empirical justification for describing aggregate production in this way.

In a series of papers, Franklin Fisher explored the theoretical conditions needed to ensure the existence of aggregate production functions and of aggregate measures of capital, labor, and output.[15] One of Fisher's key insights – which ought to make the problem tractable, but doesn't – is that a production function is intended to measure the *maximum* amount of output that can be produced using given inputs. The reason this simplifies things is that if factors are distributed efficiently among firms (say by competitive markets), then the maximum level of output will only depend on the overall quantity of factors in the economy.

Unfortunately, that assumption turns out not to be strong enough to ensure that aggregation of output or factors across firms can take place, even if all factors are completely mobile across firms. As Fisher (1993, chapter 5) demonstrates, in order to obtain these aggregates, we first need to assume that every firm's production function has constant returns to scale (this is vital) and also takes the form:

$$Y^i = f^i(X^i, L^i) = F^i(\phi^i(X^i), L^i), \tag{4.14}$$

---

[13] Total factor productivity (TFP) is typically used in applied settings; other modelling exercises sometimes assume the presence of factor productivity changes that augment one or more inputs.

[14] CBO's methodology exemplifies the best practice for this approach to estimating potential output. In brief, potential labor input is obtained by extracting trends from cyclically adjusted employment and hours; productive capital is computed by weighting disaggregated BEA wealth stocks with estimated Hall–Jorgenson rental rates; the Cobb–Douglas weights are computed from the Hodrick–Prescott trend of the measured capital share; and trend TFP is extracted from a cyclically adjusted estimate (with some judgment applied to certain periods). See Shackleton (2018) for a detailed description.

[15] Most of the relevant papers are collected in Fisher (1993); also see Felipe and Fisher (2003) for a useful overview of the literature.

with $\phi^i(\cdot)$ a scalar-valued function and where X denotes the factors that we want to aggregate.[16] As Fisher notes, this assumption is already pretty restrictive. Then, except for some trivial cases, aggregation across firms will be possible if and only if one of two things is true: Either all of the $F^i(\cdot, \cdot)$ are the same or all of the ϕ^i are the same (or both). Neither condition is likely to hold even for a single firm, let alone for all firms.

Even if we can't do this precisely, is there a way to at least *approximately* satisfy the conditions required to obtain an aggregate production function that has economywide factor aggregates as its arguments? In other words, while an "exact" aggregate production function might not exist, perhaps it is possible to come up with an approximate production function that is accurate so long as the variables that make up its arguments don't move too far outside a particular range. Unfortunately, as Fisher (1993, chapter 7) showed, even this is beyond our reach. In order to get a good approximate aggregate production function, either we need almost all of the economy to meet the (again restrictive) aggregation conditions, or we need the rates of change of certain derivatives of the approximating function to swing up and down wildly (or even to become unbounded) as we look at a sequence of functions that meet the approximation criterion.[17]

What about empirics? Don't you get "sensible" results when you regress GDP on aggregate measures of labor and capital – similar to what you'd expect if a Cobb–Douglas or CES production function were lurking behind the scenes? Again, not really.[18] Using simulations, Fisher (1993, chapters 8 and 9) demonstrated that a Cobb–Douglas production function will appear to fit the data well so long as labor's share of income is roughly constant, not because the function reflects the underlying technological relationships in the economy. For CES production functions, aggregate estimates also fit well in the sense of having high R-squared values (most of these simply amounted to a regression of one trending series on another). But the estimated parameters often bore no relation to the parameters of the microeconomic functions that were used to generate the data – for example, an aggregate elasticity of substitution was estimated even though such a parameter was meaningless *by construction* because the model economy was set up such

---

[16] We can also redefine the problem so that X is output and $f(\cdot)$ is a factor requirements function.

[17] There is no economic interpretation of this result, except to note that functions whose derivatives have this property are unlikely to describe any sort of real-world relationship.

[18] In both senses: Not only are estimates like these meaningless, but they sometimes look kind of crazy as well – remember Romer (1987)?

that the requirements for aggregation didn't hold. In a related vein, Nelson and Winter (1982, chapter 9) simulate an evolutionary model in which firms don't even maximize profits and production involves fixed coefficients; even so, a Cobb–Douglas production function seems to fit the simulated data well. More recently, Felipe and McCombie (2003) demonstrate that the fact that GDP, Y, can be written in terms of the sum of payments to labor wL and capital uK:

$$Y_t = w_t L_t + u_t K_t \tag{4.15}$$

(we ignore things like indirect taxes) ensures that growth accounting exercises will appear to work, and that we will always be able to recover a constant-returns-to-scale expression with the functional form $Y = F(K, L, t)$ (how well it or the growth accounting exercise will end up fitting depends on the behavior of observed factor shares and how any dependence on calendar time is modelled). Again, equation (4.15) is merely an accounting identity – it's one way to consistently *measure* aggregate value added – and doesn't tell us anything about any sort of technological relationships in the economy.[19]

The fact that economists continue to use production functions for theoretical work and continue to assign any meaning to complicated growth accounting exercises using labor and capital aggregates is more than a little embarrassing. The points discussed above were largely settled by the early 1980s, and involved "serious" mainstream economists.[20] The conclusions are also very stark: The economy's supply side cannot be characterized by a production function – even approximately – except under ridiculously unrealistic conditions; manipulation of a production function in a model or to inform empirical work tells us nothing worth knowing; and labor and capital aggregates that are relevant to production can only exist under conditions that are unlikely to ever be met by a real-world economy.[21] And by extension, even the most carefully constructed estimates of total factor productivity will be meaningless.

The reason that this cringeworthy situation persists, I suppose, is similar to why representative agents are still widely invoked in macromodels:

---

[19] See Shaikh (1974) and Simon (1979) for related discussions.

[20] Franklin Fisher won the John Bates Clark medal in 1973; in addition, Herbert Simon won a Nobel Prize in 1978 (though not for his work on this topic).

[21] That is not to say that a well-defined *index* of the aggregate capital stock can't be constructed (recall the discussion of BEA's series on wealth stocks in the previous chapter). But this index will have nothing to do with the economy's productive potential, except by accident.

No one ever got a paper rejected from a (mainstream) journal because they used a production function. There is also the fact that fewer people nowadays even remember that production functions were once looked on skeptically by a broad swathe of the profession, while fewer still have the patience or interest to think about frustrating and ultimately intractable questions related to measurement and aggregation. Finally, assuming a production function lets economists be rather lazy about how they explain distribution in the economy, since they can invoke the "marginal product" of some aggregate factor to explain the income received by the owners of the factor (more on this below). But none of these reasons provides an especially good defense of the status quo.

4.4 Allocation and Labor's Share of Income

Ever since Hicks (1932, chapter VI), economists have sought to explain factor shares in terms of the substitutability of capital and labor and the direction of technological change. If we believe that output is characterized by a constant-returns-to scale production function $F(A_t^K K_t, A_t^L L_t)$, where A^i is a measure of factor-augmenting technological change for factor i, then as Solow (1958) showed, the elasticity of the labor share $(1 - \alpha_t)$ with respect to the effective capital–labor ratio $k_t \equiv A^K K / A^L L$ is equal to

$$-\alpha_t \left(1 - \frac{1}{\tau} \right),$$

where τ is the elasticity of substitution. Hence, if $\tau > 1$, an increase in k_t reduces labor's share of income.

Back when labor's share of income was thought to be (nearly) constant, the explanation for this relative stability was couched in terms of an increasing K/L ratio combined with technological change that was "biased" toward labor (thus keeping k stable).[22] It's actually not straightforward to measure labor's share in the United States nor does everyone agree about what should

---

[22] Actually, the literature on directed technological change or "induced innovation" tried to explain why the economy would reach a corner solution such that *all* technological progress was labor-augmenting (Harrod-neutral). The reason this is desirable is that only Harrod-neutral technological change is consistent with the existence of a steady-state "balanced" growth path in the standard growth model setup. The intuition for why technological change is biased in this direction is that labor, unlike capital, can't be accumulated through investment. See Samuelson (1965, 1966b), Kennedy (1966), and Drandakis and Phelps (1966) for some early papers that are much more interesting than recent discussions of the topic.

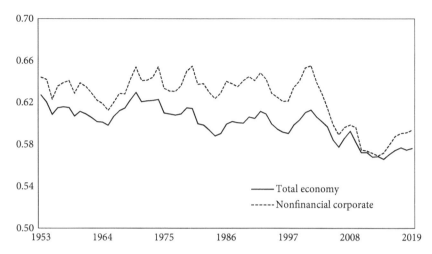

Figure 4.6 Two measures of labor's share of output (annual data).

be in the denominator (namely, whether it should be gross or net output). One important issue concerning the numerator is how to handle proprietors' income, which has both capital and labor components. In producing nonfarm business estimates of total compensation, the BLS impute labor income to proprietors by assuming they receive the same rate of hourly compensation as employees working in their sector; as BLS acknowledge, this is a problematic assumption (Giandrea and Sprague, 2017).

Figure 4.6 plots two labor's share measures that try to address this issue; both indicate that labor's share has declined in recent decades. The first measure computes a labor share for the entire economy by dividing employee compensation by gross domestic income less proprietors' income. (One can show that this is equivalent to assuming that the labor income share of proprietors' income is the same as it is elsewhere in the economy.) The second measure is for the nonfinancial corporate sector only, which means that proprietors are entirely absent.[23] While both labor share measures decline on net, the imputed share for the full economy declines by somewhat less. Table 4.3 decomposes the 1998–2019 change in the full-economy labor share, $s_t - s_0$, by sector using the formula:

---

[23] Karabarbounis and Neiman (2014) advocate using (total) corporate-sector data for this reason. Grossman and Oberfield (2022, p. 98) cite research that suggests that this approach is not foolproof, both because income is often reclassified for tax purposes and because firms with high labor shares have incentives under the current tax code to leave the corporate sector and reorganize as a partnership.

Table 4.3. *Decomposition of change in labor's share, 1998–2019 (percentage points)*

	Within sector	Across sector
Natural resources	−0.2	0.2
Trade/transportation/utilities	−0.8	−1.0
Construction	0.3	0.0
Durable goods manufacturing	−0.8	−1.8
Nondurable goods manufacturing	−0.8	−0.6
Information	−0.4	0.2
Finance, insurance, and real estate	−0.4	0.5
Professional and business services	0.1	2.3
Education and health	−0.1	1.8
Leisure and hospitality; other services	0.3	0.1
Government	0.2	−0.7
Sum	**−2.6**	**0.7**

Note: Industry definitions based on NAICS.

$$s_t - s_0 = \sum_i \underbrace{\omega_{i0}(s_{it} - s_{i0})}_{\text{Within−sector}} + \underbrace{(\omega_{it} - \omega_{i0})s_{it}}_{\text{Across−sector}}, \qquad (4.16)$$

where i indexes sectors, s_{it} is sector i's labor share in period t, and ω_{it} is the sector's share of total value added in period t. (The farm sector is excluded for this calculation.) From the table, we see that the total decline is attributable to declines in labor shares within individual sectors (left column), rather than a shift in the fraction of value added that is accounted for by sectors with low labor shares (right column) – in fact, the shift *toward* higher-labor-share sectors has helped to keep the aggregate measure from declining by even more.[24]

One explanation for the decline in the US labor share that is often advanced is that the elasticity of substitution between capital and labor is greater than one, which means that an increase in the effective capital–

---

[24] The sectoral labor shares are defined as the sector's wage bill divided by the sector's value added less its proprietors' income. Although they come from the NIPAs, these sector-specific proprietors' income measures aren't as well measured as total proprietors' income (the latter makes adjustments that better capture income generated by production); for the table, the difference between the two totals is allocated across industries according to the industry's share in the industry total.

labor ratio has put downward pressure on the labor share.[25] We might be skeptical of this explanation given that the elasticity of substitution and capital–labor ratio have no actual meaning, so it's unclear what, if anything, is being measured or described in order to support this conclusion.[26] In addition, even if we take the production function approach seriously, Elsby et al. (2013) show that it is not internally consistent given actual changes in wages, productivity, and measures of the capital–labor ratio. As it turns out, quantitative explanations for the decline in the US labor share, if totalled together, can explain it many times over – see Grossman and Oberfield (2022), who cite publication bias as one of the reasons, along with an inability to identify "fundamental" causes of the decline (which leads to double counting). But more to the point, our inability to coherently explain an apparently large shift in distribution by appealing to the neoclassical model of production highlights that the model is not only meaningless, but worthless.[27]

4.5 Digression: A Result that Probably Isn't

The relative stability of US economic growth over a long span of time, even if mostly accidental, is nevertheless remarkable when we think of the numerous factors at play in determining an economy's overall growth rate. Similarly, economists' continued inability to explain the post-1960s productivity slowdown, even with the advantage of considerable hindsight, highlights how difficult it is to say anything useful about the sources of growth in an economy.

---

[25] Karabarbounis and Neiman (2014) use this argument to describe labor share declines throughout the world.

[26] This is an unfortunate weakness of Piketty (2014), whose argument depends importantly on the claim that the elasticity of substitution is greater than one. A more useful demonstration of his basic point, which doesn't rely on features of the production technology, comes from a model of wealth evolution like that described by Berman et al. (2021).

[27] At this point, a microeconomist would correctly point out that the shortcomings associated with aggregate production functions in no way bear on the doctrine that marginal products determine factor remuneration. Even so, it seems hard to explain the aggregate earnings distribution according to marginal productivity theory without introducing some additional allocation mechanism. Because individual attributes result from a combination of numerous independent outcomes, they will be characterized by a Gaussian distribution; by contrast, empirical studies find that earnings are characterized as a Pareto distribution (see Pluchino et al., 2018 for further development of this point). We therefore need some mechanism to transform normally distributed inputs into Pareto-distributed outputs; while we could posit the existence of a mechanism like the one in Gabaix and Landier (2008) to explain this, it apparently only applies to CEOs. (Pluchino et al., 2018 propose that the relevant mechanism is something called "luck.")

However, Philippon (2022) claims that the productivity slowdown never happened, and that the apparent stability of US growth is mostly illusory. He argues that rather than being exponential (and so characterized by log levels that are piecewise linear):

$$\ln A_t = a + g\,t, \tag{4.17}$$

TFP growth is actually *additive*:

$$A_t = b + d\,t, \tag{4.18}$$

where t denotes calendar time (note the lack of a $\ln(\cdot)$ term in the second equation). He argues that the additive model, together with a conventional production function, does a better job forecasting the (inverse) marginal product of capital; in terms of the capital–labor ratio k_t this is given by

$$k_t^{1-\alpha} = \frac{\alpha}{u} A_t \tag{4.19}$$

for the Cobb–Douglas production function he assumes. (Here, α denotes the elasticity of output with respect to capital and u denotes the user cost, both assumed to be constant.) With additive TFP growth, equation (4.19) becomes

$$k_t^{1-\alpha} = a_k + b_k t. \tag{4.20}$$

Philippon also states that the additive model does a better job forecasting labor productivity, $Y_t/L_t = A_t k_t^\alpha$, which given equations (4.18) and (4.20) can be written as:

$$\frac{Y_t}{L_t} = (b + d\,t)\,(a_k + b_k t)^{\frac{\alpha}{1-\alpha}}. \tag{4.21}$$

(As Philippon points out, we can get a convex trajectory for labor productivity under the additive TFP assumption because the two calendar-time terms t multiply each other.)

Let's once again take this framework at face value, and check these claims using annual US data on k, Y/L, and TFP from Fernald's (2012) updated utilization-adjusted TFP database.[28] If the additive trend model is correct, we should be able to fit separate additive trends for k_t and A_t that, when combined according to Equation (4.21), yield a good out-of-sample fit for

---

[28] Following Philippon, I use a TFP series that does not adjust for labor quality and I hold α fixed at the average level in Fernald's sample, which is 0.3336. Estimation runs from 1947 to 1983.

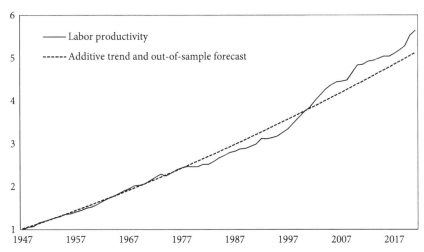

Figure 4.7 Out-of-sample forecast of labor productivity under an "additive" TFP assumption. The model used to construct the forecast is estimated over 1947–1983.

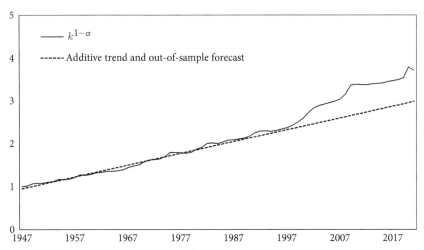

Figure 4.8 Out-of-sample forecast of $k^{1-\alpha}$ under an "additive" TFP assumption (k is the capital–labor ratio). The model used to construct the forecast is estimated over 1947–1983.

labor productivity. As Figure 4.7 shows, however, the additive model fails to do so because it is unable to produce a good forecast for $k^{1-\alpha}$ (Figure 4.8).

Philippon's model of TFP growth inherits all of the problems of the standard neoclassical production framework – both in the empirical estimates of TFP that he analyzes as well as the model of output he uses. One issue

Figure 4.9 Out-of-sample forecast of labor productivity under the assumption of an exponential trend. The figure shows log productivity along with a trend that is allowed to change after 1973. The trend is estimated over 1953–1994; values of the trend after that date are out-of-sample forecasts.

Philippon raises that *is* worth pondering a bit is whether the evidence against exponential growth is as strong as he portrays it; he argues that "[t]he exponential model is not useful because no country is able to live up to its extreme predictions." But consider Figure 4.9, which uses data on the log level of nonfarm business productivity from 1953 to 1994 to fit a single trend break after 1973. Out of sample, the model *underpredicts* labor productivity because of what appears to be a one-time level shift (the late-1990s productivity speedup). After that, the series runs parallel to (and above) the trendline. (We get qualitatively similar results if we use the TFP measure instead of labor productivity.) The point here is not to argue that this is a good way to identify changes in productivity growth, or that this model should be used to forecast productivity. Rather, it is to illustrate that a description of US labor productivity in the postwar period needs to be more subtle than simply fitting a single trend – and is not incompatible with sustained periods of exponential growth. (In addition, the post-1960s productivity slowdown seems too abrupt to attribute to a gradual petering out of innovations or whatever other drivers of growth there might be.)

Overall, a basic problem that we face in thinking about the past and future of economic growth is that it is difficult to say much about long-run trends in output or productivity without having a long span of data to examine. (Another problem is that it's difficult to learn much about the drivers of economic growth from aggregate statistics like these.) However, it is unreasonable to expect any sort of stability in an economy over a long period; changes in demographics and the economy's industrial structure (among other things) imply that there is probably not much to be gained by trying to compare the current situation with the 1950s, let alone the late 1800s. And that just applies to measuring and describing economic growth; being able to explain *why* growth has changed over time and what might cause it to change again remains well beyond anyone's ability – and likely always will.

4.6 Digression: A Solution that Definitely Isn't

A paper by Baqaee and Farhi (2019) claims to solve the problems attending aggregate production functions through the use of careful microfoundations and an application of the main result in Hulten (1978). We might be a bit skeptical of such a claim in light of Section 4.3; how, then, does the paper achieve its goal?

The paper correctly notes that it is not generally possible to meet the conditions for factor aggregation except under very special circumstances. (One might argue that being able to refer to factor aggregates is exactly the point of an aggregate production function – so we can really just stop here.) But the Fisher aggregation theorems also place stringent conditions on whether and how *output* can be aggregated. The paper deals with this by simply assuming that the condition for output aggregation is already met, which it does by specifying a homothetic final demand aggregator.[29] The paper also points to companion work (Baqaee and Farhi, 2018) that relaxes the homotheticity assumption and allows for imperfect competition. However, that paper notes that "very restrictive assumptions" (presumably the Fisher aggregation conditions) are needed to aggregate output in this case.

This sort of approach to thinking about production (and productivity) has no discernable practical relevance. In general, output aggregation requires factors of production to be perfectly mobile across firms (if they aren't, then all firms need to produce the same bundle of output, which means that producers can't specialize).[30] Because the approach leans heavily on Hulten (1978), the main condition from that paper – that the economy is always in a general competitive equilibrium – also needs to be met in order to obtain

---

[29] A not unrelated observation is that it's easy to aggregate output whenever we can assume that relative prices are fixed (we get something like a Hicksian composite commodity).

[30] See Fisher (1993, chapter 5).

any useable results. But the biggest problem with this approach is that it uses input–output tables in a very questionable way.

Specifically, a key feature of this characterization of production is its use of the input–output tables to calculate the interdependence of producers (that is, the direct and indirect ways that output by producer i is used by producer j). This interdependence can be summarized by a total-requirements matrix B that can be computed from the Leontief (direct-use) table A in the following manner:

$$B = I + A + A^2 + A^3 + \cdots,\qquad(4.22)$$

where I is the identity matrix. The idea – which is standard in input–output analysis – is that the infinite sum captures all the ways that producer j's output is used by producer i – not just directly, but also through purchases of other inputs that use j's output, and through purchases of inputs that use inputs that use j's output, and so on.

Now here's the problem. The B matrix in equation (4.22) is capturing a process that arguably takes a bit of calendar time to work through. If we think, say, of how the airline industry uses the output of oil producers, there is a reasonably direct connection between oil and jet fuel. But the use of oil also extends (eventually) to the plastic used to make the food trays and to the synthetic fabric and foam rubber used to make the seats, possibly to the electricity used to smelt the aluminium that goes into a jet's body, to the petrochemicals used to produce the paint for the airline's livery, to the gasoline used by the company cars of the airline's legal firm, and on and on. That process isn't instantaneous – nor will an iterate of the A matrix be coordinated across all producers in the same calendar period (even within the same sector) – so we can't really use B in any sort of realistic way to analyze the short-run effect that a shock to a producer's costs or productivity will have on other producers.[31] At best, then, predictions that use B will just relate one long-run equilibrium position to another, but we won't be able to use these for a period-by-period analysis.

It's interesting to note that Hulten himself seems to have been rather dismissive of this type of approach. He mentions in his 1978 paper that it is possible to define a sector i's rate of productivity change as

---

[31] A related problem arises when the B matrix is used to quantify the effect that a change in crude energy prices will have on the core PCE price index; the effect implied by B is considerably larger than what a reduced-form regression-based estimate typically finds.

$$\frac{\dot{Z}_i}{Z_i} = \sum_{j=1}^{n} \gamma_{ij} \frac{\dot{A}_j}{A_j}, \tag{4.23}$$

where the γ_{ij} terms represent the "full equilibrium response" of sector i to a change in sector j's rate of productivity growth. However, Hulten also added that "[t]his formulation does not, in general, have empirical content since the γ_{ij} are complicated functions of various substitution elasticities and commodity shares."

4.7 Can We Live without Potential Output?

The main reason we approached this problem was to see whether we could construct a sensible measure of potential output that would give us an idea of how much the economy could produce in a state of full utilization. The answer would seem to be that no suitable framework exists for doing so (as we'll see in later chapters, adding information about inflation or attacking the problem in terms of a "natural" rate of unemployment doesn't help either). But is this actually a problem from a policy perspective?

When one thinks about it, the concept of potential output seems a little bizarre: The idea that a single scalar value exists that can summarize the sustainable level of activity in an economy as large as ours is hard to take seriously (if you think otherwise, try to explain how that scalar would be relevant if there were a significant shift in the composition of final demand). The idea that we can measure potential output precisely enough that it can serve as a guidepost for policy also seems unlikely. (In the 1960s some of the best minds tried; it didn't end well.) There is also a deeper question of what a "sustainable" level of activity even means in this context. If we define it as, say, a lack of visible inflationary pressure, then the concept becomes divorced from utilization: Inflation could rise even when various groups in the workforce or sectors in the economy are far away from being fully employed. Such a definition also causes potential to become less of an inherent feature of the economy, and more the result of deliberate policy responses. For example, say that monetary policy actions could move the economy to a high rate of utilization, but at the cost of inflating asset bubbles and increasing financial fragility. We might view that level of activity as unsustainable, and therefore argue that the economy had exceeded its potential. But what if the stimulus to aggregate demand were to come from fiscal policy instead? That might be a more sustainable outcome, but it really shouldn't mean that potential output is different across the two cases.

The one time that the Federal Reserve seemed to successfully identify an increase in potential growth and respond accordingly was during the late 1990s and early 2000s. But there was little to no science involved in this exercise. Analyses that pointed to large unmeasured productivity gains in sectors like services never explained whether such mismeasurement had gotten worse over time, which was the only way that such a fact would have been relevant (if there is simply a constant wedge between what's measured and what's not, then it doesn't imply that you should be pushing *measured* output any faster than before). On the inflation side, the analytical work basically involved adding dummy variables to measure the degree to which conventional accelerationist inflation equations had started to overpredict actual inflation, and then attributing these misses to a lower NAIRU (what this analysis missed was that the level of trend inflation had shifted lower in the wake of the 1990–1991 recession and remained stable from about 1995 on, and also that the Phillips curve had flattened – things that didn't become apparent until later).[32] None of this is meant to take away from the outcome – namely, that the unemployment rate was allowed to drop to much lower levels than had previously been thought consistent with stable inflation. And it seems likely that had an economist with strong priors about the Phillips curve and the natural rate been the Fed's chair, the unemployment rate wouldn't have been allowed to go as low as it did. But the policy decision wasn't really informed by serious analysis, just a key policymaker's hunch.[33]

In terms of forecasting economic aggregates, there also isn't too much that's lost by not having an estimate of potential: The level or growth rate of potential GDP doesn't seem to have any gravitational pull for actual output or spending (that is, it's not a rest point toward which the economy tends on its own), and estimates of the GDP gap are of limited use for inflation forecasting. It is also difficult to forecast the components of potential. For instance, even if we take the "purified" TFP growth series from Basu et al. (2006) at face value, it is essentially unpredictable: The R-squared from an annual AR(1) model is 0.02, and the series' mean growth rate is indistinguishable from zero after 1963. Similarly, for the utilization-adjusted quarterly TFP measure of Fernald (2012), the R-squared from an AR(2) model

---

[32] Much of this work was commissioned from the staff by senior Federal Reserve officers; at the time, the staff's suspicion was that they were assisting then-Chair Greenspan in making his case to other FOMC members, not that the analysis was being used to actually inform his decisions.

[33] In fact, even today it is difficult to ascertain what effect the late 1990s productivity speedup had on inflation.

fit over 1975–2019 is even closer to zero – though here, at least, the constant term is statistically significant. And while it seems as though it should be straightforward to extrapolate slow-moving, demographically driven series like trend labor force participation, in practice it's not as easy as it sounds.[34] The best we can probably do to gauge the economy's state, then, is to compare variables with less-pronounced trends (like the level of the unemployment rate) to their values in previous periods when the economy was judged to be at "full" employment – the more recent the periods, the better – and hope that these provide a reasonable guide going forward as to how high the level of economic activity can get without causing any problems. With that in hand, test the waters gingerly.

The desire for an indicator like potential output reflects a desire for a quantitative policy guidepost that simply can't be met. The economy is too complicated to be reliably represented by a single summary measure like potential (or the "natural" rate of unemployment, as we'll see), and there is no sound analytical justification for trying to do so. (As an empirical matter, such estimates tend to be all over the place even under relatively normal conditions.) Policymakers should eschew the false precision that such measures provide, and policy analysts and others should stop investing so much time and effort in producing them.

---

[34] It's worth recalling that when Solow (1982) gave his retrospective assessment of why potential output projections from the 1960s had turned out so poorly, he pointed to bad forecasts of population growth as the main culprit.

The Macroeconomics of "the" Labor Market

The most barbarous fact in all Christendom is the labor market. The mere term suffi-
ciently expresses the animalism of commercial civilization.

Eugene V. Debs (1904)

The labor of a human being is not a commodity or article of commerce.

15 U.S.C. §17

Probably the least useful way to think about the overall amount of employment in an economy is in terms of a giant supply and demand diagram
with the real wage on the *y*-axis. (It's also a bad way to think about the
real wage.) However, there do exist macroeconomic relationships among
employment, unemployment, and real activity, and some of them can be
vaguely useful. In this chapter, we'll look at a few of these relationships and
see how well we can explain them. We'll also consider a couple of cases where
an aggregative approach, which ignores the heterogeneity of labor markets
and labor market outcomes, is extremely misleading.

5.1 The Beveridge Curve

Like the Phillips curve, the Beveridge curve is a kinda-sorta empirical regularity (it shifts around a lot) that economists have spent a large amount of
time trying to explain on a deeper level.[1] In its basic form, the Beveridge
curve is a downward-sloping relationship between job vacancies and unemployed workers that is apparent over the course of a business cycle. What

---

[1] It's named after William Beveridge, who – along with Aneurin Bevan, founder of the NHS –
laid the ground for the British welfare state. (Of the two, Bevan was by far the more
admirable.) A lot of lazy people who don't know where the library is cite Beveridge (1944)
as a reference for the Beveridge curve; don't, because it's not actually in there.

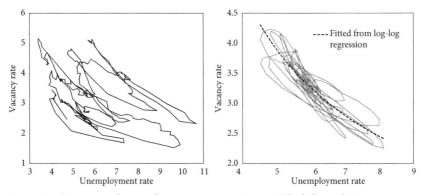

Figure 5.1 Vacancy and unemployment rates, 1955–2016. The left panel gives raw values; the right panel shows the business-cycle components of the series, obtained with a bandpass filter (the sample means are added to the components). The dashed line gives the fitted values from a log-log regression.

this relation captures is that when the level of economic activity is high, vacancies tend to be high as well (because firms are trying to hire workers) and unemployment tends to be low (because workers are finding jobs more readily). Likewise, when real activity and labor demand slacken, firms post fewer vacancies and lay off more workers, which in turn causes unemployment to rise.

Figure 5.1 gives an idea of what this looks like. The left panel shows raw values of the vacancy and unemployment rates from 1955 to 2016.[2] The right panel plots the components of these series at business-cycle frequencies obtained from a bandpass filter.[3] From the left panel we get a hint of a slightly convex relationship that shifts outwards and inwards; at business-cycle frequencies (right panel), we see more evidence of convexity – the dashed line gives the exponentiated fitted values from a log-log regression – and some evidence of "loops." As is evident from Figure 5.2, which plots these series around the 1990–1991 and 2001 recessions, these loops tend to be counterclockwise.

All that seems intuitive enough (except maybe for the direction of the loops), but there is a bit more going on here behind the scenes. At any point

---

[2] We'll discuss how vacancies are measured a little later.

[3] The filter cutoffs are 6 and 32 quarters; the window width is 25 quarters (12 quarters on either side). The end of the sample period, 2016:Q4, is chosen so that none of the pandemic period observations is used. To allow easier comparability across panels, the sample means for the raw series are added back to the business cycle components; this is only a half-measure, though, since the low-frequency components of these series are not constant.

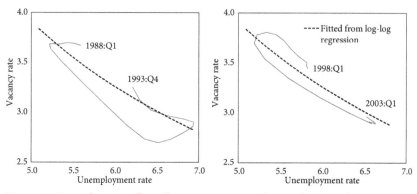

Figure 5.2 Beveridge curve "loops" in two recessions. The gray lines are the business-cycle components of the vacancy and unemployment rates (plus their sample means) around the 1990–1991 and 2001 recessions (the dashed lines reproduce the fitted values from the log–log regression in Figure 5.1). Left panel: 1988–1993; right panel: 1998–2003.

in time, firms are hiring and firing people. Similarly, workers are finding or losing jobs (or quitting) or moving from one job to another; and people are entering or leaving the labor force. Combined, these various flows – which can be surprisingly large in gross terms – determine the aggregate values of unemployment, employment, and the labor force at a point in time, and the responses of these flows to a shock show up as movements along (actually around) the Beveridge curve, or as shifts of the curve.

The situation cries out for a system of differential equations; there are several different ways we can meet the need. The first way involves carefully describing job market flows, and then backing out what the value of the steady-state unemployment rate will be based on what these flows are at a point in time.[4] A good example is provided by Petrongolo and Pissarides (2008); let's work through their exercise (but using a slightly less opaque notation).

We assume that a worker can be in three different states: unemployed (U), employed (E), or not in the labor force (N). Denote the transition rate between states i and j as τ_{ij}; for example, the transition rate from employment to unemployment is given by τ_{EU}. (These transition rates can change over time.) Using the fact that $L = U + E$, so $E = L - U$, we have two differential equations for U and N:

---

[4] This approach has a long history; one of the first papers to think about the labor market in these terms – and one that is still worth reading today – is Holt and David (1966).

$$\frac{dU}{dt} = \tau_{EU}(L - U) + \tau_{NU}N - \tau_{UN}U - \tau_{UE}U,$$

$$\frac{dN}{dt} = \tau_{EN}(L - U) + \tau_{UN}U - \tau_{NU}N - \tau_{NE}N. \tag{5.1}$$

What we do to find the flow-implied or steady-state unemployment rate u_t^* (which is defined in the usual way as U_t relative to the labor force $U_t + E_t$) is to set dU/dt and dN/dt equal to zero and solve system (5.1). Several pages of tedious algebra later, we obtain the following expression for u_t^*:

$$\frac{\tau_{EU} + \iota_0}{\tau_{UE} + \tau_{EU} + \iota_0 + \iota_1}, \tag{5.2}$$

where ι_0 and ι_1 are given by

$$\iota_0 = \tau_{EN}\frac{\tau_{NU}}{\tau_{NU} + \tau_{NE}} \quad \iota_1 = \tau_{UN}\frac{\tau_{NE}}{\tau_{NU} + \tau_{NE}}. \tag{5.3}$$

Although messy, the last two expressions have an intuitive interpretation. The ι_0 term represents an indirect inflow of employed workers into unemployment, where "indirect" refers to the fact that they are moving from E to U via nonparticipation. Likewise, ι_1 is the outflow of unemployed workers into employment, again via nonparticipation. These participation flows can be important contributors to movements in actual unemployment (and, by extension, to Beveridge curve dynamics): As Elsby et al. (2015) document, the 2007–2009 recession saw a large drop in the outflow rate (ι_1) as unemployed workers remained in the labor force, and an increase in the inflow rate (ι_0) as people entering the labor force moved directly into unemployment.

If we plot the actual unemployment rate against the value of u_t^* implied by time-t flows (Figure 5.3), we see that the actual unemployment rate tends to be very close to the steady-state rate, and that large changes in unemployment are led by the steady-state rate. Under normal circumstances, the relevant flows into and out of unemployment are large enough that it takes very little time for the actual rate to converge to its steady-state value. That means that the actual rate is largely determined by the same thing that determines u^* – namely, the transition rates τ_{ij} – and it is changes in these flow rates that account for much of the movement in the actual unemployment rate.[5]

---

[5] For example, the small gap that opens up between the two series in early 2009 only amounts to a four-month lag. In the figure, the large spike in the unemployment rate that resulted from the pandemic-related shutdown of the economy is cut off by the scale. In one month (March 2020), the numerator in equation (5.2) rose by a factor of 5.6 as τ_{EU} jumped, and the denominator fell by 23 percent. The result was to boost March 2020's flow-consistent rate of

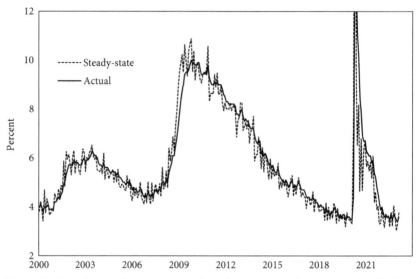

Figure 5.3 Actual unemployment rate and steady-state unemployment rate implied by labor market flows.

How do vacancies get into the mix? Here's where we cross the fine line between clever and stupid. For the time being, we are going to assume that there exists an object called an aggregate *matching function* $m(\cdot)$, which tells us how many hires per unit time take place given the current levels of U and V. (The idea is similar to a production function, where "output" is a flow of hires, and the inputs are job postings together with the pool of unemployed workers searching for a new job. That is, more job postings, more workers looking for work, or both will increase the flow of new hires.) We can write the matching function as

$$h_t = \alpha_t m(U_t, V_t), \tag{5.4}$$

where h denotes flow hires out of unemployment and α is a shift term (like TFP in a production function) that raises the number of hires for given values of U_t and V_t. (The term of art for α is that it measures "matching efficiency.") Now, flow hires out of unemployment is the same thing as $\tau_{UE}U$, which is the last term in the first equation of system (5.1) and the first term in the denominator of (5.2). So we can equate $\tau_{UE}U$ with $\alpha m(U, V)$. In addi-

---

7.8 percent by a factor of 7, resulting in a one-month spike in u^* to 56.5 percent. Fortunately, those flows didn't persist long enough for the actual unemployment rate to converge to u^*.

tion, under the assumption that $\alpha m(\cdot)$ exhibits constant returns to scale, we can divide both sides by U to obtain:

$$\tau_{UE} = \frac{\alpha m(U, V)}{U} = \alpha m(1, V/U) = \alpha m(1, v/u), \tag{5.5}$$

where v and u are the vacancy and unemployment *rates* (we can divide the top and bottom of V/U by the labor force).

Why would we do all this? Well, the τ_{ij} terms are in principle measurable: We can use matched panels of the Current Population Survey (CPS) to compute these various transition rates.[6] Then, if we assume a functional form and specific parameter values for $m(\cdot)$, we can pin down the sources of any observed shifts in the empirical Beveridge curve and quantify their effects.[7] Alternatively, we can decompose changes in the unemployment rate into the contributions of changes in these various transition rates, which is what Petrongolo and Pissarides (2008) do.[8]

From a macroeconomic standpoint this is probably not the most interesting decomposition that we can come up with. We would prefer to know something about dynamics; namely, why the vacancy and unemployment rates tend to trace out loops, and – more broadly – how the Beveridge curve is likely to behave following different types of shocks. That will in turn let us infer whether a particular shock has hit the labor market by observing actual movements in unemployment and vacancies, and – hopefully – will let us draw conclusions about the state of labor market functioning. But to do so, we need to approach the problem in a different way.

Specifically, let's consider a model of Beveridge curve dynamics developed by Blanchard and Diamond (1989).[9] The model still assumes a matching function $\alpha m(U, V)$ (with the usual constant returns to scale property), but

---

[6] The CPS – also known as the *household survey* – is the source of the data used to compute the unemployment and labor force participation rates, and contains a number of questions about labor market status. Because of the way the sample is constructed, it is possible to observe what are inferred to be the same individuals over consecutive months, which allows us to estimate the τ terms. Flows data are available as far back as 1990 on the BLS website.

[7] See Elsby et al. (2015) for an excellent example of this sort of exercise. An alternative is to use the measured flows and observed paths of V_t and U_t to back out an estimate of matching efficiency; see Veracierto (2011).

[8] There are two issues regarding this exercise that we've breezed past. First, we are implicitly assuming that the matching function only determines U to E flows; flows from N to E just happen. Second, the τ terms are actually continuous-time transition rates, so ideally we would convert the observed transition rates into continuous-time equivalents. (That's not always easy to do – see Petrongolo and Pissarides, 2008 for an example.)

[9] Arguably, this paper did more than any other to make people interested in the Beveridge curve again.

it also allows the rates of job creation and destruction to vary (and so can analyze cyclical movements and changes in reallocation).

The model assumes that there is a capacity level for the economy (in employment terms) equal to $\bar{E}$. Jobs can be filled, F; unfilled with a vacancy posted, V (so the employer wants to fill it); and unfilled with no vacancy posted, I ("idle capacity"). The model is in continuous time; there is a flow probability π_0 that a productive job becomes unproductive (and so enters idle capacity) and a probability π_1 that an unproductive job becomes productive. If there are P ($= F + V$) productive jobs and $\bar{E} - P$ unproductive jobs, then in flow equilibrium $dP/dt = 0$, which requires $\pi_1(\bar{E} - P) = \pi_0 P$. Hence, the share of $\bar{E}$ that is productive, $P/\bar{E}$, equals $\pi_1/(\pi_0 + \pi_1)$. Blanchard and Diamond call this c, for $cyclical$, as it serves as a measure of aggregate activity in employment terms. Blanchard and Diamond also define a term s, which determines the steady-state flow of jobs going from productive to unproductive,

$$s\bar{E} \equiv \pi_0 \left(\frac{\pi_1}{\pi_0 + \pi_1} \right) \bar{E}, \tag{5.6}$$

which they interpret as the intensity of reallocation taking place in the economy.

If workers quit at a rate q, then the following system determines employment and vacancy flows

$$\frac{dE}{dt} = \alpha m(U, V) - qE - \pi_0 E, \tag{5.7}$$

$$\frac{dV}{dt} = -\alpha m(U, V) + qE + \pi_1 I - \pi_0 V, \tag{5.8}$$

which is intuitive: Employment increases with new hires, declines with quits, and declines when a job becomes unproductive; likewise, vacancies decline when a job is filled, and rise when a worker quits a productive job or when a previously unproductive job becomes productive (and needs to be filled), and declines when a productive job for which a vacancy was open becomes unproductive. Using the fact that $L = E + U$ and $\bar{E} = E + V + I$ allows us to rewrite the system as

$$\frac{dU}{dt} = -\alpha m(U, V) + (q + \pi_0)(L - U),$$

$$\frac{dV}{dt} = -\alpha m(U, V) + (q - \pi_1)(L - U) + \pi_1 \bar{E} - (\pi_0 + \pi_1)V, \tag{5.9}$$

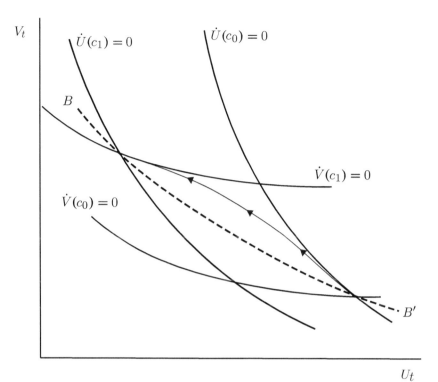

Figure 5.4 Effect of an increase in aggregate activity c in the Blanchard–Diamond model. Higher activity shifts in the $\dot{U} = 0$ locus and shifts up the $\dot{V} = 0$ locus. Arrows indicate the dynamic path (which gives a countercyclical "Beveridge loop"); the steady-state U, V combinations traced out by different values of c yield the Beveridge curve in this model (the dashed line $B\,B'$).

which determines Beveridge curve dynamics. Specifically, Blanchard and Diamond show that the system gives two loci for $\dot{U} = 0$ and $\dot{V} = 0$ whose intersection gives a point on the Beveridge curve. A shock to aggregate activity c has the effect shown in Figure 5.4; these shocks trace out a Beveridge curve (the dashed line) and induce a dynamic response that involves counterclockwise loops in a diagram with V on the y-axis and U on the x-axis.[10] In addition, shocks to reallocation s have the effect of

---

[10] Whether a counterclockwise loop will be present is ambiguous, though it can be shown that it is likely to happen in this model. (Loosely, the model implies that $\dot{V}$ increases by more than $\dot{U}$ when there is an increase in c.)

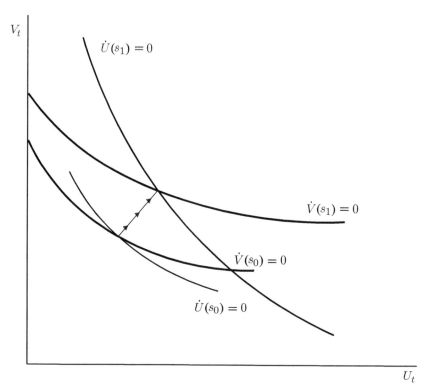

Figure 5.5 Effect of an increase in reallocation intensity s in the Blanchard–Diamond model. Greater reallocation intensity shifts out the $\dot{U} = 0$ locus and shifts up the $\dot{V} = 0$ locus, resulting in higher vacancies and unemployment. In this model, the dynamic path (shown by the arrows) lies along a 45-degree line.

shifting the curve out and cause V and U to move toward the northeast of the diagram (Figure 5.5).[11]

This model provides an intuitive macroeconomic account of the Beveridge curve that matches the main stylized facts about U and V dynamics. Even better, Blanchard and Diamond show how to empirically identify c and s shocks (and, in a modified version of the model, shocks to the labor force). The idea is to use a VAR model and then define shocks to c as innovations that move U and V in opposite directions for at least n months, and shocks to s as innovations that move U and V in the same direction for at least

---

[11] In the version of the model that includes labor force shocks, such a shock causes an initial increase in unemployment and then a decline in both U and V as the additional workers are absorbed into employment.

n months.[12] These conditions imply restrictions on the matrix that transforms the structural shocks into the reduced-form residuals; imposing some additional restrictions allows us to back out these shocks.[13] Finally, we can decompose the movements in unemployment and vacancies (and the labor force) into the accumulated contributions of these various shocks.[14]

Blanchard and Diamond use a nonstandard transformation of the data to obtain a more-direct mapping from their theoretical model to their empirical results. However, their identification procedure is easy enough to implement in terms of the unemployment, vacancy, and labor force participation *rates*, and doing so preserves additivity and makes the interpretation of the results simpler.[15] Figure 5.6 gives the results obtained from a 12-lag VAR fit to monthly data over the sample period 1955–2019. The first panel shows the contribution of the cyclical shock to movements in the unemployment and vacancy rates; a clear Beveridge relation emerges (though some kind of downward-sloping relation is almost guaranteed given how the estimation procedure is set up). On net, the labor force shocks result in a small backward drift in the Beveridge curve over this period (mainly by reducing the unemployment rate); in contrast, the estimated reallocation shocks have little net effect. Finally, the baseline forecasts are vaguely hill shaped after the early 1960s, implying an outward shift of the relation through the early 1980s followed by a partial retracement.

The first panel of Figure 5.6 suggests very little convexity in the cyclical Beveridge relation.[16] Figure 5.7 provides a different perspective by looking for nonlinearity in the bandpass filtered data from Figure 5.1. Fitted values from either a log-log regression or a regression of the filtered vacancy rate on

---

[12] Labor force shocks are defined as the portion of an innovation to L that is not related to an innovation to E; the idea is that a large fraction of labor force movements occur as increases in E draw workers into the labor market (or as decreases in employment lead people to exit).

[13] The system is actually overidentified once these additional restrictions are imposed; without them, we can only identify ranges of parameter values that meet the criteria for the direction and duration of the impulse responses.

[14] This is sometimes called an *historical decomposition*; because what we are doing here is divvying up the moving-average representation of the series, the baseline forecasts plus the shock contributions exactly recover the actual values.

[15] Specifically, the cyclical shock is defined so as to cause the unemployment *rate* and vacancy *rate* to move in different directions for at least *n* months, and the reallocation shock is defined to move the series in the same direction for at least *n* months (here, *n* = 9). The labor force shocks are then described in terms of the participation rate.

[16] Although one might expect that the convexity that Blanchard and Diamond found is attributable to their having used what is essentially a log-level specification, I also find no evidence of convexity when I re-run their version of the model on my dataset.

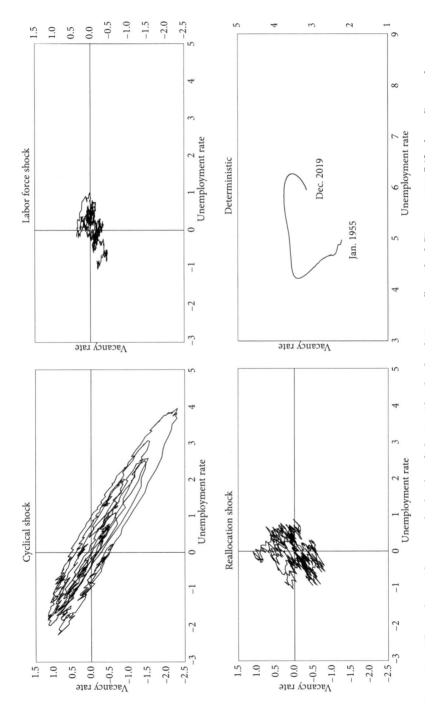

Figure 5.6 Effects of Beveridge curve shocks identified using Blanchard and Diamond's method. "Deterministic" (final panel) gives the contribution from the baseline projection. Sample period is 1955–2019.

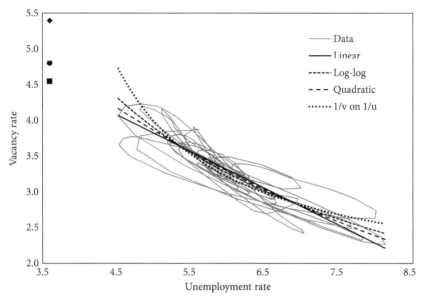

Figure 5.7 Attempts to find evidence of Beveridge curve convexity with specifications that allow for nonlinearity (uses the business-cycle components of the vacancy and unemployment rates plus their sample means). Markers extend estimates to a 3.6 percent unemployment rate (diamond = log-log; circle = quadratic; square = linear).

the level and square of the filtered unemployment rate are not appreciably different from the fitted values from a linear model; as shown by the markers, the various fitted curves show more dispersion at low rates of unemployment.[17] The 3.6 percent unemployment rate used for this extrapolation is the rate that prevailed in the fourth quarter of 2022; the actual value of the vacancy rate in that quarter was 6.6 percent, which suggests either that a much greater degree of nonlinearity is present in extremely tight labor markets, or that other non-cyclical factors pushed unemployment and vacancies well away from their usual relationship.[18]

The vacancy measure that we have been using for our analysis is the composite help-wanted index (HWI) developed in Barnichon (2010); to obtain a vacancy rate, I divide this measure by the civilian labor force. Until 1995, the

---

[17] The sample means are added back to the filtered series before they are used in the regressions; note that the average values for the filtered series are essentially zero.

[18] If we regress $1/v$ on a constant and $1/u$, we can get much more curvature (the implied vacancy rate at a 3.6 percent unemployment rate is 9.3 percent). However, this result goes away if we allow for a linear term as well (the data really prefer something close to a straight line).

composite HWI uses an older series on help-wanted listings in newspapers that was produced by the Conference Board starting in 1951; from 1995 until the end of 2000, the composite series includes a correction for the increased use of online job listings; and from the end of 2000 to the present, the series is equal to the job openings measure from the BLS's Job Openings and Labor Turnover Survey (JOLTS).[19] The newspaper HWI is commonly used in historical work on the Beveridge curve – it is basically the only source of data on job openings for the full economy over this period – but it is not necessarily a good measure.[20] As Abraham (1987) notes, changes in newspaper competition, the occupational composition of employment, and other factors likely caused the relationship between the help-wanted index and "true" vacancies to change over time; by her calculations, the difference between the two series was quite large (35 percent) by 1985. Abraham computes an adjustment factor, but it only extends from 1960 to 1985 (and is annual); even so, it is worth seeing how much of a difference it makes if we use it. (Ideally, the bandpass filter should take care of a slow-moving trend such as this; the question is therefore whether the VAR results are importantly affected.) To extend the series backward and forward in time, I simply assume that the adjustment factor was unchanged from 1953 until 1960 and from 1985 until 1994; I then use it to scale the Barnichon measure and re-do the Blanchard–Diamond analysis with the alternative vacancy rate.[21] The results are plotted in Figure 5.8; they are qualitatively similar, and mostly reflect the fact that the adjustment factor shifts up the level of the vacancy rate proxy in earlier periods.

There are two additional empirical issues associated with the Blanchard–Diamond approach. One is technical: What Blanchard and Diamond are

---

[19] There is a small but noticeable discrepancy between the Conference Board measure and Barnichon's series in the 1950s. The results shown here use the Barnichon series (as downloaded on March 13, 2023). I computed a corrected series that ratio splices the Conference Board HWI to the Barnichon series in January 1961; re-running the Blanchard–Diamond model on the corrected series yields qualitatively similar results – though different enough to highlight the lack of robustness of this approach, and to suggest that *only* the qualitative features of the Blanchard–Diamond specification are worth paying attention to. (It's also a good reminder to be cautious about strange data that you meet on the internet.)

[20] Vacancy data were also collected over short spans of time in various pilot programs in the 1960s and 1970s; see Abraham (1983).

[21] Blanchard and Diamond do something similar in their own work, except that they fit a quadratic time trend to the log of the adjustment factor and use it to extrapolate the series. Plotting the log of the adjustment factor suggests that it isn't a good candidate for a quadratic trend; hence my own more pusillanimous approach. Note that the adjustment factor is transformed so that recent data (such as the JOLTS series) retain their original values.

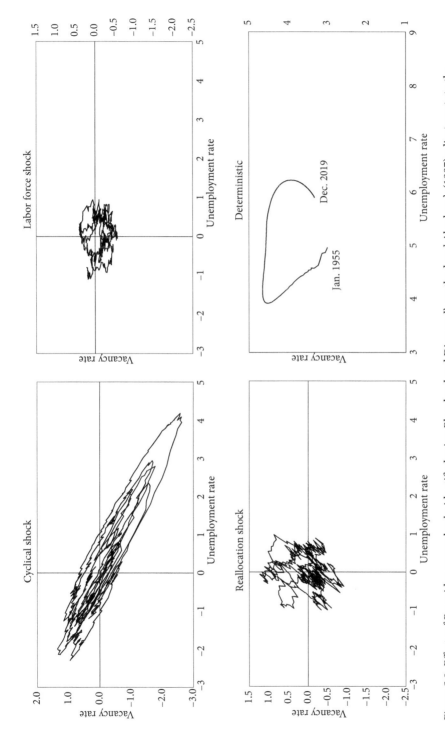

Figure 5.8 Effects of Beveridge curve shocks identified using Blanchard and Diamond's method and Abraham's (1987) adjustments to the help-wanted index. Sample period is 1955–2019.

117

doing is equivalent to identifying structural shocks with a sign-restricted VAR; however, as Baumeister and Hamilton (2015) demonstrate, standard ways of approaching this sort of estimation problem are not innocuous. Intuitively, while we might think that sign restrictions impose a relatively minimal amount of structure – in Bayesian terms, that we are bringing a relatively uninformative prior to the data – for the highly nonlinear objects we are interested in (impulse responses and the like), the prior can be quite informative. (Put differently, Baumeister and Hamilton show that the priors that implicitly underlie sign-restricted VAR models will affect the posterior distributions even as the sample size goes to infinity.) We can apply Baumeister and Hamilton's suggested procedure for fitting a sign-restricted VAR to Blanchard and Diamond's specification; Figure 5.9 shows the results for the activity, reallocation, and labor force shocks.[22] For this particular application, the results differ in only a few noticeable ways from those obtained under the original procedure: We still see little evidence of convexity in the cyclical relation, and the labor force shocks now mostly influence the unemployment rate, with a minimal effect on the vacancy rate.[23]

The other issue with the Blanchard–Diamond approach – and which is common to many descriptions of the Beveridge curve – is that it's not really clear what the empirical reallocation shock is, and what it is actually capturing. Blanchard and Diamond define their reallocation shock as a change in the flow of productive jobs that become unproductive, which seems similar to job destruction. But a reallocation shock in their model can also be consistent with an increase in the flow of unproductive jobs becoming productive (job creation); likewise, in their model an increase in the quit rate has an identical effect to an increase in the reallocation rate. In more-general models, a reduction in matching efficiency (the α term in Equation 5.4) can shift out the Beveridge curve as well; this could reflect a situation where workers in a declining sector are not well suited for other jobs in the economy, or where individuals' reservation wages are going up and (at least initially)

---

[22] I use the estimated values found from our earlier estimation exercise to specify the modes of relatively uninformative prior distributions for the various parameters; the version of the estimation procedure that I use is Ahn's (2023) modification of the original Baumeister–Hamilton setup. (For the results reported here, I use 100,000 burn-in draws followed by 200,000 additional draws.)

[23] The tighter scatterplot for the cyclical shock, by contrast, might reflect the use of posterior medians rather than posterior means. (Using medians also implies that the historical decompositions will not necessarily sum to the actual series, since this property only holds for means.) Alternatively, it could simply be evidence that the precise way in which these shocks are identified matters importantly for the results.

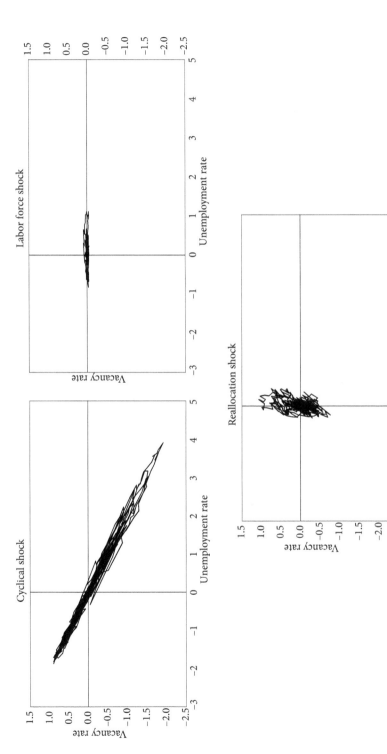

Figure 5.9 Effects of Beveridge curve shocks identified using Baumeister and Hamilton's (2015) estimation procedure for a sign-restricted VAR. Sample period is 1955–2019.

resulting in fewer matches. The reason why these various cases are interesting separately is that their implications for aggregate wage growth are
likely to be very different, even though an empirical approach that associates
outward shifts in the Beveridge curve with reallocation shocks will treat
them as all being the same.[24]

The reason for treating this approach at such length is that, as Elsby et al.
(2015) point out, something like it underpins most modern interpretations
of the Beveridge curve. The system of equations given by (5.9) are simply
accounting identities that are useful for organizing any thinking about job
flows, and the locus of U and V values that yield $\dot{U} = 0$ and $\dot{V} = 0$ basically
is how most modern work defines the Beveridge curve. What much of the
literature therefore concerns itself with is trying to explicitly model decisions
related to job creation (vacancy posting), job destruction, whether to accept
a job offer, and whether to quit as the outcomes of optimizing behavior by
workers and firms in the face of exogenous shocks. Finally, the use of an
aggregate matching function is a feature that is common to many if not most
theoretical and empirical contributions to the literature on aggregate labor
market dynamics. This last analytical element is overdue for our attention.

5.2 The Beveridge Curve without a Matching Function

In conventional accounts of the Beveridge curve, the convexity of the curve
reflects the presence of a matching "technology" that can be described by a
function like the one shown above as equation (5.4), reproduced here,

$$h_t = \alpha_t m(U_t, V_t), \tag{5.10}$$

where h_t denotes flow hires.[25] Convexity therefore results from diminishing "returns" (increments to hires) as either U or V are increased holding
the other term fixed, which arises naturally if the function exhibits constant returns to scale. The consensus of the empirical literature is that this
function does in fact take a constant-returns-to-scale form (Petrongolo and
Pissarides, 2001), which means that we can rewrite it as

---

[24] This is one reason why the aggregate reallocation shock tends not to be a very good
indicator of inflation pressures, even though it can be interpreted as an increase in
structural unemployment in some cases. See Ahn and coauthor (2023) for an attempt
to unpack the sources of reallocation shocks using ancillary data on job creation, job
destruction, and quit rates, and for an examination of some implications for wage and
price inflation.

[25] Earlier, we defined h as the number of flow hires out of unemployment; here, we simply
want to refer to all hires (as a proxy for the number of jobs or successful worker–employer
matches "formed" per period).

$$\frac{h_t}{U_t} = \alpha_t m \left(1, \frac{V_t}{U_t}\right). \tag{5.11}$$

Petrongolo and Pissarides (2001, p. 393) also note that most empirical studies find that a log-linear (constant elasticity) approximation to equation (5.11) "fits the data well," which means that we can try to estimate a specification like

$$\ln \frac{h_t}{U_t} = \beta_0 + \beta_1 \ln \frac{V_t}{U_t} + \varepsilon_t. \tag{5.12}$$

Here, any deviations of the matching efficiency term α_t from its mean will show up in the residual ε_t, and the implied elasticity on U_t will be given by $1 - \beta_1$.

This is an equation that we can bring to the data, because the JOLTS release gives us job openings and hires (and we can get data for unemployment from other sources).[26] When we estimate Equation (5.12) using monthly data from December 2000 to December 2019, we get the results shown in column 1 of Table 5.1. This parameter value seems plausible,

Table 5.1 *Empirical matching function estimates*

	1	2	3	4	5	6
$\ln\left(\frac{V}{U}\right)$	0.684 (0.013)	0.098 (0.011)	0.101 (0.011)			
$\ln U$		−1.196 (0.021)	−1.191 (0.022)			
$\Delta \ln\left(\frac{V}{U}\right)$				0.279 (0.042)	0.004 (0.038)	−0.030 (0.071)
$\Delta \ln U$					−1.101 (0.084)	−1.238 (0.253)
IV	No	No	Yes	No	No	Yes

Dependent variable is $\ln(H/U)$ or $\Delta \ln(H/U)$, where H is the JOLTS measure of hires. "IV" indicates whether estimation uses instrumental variables; estimation period is December 2000 to December 2019. Standard errors in parentheses.

---

[26] I use the JOLTS data for the private sector (which exclude farms), and unemployment for the nonfarm sector; this last variable is not seasonally adjusted, so I seasonally adjust it using the X-11 filter. Note that the JOLTS series are end-of-month values while unemployment is for a reference week within the month. To better align Equation (5.12) with the theory, we can replace V_t by V_{t-1} – that is, use start-of-month vacancies; doing so yields results that are essentially identical to what's reported in Table 5.1.

though the implied coefficient on unemployment (around 0.32) is outside the range of values that Petrongolo and Pissarides (2001) cite in their survey.

We can also directly test the assumption of constant returns to scale (keeping the assumption that the matching function takes a constant-elasticity form) by adding $\ln U_t$ to the estimation equation. Under constant returns to scale, the coefficient on this variable should be zero: If the unemployment elasticity is η^U and the vacancy elasticity is η^V, then the coefficient on log unemployment will be $(\eta^U + \eta^V - 1)$, which is zero when $\eta^U + \eta^V = 1$. As the results in column 2 indicate, this coefficient is pretty far from zero (its t-statistic, which is of course a test of the hypothesis that it can be restricted to equal zero, is -57.0). In addition, if we instrument for $\ln U$ by using its lag (in order to deal with its being on both sides of the regression), we obtain essentially the same result (column 3).

The various series are all obviously nonstationary over this period, so running the regression in first differences is probably a safer course. When we do so, we obtain the results in column 4, which yield a rather different coefficient on the V/U term relative to what we found when log-levels were used (not a good sign). And even here, adding the log-difference of U to the model implies a strong rejection of the constant-returns-to-scale assumption and wipes out the coefficient on $\Delta \ln(V/U)$ (column 5), even if we instrument for $\Delta \ln U$ (column 6).[27]

It turns out that we can't even get sensible results if we simply regress the log of h on a constant and the logs of U and V, or fit the same equation in log-differenced form. About the only way to get something that looks a bit like a conventional matching function is to omit the constant term *and* use log levels of U and V. But that last result merely tells us that because hires tend to run between unemployment and vacancies (Figure 5.10), asking the model to fit hires without a constant will simply make it deliver a convex combination of the U and V terms. And even then, estimating the specification in first differences causes the "sensible" results to vanish.

At best, therefore, it seems as though the relevant elasticities are poorly pinned down even if we impose constant returns to scale – which the data soundly reject. And the results from the other exercises should make us skeptical that we are actually recovering anything resembling a "structural" matching function in the first place. The obvious conclusion, then, is that there is not really any evidence for an aggregate matching function in

---

[27] For this specification the instrument is the lagged growth rate of nonfarm payroll employment (the first-stage F statistic is 28.4), because the lagged first-difference of unemployment growth is not very highly correlated with its time-t value.

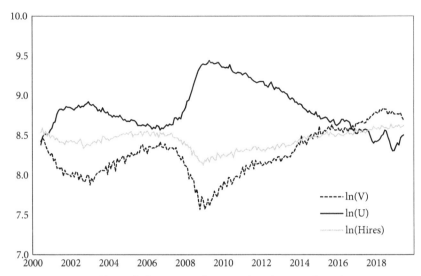

Figure 5.10 Natural logs of job openings (vacancies) V, hires, and nonfarm unemployment U (seasonally adjusted). In general, hires tend to lie between vacancies and unemployment, which is why conventional matching functions seem to fit the data.

20 years of JOLTS data. While that seems at odds with what others have found, recall that the Petrongolo and Pissarides (2001) survey antedates the JOLTS data, and that many of the attempts to fit a matching function prior to when the JOLTS data became available required a number of rather heroic assumptions to construct series that could serve as proxies for hires and vacancies. Plus, we have already seen that vacancy estimates based on the help-wanted index can give different results depending on what adjustments are made to the series over history. Hence, despite their 20-year span, the JOLTS data are probably the best that we have available for this sort of exercise, and we should take seriously our inability to find an aggregate matching function using those data.

It probably shouldn't seem too strange that we can reject the notion of a matching function empirically. (It's not as though we had much luck with the production function either.) Once again, the idea of an economywide labor market seems stylized to the point of silliness: To first order, labor markets are specific to localities, to industries, or (most likely) to both. That sort of heterogeneity won't be captured by summing the number of job openings and number of unemployed, since that procedure implicitly treats each vacancy or unemployed worker the same, no matter where or in what industry they're located. And while we might point to geographic or occupational "mismatch" as influencing the aggregate flow of hires through a shift term in an aggregate matching function, at that point it's not clear why we would want to be looking at things through the prism of an economywide matching function in the first place.[28]

Do we even need a matching function to explain the Beveridge curve? Earlier accounts didn't – in fact, they appealed to demand and supply conditions across a number of separate (and not necessarily clearing) labor markets in order to explain the existence of a (possibly convex) relationship between vacancies and unemployment. The canonical description of the Beveridge curve in these terms comes from Hansen (1970), who drew on Holt and David's (1966) earlier work. Hansen portrayed supply and demand in a *single* labor market in the usual way (Figure 5.11).[29] However, he also argued that *actual* employment at a point in time would lie along the EE' curve in the figure: In conditions of excess labor supply (the upper portions of the supply and demand curves), employment will be constrained by labor demand; similarly, in excess demand conditions employment is constrained by labor supply. In addition, if there is any friction in the market the EE' curve would lie to the left of the relevant portions of the supply and demand curves: Even a situation of excess supply will not let every employer find the workers they need at a particular point in time, just as in a situation of excess demand not every worker will be able to find employment. And when labor demand exceeds labor supply at the going wage, employers will have job vacancies.

It is intuitively clear how, if we have numerous markets in various states of excess supply or demand, we can obtain an aggregate vacancy–unemployment relation that is downward-sloping (and even convex) – see Figure 5.12. As overall labor demand increases (causing the D^0 schedules to shift out to D^1), employment will be slightly higher in markets where

---

[28] Barnichon and Figura (2015) try to examine the matching function across labor markets that are segmented by location and occupation. However, the locations they consider (Census divisions) are still quite large, and the occupational breakdown they use (professional, services, sales, and production) is crude and lumps together very different industries (for instance, construction workers and truck drivers are both in the "production" category). In addition, they do not have actual vacancy data for their segments, and their estimation procedure requires them both to assume the existence of matching functions for each segment and to assume that the elasticity parameter in those segment-specific functions is the same across all segments.

[29] As is traditional in these sorts of analyses, we are being a bit hand-wavy about the definition of the real wage $\widetilde{w}$. For the labor supply curve, the relevant deflator for the nominal wage should be a measure of consumption prices. But for the demand curve, the price should be the price of producers' output.

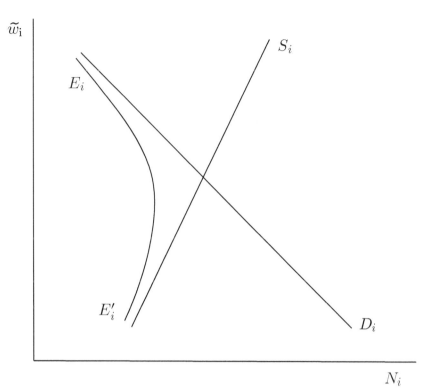

Figure 5.11 Stylized labor market in sector/locality i, as described by Hansen (1970). The EE' curve shows the level of employment that actually prevails under voluntary exchange and with the presence of hiring and job-finding frictions.

excess demand is already present or where excess demand opens up, while vacancies – the distance between the labor demand schedule D and the EE' curve at the prevailing real wage – will increase.[30] In markets with excess supply, an increase in labor demand will raise employment; vacancies will also rise (modestly at first, and then by a larger amount if the market moves into a state of excess demand). The economywide result will be an increase in total vacancies and a decline in total unemployment. Convexity of the relation can arise as a greater number of markets move into excess demand, since employment will rise (and unemployment fall) by smaller and smaller

---

[30] In the figure the asterisk denotes the actual real wage (which can be at a non-market-clearing level); we assume that the market wage rate can be slow enough to adjust that situations of excess supply or demand can emerge. Note also that intermediate cases can arise if the increase in total labor demand is unevenly spread across individual markets.

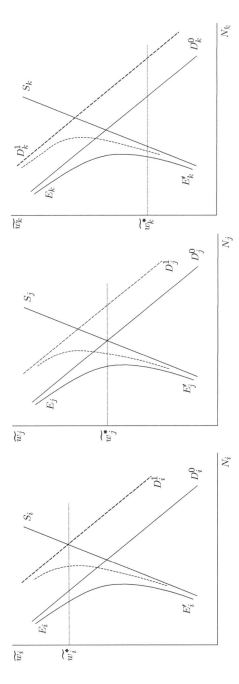

Figure 5.12 Hansen's (1970) description of the Beveridge curve. An increase in labor demand to D^1 in sectors/localities i, j, k has different effects on vacancies and unemployment depending on whether the individual market was initially in a state of excess supply (left panel), effective market clearing (middle panel), or excess demand (right panel). The total result is an increase in vacancies (largely from markets j and k) and a decline in unemployment (largely from market i), which implies a downward-sloping (V, U) relation for the overall economy.

amounts even as vacancies will continue to increase. In addition, Hansen (1970) demonstrates that it is possible to follow Holt and David (1966) and derive a dynamic model that delivers counterclockwise loops around the vacancy–unemployment relation (even *without* the matching function-like assumption that higher unemployment reduces the time that it takes to fill a vacancy).[31]

Although harder to work with, this account of the Beveridge curve is much more plausible (and useful) than one based on an aggregate matching function.[32] This alternative description also has the advantage of drawing a more-direct connection between vacancies and unemployment and the rate of wage growth, in that we would expect the state of excess supply or demand in individual markets would contribute to an overall degree of upward or downward pressure on wage growth.[33] Finally, this alternative carries different implications than those that follow from an aggregate Beveridge curve whose convexity owes to the presence of a matching function that is concave in both of its arguments. Say that we are on the steeply sloped portion of the Beveridge curve, where the aggregate vacancy rate is extremely high and the aggregate unemployment rate is very low – a situation that is likely to result in upward pressure on aggregate wage growth. Under the matching-function interpretation of the Beveridge curve, policy actions could cool down the (single) labor market and slow the rate of wage growth without much cost in unemployment, since the reduction in labor demand would mostly show up as a reduction in vacancies. But if we are talking about numerous individual labor markets, such a case will be a special one: If the policy action affects all markets to some degree, then it's not clear that it will only hit the "right" ones (that is, the ones with excess demand).

So is the Beveridge curve useful, or just interesting? Probably just interesting. In order to tie outward shifts in the aggregate curve to wage inflation, we need a much more refined breakdown of the source of the shift (for instance, what type of reallocation shock has taken place), and that requires us to look at additional pieces of data. Most of the cyclical behavior of unemployment and vacancies takes place off of the curve itself, and we can typically get a

---

[31] As in Blanchard and Diamond (1989), Hansen's formal demonstration uses a sine function to approximate the (exogenous) cyclical behavior of labor demand.

[32] Not to everyone, though: Blanchard and Diamond (1989) explicitly view this alternative formulation of the Beveridge relation as being less attractive. (They also state that it abstracts from frictions in individual labor markets, which isn't completely correct.) So read both papers and choose whom you want to believe.

[33] Hansen explicitly formulates a description of the wage Phillips curve in these terms; also see chapter 5 of Barro and Grossman (1976).

better picture of what's happening in that regard by looking at data on job flows. Finally, since the matching function seems to have no real-world basis, there isn't a way to reliably parameterize the Beveridge relation in a manner that would be useful for generating quantitative predictions as to how unemployment is likely to change given a specified change in labor demand. Hence, while it's always gratifying to see patterns in macroeconomic data that aren't simply the result of pareidolia, we're unlikely to get very far by staring hard at the Beveridge curve.

5.3 Two Other Simple Aggregate Relations

If you were to ask a neoclassical macroeconomist how much additional output would be associated with a 1 percentage point reduction in the unemployment rate, they would likely give you a figure on the order of 0.7 percent. How they would get there is as follows. If we hold the size of the labor force constant, then a 1 percentage point decline in u requires a one-percent increase in employment E (this follows because $\Delta \ln E \approx -\Delta u$ if the labor force doesn't change). If the labor elasticity of output is around 2/3, then an increase in employment of one percent is associated with an increase in output of 2/3 percent. However, when we check this prediction empirically, we obtain an eventual decline in the unemployment rate of about 0.3 percentage point from a 2/3 percent increase in output – just half as large as the neoclassical estimate of a 0.7 percentage point decline.

The reason for this difference is that many other margins – labor productivity, the workweek, labor force participation, and others – also tend to change when output changes, and in such a way that a smaller reduction in the unemployment rate is needed to yield a given increment to output. Collapsed into a single equation, these other relations give rise to a relation between the unemployment rate and output that is known as Okun's law. As it turns out, that single-equation shortcut works better than trying to estimate and combine each margin separately, and for a very intuitive reason.

Table 5.2 shows coefficient estimates from a set of Okun's law specifications of the following form,

$$\Delta u_t = a + A(L)\Delta \ln y_t + B(L)\Delta u_{t-1} + \varepsilon_t, \qquad (5.13)$$

with real GDP denoted by y and the unemployment *rate* denoted by u. The equation is estimated over 1953–2019 and – to see how robust the relation is over time – over several subperiods. (Everything is done

Table 5.2 *Estimated Okun's law specifications*

	Sample period	Coefficient sums		Long-run	Implied g
		$\Delta \ln y$	Δu		
1.	1953:Q1– 2019:Q4 (full)	−0.283 (0.031)	0.361 (0.062)	−0.443	3.0
2.	1953:Q1– 1972:Q4	−0.389 (0.056)	0.119 (0.123)	−0.442	4.0
3.	1973:Q1– 1992:Q4	−0.384 (0.062)	0.119 (0.126)	−0.436	3.1
4.	1993:Q1– 2005:Q4	−0.303 (0.070)	0.365 (0.147)	−0.476	2.9
5.	2006:Q1– 2019:Q4	−0.449 (0.096)	0.379 (0.126)	−0.723	1.6
6.	2009:Q2– 2019:Q4	−0.236 (0.117)	0.313 (0.122)	−0.344	0.4

Note: "Long-run" gives the sum of the coefficients on $\Delta \ln y$ divided by one minus the sum of the coefficients on lagged Δu. "Implied g" is the implied rate of potential output growth. Standard errors in parentheses.

in first differences because these variables scream "nonstationary.") The remarkable thing about these estimates is how stable they appear to be: Until 2005, the long-run semi-elasticities (third column of figures) are roughly the same in each period. The behavior of the estimates after 2005 is also interesting: If the sharp increase in unemployment during the 2007–2009 recession is included in the sample (row 5), then the sensitivity of unemployment to output rises as well; at the time, anecdotes suggested that firms had fired people at a quicker-than-usual pace during the downturn. If we start the estimation at the recession's trough (row 6), the coefficient sums are similar to the full-sample estimates, though the lag structure shifts inasmuch as later lags of output growth receive the largest coefficients.

The reason Okun's law works as well as it does stems from its being based on an identity (Clark, 1983). We can write real GDP in the following way:

$$\text{GDP} = \frac{\text{GDP}}{\text{NF output}} \cdot \underbrace{\frac{\text{NF output}}{\text{NF hours}}}_{\text{Productivity}} \cdot \underbrace{\frac{\text{NF hours}}{\text{NF empl.}}}_{\text{Workweek}} \cdot \frac{\text{NF emp.}}{\text{CPS emp.}} \cdot \underbrace{\frac{\text{CPS empl.}}{\text{Lab. force}}}_{1-u} \cdot \underbrace{\frac{\text{Lab. force}}{\text{Population}}}_{\text{LFPR}} \cdot \text{Population},$$

(5.14)

where each variable is something we can measure with available data.[34] In Equation (5.14), "NF" stands for "nonfarm," which is one of the sectors for which productivity measures are available; also, note that employment takes two forms, nonfarm and "CPS" (for "Current Population Survey"), where the CPS measure is the estimate of employment from the survey that's used to estimate the labor force participation rate (LFPR), the unemployment rate, and other statistics. (As was noted earlier, the CPS is also known as the "household survey," as opposed to the "establishment survey" or Current Employment Statistics survey, which is the survey of business establishments used for the nonfarm payroll, workweek, and average hourly earnings statistics.) In addition, the concept of population that's being used is the civilian noninstitutional population aged 16 years or more (rather than the total US population), since that's what's used in the denominator of the participation rate. Finally, the term labelled $1 - u$ is the *employment rate* (CPS employment relative to the labor force); it equals one minus the unemployment rate because (by definition) the labor force is the sum of employment and unemployment.[35]

If we take logs, we can move the population term over to the left-hand side and express things in terms of the GDP-to-population ratio, y^{pop}. Now the linear system that we get from regressing the log-difference of all the remaining right-hand-side variables in (5.14) on current and lagged GDP-to-population growth looks like Equations 5.15 to 5.20:

$$\Delta \ln \left(\frac{\text{GDP}}{\text{NF output}} \right)_t = a_0 + A(L) \Delta \ln y_t^{\text{pop}} + \varepsilon_t^a, \qquad (5.15)$$

---

[34] Normally, one should never take the ratio of two chain-weighted aggregates (as is done in the first term of equation 5.14); here, though, it's simply being used as a piece of the identity without investing it with any deeper economic content.

[35] One caution should be kept in mind when using the household survey data. Periodically, the BLS introduce "population controls" that reflect either the decennial Census or revised estimates of immigration and emigration. These controls introduce discontinuities in the population, labor force, employment, and unemployment figures; typically, though, the effect on ratios like the unemployment rate or participation rate is much smaller (since the adjustment affects both the numerator and denominator of these series). In addition, there have been adjustments to the CPS estimation procedure and questionnaire over time (most notoriously, the 1994 "CPS redesign," which scarred many labor economists of a particular vintage). It is possible (and best practice) to smooth out the effects that the population controls have on the CPS data; although the data I've used throughout are simply the published data (no smoothing), re-running the matching function estimates using smoothed *total* unemployment yields essentially identical results. (The smoothed series do not extend far enough back in time to be able to use them in the Blanchard–Diamond specification; as noted, though, the unemployment and participation *rates* are mostly unaffected by the population controls.)

$$\Delta \ln(\text{NF productivity})_t = b_0 + B(L)\Delta \ln y_t^{\text{pop}} + \varepsilon_t^b, \qquad (5.16)$$

$$\Delta \ln (\text{Workweek})_t = c_0 + C(L)\Delta \ln y_t^{\text{pop}} + \varepsilon_t^c, \qquad (5.17)$$

$$\Delta \ln \left(\frac{\text{NF empl.}}{\text{CPS empl.}} \right)_t = d_0 + D(L)\Delta \ln y_t^{\text{pop}} + \varepsilon_t^d, \qquad (5.18)$$

$$-\Delta u_t = e_0 + E(L)\Delta \ln y_t^{\text{pop}} + \varepsilon_t^e, \qquad (5.19)$$

$$\Delta \ln \text{LFPR}_t = f_0 + F(L)\Delta \ln y_t^{\text{pop}} + \varepsilon_t^f, \qquad (5.20)$$

where Equation (5.19) uses the approximation $\ln(1 - u) \approx -u$.

If all of the equations use the same number of lags of Δy_t, then because of the underlying identity the system will have the following cross-equation properties:

$$a_0 + b_0 + \cdots + e_0 + f_0 = 0,$$
$$a_1 + b_1 + \cdots + e_1 + f_1 = 1,$$
$$a_i + b_i + \cdots + e_i + f_i = 0,$$

where the subscript-one coefficients are the coefficients on the $\Delta \ln y_t^{\text{pop}}$ terms in the various equations and the subscript-i coefficients (where $i > 1$) apply to the $\Delta \ln y_{t-i}^{\text{pop}}$ terms.

What this implies is that there are two ways to obtain a forecast of the unemployment rate: directly, through Equation (5.19), or the hard way, by combining the separate forecasts from the other equations in the system and then subtracting them from $\Delta \ln y_t^{\text{pop}}$. What Clark pointed out was that the direct way of forecasting the unemployment rate will typically tend to work better, because in several cases a positive shock to one variable in the system (say the workweek) would likely show up as an offsetting negative shock to another series (here, productivity). In more technical terms, what's happening is that the presence of the identity means that the variance–covariance matrix for the six-equation system will have rank 5 instead of rank 6, with the reduction occurring through a number of negative off-diagonal elements (these provide the offsets). We can confirm that this occurs in our sample as well, with especially large negative correlations between the residuals in the productivity and workweek equations, as well as between the residuals for the participation rate and the nonfarm-to-CPS employment ratio.

Things become a little more complicated if we include lagged dependent variables in each equation. When we had the same set of right-hand-side variables in all of the equations, we could estimate each by OLS (in fact,

FGLS estimation of the full set of equations as a seemingly unrelated regression model would be impossible given the singularity of the variance–covariance matrix).[36] The singularity problem can be sidestepped by dropping an equation from the system – say the $-\Delta u$ equation – and then recovering its coefficients by applying the cross-equation restrictions implied by the identity to the coefficients of the other equations obtained from iterated FGLS or (equivalently) maximum likelihood.[37] We can take this latter approach to assess by how much Okun's law improves on an estimate of unemployment obtained by combining the other equations in the identity; depending on the sample period, the difference can be relatively minor (the smallest improvement in the adjusted R-squared is about 4 percentage points) or reasonably big (the largest improvement is around 13 percentage points).

Although Okun's law was originally used as a way to quantify how much output would be realized from a 1 percentage point reduction in the unemployment rate (though see note 41 below), the primary interest in Okun's law has been as a way both to estimate potential output and to diagnose when assumptions about the components of potential might be incorrect.[38] Since Equation (5.14) is an identity, it will also hold for the trend values of each variable (including the "trend" level of the unemployment rate) so long as those trends are defined so as to respect the equality. We can therefore rewrite the system such that each left-hand-side variable is expressed in terms of log-deviations from its own trend, or as deviations of its growth rate from its trend growth rate, and then use real GDP relative to its trend (in log-levels or growth rates) as the cyclical indicator. (By convention, population is always equal to its trend level and so drops out of the system; its level

---

[36] When the same set of regressors are used in each equation, equation-by-equation OLS is identical to iterated FGLS – intuitively, each y vector is being projected onto an identical column space.

[37] A similar sort of problem arises in the estimation of demand systems; the solution is essentially the same. Note that when lagged dependent variables are present, some statistical packages will be able to mechanically generate estimates for the singular (six-equation) system using iterated FGLS; however, the result is typically achieved by restricting the coefficients on the lagged dependent variables to be the same across equations. (Another telltale sign that something's amiss is that the log-likelihood for the estimated system deteriorates markedly.)

[38] Okun's analysis was commissioned by James Tobin, who was at the time a member of President Kennedy's Council of Economic Advisers (Okun was a staff economist there, and knew Tobin from Yale); the original purpose was to convince the President of the likely benefits of a tax cut. (See Bernstein, 2001, pp. 133–36.) Shortly thereafter, Okun used it as a way to estimate potential output (Okun, 1962).

is needed, though, if we want to compute trend GDP.) But because Okun's law tends to do better than the individual components, we can instead use an estimate of trend unemployment u^* (which we might obtain through an analysis of labor market functioning) and then define the output gap so that it is consistent with Okun's law written as:

$$u_t - u_t^* = B(L)(\ln y_t - \ln y_t^*),\tag{5.21}$$

with maybe a few lags of the unemployment and output gaps thrown in to better capture dynamics. Once we back out that potential level, we can use it to cyclically adjust the other pieces of the identity; that in turn should make extraction of *their* trends easier. In addition, if we take equation (5.21) seriously (and add some lags), we can write it in first differences,

$$\Delta u_t = B(L)\Delta \ln y_t - B(L)\Delta \ln y_t^* + G(L)\Delta u_{t-1},\tag{5.22}$$

where we have assumed that Δu_t^* is zero. This allows us to back out the average rate of potential growth over a given estimation period if we replace $\Delta \ln y_t^*$ in regression (5.22) with a constant term, take its negative, and then divide the result by the sum of the coefficients on $\Delta \ln y_t$ – that is, by $B(1)$. These implied average growth rates are shown in the last column of Table 5.2.[39]

All this sounds sensible, but it's really not. First, everything is (at best) extremely circular. Second, because we're playing with an identity, we can set a particular component's trend to anything we like and maintain the same trend for GDP by making offsetting adjustments to another trend. Ideally these trends could be measured separately: For example, conventional estimates of trend labor productivity are often based on some sort of appeal to a production function and measures of capital and (trend) TFP; estimates of the trend labor force participation rate can be generated by looking at the age distribution of the population and cohort-specific participation rates; and it used to be possible to back out u^* estimates from inflation equations (assuming that's how we wanted to define it).[40] We might also try fitting some sort of flexible trend for each variable. But since many of these trends

[39] The relatively low rate of implied potential growth in the 2009–2019 sample period reflects the fact that the unemployment rate fell steadily over this period (by about 6 percentage points in total) despite an uninspiring average rate of GDP growth (about 2.2 percent per year). Of course, a believer in this sort of exercise might also point out that the constant term could be contaminated by a nonzero change in u^* over this period.

[40] Typical practice involves using the current level of the capital stock in the trend productivity calculations, rather than the long-run steady-state value that would be implied by a growth model.

are going to be hard to discern in real time (or hard to estimate over history) without some sort of cyclical correction, we're again stuck with needing an estimate of the output gap. Likewise, forecasting the future evolution of these trends is unlikely to be much more than informed guesswork, especially since most of them actually can't be estimated all that well over history.

Now if we have any of those trends (and therefore trend GDP) wrong, we will see errors emerge in our fitted Okun's law regression. These will also show up as errors in one or more of the component equations (they might also involve an error in our u^* assumption), which can serve as a signal to adjust the relevant trend to bring the equation back on track. But as well as Okun's law fits, it is still an extremely noisy relationship in first differences (and a problematic one in log-levels, as the output and unemployment gaps inherit the high degree of persistence that is present for the actual values of $\ln y$ and u). We might also think of combining Okun's law with additional equations and then estimating y^* and u^* as latent variables; however, it's not clear to what extent the estimates of these terms will be determined by the need to fit the dynamics of unemployment and output (or other variables in the system), as opposed to being good estimates of the full-utilization values of these variables.

So is Okun's law a useful macroeconomic relationship? It's probably the best way to forecast the unemployment rate conditional on a path for output – but then that assumes that you have a good GDP forecast to begin with. As for estimating potential output, it might be a useful relation were the concept of potential itself meaningful (which, as we saw in Chapter 4, it's not), and if someone dropped a series for the full-employment unemployment rate in your lap (which is unlikely to happen in practice).[41] Hence, here too we have a relation that is interesting to think about, but that is probably only useful for a narrow purpose – namely, as a way of checking the consistency of an output forecast relative to an unemployment rate forecast. (And that's a real shame – one almost never comes across a macroeconomic relation that's this stable over such a long period of time.)

---

[41] In fact, this was how Okun used the relation – the assumption at the time was that full employment corresponded to a 4 percent unemployment rate, which was then substituted into Okun's law to back out the corresponding level of potential. As Plosser and Schwert (1979) noted, there was a problem with how this was actually done: Okun ran the regression with the unemployment gap as the dependent variable and then took the reciprocal of the coefficient on output to translate the unemployment gap into an output gap – but you can't use the reciprocal in that way unless the R-squared of the Okun's law regression is one (which it isn't).

Table 5.3 *GDP elasticity of employment*

Sample period	Total GDP	Nonfarm GDP
1953:Q1–2019:Q4 (full)	0.873	0.695
1953:Q1–1972:Q4	0.907	0.722
1973:Q1–1992:Q4	0.843	0.647
1993:Q1–2019:Q4	0.968	0.773

If all we are really interested in is the response of employment growth to real GDP growth (say as a way of computing the response of the wage bill to a change in output), then a perfectly serviceable relation involves a regression of the log-difference of nonfarm employment on its own lags and on the contemporaneous and lagged log-difference of real GDP (we are, of course, taking a stand on causality by using the contemporaneous value of output growth in the regression; the same was true of our Okun's law estimates). This relation yields a relatively stable long-run elasticity over the full sample and various subperiods, whether we use total real GDP or real GDP for the nonfarm sector (see Table 5.3).[42]

5.4 What We Miss with Aggregation

We would expect there to be limits on how well aggregate relationships can capture developments in labor markets (either in theory or empirically); our discussion of the Beveridge curve provides one example. Additionally, the introduction to this chapter noted that connecting aggregate employment to the aggregate (real) wage is not especially helpful; one reason is that labor markets don't seem to "clear" through price adjustment, and another is simply that wages are determined at a high level of disaggregation in separate markets that are often, for all practical purposes, unrelated to one another. In other words, "the" labor market doesn't exist, so *a fortiori* "the" real wage isn't determined in it. And while the aggregate real wage is certainly something that can be (imperfectly) measured, it has no important bearing on the aggregate volume of employment except to the extent that labor income matters for aggregate spending (after all, there's a reason why labor economists work with microdata).[43]

---

[42] Each model uses the contemporaneous value and four lags of output growth and two own lags.

[43] That isn't to say that aggregate (nominal) wage growth isn't partly determined by aggregate real activity (as we'll see in the next chapter), though here too the phenomenon is best

In the labor market context, another simple illustration of a case where aggregation leads us astray involves the employment effects of the minimum wage. To an economist accustomed to thinking purely in terms of a big supply and demand diagram, imposing a minimum wage should pretty much unambiguously reduce employment (unless the minimum wage is so low that it's irrelevant).[44] However, empirical studies often find *no* employment effect, and certainly not one that is large enough to be visible in aggregate data. A popular explanation for this finding is that employer monopsony power is present, though that explanation makes little sense at the aggregate level.[45] However, as Azar et al. (2019) point out, one simple way to square the circle is to note that labor markets are heterogeneous; specifically, that the degree of monopsony power that employers enjoy can depend importantly on what occupations are involved, as well as on how important the employer is in a particular labor market. They provide evidence that the employment effects of an increase in the minimum wage are less negative (and even become positive) in more highly concentrated labor markets, in line with the idea that monopsony power can be relevant, and note that the finding of a small or zero aggregate effect likely reflects the averaging of these heterogeneous outcomes across markets. Besides being interesting in its own right, this result also suggests another reason why thinking about the Beveridge curve in terms of aggregated individual labor markets is more likely to be correct than thinking about it in terms of a single homogenous market with an aggregate matching function.

Another, more important source of heterogeneity that is lost by only looking at economywide totals involves labor market outcomes across demographic groups. Figure 5.13 plots three-month moving averages of the monthly unemployment rates for various races or ethnicities.[46] There is a clear and persistent difference in the levels of the various unemployment rates, and the rates for Hispanics and blacks appear to be more sensitive to

---

understood without an appeal to an economywide labor market where supply and demand are brought into alignment by a market-clearing real wage.

[44] This isn't a straw man – some prominent mainstream economists actually do make arguments like this.

[45] If it were true, though, it would provide another reason not to take new Keynesian models seriously, since these models typically describe wage determination in terms of monopolistic sellers of labor (workers).

[46] These categories are how the Census Bureau classifies race or ethnicity. Note that the groups are not mutually exclusive, because people reporting as "Hispanic" can be white or black. These data are only available since 1973; the data for Asian unemployment rates start in 2003. In 2003 there were significant revisions to the questions on race and ethnicity in the CPS; the main effect was to raise the unemployment rate for Hispanics by about half a percentage point (other groups' unemployment rates were essentially unchanged).

Table 5.4 Okun-style models by demographic group

	Black	Hispanic	White	Total
1973:Q1–2019:Q4 (full sample)*	−0.632	−0.659	−0.437	−0.464
Average gap with total, pct. pts.	5.6	2.5	−0.8	–
1973:Q1–1992:Q4*	−0.597	−0.679	−0.417	−0.436
Average gap with total, pct. pts.	6.9	3.1	−0.8	–
1993:Q1–2019:Q4*	−0.719	−0.637	−0.496	−0.556
Average gap with total, pct. pts.	4.6	2.0	−0.7	–

*Sum of coefficients on $\Delta \ln y$ divided by one minus the sum of the coefficients on lagged Δu.

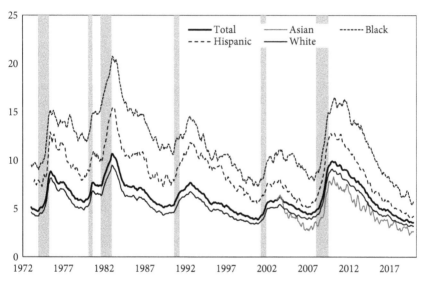

Figure 5.13 Overall unemployment rate and unemployment rates for different races or ethnicities (three-month moving averages of monthly data). Gray bars denote NBER recessions.

the state of the business cycle. These impressions are confirmed by Table 5.4; for each period shown and for each group, the table gives the long-run coefficient on total GDP from Okun-style regressions and the average gap between each group's unemployment rate and the total unemployment rate.[47]

---

[47] Results for the Asian unemployment rate are not shown because the span of available data is too short. Each model regresses the first difference of the relevant unemployment rate on the contemporaneous value and two lags of log-differenced real GDP, along with two own lags.

In a study of racial and ethnic disparities in labor market outcomes that also accounted for differences across women and men, Cajner et al. (2017) used CPS microdata to try to determine what portion of these differentials could be explained by individual characteristics (including age, educational attainment, marital status, and state of residence). They found that very little of the black–white differential could be explained by these observables, and that this differential mainly reflected a higher risk of job loss for black workers. By contrast, the differential between Hispanic and white unemployment rates could be largely explained by lower average educational attainment among Hispanics; in addition, the risk of job loss for this group was also high relative to white workers, which helps to explain the greater cyclical sensitivity of Hispanic unemployment rates.[48]

5.5 The Concept of Labor Market Slack

Only the most obtuse would argue that unemployment or underemployment invariably represents the efficient outcome of fully clearing markets (or even that it does so in many cases). Instead, there can be prolonged periods in which large numbers of people who are willing to work at prevailing wage rates are unable to find jobs, which is another way of saying that a portion of actual unemployment or underemployment can reflect insufficient labor demand – a situation that is often referred to as a "slack" labor market. For a policymaker, being able to assess how much slack is present in the labor market would be a useful way to determine how much stimulus to provide to aggregate demand, or whether such stimulus is at risk of causing the labor market to run "too hot" (though if there are minimal or no inflationary consequences, it is hard to see a way in which the labor market *could* be too hot).[49]

---

[48] The study used data from the 1976–2016 period, and also examined differences in other labor market outcomes, including labor force participation rates. Note that the industry of previous employment was not included among the individual characteristics.

[49] Not that some haven't tried. In new Keynesian models, labor contracts do not respect the principle of voluntary exchange, and so require workers to (over-)work as much as an employer asks at the contracted wage. (For obvious reasons, including the 13th Amendment to the US Constitution, there's little reason to entertain that possibility.) Similarly contrived stories include the notion that a period of prolonged labor market tightness might lead people to cut their education short and enter the labor market too early, or that a tight labor market might cause workers to change employment too frequently. Neither of these speculations has any empirical support that I'm aware of, though they are sometimes enlisted by central-bank types as a convenient way to rationalize unpleasant approaches to inflation control.

Can we find a way to define and measure the degree of underutilization in the labor market? If we believe that – absent any shocks – the economy will naturally tend to a state in which resources are fully utilized, then a reasonable candidate would be the difference between the actual unemployment rate and the rate that would prevail after the effects of any shocks to the economy had completely died out. This is essentially Friedman's (1968) concept of the *natural rate* of unemployment, which he defined as "the level that would be ground out by the Walrasian system of general equilibrium equations, provided there is imbedded in them the actual structural characteristics of the labor and commodity markets, including market imperfections, stochastic variability in demands and supplies, the cost of gathering information about job vacancies and labor availabilities, the costs of mobility, and so on." Empirically, such a definition corresponds to a Beveridge–Nelson trend – assuming, of course, that we have an adequate model of the economy that can capture these various potential influences on the natural rate.

Friedman's concept of a natural rate is probably closest to what most economists have in mind as a benchmark for labor market slack. It has the advantage of being very clearly defined, and it dovetails nicely with a well-established empirical definition of a series' trend. However, there are good reasons to be skeptical of the theoretical soundness and practical workability of this concept. As we saw earlier, there is a strong theoretical argument for dismissing the notion that there is a "real side" of the economy that eventually makes its influence felt following a shock (recall the issues associated with proving the stability of a general economic equilibrium). Similarly, once we start trying to apply the natural rate concept to real-world questions, we find that Friedman's definition doesn't provide an unambiguous guide to what we should be measuring. For example, take a situation where currently unemployed workers are not a good fit (in terms of skills or location) for existing job openings. Should this be embedded in the mythical enhanced Walrasian equations of Friedman's natural rate concept, or is it something that would be resolved if relative prices and wages were sufficiently flexible and workers sufficiently mobile? Would the situation resolve itself if workers and firms were given enough time to adapt, in which case it shouldn't be allowed to affect the Beveridge–Nelson trend? Should the Beveridge–Nelson trend be conditioned on the current skill mix of workers, or should changes in the skill mix be treated as transitory shocks that will (eventually) dissipate as new generations of workers enter the labor market and older generations leave? None of these questions has an easy answer, and there is no model that provides a sufficiently good representation of the world that it would allow us to translate any answers that we come up with into a solid empirical estimate. (Section 5.6 uses a torn-from-the-headlines example to illustrate these difficulties.) Moreover, if persistent strong labor demand can itself reduce structural unemployment (a phenomenon known as hysteresis), then the natural rate concept becomes less meaningful even on its own terms.

An alternative is to try to back out a benchmark for labor market slack by looking at wage and price behavior, the idea being that a particular degree of labor market tightness is not "sustainable" (given how the Fed sets policy) if it results in increases in price inflation or labor cost growth. Such a proposal assumes we can control for all other influences on wages and prices, which is difficult to do in practice; in addition (and as we'll see when we get to the discussion of inflation), such a definition depends importantly on the nature of the inflation process, as does the precision with which any such benchmark can be estimated.

A related but probably unanswerable question is whether there is a hard limit (other than zero) on how low the unemployment rate can actually fall – in other words, what is the irreducible amount of structural and frictional unemployment present in the economy at a particular point in time.[50] One possible way to answer the question is to look at previous periods in which the unemployment rate has dropped to relatively low levels; for example, in the post–World War II period the lowest unemployment rate on record is 2.5 percent, which was achieved in May and June of 1953. However, this level of the unemployment rate came at the end of the Korean War, and in a period where both the demographic composition and the industrial structure of the economy were very different to today. More recently, the unemployment rate reached lows of 3.8 percent (in April of 2000) and 3.5 percent (in September of 2019), so at a minimum these would seem to be attainable rates of aggregate unemployment. We might also look at the rate of short-term unemployment (those unemployed for less than five weeks) as a reasonable proxy for the frictional unemployment rate, though this will overstate the frictional rate to the extent that some of these workers are unemployed because of structural factors, and it is also unclear whether we should consider workers who are in the first stages of a longer spell of unemployment – and hence included in the short-term rate – to be frictionally unemployed. Over the 25 years that preceded the pandemic, this rate was typically less

---

[50] Arguably, even this concept would not correspond to true full employment if a portion of structural unemployment reflected persistent noneconomic factors that kept some groups from being able to find jobs readily.

than 2 percent outside of recessions and dropped as low as 1.1 percent for a single month in 2019.

The unemployment rate is not the only measure of labor underutilization; in fact, it is number three out of a total of six measures that the BLS report. In order to be counted as unemployed, a jobless worker needs to have made a specific and active attempt to find a job over the preceding month or needs to be on temporary layoff and expecting to be recalled to their job (otherwise, they are not counted as being in the labor force). The BLS also have a broader category, "marginally attached to the labor force," if a person is not working or not looking for work, but say that they want a job and have looked for one over the past year. Within the marginally attached, there is a subgroup called "discouraged workers" – these are people who tell the interviewer that they aren't looking for work because of a reason related to the job market. Finally, there is a category of workers who want to work full time but who have only been able to get part-time work (these workers are classified as "part time for economic reasons").

These various definitions can be used to make alternative measures of underutilization that differ in scope; likewise, there are measures that capture the share of the labor force that has been unemployed for more than 15 weeks (the official term for this series is "U-1"), and the share of the labor force that is accounted for by people who have lost their job or completed a temporary job (U-2).[51] The official unemployment rate is denoted as U-3, while U-4 includes discouraged workers in its definitions of underemployed and the labor force. The U-5 rate broadens U-4 to include all marginally attached workers; finally, the U-6 rate is the ratio of unemployed workers, marginally attached workers, and those working part time for economic reasons to the total labor force plus those who are marginally attached. Figure 5.14 plots these various measures from 1989 to 2019 (consistent U-4, U-5, and U-6 series start in 1994). Unsurprisingly, all of these series have the same contour over the business cycle; in addition, in the wake of a recession the gap between U-5 and U-6 widens noticeably as the number of workers who are part time for economic reasons increases. Together with the statistics on unemployment rates by race or ethnicity, these series also highlight how far the economy remains from true full employment even when the total unemployment rate declines to relatively low levels.

The ultimate purpose of these exercises is to provide a rough idea of how far the economy is from full employment – in this last example, to gauge how many "potential" workers might rejoin the labor force were the labor market

---

[51] Note that U-1 and U-2 are not mutually exclusive.

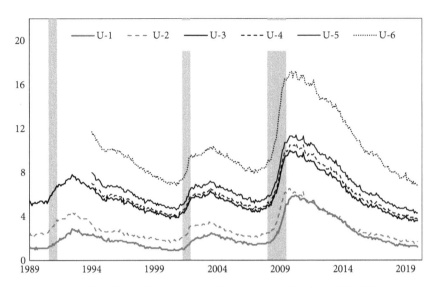

Figure 5.14 Alternative measures of labor underutilization, 1989–2019.

to become tight enough. Should the "natural" rate of unemployment play a role in any of this? Probably not. The lack of a useable definition or well-founded empirical estimate of the natural rate (especially in the inflation regime that prevailed from around 1997 to 2019) means that using such a guidepost for policy simply introduces another badly measured and ill-conceived unobservable to the mix. In practice, policymakers will either pick whatever estimate suits them (and there is a wide range of such esti-mates to choose from), or they will take an attitude of "I'll know full employ-ment when I see it." (That latter attitude would probably be adequate if not for the fact that all too often the only thing that they end up looking at is the headline unemployment rate – or the inflation rate.)[52] Of course, anyone who slogged through the discussion of potential output in Chapter 4 proba-bly could have guessed well in advance that it would be hard to come up with a theoretical or empirical justification for a single scalar measure of capacity employment. But, like Ken Arrow's zero-accuracy weather forecasts, these concepts are likely to remain important for planning purposes. So it's good to have some idea of the intellectual incoherence of both.[53]

---

[52] Hence, a more interesting question is why in practice full employment is consistently ranked lower than inflation control as a policy goal; for a suggestive but somewhat incomplete answer, see Kalecki (1943).

[53] For those who don't get the reference: Kenneth Arrow worked on producing weather forecasts for the Army Air Corps in World War II. (Remember Arrow–Debreu? Same Arrow.) Eventually he asked his superior officer to convey to *his* superiors that their

5.6 Digression: Defining the Natural Rate in a Pandemic

One way to illustrate the practical difficulties that arise in trying to define the natural rate – or a closely related measure that uses inflation to gauge proximity to full employment – is to ask whether the rise in unemployment that resulted from the mandated business closures during the COVID pandemic should have been treated as an increase in the natural rate.

Under the Friedman definition, we might decide that the direct effect of the closures on unemployment should correspond to an increase in the natural rate – because they occurred through government *diktat*, they can be viewed as an institutional constraint on the labor market. Then again, one could reasonably consider these closures to be factors that would eventually be ironed out by a return to a Walrasian equilibrium after wages and prices had adjusted sufficiently so as to absorb workers from closed sectors into still-operating sectors. *That* would imply no change to the natural rate. Under this latter interpretation, the unemployment caused by shutdowns would need to be classified as frictional or structural unemployment: A waiter is thrown out of work because their restaurant is closed, they can't get work in any other restaurant (they're *all* closed), and so needs to find work in some other sector of the economy.[54] This suggests that it's not even clear whether structural unemployment should be something that raises the natural rate under Friedman's definition: In the idealized Walrasian world, the (incorrect) presumption is that the theory implies that real wages will always fall enough to employ everyone, unless labor demand curves are completely flat. (But here too, there's that annoying stability issue to contend with …)

---

forecasts were about as good as random guesses. Arrow waited a few days, and then heard back that "The General understands that the weather forecasts are no good. But he needs them for planning purposes." (The metaphor translates directly to economic forecasting in policy settings.)

[54] The worker might be considered out of the labor force – not unemployed – because they're waiting for the economy and their former employer to reopen. In the official statistics, such a person is considered unemployed if they are on temporary layoff; if they aren't – for example, if their restaurant is closed permanently and all the other restaurants are closed too, so they end up not looking for work for longer than four weeks and don't think they'll be called back to work – they are considered to be out of the labor force. This was an actual problem that the CPS interviewers faced during the first part of the pandemic; at the time, interviewers were given special instructions to count people as "unemployed on temporary layoff" even if they were uncertain when or if they'd be recalled, or whether they'd be recalled in six months (unless they have a definite recall date, the official definition of "on temporary layoff" requires a worker to expect to return to work within six months).

Friedman also associated his concept with stable inflation; perhaps that characteristic of the natural rate would help us? Under that definition – the natural rate is the level of employment that puts neither downward nor upward pressure on inflation – we might also treat the change in unemployment that directly results from the shutdowns as a change in the natural rate. Here's why. Say there are two sectors in the economy, and sector 1 is shut down because of mandated business closures. Say also that by themselves, these closures cause the aggregate unemployment rate to rise to 15 percent. If the government could step in to offset the resulting hit to sector 2's demand (where that hit to demand results from the extent to which sector 1's workers and capital owners no longer buy sector 2's output), then sector 2's production and employment would remain unchanged and the firms in sector 2 would have no reason to change their price-setting behavior. So long as the government continued to do this and sector 1 remained closed, this situation would yield stable inflation with an unemployment rate of 15 percent, which should be our new estimate of the natural rate. (Whether we could measure this in practice – and whether it would actually be useful for anything – is another matter, of course.)

There are also serious conceptual difficulties with that conclusion, even in this stylized world. Such a definition requires us to believe that the sector 1 unemployed would have no effect on sector 2 wages. We also need to assume that sector 2's workers won't change their behavior even though there's been a large rise in unemployment elsewhere in the economy. Finally, another implicit assumption is that after sector 1 reopens, the price-setting behavior of its firms is exactly the same as before (so no attempt to boost markups in the face of pent-up demand or as a way of making up for lost profits), and that the workers in sector 1 also make no change to the wage they are willing to accept.[55] But at this point, a fair question is what practical use such a measure has. Not only is it unlikely to yield an unemployment gap that is informative about wage or price inflation (or anything else), but it seems perverse to claim that these events resulted in a drop in potential (though the logic of the definition seems to compel it) – it's not as though the capital stock was destroyed by a natural disaster, or a large number of workers emigrated.

---

[55] There is also a pedantic technical difficulty to contend with. First, if there is a difference across sectors in their trend inflation rates, closing sector 1 will automatically leave an imprint on inflation. Relatedly, given how aggregate price statistics are computed in the NIPAs, it would take two periods before sector 1's prices stop mattering for the index; if those prices were rising prior to the shutdown, then there will be a dip in measured inflation if sector 1's price changes are considered to be zero for as long as it's closed down.

These issues associated with making a consistent definition of the natural rate of unemployment aren't special to a pandemic – they are always present in some form. (And all of this assumes that we take Friedman's definition at face value, and that we could even come close to estimating the economy's fictitious Walrasian equilibrium or stable-inflation unemployment rate in the first place.) Add to this the fact that not everyone views Friedman's definition of the natural rate as the best one (a commonly suggested alternative is to define the benchmark unemployment rate as the portion of unemployment that is immune to changes in aggregate demand at a given point in time), and it's clear that such a concept is almost certain to cause far more mischief than it's worth.

6

Understanding US Inflation Dynamics

I cannot give any scientist of any age better advice than this: the intensity of the conviction that a hypothesis is true has no bearing on whether it is true or not.

Sir Peter Medawar (1979)

Perhaps the most important determinant of labor market conditions in the United States is the rate of wage and price inflation – not because of a deep structural linkage, but because of the policy response that inflation elicits. Despite this importance, it has proved to be exceedingly difficult to attain even a basic understanding of inflation's drivers – empirically as well as theoretically. Empirically, we are hamstrung by having only one realization of the postwar inflation process to study, particularly because that single realization has been subject to at least one important regime change over the past sixty years. Useful theoretical models of inflation have also been hard to come by; while there is reasonable evidence that many prices are sticky in some sense, the utterly ad hoc way in which that apparent slow adjustment has been modelled has resulted in commonly used models that are nowhere near structural, impossible to estimate, and whose theoretical predictions are directly at odds with the data.

Even an attempt to characterize stylized empirical facts about the inflation process is unlikely to convince everyone. First, there are several reasonable measures of inflation that one can use, each with different properties, and each with its own diehard adherents. Inflation is also characterized by a large amount of idiosyncratic variation, which for several reasons makes it difficult to come up with robust or sensible correlations that can plausibly be called structural features of the inflation process. Most importantly, though, the presence of largely unexplained regime shifts raises the possibility that inflation might not be an ergodic process at all, or might be the result of emergent dynamics that will be unreliably captured by an aggregate model.

As always, we should be a little skeptical that we *can* come up with a reasonable aggregate characterization of inflation. There are a plethora of markets for goods and labor in our extremely large and geographically dispersed economy, so the notion that the broad movement of US prices and wages can be tied to other aggregate variables in any sort of systematic way seems slightly suspect on its face. But if we push this logic further, it suggests that the *only* place that we will be able to find a useful empirical model of inflation dynamics is at the economywide level. Even if we (sensibly) believe that the state of excess demand or supply in individual final goods markets has an important effect on the rates of price change in those markets, many of these markets are not confined to a single narrow geographic area but are much more widespread. Similarly, the input costs that producers face are likely to have an important national element, especially if those inputs are imported.[1] For wages, we saw in the previous chapter how aggregating individual labor markets could conceivably give rise to a relation between economywide real activity and wage growth; such a relation would be strengthened if wage growth depends on price inflation, and if that inflation in turn reflects more than just price changes for locally produced goods. Hence, local demand and supply conditions are likely to be less relevant than national conditions in determining the co-movement of many observed price changes, and their effects should hopefully (mostly) wash out in an aggregate inflation equation.[2]

For this last reason, attempts to enlist regional or disaggregated data to uncover the determinants of price inflation have failed to generate useful insights into the nature of the aggregate inflation process. At best, these approaches simply capture the same correlations that can be found in the aggregate data (but in a manner that is more opaque and less well founded); at worst, these studies simply find that price changes in a region are strongly tied to developments in the region's housing markets. Regarding this latter point, an important shortcoming of using regional price data to think about aggregate inflation dynamics is that these data are strongly influenced by

---

[1] Put more pithily, General Motors' pricing decisions are probably not heavily influenced by the state of demand in Detroit, while the price of tomatoes in the United States is likely to depend on weather conditions in Florida or California, not the demand for ketchup in those places.

[2] There is an important caveat to be made here: As the experience with the COVID-19 pandemic shows, developments in specific sectors *can* have important effects on overall inflation (especially if they persist); moreover, as was noted above, idiosyncratic shocks can have noticeable effects on inflation even under more-normal circumstances. So don't expect an aggregate inflation equation to have an especially high R-squared – or to perform especially well as a forecasting model – even in the best of times.

housing services prices – housing being one of the most cyclically sensitive components of consumer prices and so not representative of the average – and one that also receives a large weight in the CPI (the price index used by most regional studies).[3] Regional prices for housing services are likely to be tied to local economic conditions such as employment and income in an area (though with an important national component, as mortgage rates will influence the demand for rental housing by making homeownership more costly). But this isn't the usual way one motivates an aggregate Phillips curve.[4] In any event, once housing services prices are excluded, Phillips curves based on regional data explain very little of the variation in economywide inflation, especially in recent decades (for an example, compare figure VI in Hazell et al., 2022, with their appendix figure C.3). Likewise, attempts to document the frequency and size of price changes at the microeconomic level have failed to live up to their initial promise: Rather than telling us something informative or practically useful about the inflation process, the best that this literature has been able to do is to provide some microeconomic evidence against certain types of theoretical inflation models that probably shouldn't have been taken all that seriously in the first place. (In its more degenerate state, the literature simply provides empirical values that can be used to "calibrate" these models and give an appearance that the modeller has actually engaged with the real world.)

As we'll see, we can come up with an empirical description of aggregate inflation that is reasonably robust along some dimensions – albeit tied to a specific econometric approach – and that helps to explain some of the puzzles about inflation's behavior that other researchers have found vexing over the years. However, we'll have considerably less luck in coming up with deeper (or deeply compelling) explanations for these results, nor will we have much success where wage determination is concerned.

---

[3] One clarification about housing services prices: Since the early 1980s, the CPI has measured owner-occupied housing services prices on a rental-equivalence basis – that is, by re-weighting an area's sample of tenants' rents in accordance with the relative concentration of owner-occupied housing in that area. (The PCE price index uses the CPI series, though it ends up giving housing a much smaller weight in the total index; it also never included mortgage interest costs in its owner-occupied housing price measure, which the CPI did until it switched to its rental equivalence procedure.) Hence, house *prices* do not directly enter measured prices for housing services, though they can have an indirect effect by affecting the affordability of owner-occupied housing and hence the demand for rental housing.

[4] Note too that during the influential outlier known as the 2007–2009 recession, the causality likely ran the other way, with the state of local housing markets itself an important contributor to local-area economic conditions through its effect on wealth and consumer confidence.

6.1 An Empirical Characterization of Postwar US Inflation Dynamics

We would like a parsimonious way of summarizing observed inflation dynamics that allows the process to evolve over time. The approach we'll take here is to use a VAR model that incorporates time-varying parameters and stochastic volatility, and that includes enough relevant drivers of inflation to have at least some chance of capturing and describing key features of the inflation process. An approach like this one is not perfect, as it requires a simpler dynamic specification – in particular, fewer own lags – than would typically be found in other types of empirical wage and price equations (such as a Phillips curve). It also inherits the same questionable claim to being a structural model that any recursively identified VAR model does. But using an estimation technique that explicitly models parameter drift and that incorporates information from the full sample seems desirable, with the hope being that it will be less susceptible to the sampling variability that can attend other procedures (for example, rolling regressions or estimation over arbitrarily defined subperiods). Relatedly, allowing the volatility of shocks to vary over time reduces the chances of identifying a shift in the parameters of the inflation process when none is actually present.[5]

In general, an n-variable recursively identified VAR can be written as

$$y_t^1 = a_0^1 + A^{11}(L)y_{t-1}^1 + A^{12}(L)y_{t-1}^2 + \cdots + A^{1n}(L)y_{t-1}^n + \varepsilon_t^1,$$
$$y_t^2 = a_0^2 + A^{21}(L)y_{t-1}^1 + A^{22}(L)y_{t-1}^2 + \cdots + A^{2n}(L)y_{t-1}^n + a_1^2 y_t^1 + \varepsilon_t^2,$$

$$\vdots$$

$$y_t^n = a_0^n + A^{n1}(L)y_{t-1}^1 + A^{n2}(L)y_{t-1}^2 + \cdots + A^{nn}(L)y_{t-1}^n + a_1^n y_t^1$$
$$+ a_2^n y_t^2 + \cdots + a_{n-1}^n y_t^{n-1} + \varepsilon_t^n, \tag{6.1}$$

where the $A^{ij}(L)$ terms denote lag polynomials and ε_t^i is the structural residual associated with equation i. (As the system is written here, the variables are ordered $y_t^1, y_t^2, \ldots, y_t^n$.) The values of $A^{ij}(L)$ and a_j^i and the standard deviations of the ε_t^i terms are allowed to drift over time (they are modelled as random walks). We can then use the relevant sets of parameter values to look at impulse response functions at various points in time, and can also use the VAR to decompose the historical movements in a given variable into the

---

[5] An approach like this has been used by a number of authors to study historical changes in inflation dynamics; Cogley and Sargent (2005) and Clark and Terry (2010) are two noteworthy examples. The computer code that I use for these estimates was originally written by Todd Clark.

cumulative contributions of the various structural shocks (similar to what we did in the previous chapter with Blanchard and Diamond's empirical Beveridge curve). In addition, as Cogley et al. (2010) demonstrate, the model can be used to produce estimates of the variables' stochastic trends. To see this, write the VAR in its companion form as

$$z_{t+1} = \mu_t + B_t z_t + e_{t+1}, \tag{6.2}$$

where z_t stacks the current and lagged values of the variables y_t^i, μ_t contains the time-varying intercepts from each VAR equation, and B_t contains the VAR's autoregressive parameters (which are also time varying). At time t, we can obtain estimates of the stochastic trends $\bar{z}_t$ from

$$\bar{z}_t = (I - B_t)^{-1}\mu_t, \tag{6.3}$$

where I denotes the identity matrix. (Here we once again meet up with our old friend, the Beveridge–Nelson trend: Equation 6.3 represents the expected long-run levels of the VAR's left-hand side variables once the effects of any shocks have died out.)

The VAR system that I use includes two lags of a relative import price measure, trend unit labor cost growth, core market-based PCE price inflation, and the difference between actual unemployment and the CBO's current estimate of its "noncyclical" rate, with that causal ordering.[6] Estimation starts in 1965:Q1 and ends in 2019:Q4. I use market-based PCE prices in the VAR because several nonmarket components of PCE are priced using input cost indexes that are in turn based on wage or compensation measures (on average, core market-based prices account for roughly 90 percent of the overall core index). In addition, I define core inflation with the PCE price index rather than the Consumer Price Index (CPI) because the published CPI contains methodological breaks and uses mortgage interest rates to measure housing costs in the 1960s and 1970s.[7] The focus on *core* inflation reflects the importance of food and energy price shocks during the 1970s and early 1980s; such shocks are generally (though not universally) viewed as having resulted from factors unrelated to the level of resource utilization in the United States and abroad, and so are plausibly exogenous as far as domestic inflation developments are concerned.

---

[6] Complete definitions of the data series can be found in the appendix to this chapter (Section 6.9); note that the labor cost series uses the Productivity and Costs (P&C) measure of hourly compensation (wages plus benefits) in the nonfarm sector.

[7] The inflation measure used here also includes an adjustment for the effects of the Nixon-era price controls.

Including a measure of unit labor costs (defined here as hourly compensation growth minus a measure of trend labor productivity growth) is useful for a couple of reasons.[8] First, because most of the variation in trend unit labor cost growth reflects changes in compensation growth (rather than changes in trend productivity growth), we can gain some insight into how wage determination might have varied over time by including this measure. Relatedly, the labor cost term allows the model to capture the dynamics associated with wage–price feedbacks in periods when they are present. That last feature is important, in that much of the effect that the food and energy price shocks of the 1970s and early 1980s had on *core* inflation likely reflected their effects on wage and labor cost growth (without such a channel, it's difficult to explain why food prices appeared to have had such a large effect on the core, or why higher food and energy price inflation left such a persistent imprint on broader inflation). The use of a trend productivity measure reflects an assumption (which is *only* an assumption) that firms set prices on the basis of a "normal" or smoothed level of productivity because actual productivity fluctuates so much from one quarter to the next. We don't really know what that smoothed measure is, and so we use an estimate of trend productivity as a proxy. (For what it's worth, it is difficult to find an empirical role for actual productivity in an inflation equation once trend productivity has been controlled for.)

The use of CBO's natural rate estimate to compute the unemployment gap represents an unsatisfactory compromise. Although it is standard practice to include a measure of the unemployment gap as a proxy for labor and product market slack, the discussion from the previous chapter should make us wary of doing so. In addition, conventional measures of utilization like the unemployment gap or output gap tend to be informed in some manner by the behavior of inflation itself – for example, one common way to measure the "natural" rate of unemployment involves backing it out from a Phillips curve. The latter problem is minimized by the CBO measure. Up until 2004, the CBO natural rate series is constructed by applying

---

[8] Unit labor costs equal the dollar amount of labor needed to produce a unit of output; they can be measured as the hourly compensation rate divided by labor productivity. (Intuitively, labor productivity determines how many hours of labor are needed to produce one unit of output; multiplying this number of hours by the wage rate gives the total labor cost needed to produce a unit of output.) Unit labor cost is commonly used as a cost measure because labor costs are the single largest component of overall costs; also, because increased production typically requires hiring additional labor to work at existing production facilities, unit labor costs will be a reasonable proxy for the increase in total costs that results from producing an additional unit of output (*a/k/a* marginal cost).

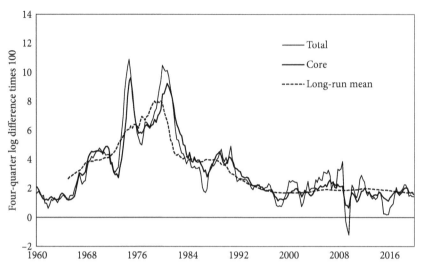

Figure 6.1 Stochastic trend (long-run mean) of PCE price inflation from a VAR with time-varying parameters and stochastic volatility.

demographic adjustments to a (constant) NAIRU estimate; after 2004, the CBO measure is constructed under the assumption that the 2005 unemployment rates for various demographic groups equalled the natural rates for those groups, with the aggregate natural rate changing over time with the relative sizes and estimated "potential" labor force participation rates of each group (see Shackleton, 2018, appendix B).[9] Hence, most of the variation in the CBO series reflects slow-moving demographic changes, rather than inflation's behavior in a particular period.

The first noteworthy results that we get from the estimated VAR are the stochastic trends (long-run means) for inflation and labor cost growth (Figures 6.1 and 6.2). The contours of these trends roughly mirror each other, which hints at some sort of connection between wages and prices in the first part of the sample. What is equally interesting, however, is that the trends become relatively stable after the mid-1990s; in particular, they appear largely invariant to economic conditions, including actual inflation or labor

---

[9] NAIRU is an acronym for "non-accelerating inflation rate of unemployment" – though technically, "accelerating" should be "increasing." (As we'll see later, the NAIRU is only a valid concept if the presence of a nonzero gap results in a steady change in inflation; for that reason, the term became obsolete when the inflation process became effectively mean-reverting after the mid-1990s.)

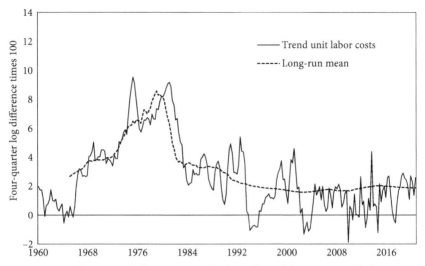

Figure 6.2 Stochastic trend (long-run mean) of trend unit labor cost growth from a VAR with time-varying parameters and stochastic volatility.

cost growth as well as the 2001 and 2007–2009 recessions.[10] The contributors to the increase and later decline of these long-run means are also worth noting, although hard to explain. As Figure 6.3 indicates, the time-varying intercept of the inflation equation is not the source of the change in inflation's long-run mean: The intercept *declines* through the 1960s and 1970s, and then rises after the 1980s. Instead, the main source of the increase in the trend is a steady increase in "intrinsic" inflation persistence, as captured by the sum of the coefficients on the own lags in the inflation equation (see Figure 6.4).[11] All else equal, higher own-persistence can raise inflation's long-run mean even if the intercept of the inflation equation declines; a rough analogy is to the long-run mean of an AR(1) process with time-varying coefficients:

$$AR(1)\ process: y_t = \alpha_t + A_t(L)y_{t-1} + \varepsilon_t, \quad A_t(1) < 1,$$

$$Long\text{-}run\ mean\ at\ time\ t: \bar{y}_t = \frac{\alpha_t}{1 - A_t(1)}, \tag{6.4}$$

---

[10] See Peneva and coauthor (2017) for an earlier discussion of this point.

[11] There is also an increase in the sensitivity of labor cost growth to inflation, which has the effect of modestly increasing the "effective" weight on lagged inflation in the inflation equation.

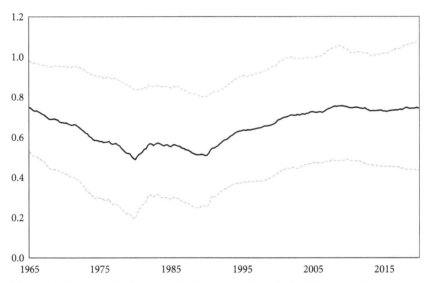

Figure 6.3 Time-varying intercept (inflation equation). Dashed lines give 70 percent credible set.

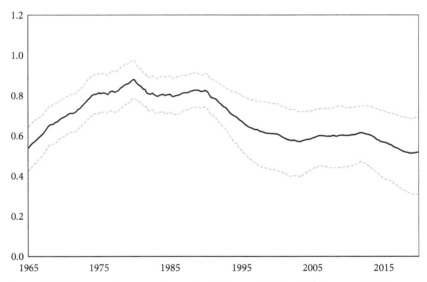

Figure 6.4 Time-varying sum of lagged inflation coefficients (inflation equation). Dashed lines give 70 percent credible set.

where either an increase in the intercept α or an increase in the sum of the lag coefficients $A(1)$ will raise the series' long-run mean (though see note 12 below). But what *economic* interpretation should we give to the rise in inflation persistence over this period?

One possible interpretation is suggested by Cogley et al. (2010), who associate the stochastic trend in inflation with the Federal Reserve's inflation target. Under that telling, the own-persistence of inflation at a point in time contributes to the persistence of the "inflation gap," which they define as the deviation between actual inflation and the Fed's long-run inflation goal; a rise in the persistence of the inflation gap might then be attributed to the Fed's becoming less willing to bring actual inflation back to its target quickly.[12] Here, though, the interpretation runs into trouble. As noted, even if the intercept in the inflation equation is fixed, a rise in own-persistence will raise inflation's long-run mean. But it is unclear why we should then associate the resulting increase in inflation's stochastic trend with an increase in the Fed's long-run inflation target, which seems as though it would be more naturally captured by an increase in the inflation equation's intercept. (Of course, we might be skeptical that a model such as this one would actually be capable of making this sort of distinction, which further complicates the task of giving economic interpretations to the VAR's trends – let alone structural ones.)

It's also interesting to note that the main driver of the stochastic trend in labor cost growth is the stochastic trend in inflation. The intercept of the labor cost equation also declines until around 1980, and then moves up in fits and starts over the rest of the sample period. In addition, the own-persistence of labor cost growth is very small (the sum of the lagged dependent variables in the labor cost equation never goes much above 0.1 in absolute terms). Instead, the main thing that varies in the equation is the sum of the coefficients on lagged inflation – Figure 6.5 – which is very close to one by the end of the 1970s.

What these results suggest is that a so-called wage–price spiral was operative in the 1970s. That term means different things to different people, so let's go through the correct definition and distinguish it from one that's been much less relevant in recent decades.

---

[12] This discussion, like the one in the previous paragraph, is loose – the persistence of the "inflation gap" in the sense of Cogley et al. (2010) and the value of inflation's stochastic trend both depend on the full-system properties of the VAR – but it is not too misleading in this particular case.

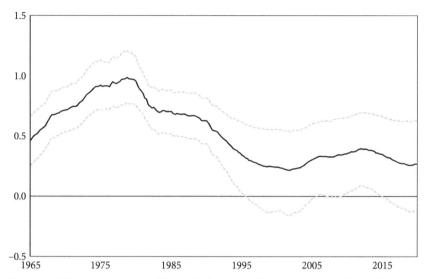

Figure 6.5 Time-varying sum of lagged inflation coefficients (equation for trend unit labor cost growth). Dashed lines give 70 percent credible set.

6.2 The Wage–Price Spiral, Then and Now

A wage–price spiral simply means that there is a feedback between wage growth π^w and price inflation π^p:

$$\pi_t^p = a + A(L)\pi_{t-1}^p + B(L)\pi_{t-1}^w,$$
$$\pi_t^w = c + C(L)\pi_{t-1}^p + D(L)\pi_{t-1}^w, \tag{6.5}$$

which might be the case if firms set their prices with reference to labor costs and if workers care about the cost of living when deciding whether their wages are high enough.[13] In general, the presence of this feedback will make a shock to inflation more persistent than it would be if price inflation didn't affect wage growth: Not only do we have to worry about inflation's own persistence, $A(1)$, but we also need to account for the fact that higher inflation will boost wage growth through the $C(L)$ terms, thus putting further upward pressure on inflation, then back to wage growth, and so on. (We're assuming that the coefficients of the system are such that the process doesn't contain unit roots or yield explosive dynamics.)

What people often mean when they refer to a wage–price spiral is a special case of Equation (6.5) that appeared to be present in the 1970s (and was

---

[13] Once again, we're being a bit fuzzy here about the difference between the price of domestic business output and consumer prices. That's macro for you.

likely also a feature of the inflation process from the 1960s through the mid-1990s. In this special case, labor cost growth is (eventually) passed through one-for-one into price inflation, while inflation also raises wage growth one-for-one (again eventually). In a very simple specification that doesn't worry about the "eventually" part, we can think about prices as being set as a constant markup μ over a measure of unit labor costs,

$$p_t = \mu \, \frac{w_t}{z_t^f}, \tag{6.6}$$

where w_t is the nominal wage and z_t^f is the value of labor productivity that *firms* use when deciding how to set their price. (For now we are not explicitly including other sorts of cost shocks, or shocks to consumer inflation that might arise from things that are unrelated to the state of demand in the economy – like bad harvests or an oil embargo – but keep these things in mind.) In log-differenced form, the markup equation becomes

$$\pi_t^p = \pi_t^w - \Delta \ln z_t^f. \tag{6.7}$$

We then assume that wage growth is a (declining) function of labor market slack (let's use the unemployment rate u_t minus some reference rate u_t^*); recent price inflation; and some measure of labor productivity growth $\Delta \ln z_t^w$ that *workers* think should be reflected in their wage increases:

$$\pi_t^w = -\beta(u_t - u_t^*) + C(L)\pi_{t-1}^p + \Delta \ln z_t^w \quad (\beta > 0). \tag{6.8}$$

Here, the key feature of the inflation equation is that the sum of the coefficients on lagged inflation, $C(1)$, equals one, so that price inflation is eventually fully reflected in wage growth. If we combine these equations, we have what is known as an *accelerationist* price Phillips curve:

$$\pi_t^p = -\beta(u_t - u_t^*) + C(L)\pi_{t-1}^p + \Delta \ln z_t^w - \Delta \ln z_t^f, \tag{6.9}$$

where the term accelerationist refers to the idea that inflation will continue rising so long as the actual unemployment rate is lower than u^* (and conversely) – that is, in such a situation *prices* will accelerate.[14] In addition, any shock to inflation or wage growth (even if it's temporary) will have a permanent effect on the inflation rate because it permanently raises wage growth. The presence of the unit sum also implies that we can write the inflation equation in first-differenced form,

---

[14] You sometimes hear people referring to an acceleration in *inflation* when the inflation rate rises. That's one derivative too many – again, it's prices that are accelerating; inflation is only increasing. (Now you can feel smug whenever you see this done in the business press.)

$$\Delta \pi_t^p = -\beta(u_t - u_t^*) + G(L)\Delta \pi_{t-1}^p + (\gamma \Delta \ln z_t^w) - \Delta \ln z_t^f, \quad (6.10)$$

which in addition to imposing the unit sum on lagged inflation also makes the accelerationist property of the equation clearly evident.[15] When the Phillips curve takes this form, the u_t^* term is sometimes known as a NAIRU (recall footnote 9); the only way to keep inflation constant in such a world (barring any other shocks) is to keep actual unemployment equal to the NAIRU.[16]

If the price Phillips curve does take an accelerationist form – and there are other ways to motivate this sort of equation without using a wage–price system – another concept that can be talked about is the so-called *sacrifice ratio*. The sacrifice ratio gives the number of "point-years" of unemployment that are required to permanently reduce inflation by one percentage point; for example, a sacrifice ratio of two means that reducing inflation by a percentage point requires keeping the unemployment rate a percentage point above the NAIRU for two years, two percentage points above the NAIRU for one year, and so on. One can show that the sacrifice ratio implied by a quarterly model equals four times the absolute value of the coefficient on the unemployment gap (β, above) divided by the "mean lag" implied by the coefficients $C(L)$ in Equation (6.9) (the factor of four converts the mean lag in quarters into a mean lag in years). Specifically, if the individual coefficients on $\pi_{t-1}, \pi_{t-2}, \ldots, \pi_{t-n}$ are given by $c_1, c_2, \ldots, c_n$, then the mean lag (in quarters) can be computed as

$$\sum_{i=1}^{n} i \cdot c_i, \quad (6.11)$$

or, using the coefficients from the first-differenced form of the inflation Equation (6.10), as $1 - G(1)$.[17]

An accelerationist Phillips curve or a wage–price system of this sort was used to explain the inflation experience of the 1960s, 1970s, and 1980s; that

[15] This is easy to see once we realize that the coefficient on the $(t-1)$ inflation lag in Equation (6.9) can be written as one minus the sum of the other lags. Note also that the order of $G(L)$ in Equation (6.10) will be one less than the order of $C(L)$.
[16] If the NAIRU were fixed (and if it really existed), it could be backed out of Equation (6.9) or (6.10) by replacing the gap term with actual unemployment and a constant; alternatively, in place of the constant we could use a spline or use a Kalman filter to capture any time variation in the intercept. When Staiger, Stock, and Watson did this in 1997 – almost exactly when accelerationist models stopped working – they found that the confidence intervals around estimates of the NAIRU were pretty wide, and arguably too wide to make them a useful benchmark for policy.
[17] You can show this by manipulating Equation (6.9) to put it into first-differenced form, and then comparing $1 - G(1)$ with the mean lag implied by Equation (6.11). Note too that the coefficient sum $G(1)$ will be negative if the inflation equation is accelerationist.

explanation has several pieces. The first claim is that the unemployment gap was negative on average (the unemployment rate tended to be below the NAIRU), with conventional accounts attributing much of the blame to policymakers who didn't realize that the NAIRU was rising and trend productivity growth was slowing, and who also kept monetary and fiscal policy on an expansionary footing for too long. A second piece of the story is that the decade of the 1970s was bookended by very large food and energy price increases. At a minimum, shocks like these would leave a permanent imprint on inflation – even core inflation – by raising consumer price inflation and so pushing up wage growth; in addition, to the extent that these prices were a nonlabor component of producer costs (which makes sense for energy prices, not so much for food), they could have entered domestic inflation through that channel as well, and with additional second-round effects through wage growth.[18] Finally, starting around the mid-1960s there was a slowdown in (trend) productivity growth. If such a slowdown raises price inflation faster than it lowers wage growth – say because firms see the effect on their costs more quickly than workers adjust their view of what their own productivity is – then this will be another source of upward pressure on inflation, as the term $\Delta \ln z_t^w - \Delta \ln z_t^f$ in Equation (6.9) will be positive.

When people fret over the prospect of a wage–price spiral emerging, it is this latter situation they are referring to: one in which there is not only feedback between wages and prices, but where that feedback is strong and persistent enough that it causes price inflation to ratchet up steadily and inflation to behave as a unit-root process (just like it seemed to do in the bad old days of wide lapels and hideous neckties). It certainly does seem that something like accelerationist inflation dynamics were present from the 1960s until the late 1980s or mid-1990s: It's not hard to find evidence of something close to a unit coefficient sum in inflation equations fit to data from this period (in fact, the coefficient sum is often less than a single standard error away from one), and further evidence that there was some kind of unit root present in inflation comes from the upward drift in inflation's estimated long-run mean, along with the fact that the back-to-back recessions of 1980–1982 seemed to persistently lower core PCE price inflation by about two percentage points. (The 1990–1991 recession also seemed to cause inflation to ratchet lower.) In addition, the idea that there was nearly full passthrough of price inflation to wage growth would seem to be supported by the coefficient sums shown in Figure 6.5.

---

[18] See Blinder and coauthor (2013) for a discussion of the role food and energy price shocks played in the high inflation of this period.

What is most relevant for today, however, is that none of these concepts –
the NAIRU, sacrifice ratios, accelerationist inflation dynamics – remains
meaningful when the inflation process has a stable stochastic trend (though
that fact isn't sufficient to prevent people who should know better from
rabbiting on about them). In this happier situation inflation will be mean-
reverting, a transitory shock will have no long-run effect on inflation,
and a persistent unemployment gap will only result in a one-time change
in inflation. In particular, under these circumstances the Phillips curve
relation will take a form that's something like the following:

$$\pi_t^p = a - \beta(u_t - u_t^*) + A(L)\pi_{t-1}^p, \tag{6.12}$$

where $A(1)$ is *less* than one. Here, inflation's long-run mean will equal $a/(1 -
A(1))$, and u^* is not a NAIRU, but is instead the level of the unemployment
rate that is consistent with inflation's being at its long-run mean. Similarly,
keeping the unemployment rate a percentage point below u^* simply results
in an (eventual) increase in inflation equal to $\beta/(1 - A(1))$, so a long-run
trade-off exists between the level of real activity and the level of inflation.[19]
An equation like this one seemed to describe the relationship between inflation and slack from roughly the mid-1990s until 2019 – that is, over the
period when the stochastic trend for inflation appeared effectively invariant
to economic conditions – and might even continue to characterize the inflation process in the post-pandemic period. (At the time of this writing, that
question remained an open one.)

6.3 Some Stylized Facts about Inflation Dynamics

There is still more to be discovered in the VAR results. Figure 6.6 plots how
inflation responded at various dates following a one-standard-deviation
shock to trend unit labor costs (which equals about 2.8 percentage points in
this sample). Although wage–price passthrough seems to have been present
in earlier decades – zero lies out of the 70 percent credible set (not shown)
for about two years for the 1975 response, and for about a year for the
1985 response – it appears to essentially vanish in more-recent periods.[20]

---

[19] Hence, instead of talking about a sacrifice ratio, we should describe the relevant trade-off
as a long-run level shift.

[20] As Peneva and her coauthor (2017) document, there is some evidence that the passthrough
to inflation of trend unit labor costs defined using the employment cost index (ECI) has
remained relatively stable – and economically significant – since the 1980s. But because
the ECI only begins in 1980, we can't know whether the response was different in earlier

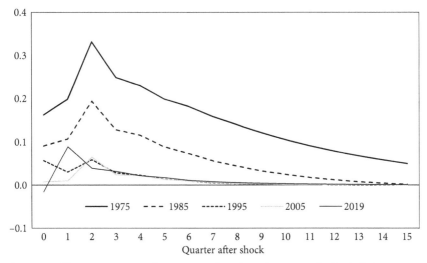

Figure 6.6 Time-varying impulse response functions: Response of price inflation following a one-standard-deviation shock to labor cost growth. (Percentage-point deviation from baseline.)

Next, Figures 6.7 and 6.8 plot the responses of core inflation and labor cost growth to a one-standard-deviation *negative* shock to the unemployment gap.[21] What these results seem to indicate is that the sensitivity of inflation to the unemployment gap has declined over time – the price Phillips curve has flattened – while the sensitivity of compensation growth to the gap doesn't change much (the slope of the *wage* Phillips curve seems to have been relatively stable).[22] To make this point more rigorously, we can look at the "integral multipliers" for the price and wage responses; doing so allows us to control for the fact that the persistence of the unemployment rate (and so its response to an own shock) has varied over time. Specifically, we can compute

decades. (Note also that the ECI is much less volatile than the compensation measure used here.)

[21] As they come from a VAR, these estimates also include the indirect effects that the gap has through its influence on other variables in the system. Then again, the coefficient on the gap in a typical Phillips curve is likely capturing some of these indirect effects too.

[22] Looking at the disaggregated data indicates that one price component that is especially insensitive to the unemployment gap is goods prices. A colleague of mine (Ekaterina Peneva) suggested that a contributor to this might be better management of final goods inventories, as that makes it less necessary to aggressively reduce prices when demand weakens.

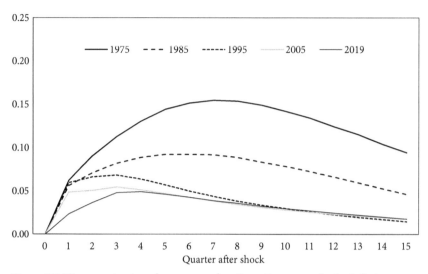

Figure 6.7 Time-varying impulse response functions: Response of price inflation following a one-standard-deviation shock to the unemployment gap. (Percentage-point deviation from baseline.)

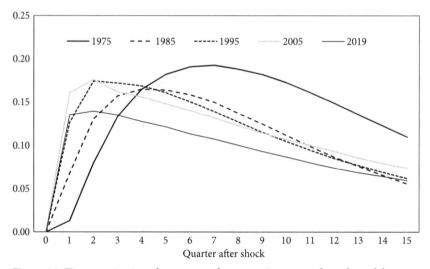

Figure 6.8 Time-varying impulse response functions: Response of trend unit labor cost growth following a one-standard-deviation shock to the unemployment gap. (Percentage-point deviation from baseline.)

Table 6.1 *Integral multipliers from an unemployment gap shock*

	1975	1985	1995	2005	2019
1. Price inflation					
Four quarters	0.32	0.24	0.21	0.17	0.14
Six quarters	0.38	0.26	0.20	0.15	0.14
Eight quarters	0.46	0.29	0.19	0.15	0.14
2. Trend ULC growth					
Four quarters	0.31	0.42	0.53	0.53	0.46
Six quarters	0.42	0.45	0.52	0.50	0.44
Eight quarters	0.52	0.49	0.52	0.48	0.43

$$\frac{\sum_{i=1}^{N} \phi^x(i)}{\sum_{i=0}^{N-1} \phi^u(i)}, \tag{6.13}$$

where $\phi^x(i)$ is the impulse response function for either inflation or labor cost growth and $\phi^u(i)$ is the impulse response function for the unemployment gap; for N let's use four, six, or eight quarters.[23] These multipliers are shown in Table 6.1; they confirm that inflation is much less responsive to the gap after the mid-1990s, while the response of labor cost growth stays roughly the same.[24]

If correct, this result is interesting because it suggests that the flattening of the price Phillips curve reflects changes in the pricing practices of firms. Put differently, we could imagine three reasons why the price Phillips curve might become flatter over time: The *wage* Phillips curve could have flattened, implying that firms' (labor) costs will change less when real activity changes; the passthrough of labor costs to prices could have diminished; or a change in the cyclicality of firms' markups could work so as to partly offset the rise in labor (and other) costs that occurs as the economy tightens. This latter explanation also highlights that the unemployment gap is likely a proxy for both labor *and* product market slack; that is, it will be correlated with aggregate demand as well as with labor demand. But if the wage Phillips curve hasn't flattened, then the source of the reduced sensitivity of inflation

---

[23] The difference in the range of the summation indexes in the numerator and denominator of (6.13) reflects the fact that inflation's place in the recursive ordering implies that it does not respond in the period when the unemployment gap shock hits.

[24] The signs of the multipliers in the table are positive because the calculation uses the *negative* of the inflation impulse response following a *positive* shock to the unemployment gap; though confusing, it means that we don't need to have a negative sign in front of every entry in the table.

to aggregate demand needs to come from a change in pricing behavior in product markets, where pricing behavior also encompasses how costs are passed through to prices.

We don't actually need a VAR to find mildly convincing evidence of a flatter price Phillips curve, though we do need to take into account the shift in the inflation regime – specifically, the change from a difference-stationary process, where we need to model inflation with an accelerationist specification, to a process with a stable long-run mean. That last point is worth emphasizing: If you use an accelerationist specification once it no longer provides a good description of the data, the resulting empirical model will usually respond by squeezing the coefficient on slack – especially if a recession or two are present in the sample. It won't have any trouble with the coefficients on lagged inflation being forced to sum to one: It needs that to fit the 1970s and 1980s, and afterward actual inflation is sufficiently stable that even a unit sum generates fitted values that don't look awful (because the lagged inflation terms basically recover the mean inflation rate).[25] The failure to take this shift into account has led to some unnecessary confusion in the past, as researchers have used the obsolete accelerationist framework to identify supposed puzzles or anomalies that aren't actually there.[26] Figure 6.9 looks at the partial correlation of overall core PCE price inflation and the unemployment gap after removing the effect of weighted relative import price changes. (To smooth things out a little, inflation is defined as a log difference of the annual-average price index.) In the left panel, which covers the period 1963–1987, we use the first-difference of inflation as the dependent variable. In the right panel, which uses the inflation rate minus two percent as the dependent variable, the sample period extends from 1995 to 2019 (when inflation was arguably mean-reverting) and the partial correlation removes the effects of import price inflation and once-lagged inflation. The flattening of the price Phillips curve is readily apparent, and even though they don't look it, both correlations are statistically significant at conventional levels.[27]

We can do something similar for hourly compensation (Figure 6.10). Here, instead of trying to find a reasonable relation between wage growth and other correlates (like lagged inflation), we can instead simply treat

---

[25] Running a dynamic simulation, however, will reveal how badly the model fails in the latter part of the sample – see note 29, below.

[26] One example is the debate over whether the unemployment rate of the short-term unemployed was a better measure of slack during and after the 2007–2009 recession (Gordon, 2013); another – which we'll discuss further below – is whether there was "missing disinflation" over this period (Coibion and Gorodnichenko, 2015; Watson, 2014).

[27] In the early sample the absolute value of the *t*-statistic is 2.5; in the later sample it's 2.7.

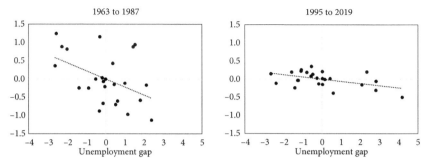

Figure 6.9 Flattening of the price Phillips curve over time. (Partial correlation between unemployment gap and inflation series after controlling for the influence of weighted relative import price changes.) Left side uses first difference of core PCE price inflation adjusted for effects of 1970s price controls; right side uses core inflation rate minus 2 percentage points.

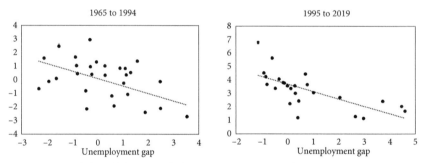

Figure 6.10 Stability of the wage Phillips curve over time. Left side uses first-difference of P&C hourly compensation growth; right side uses level of hourly compensation growth.

annual compensation growth as a difference-stationary process in the first regime and as a mean-reverting series in the other; unlike in the previous case, the wage model doesn't really want a lagged dependent variable included in the second period.[28] Here we also see some confirmation of the VAR result, with a relatively stable relation with the unemployment gap in both periods.

How seriously should we take the VAR results as evidence that the price Phillips curve has flattened (and the wage Phillips curve hasn't)? A good general rule about empirical inflation work is that most results are rubbish, a handful are suggestive, and none is dispositive. Inflation – even core

---

[28] That implies a specification that's very close to Phillips's (1958) original one. Plus ça change, plus c'est la même chose …

inflation – is highly volatile, which implies that it can often be "explained" by a variable that captures a handful of important outliers in the data despite its not being a true causal determinant.[29] Where the relation between inflation and slack is concerned, we are further hampered by the fact that most of the important variation takes place during recessions, which means that we effectively have just half a dozen observations to work with over the past fifty years. (We also can't measure slack very well.) Finally, if we accept that there seems to have been at least one major break in the inflation process, we need to be careful not to extrapolate the results from one regime into another – including by using data from the full sample – which means that we're typically going to be dealing with pretty restricted sample sizes where everything is basically slush. And all this holds twice as strongly for models of wage inflation.

With that caveat in mind, we've now come to a point where we can list the following stylized facts (or "suggestive" stylized facts) about the evolution of the inflation process in the postwar period, as well as a description of how that process looked on the eve of the pandemic. In declining order of certainty (or robustness):

- Inflation's stochastic trend became essentially invariant to economic conditions after the mid-1990s (specifically, a few years after the 1990–1991 recession), remaining stable even during the 2001 and 2007–2009 recessions. So, for all intents and purposes, inflation was a mean-reverting process over the quarter-century that preceded the pandemic.
- In addition, the stochastic trends for price inflation and labor cost growth manifest very similar contours. In the earlier period, a wage–price spiral appears to be present; more recently, the joint stability of the two trends *hints* that some other factor might be at work.
- The price Phillips curve has flattened relative to the 1970s and 1980s. The wage Phillips curve, by contrast, appears to have been more stable.
- There is evidence that the passthrough of labor cost growth to price inflation also declined, though it depends on the compensation measure used: The evidence is strong for the series used in the VARs (hourly compensation from the P&C data), but other research suggests that the passthrough of labor costs defined using the ECI compensation measure has been roughly stable.[30]

---

[29] One way to guard against this problem is to look at dynamic simulations from an inflation model rather than the model's fitted values: Often, the tracking performance of a simulated model will be very poor even though the fitted values look reasonable.

[30] Note that the claim here isn't that compensation costs – which in the aggregate represent about two-thirds of firms' total production costs – are unimportant for firms' pricing

Finally – and this probably should have gone at the top – an extremely large portion of quarter-to-quarter and even year-to-year movements in wage and price inflation can't be explained by "fundamental" determinants. (That's one of a host of reasons why being an inflation forecaster is not a pleasant job.) In particular, idiosyncratic relative price shocks can have noticeable effects on overall inflation; on occasion, these shocks can be explained *ex post* (for instance, an increase in medical services prices that results from a change to Medicare reimbursement rates), but mostly they show up as noise. The presence of these sorts of shocks gives us another reason to focus on market-based PCE prices: The nonmarket component of the PCE price index, which is largely imputed, is highly erratic and contains little signal about the future direction of inflation.[31]

6.4 Supply (and Related) Shocks

Another source of idiosyncratic relative price movements – *supply shocks* – is important enough to be treated separately. In older inflation specifications, supply-shock terms were typically measures of relative food and energy price inflation (possibly weighted by their importance in GDP or consumption), as food and energy price changes seemed to be an important empirical determinant of *core* inflation.[32] The term *supply shock* comes from the idea that most of the variability in these series is exogenous to the state of domestic aggregate demand (hence "shock"), while events like energy price shocks were seen as something that would shift up an aggregate supply curve in an AS/AD framework by raising the cost of an important input to production. (The other important way firms' costs could rise – and probably the only way when food prices are concerned – is through higher nominal wages.) There no longer appears to be much role for energy or food shocks in driving core inflation, which might reflect

---

decisions. Rather, the point is that *independent* movements in the P&C measure of compensation no longer seem all that material for price inflation.

[31] Nonmarket PCE includes components of spending that national income accountants need to measure, but whose prices have a tenuous connection to the prices people actually face or think about. (Oddly, though, imputed rents for owner-occupied housing are defined to be a *market*-based price.) Appendix C discusses other inflation measures that try to control for idiosyncratic price changes.

[32] "Relative" here refers to the price change of food or energy relative to the core. One simple way to obtain a *combined* relative price change for food and energy that is weighted by the relevant expenditure shares in the headline (total) index is to subtract core inflation from the headline rate. (To show this, note that the expenditure weights on the core, food, and energy sum to one.)

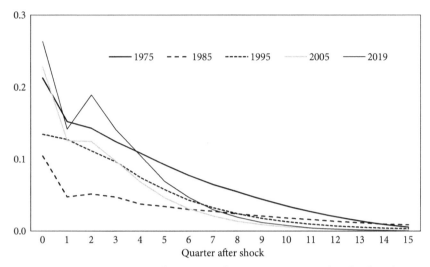

Figure 6.11 Time-varying impulse response functions: Response of market-based core PCE price inflation following a one-standard-deviation shock to weighted relative import price growth. (Percentage-point deviation from baseline.)

reduced passthrough of consumer prices to wages.[33] Nowadays, inflation specifications often include a term to capture the effects of relative price changes for nonoil goods imports; so long as the term is weighted by a measure that captures the rising importance of imports over time (such as their share in nominal GDP), the coefficient on relative import prices is reasonably stable (see Figure 6.11).[34] Since a nontrivial fraction of personal consumption is imported, it's not too surprising that import prices affect consumer prices; what is surprising is how rapid the passthrough appears to be – in the VAR models above, the effect is largely contemporaneous. (For that reason, the relative import price terms are defined as the current import price change minus once-lagged core inflation; this allows them to be ordered above consumer price inflation in the VAR and hence to potentially have a current-quarter effect.)

It's worth pointing out that although supply-shock terms typically enter empirical inflation models, the theoretical rationale for including them is

---

[33] For energy shocks, see Clark and Terry (2010), together with the literature cited in that paper. It is also possible to use a methodology like theirs to assess the effects of food price shocks on core inflation; these appear to have diminished over time as well.

[34] The effect of the real effective exchange rate on core inflation also tends to be relatively stable through the 2010s, as a decline in the passthrough of exchange rates to import prices appears to have been mostly offset by the greater importance of imports to the US economy.

relatively underdeveloped. One theoretical *objection* to including them that is occasionally raised is the claim that changes in relative prices cannot affect the overall price level, so including any sort of relative price term is inappropriate. The argument, which is essentially an appeal to the so-called *classical dichotomy*, states that an increase in the relative price of one good should show up as a higher nominal price for that good and lower nominal prices elsewhere; only a change in the money supply can affect the overall price level.[35] Typically, the point is made simply by appealing to a famous quote by Friedman (1975): "Why should the *average* level of all prices be affected significantly by changes in the prices of some things relative to others?"

Besides the wage channel discussed above, a natural way for the overall price level to be affected by a relative price change is through sticky prices: If the required reductions in other prices are small enough, then they very likely won't take place (at least not for some time).[36] A similar point, which was possibly applicable during the pandemic, relates to how a price increase caused by a large shift in demand for a particular sector's output can have an effect on the overall price level. If the reductions in demand for other goods are small – say because they are spread out over a large number of different markets – then price reductions in those other markets might not occur and an increase in the overall price level can result.[37]

But that isn't to say that supply-shock terms have much more than an intuitive justification in empirical inflation models. For example – and despite having invoked the presence of nominal rigidities in the preceding paragraph – we can't really turn to the standard Keynesian aggregate supply/aggregate demand (AS/AD) framework to think about the effects of relative price shocks. A relative price change that doesn't immediately show up in nominal wages or have an important effect on other production costs will move us *off* of the aggregate supply curve, but the model is silent about the dynamics that follow and that are key to figuring out the resulting paths of output and inflation.[38] More importantly, the AS/AD model doesn't help

---

[35] A version of this argument was enlisted by Barsky and Kilian (2002) in the context of oil price shocks, and by Ball (2006) in the context of globalization.

[36] Naturally, this argument won't convince someone who believes in full market clearing at all times through fully flexible price adjustments.

[37] Even Friedman (1975) conceded this point, in a sentence that follows his more-famous quote: "Thanks to delays in adjustment, the rapid rises in oil and food prices may have temporarily raised the rate of inflation somewhat." Here, "somewhat" is shorthand for "by as much as five percentage points" – see Blinder and coauthor's (2013) table 2.4.

[38] A new-Keynesian inflation equation also won't be much help in this regard, as it will simply classify such an inflation increase as being caused by yet another fancifully labelled residual whose dynamics are imposed by assumption.

us think about the consequences for inflation and output growth under conditions of general excess demand, or when supply problems in some sectors prevent producers from being able to fully meet the demand for their output.[39] Although it seems natural to appeal to the notion that we are on the "steep part" of the aggregate supply curve in these situations, that explanation is inconsistent with the logic of the model, which assumes that goods markets always clear and that firms are always on their labor demand curves. In particular, the reason why the aggregate supply curve steepens in the AS/AD model is because firms face diminishing returns to labor (capital is assumed fixed). As a result, they require larger and larger increases in the price level in order to reduce real wages sufficiently that it becomes profitable to produce additional output given these diminishing returns. That explanation doesn't feel as though it really describes a situation of excess demand for goods and labor, nor does the assumption of a fixed nominal wage seem like a good one in this case. (The mechanism by which the AS/AD model brings aggregate demand back into line with aggregate supply is also implausible, since the sensitivity of spending to changes in real wealth is so low in practice.)[40]

These topics came to the fore after the shutdown and reopening of the world economy in response to the COVID pandemic, as there was understandable interest among policymakers in figuring out how much of the resulting swings in inflation reflected supply-side developments (like production constraints or supply-chain disruptions), and how much was attributable to aggregate demand. From a policy perspective, the question is relevant because you can ostensibly do something about demand – supply issues can only be left to resolve themselves – but you first need to be able to gauge *how much* you need to do. Most of the empirical estimates amounted

---

[39] Once again, the way that supply is modelled by new-Keynesian models won't provide us with any useful guidance either, because price and wage contracts in these models are assumed to require producers and workers to supply as much as is demanded at the contracted price or wage. (Interestingly, relaxing the assumption about wage contracts causes the model to basically become a real business cycle model – see Huo and Ríos-Rull, 2020.)

[40] The AS/AD model represents a special case that is captured by more-general models of non-market-clearing outcomes; specifically, a situation where the goods market is always clearing but sticky nominal wages keep the labor market in a situation of excess supply (see Barro and Grossman, 1976; Sargent, 1987). In a more-general model, a state of general excess demand causes workers to save more and work less – that is, plan for future consumption and consume more leisure today – because they are unable to sate their current demand for goods. (One might wonder whether that prediction is applicable anywhere, except perhaps in a command economy.)

to more-or-less educated guesses that looked at things like abnormal price behavior relative to past trends, or price changes in sectors where there were news reports and other evidence about significant supply problems (like auto manufacturing). But the theoretically grounded estimates were even less useful.

For example, take one well-known theoretical analysis by Baqaee and Farhi (2022). Stripped to its essentials, the demand side of the Baqaee–Farhi model takes the form of the following first-order condition for a representative household with log utility:

$$C = \alpha \, \frac{1}{D} \cdot \frac{1}{P}, \tag{6.14}$$

where C is current real consumption, P is the current value of an "ideal" CES aggregate price index, α subsumes various constants, and D is related to the consumer's discount factor, $D = \beta/(1 - \beta)$. (This doesn't look like the typical Euler equation because future consumption and the future price level are assumed to be exogenous; I've also ignored an interest rate term that turns out to be immaterial.) The model equates current real consumption with current real GDP, Y, and assumes that any aggregate demand shock reflects a change in the consumer discount factor, or $d \ln D$. This yields the following expression for aggregate demand:

$$d \ln Y = (\text{AD shock}) - d \ln P. \tag{6.15}$$

The model's aggregate supply relationship is given by

$$d \ln Y = d \ln A + \sum_i s_i \cdot d \ln L_i, \tag{6.16}$$

where A is a technology term and s_i is the income share of (variable) factor L_i (capital is fixed). Under the further assumption that "technology" is unchanged, we can just go ahead and measure the AS shock as the change in real GDP; the AD shock is just the change in nominal output (actually expenditures) $d \ln(P \cdot Y)$.

Now, think about what's actually being done here. The aggregate demand relation has a price-level elasticity of -1 (by assumption). Likewise, the price elasticity of aggregate supply is zero (again by assumption). Under those circumstances, it's obvious that we can associate any change in real output with a shift in the (vertical) supply curve, while the portion of the change in nominal expenditures $P \cdot Y$ that isn't accounted for by a change in Y – in other words, the change in P – is taken to be a shift in demand. All of this also ignores the fact that the model also assumes a full competitive equilibrium with market clearing and a production network summarized at every point in time by the complete Leontief inverse (that infinite sum of the direct requirements table discussed in Chapter 4) in order to analyze the economic disruptions induced by the pandemic – specifically, the period from February to May 2020. (The model also appears to predict sector-specific price changes that are completely unrelated to actual price changes, as documented by the paper's Appendix Figure A2.) So beyond providing a precise but wrong answer, it's hard to see what useful insights models like these give us.

For an inflation forecaster, one significant practical difficulty associated with supply shocks is that their arrival and likely evolution are very difficult to predict. While futures prices for energy goods, farm commodities, and certain industrial inputs can provide a little guidance, things like import price shocks depend importantly on exchange rate movements. Here too the experience since 2019 provides a useful case study. The portion of the inflation surge that occurred over 2021 and into 2022 that wasn't the result of an acceleration in food and energy prices appears to have had its roots in a set of unusually persistent (and largely sector-specific) relative price shocks; these shocks occurred as a large and rapid realignment of demand across broad categories of consumption ran up against a temporary inability of producers and suppliers to fully meet that demand. To the extent supply disruptions were involved, there was no good way to measure their severity, to predict their likely speed of resolution, or to quantify their effects on inflation. And that situation would unfortunately be the same today were another such event to take place.[41]

6.5 Measuring Slack

A Phillips curve wouldn't be a Phillips curve if it didn't include a measure of real activity. However, the usual interpretation for why real activity matters is that it is an indicator of the level of resource utilization in the economy. That requires comparing real activity to some benchmark level, with the resulting differential treated as a measure of economic slack. In Chapter 5, we discussed some of the conceptual problems associated with defining a measure of labor market slack; in a price Phillips curve, a measure of slack also needs to capture the state of demand in product markets. These two measures can differ in principle – for example, in the simple markup

---

[41] Based on evidence from the CPI fixings market, financial markets consistently got things wrong as well.

Equations (6.6) and (6.7) shown earlier, we could have written the change in the markup as a function of some indicator of product market slack (say because firms tend to boost prices by more than their costs increase in conditions of strong demand) with labor-market slack determining wage and labor cost growth. In practice, however, the two influences can't really be disentangled, and so something like an unemployment gap is assumed to capture both. (That there is a difference between the two concepts is suggested by the fact that the slopes of the price and wage Phillips curves aren't the same.)

The unemployment gap is typically measured as the level of the actual unemployment rate relative to some benchmark level that is allowed to vary over time; this benchmark level is typically treated as an unobservable and inferred from the behavior of inflation conditional on its other determinants.[42] In a single-equation setup, we will only be able to do this under certain circumstances. Say that the "true" model of inflation π_t takes the form

$$(\pi_t - \pi_t^*) = A(L)(\pi_{t-1} - \pi_{t-1}^*) - \beta(u_t - u_t^*) + \zeta Z_t, \qquad (6.17)$$

where Z_t denotes a set of other inflation determinants (including any idiosyncratic influences), u_t^* is the (time-varying) benchmark unemployment rate, and π_t^* is the level of inflation that would (eventually) prevail if both Z_t and the unemployment gap were zero. It's clear that in this case there is no way to pin down u_t^* and π_t^* separately even if both variables are constant over time: Any assumed value for one can be made consistent with observed inflation by suitably varying the other.

We can handle this problem if we condition on additional dynamic relationships that tie u_t^*, π_t^*, or both to other observables.[43] For example, we might assume that the behavior of other labor market variables (nominal or real) depends on $(u_t - u_t^*)$ (or that some common measure of the cyclical state of the economy drives both), and that wage growth is also influenced by π_t^*. Besides allowing us to identify both unobservables, using additional labor-market information in a fully specified multi-equation system might help us to better pin down the level of u^* in a given period (the implicit assumption is that things that matter for labor market dynamics or labor market functioning can also have some relevance for inflation – and vice-versa – inasmuch as they reflect supply-side developments in

---

[42] As with any statistical (or judgmental) filtering procedure, this inference is difficult to get right in real time (that is, when we are at or near the end of our sample).

[43] In the case of a single-equation accelerationist model of inflation, the solution involves recovering u^* by explicitly setting the π_t^* terms equal to the preceding period's actual inflation rate in Equation (6.17).

the economy). What tends to happen in practice, though, is that the estimate of u^* is mostly determined by the need to fit the dynamics of the unemployment rate or other labor-market variables; with a flat Phillips curve, being wrong about the estimate of the gap isn't going to degrade the model's ability to fit price inflation very much.[44] In any case, while point estimates of slack depend importantly on the specific model that's used to estimate them, they tend to have similar contours across models because movements in the gap largely reflect movements in actual unemployment (or actual output) around a slower-moving trend.[45]

Are there other indicators of slack that we might consider using besides one based on the unemployment rate? There doesn't seem to be a candidate that consistently works much better (or at all). On the production side, we are stuck with the problem that we need an estimate of potential output to construct an output gap, which in turn requires a measure of the full-employment unemployment rate as well as other supply-side trends. (If we had the former, of course, we could just cut out the middleman and use an unemployment gap.) We also know from our discussion of Okun's law that unemployment and output changes are typically closely linked. Capacity utilization, which is another reasonable candidate for a measure of slack, only covers the industrial sector of the economy.[46] In terms of alternative labor-market indicators, one suggestion that crops up occasionally is to measure slack as the difference between the vacancy and unemployment rates or as the ratio of vacancies to unemployment, on the grounds that this sort of measure provides a conceptually sounder way to measure excess demand in the labor market. (This idea goes back at least as far as the 1960s; more recently, the justification comes from models of Beveridge curve dynamics based on constant-returns-to-scale matching functions, in which the relevant theoretical measure of labor market tightness is V/U.) However, the vacancy and unemployment rates have also tended to move in tandem over history, so it's not clear how much additional information is present in the vacancy rate (in addition, good measures of job vacancies only begin after

---

[44] While the wage Phillips curve is steeper, the actual improvement in precision that comes from adding a wage equation to these sorts of systems tends to be small, partly because wage growth is itself volatile.

[45] This statement is mostly true for statistical models; it's less true for models whose specifications are heavily informed by theory. Note also that mismeasuring slack in periods when it makes an important contribution to actual inflation can contaminate the estimated slope of the Phillips curve, and even the coefficients on other inflation determinants.

[46] In older macromodels like the MIT–Penn–SSRC (MPS) model, capacity utilization was actually used in a markup equation as a separate indicator of product–market slack.

2000 with the JOLTS data). And while a very recent paper by Ball et al. (2022) claims that the surge in US inflation after 2020 is better explained with a model that uses linear and nonlinear transformations of V/U, out-of-sample dynamic simulations that include a lagged dependent variable in the specification indicate that neither the linear nor nonlinear V/U terms add anything to the model's tracking performance, and that the best-fitting specification is simply one that uses the unemployment gap as a measure of slack.[47]

6.6 Digression: What Missing Disinflation?

A widely cited paper by Coibion and Gorodnichenko (2015) argues that inflation remained puzzlingly high in the wake of the 2007–2009 recession – in particular, that there was "missing disinflation" over this period. After rejecting the idea that a flattening of the Phillips curve could explain the discrepancy, the authors claim that the puzzle is resolved by looking at household inflation expectations (year-ahead inflation expectations from the Michigan survey) – which they further claim provide the best proxy for *firms'* inflation expectations. Because of a sharp rise in oil prices from early 2009 to early 2012, these unanchored short-run expectations rose, thereby propping up actual inflation and preventing a larger deceleration in prices. The implication is that short-run inflation expectations play a key role in understanding the behavior of inflation over this period.

The Coibion–Gorodnichenko paper provides another example of how failing to recognize that the US inflation process has changed over time can lead to extremely misleading conclusions. The benchmark that the paper uses to assess how much disinflation is "missing" imposes a unit coefficient on either lagged inflation or a measure of expected inflation that is itself closely related to lagged inflation (namely, the year-ahead inflation forecast from the Survey of Professional Forecasters). The paper therefore uses an

---

[47] The paper provides a useful illustration of the two pitfalls associated with inflation modelling that were noted earlier. First, fitted values can be an extremely misleading guide to whether a model is any good (though in this particular case, the fitted values aren't great either). Second, one needs to be extremely careful that an "improved" inflation model isn't simply overfitting some influential outliers. Here, the past couple of years represent the only instance in which the vacancy rate has moved so noticeably out of line with the unemployment rate, so a model that includes a V/U term has a good chance of (spuriously) explaining this period's inflation surge. (During and after the 2007–2009 recession, a similar role was played by the unemployment rate for the short-term unemployed – see note 26.)

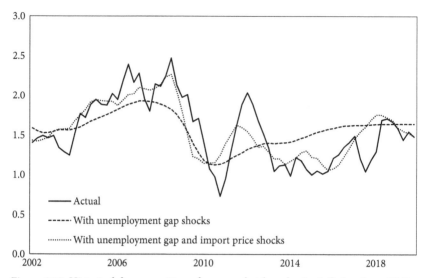

Figure 6.12 Historical decomposition of core market-based price inflation from VAR model with time-varying parameters, 2001:Q1–2019:Q4. (Four-quarter log differences.)

accelerationist specification over a period in which that specification was no longer relevant.

What happens if we instead use an empirical model that assumes a flat Phillips curve and stable long-run mean for inflation? Figure 6.12 plots an historical decomposition of this period using the coefficients from the VAR model.[48] The dashed line plots the baseline inflation forecast from the model plus the contribution of the unemployment gap shocks together with actual core inflation (the solid line). The reduction in inflation that resulted from the increase in the unemployment rate is clearly apparent, and tracks the contour of actual core inflation relatively closely. And we can get closer still if we also include the contribution of shocks to relative import price inflation over this period (the dotted line).[49]

The paper also demonstrates why the Michigan survey data need to be used with caution. Table 6.2 gives results from monthly regressions of

---

[48] Over this period, the VAR's inflation equation is basically just a regression of market-based core inflation on its lags, the unemployment gap, and the relative import price term, along with a constant term to pick up the stable long-run mean.

[49] In the figure, inflation is defined as the four-quarter log difference of the market-based PCE price index. Note that Coibion and Gorodnichenko also use the CBO unemployment gap as their estimate of slack, though the specific natural rate series they use was later discontinued (it included a one-time upward adjustment to capture the effect of the 2007–2009 recession on labor market functioning). Although the historical decomposition is really using the *shocks* to the unemployment gap and relative import price terms, these

Table 6.2 *Dependence of expected inflation coefficient on its timing*

	Sample period	Coefficients		
		$\Delta\pi_t^e$	$\Delta\pi_{t-1}^e$	π_{t-1}^{CPI}
1.	1987–2019	3.488		0.377
		(0.407)		(0.042)
			−0.214	0.440
			(0.481)	(0.050)
2.	1997–2019	4.016		0.337
		(0.519)		(0.051)
			−0.141	0.415
			(0.633)	(0.062)
3.	1997–2007	3.937		0.160
		(0.654)		(0.077)
			−0.558	0.263
			(0.835)	(0.098)
4.	2011–2019	2.710		0.371
		(0.866)		(0.086)
			0.569	0.355
			(0.944)	(0.094)
5.	2001–2019	4.064		0.363
		(0.556)		(0.055)
			−0.088	0.440
			(0.689)	(0.068)

Note: Standard errors in parentheses. π^e is median expected price change over the next 12 months from the Michigan survey; π^{CPI} is the annualized log difference of the monthly headline CPI.

headline CPI inflation on its first lag and on the first difference of the year-ahead expected inflation measure from the Michigan survey.[50] Although the contemporaneous change in the Michigan survey seems to enter the

---

shocks turn out to explain virtually all of the variation in their respective series over this period.

[50] The Michigan survey question asks about the expected "price change" over the next 12 months, not about a specific price index. However, it's conventional to compare the Michigan measure with the headline CPI change, probably because the CPI is seen as better capturing prices paid "out-of-pocket" by consumers. (If we seriously believed that the PCE price index is a better price measure on welfare-theoretic grounds, we should probably use it instead.)

regression, lagging it by even a single month – and again, this is the year-ahead expectation – causes its coefficient to vanish. The reason is that the Michigan survey is taken over the course of a month, when consumers are revising their views about inflation based on the price changes they are seeing in that same month (including for volatile categories like food and energy).[51] Hence, regressions of actual inflation π_t on the Michigan measure are closer to a regression of time-t inflation on itself, rather than on a proxy for $E_t\pi_{t+1}$. (The problem is further complicated when quarterly data are used because of the way in which underlying monthly changes are weighted in a quarterly average change – see Appendix E.)

6.7 Can We Explain Any of This?

Although the Phillips curve has been an object of fascination since it was first introduced, we have no compelling theory of inflation dynamics that would allow us to understand the Phillips correlation – or the historical shifts in the Phillips curve – on anything like a deep level. What this means is that we also have no good way to explain the two most important changes to the inflation process that have taken place over the past fifty years; namely, the near-constancy of inflation's stochastic trend after the mid-1990s, and the reduced sensitivity of price inflation to real activity.

The usual explanation for the first change is that it reflects better "anchoring" of the public's expectations of inflation.[52] Since the 1970s, theories of inflation dynamics have emphasized the role of inflation expectations in driving actual inflation; in those earlier models, inflation was assumed to depend on last period's expectation of current inflation, implying a Phillips curve like

---

[51] We get the same result if we use CPI data that aren't seasonally adjusted, which are a little closer to what consumers are actually seeing. It's a little remarkable that households are able to think about inflation in a coherent fashion – especially for items that are rarely purchased – since backing out a rate of inflation from an observed price change requires you to recall *when* the price last changed, so that you can correctly gauge the *rate* of change. It would be interesting to try to discern whether consumers simply notice price changes when they occur, and then form their views about inflation as a sort of "intensity" measure that reflects how many price changes they happen to have noticed.

[52] In effect, Coibion and Gorodnichenko (2015) provide evidence *against* a role for inflation expectations in the inflation process, since the explanation they come up with – inflation expectations are important *and* are unanchored because they respond to actual price changes – doesn't square with the observed stability of inflation's stochastic trend since the mid-1990s.

$$\pi_t = -\beta(U_t - U^*) + \zeta Z_t + E_{t-1}\pi_t, \tag{6.18}$$

using similar notation to Equation (6.17). The usual motivation for including expected inflation was to prevent purely nominal influences from
permanently affecting real outcomes (the classical dichotomy again), which
is why changes in expected inflation were assumed to (eventually) have a
one-for-one effect on actual inflation.[53] In Friedman's case, the way this
worked was through wage bargaining: Workers were concerned over their
anticipated real wage, and would adjust their wage demands accordingly
if they expected higher inflation. If inflation *did* come in higher than
anticipated, then the resulting reduction in the *ex post* real wage would
result in an increase in employment and reduction in unemployment.[54]
The more interesting prediction of the model, however, involved what
would happen if the unemployment rate were kept below its "natural" rate
U^*. In Friedman's telling (and with $Z = 0$), this could only happen if actual
inflation were persistently greater than $E_{t-1}\pi_t$. But after a while, workers
would come to expect this *new* rate of inflation and raise their nominal wage
demands accordingly. The end result would be that the real wage would
rise (returning unemployment to its natural rate) and inflation would be
permanently higher.[55] The only way to *keep* the unemployment rate below
its natural rate was to keep raising inflation and so produce "accelerating
inflation [sic]."[56]

In this model – which arguably still guides the intuition of a lot of
economists – we can explain the shift from an accelerationist to a mean-
reverting inflation process as a consequence of a change in the way inflation
expectations are formed. In particular, if inflation expectations become
anchored at some level $\bar{\pi}$ and no longer respond to actual inflation or
other economic conditions (say people are asleep), then the Phillips curve
becomes

$$\pi_t = \bar{\pi} - \beta(U_t - U^*) + \gamma Z_t, \tag{6.19}$$

which implies that inflation will return to a fixed level whenever the economy is at the natural rate and there are no other shocks ($Z_t = 0$). What

---

[53] Phelps (1967), Friedman (1968).

[54] Firms were assumed to always be on their labor demand curves, so Friedman's setup
involves the same knife-edge case used by the AS/AD model.

[55] At the time he wrote, Friedman thought this adjustment process would fully play out after
"a couple of decades" (p. 11).

[56] Hence the term "accelerationist" Phillips curve (note that Friedman muffed the derivative
too).

keeps people asleep? The monetary authority.[57] By gaining a reputation for maintaining inflation at some specific (low) level on average – so the story goes – people come to expect that this level will prevail and so feel free to divert their attention to other matters of more pressing concern to them. And all that monetary policymakers need to do to keep this situation going is to ensure that their reputation for inflation control remains solid – in other words, that they have inflation-fighting "credibility" – which they preserve by standing ready to raise the unemployment rate (read: throw people out of work) whenever inflation gets too high.[58]

The fact that the sustained inflation increases of the 1960s and 1970s appeared to be associated with outward shifts of estimated Phillips curves was generally seen as validating the Phelps–Friedman description of inflation dynamics. But the *direct* evidence for an expected inflation channel was never very strong. Most of the empirical debate over the Phelps–Friedman model concerned whether there was a long-run level trade-off between activity and inflation; the way this was tested involved seeing whether the coefficients on lagged inflation in an empirical inflation equation summed to one (in other words, whether $C(1)$ equalled one in Equation 6.9).[59] In addition, because theoretical models often assumed that expectations were formed adaptively, people drifted into a habit of thought in which the presence of lagged inflation terms in empirical Phillips curves was seen as equivalent to a role for expectations in the inflation process.[60]

More modern models of inflation also assign a key role for inflation expectations. In the new-Keynesian Phillips curve, exogenously specified contracting mechanisms or price adjustment costs generate a nominal rigidity (sticky prices). The presence of sticky prices induces a concern among firms over their future costs and future demand conditions, because they want to set their current price in a way that will be most profitable not just in the current period, but over the period of time in which their price is expected to remain fixed. (Put more plainly, the firm is trying to keep its price as close to its optimal price "on average," given where it expects that

---

[57] Here we see a role for central bank communications.

[58] It's more than a little telling that central bank credibility only comes up in the context of inflation control, never in the context of delivering full employment (in fact, the former seems to require that the latter be completely absent).

[59] This unit sum became easy to find empirically around the mid-1970s – see Gordon (1976).

[60] Attempts from this period to use survey-based or commercial inflation forecasts to ascertain whether these lagged inflation terms reflected an expectations channel or merely some sort of "inertia" in wage setting were inconclusive. (See Kaufman and Woglom, 1984 and the other studies that they cite.)

optimal price will be in the future.) In their simplest form, these models imply that current inflation will depend on current expectations of *future* inflation; in other words, an inflation equation along the lines of

$$\pi_t = ax_t + bE_t\pi_{t+1}, \tag{6.20}$$

where $E_t\pi_{t+1}$ is the expectation of next period's inflation rate, and where x_t denotes the firm's current real marginal cost (which is usually just associated with a measure of real activity relative to some benchmark level).

There's not really a natural way to think about what it means to have anchored inflation expectations in the new-Keynesian framework. Because $E_t\pi_{t+1}$ is a *rational* expectation, it isn't freely determined but depends on other elements of the model economy (including how the central bank conducts policy). As a result, the way people describe periods like the late 1960s and 1970s is that the central bank was insufficiently aggressive in tightening policy to lean against inflation shocks.[61] When that happens in models like these, self-fulfilling expectations of inflation can result ("sunspot" equilibria) that adversely influence macroeconomic outcomes. But to address this problem, there's no reason for the central bank to actually do anything about inflation expectations (or even to monitor them) – all it needs to do is follow the Taylor principle, which calls for raising its policy rate by enough that the *real* short-term interest rate rises after an inflation shock. And it's far from clear that the Fed ever *failed* to respect the Taylor principle, even in the 1960s and 1970s.[62]

Empirical tests of the importance of expected inflation using new-Keynesian Phillips curves provide no real evidence one way or the other – nor are they likely to, as Mavroeidis et al. (2014) discuss. The usual way that this question is approached involves estimating the following "hybrid" version of the new-Keynesian Phillips curve,

$$\pi_t = ax_t + b_1E_t\pi_{t+1} + b_2\pi_{t-1}, \tag{6.21}$$

and then comparing the relative weights on lagged inflation and expected inflation. As $E_t\pi_{t+1}$ is a rational expectation, the estimation strategy is to instrument for actual π_{t+1}, where anything in agents' time-t information set is fair game as an instrument (since it should be uncorrelated with the time-t forecast error). What Mavroeidis et al. (2014) point out is that a weak instrument problem will almost certainly arise in this case: Since π_{t-1} (and x_t)

---

[61] Clarida et al. (2000).
[62] This point is made by Orphanides (2004) and Sims and Zha (2006a), among others.

will be in the first-stage regression, the instruments will only be able to pin down the importance of the expected inflation term if a large portion of the predictable variation in inflation is unrelated to lagged inflation. As an empirical matter, very little is. In addition, seemingly innocuous changes in specification (for example, the price index used to measure inflation or the choice of x_t) can have a large effect on the resulting parameter estimates (this is also true for estimates of the model that proxy for $E_t\pi_{t+1}$ using survey measures of expected inflation).[63]

As further evidence that the new-Keynesian model probably doesn't describe actual inflation dynamics all that well, models of this sort that account for nonzero (and time-varying) trend inflation imply that the effect of real activity on inflation should be smallest in periods like the 1970s, when trend inflation is high (Ascari and Sbordone, 2014, fig. 6); that prediction exactly contradicts the evidence on how the slope of the price Phillips curve has changed over time. (While it is possible to partly correct for this problem by allowing the frequency of price adjustment to vary endogenously, the model then predicts that inflation *persistence* should be lowest in periods when trend inflation is high – another counterfactual implication.)[64] In addition, the way that the model explains the subpar economic outcomes of the 1960s and 1970s is unconvincing: As advanced by Clarida et al. (2000), failure to adhere to the Taylor principle allowed sunspot shocks to affect the economy while also making it more vulnerable to "fundamental" shocks. However, this interpretation of the 1970s *stag*flation requires the food and energy price shocks of this period to have resulted in a large and rapid decline in the level of potential output; had non-fundamental inflation shocks been the source of the Great Stagflation, output would have been *above* potential throughout this period. A large drop in potential seems highly unlikely in the case of a food price shock; for an energy price shock, most of the effect on output actually comes from a hit to aggregate demand, not supply.

So far, the empirical support for the proposition that inflation expectations drive US inflation dynamics looks pretty thin: Either we need to associate the lagged inflation terms found in earlier empirical inflation specifications with some sort of expectations formation process; or we need

---

[63] In a related contribution, Coibion et al. (2018a) acknowledge that this problem exists, but then proceed to ignore it completely.

[64] An important shortcoming of the Hazell et al. (2022) study of the 1980s inflation experience is its use of a variant of the new-Keynesian Phillips curve that does not allow for changes in trend inflation and that is only valid if inflation is typically close to zero.

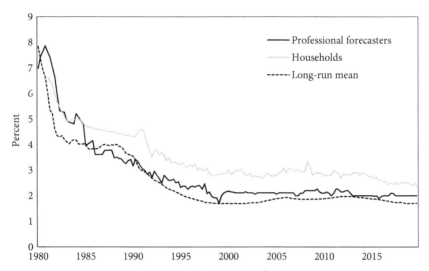

Figure 6.13 Circumstantial evidence that long-run inflation expectations matter for inflation's long-run mean (or possibly the other way around). Household expectations are median five-to-ten-year expectations from the University of Michigan's Surveys of Consumers. Expectations for professional forecasters are derived from the Survey of Professional Forecasters (SPF), Federal Reserve Bank of Philadelphia.

to ignore the fact that empirical estimates of the importance of expected inflation in the new-Keynesian Phillips curve are all over the place (and that the model fails badly along other dimensions), and simply assume that expectations matter because the theory tells us that they do. Figure 6.13 presents what is essentially the only evidence that we *can* point to, which also happens to be the shred of evidence that central-bank types tend to find dispositive. The figure plots the stochastic trend for inflation from our VAR system against two survey measures of *long-run* inflation expectations.[65] A suggestive correlation is present, but no more than that. (And if we want to put a ridiculously fine point on it, during the Volcker disinflation the stochastic trend seems to be leading the expectations series by several quarters.) The correlation with the Survey of Professional Forecasters (SPF) measure of long-run expectations is also the only serious empirical evidence that Hazell et al. (2022) adduce in support of their claim that inflation expectations are an important driver of inflation (except that they make their case by plotting the SPF against actual inflation instead of against an

---

[65] See Appendix A for a description of several of the most commonly used measures of long-run expected inflation for the United States.

estimate of its stochastic trend). Note again, though, that the expectations series shown here are *long-run* expectations, not the short-run expectations that both the Phelps–Friedman and new-Keynesian models predict should be relevant for current inflation.[66] So there isn't much of an intersection with existing theory here; nor is there a way to identify causality: For all we know, longer-run expectations declined because people were making roughly correct forecasts in response to lower actual inflation.

If we think that improved monetary policy credibility (however defined) was responsible for anchoring inflation's long-run trend, we're faced with another puzzle. After the Volcker disinflation, core PCE price inflation averaged about 4 percent per year until the 1990–1991 recession. In the wake of that recession, core inflation ratcheted down once again, reaching 2 percent by the middle of the decade (these movements are also visible in inflation's long-run mean); only after that did the trend seem invariant to economic conditions (for example, during the 2001 recession). What this history suggests is that inflation continued to behave in an accelerationist manner, with recessions able to effect permanent declines in inflation, well after Volcker had demonstrated that the Fed stood ready to use drastic measures to control inflation. It's possible, of course, that it took time for whatever happened to anchor the trend to actually happen – for example, that credibility somehow grew over time despite no additional object lessons. But it's equally plausible that it was an outcome – low inflation itself – that helped the trend to become stable.[67]

A number of studies have tried to use microdata on inflation expectations from household and business surveys or experiments in which agents are given some piece of information about inflation in order to investigate how these expectations are formed, or whether changes in expectations affect economic decision-making in any way. What do these studies tell us about the role of inflation expectations in the US inflation process? As of the time of this writing, virtually nothing.

- An older study by Blinder et al. (1998) finds that firms pay little attention to forecasts of aggregate economic conditions, including inflation. (Note that the survey of firms that was used in the study was conducted

---

[66] Even new-Keynesian models that explicitly allow for a time-varying long-run inflation trend (typically to capture changes in the central bank's inflation target) predict that short-run inflation expectations should have an important influence on actual inflation.

[67] However, it seems difficult to invoke some sort of rational inattention story here: Empirically, survey measures of consumer sentiment are correlated with actual inflation, even after the mid-1990s.

from 1990 to 1992 – a period when the aggregate data suggest that inflation's long-run trend was still responding to economic conditions.)

- Bryan et al. (2015) analyze 2011–2014 results from a survey of business expectations conducted by the Federal Reserve Bank of Atlanta (the survey only covers firms in the Atlanta Fed's district). The study documents a cross-sectional correlation between firms' reported *current* unit cost growth and their *expected* unit cost growth. (The study has no data on firms' prices.) Such a finding is unsurprising if these costs are autocorrelated, but it says nothing about how expectations influence firms' price-setting behavior.
- If we cast a wider net and look outside the United States, a study by Coibion et al. (2020) looks at firms who are randomly treated with information about inflation. Although the treatment influences the firms' expectations, the effect of the change in expectations on their actual prices is "only small and relatively transitory" (p. 184). Note also that these are *short-run* (year-ahead) inflation expectations.[68]
- Most other studies simply analyze the determinants or properties of household expectations – see the extensive survey by D'Acunto et al. (2022). But as these authors emphasize, none of these studies considers how inflation expectations "… shape agents' wage expectations, their wage bargaining decisions, and their labor supply" (p. 36).

An overarching problem with this literature is that it starts from the position that households' or firms' inflation expectations are terribly important and worthy of detailed study without providing much evidence for that view.[69] It is also worth noting that many of the entries in this literature find contradictory results: In country A, expectations do one thing to inflation/consumption/something else; in country B, they have no discernable effect; and in country C, they do something opposite to what they do in country A. Maybe we can conclude that these results suggest that expectations matter in some way… for something.[70] At a minimum, though, I think it is fair to say that existing work sheds no light on whether or how inflation expectations influence price- or wage-setting, and definitely provides no insight into whether changes in the formation of inflation expectations contributed to the features of the post-1995 inflation regime.

---

[68] Similar work by Coibion et al. (2018b) for firms in New Zealand finds even smaller effects on prices and wages.

[69] For example, Bryan et al. (2015) open their paper with the assertion that "[i]nflation expectations matter" – because they enter the new-Keynesian Phillips curve.

[70] More likely, a solid meta-analysis of this literature is needed.

What about explaining the second empirical feature of the post-1995 inflation regime, the relatively flat price Phillips curve? We've already noted that new-Keynesian models aren't of any use in this regard because they predict the opposite of what actually happened from the 1970s until now.[71] In addition, the *timing* of the flattening – which seems to have been largely complete by the mid-1990s – makes it difficult to invoke explanations based on changes in globalization or greater industrial concentration unless we think that these developments were fully in place by the late 1990s.[72]

What all this implies is that we *simply don't know* what caused the US economy to transition into an inflation regime where inflation became a mean-reverting process and the price Phillips curve flattened. That fact is embarrassing from a professional standpoint, because it highlights that we still understand close to nothing about how inflation works despite seven decades' worth of research. But it's also a serious problem where policy is concerned: For obvious reasons, remaining in this sort of inflation regime is highly desirable, so we'd like to know what policy actions would prevent us from leaving it. This issue came to the fore during the pandemic-related inflation surge, since the key question for monetary policy was whether such a visible and prolonged runup in consumer price inflation would be enough to move the economy into an inflation regime similar to the one that prevailed in the 1970s and 1980s. But there was no way to make a credible assessment of the likelihood of this outcome, or what, if anything, could prevent it from happening.

Another implication is that central bank shibboleths like expectations management, the need for communications and transparency, and a concern over maintaining "credibility" have no real analytical or empirical basis. One can just as well conclude that these things only matter to financial

---

[71] A related criticism can be leveled against McLeay and Tenreyro (2020), as their framework predicts that the Phillips correlation should be *weaker* in periods like the 1970s, when large cost shocks occur (p. 245). Moreover, a large demand shock that the Fed didn't lean against very well (the 2007–2009 recession) resulted in a degree of disinflation that was consistent with a (structurally) flatter Phillips curve, while the Fed's attempt to push up inflation in the decade following the recession only resulted in an unemployment rate below 4 percent (again what one would expect if the flattening of the Phillips curve were structural).

[72] Globalization is also hard to point to insofar as our empirical models control for changes in imported goods prices and (roughly) for import penetration into the US economy, though perhaps a more-subtle set of controls are needed to capture the influence of these forces on domestic inflation. Greater concentration seems like it could be a promising explanation given the relative stability of the wage Phillips curve – as competition becomes more imperfect, profit functions become flatter – but the timing again seems off, and it seems like that story would be more about price levels than about inflation rates.

markets (whose effective horizon is probably best measured in days, if not minutes), and not to the people actually making decisions about hiring, price setting, and spending.

6.8 Digression: Markups and Margins

Economists think that in imperfectly competitive markets firms will set their prices as a markup over their marginal costs. In addition, theoretical pricing models like the new-Keynesian Phillips curve view the actual level of this markup as an important determinant of inflation: Intuitively, these models assume that firms try to keep their markup of prices over marginal costs at some target level that maximizes profits, but also that price adjustment takes time. Hence, relatively low markups are associated with upward price pressures, while high markups put downward pressure on prices.[73]

However, marginal costs are not straightforward to measure, even at the firm level.[74] As aggregate proxies, economists look at several alternative measures of price–cost margins that, in principle, should tell us something about the markup that is relevant for firms' pricing decisions.[75] As it turns out, though, differences in exact data definitions or in the sector that is considered can lead to surprisingly large differences across conceptually similar measures.

As was noted in Section 6.1, one proxy for firms' variable cost is their unit labor cost, which is defined as the dollar amount of labor needed to produce a unit of output. Again, the justification is that labor costs are the single largest component of overall costs; in addition, increased production usually requires hiring additional labor to work at existing production facilities. So on a quarter-to-quarter basis, unit labor costs seem like a reasonable way to capture the increase in total costs that results from producing an additional unit of output.[76]

---

[73] More intuitively, it seems plausible that high markups will get competed away over time, while an increase in costs that lowers firms' markups will eventually passed through as a price increase and so boost inflation for a time.

[74] In some DSGE models, marginal cost is treated as an unobserved variable that is backed out from a filtering exercise.

[75] For example, Philippon (2019, chapter 7) argues that US prices are "too high" relative to Europe by comparing markup growth across the two locations; his definition of the markup is the ratio of prices to unit labor costs.

[76] It is possible to show that under certain (unrealistic) assumptions, unit labor costs will be proportional to marginal costs; this is why a measure of real unit labor costs – otherwise known as labor's share of income (see below) – was commonly used as the driving variable for empirical implementations of the new-Keynesian Phillips curve. That said, there are

Unit labor costs can be measured as hourly compensation divided by labor productivity.[77] We therefore need to choose what compensation and productivity measures to use; then, to compute a markup, we also have to settle on a price measure to use. In particular, the markup can be defined using:

- Trend productivity or actual productivity;
- The Employment Cost Index (ECI) as the measure of hourly compensation or a measure of compensation per hour from the Productivity and Costs (P&C) data; and,
- Compensation, price, and productivity data for various sectors, including the overall economy, the full business sector, nonfarm business, or nonfinancial corporate business.

Since empirical models still find some passthrough of ECI-based unit labor cost growth into inflation (as noted earlier in the chapter, the evidence is much weaker for the P&C measure), a mild case can be made for using the ECI as the compensation concept. In economic terms, the ECI tries to control for changes in the "mix" of jobs across industries and occupations (loosely, it measures compensation for a specific basket of jobs); we might therefore view the ECI as providing a better read of what firms view as their normal hourly compensation cost.[78] At a minimum, the ECI smooths through variability and noise that do not appear to matter much for price inflation empirically. On the other hand, the wage component of the P&C measure is benchmarked to a sample that includes close to the full universe of employers (the Quarterly Census of Employment and Wages, QCEW, which captures more than 95 percent of all jobs), and the series has a much longer history than the ECI.[79]

---

well-known puzzles regarding the cyclical behavior of unit labor costs that suggest it might not be as good a proxy for marginal costs as one might hope (see Rotemberg and Woodford, 1999, but note that subsequent data revisions leave some of their specific conclusions outdated). In addition, the new-Keynesian Phillips curve continues to fit the data abysmally even when labor's share of income is used as a driving variable.

[77] Using compensation, which is wages and salaries plus benefits, is preferable to using a wage and salary measure (such as average hourly earnings) on the grounds that compensation better captures both overall labor costs to a firm and the pecuniary benefits of a job to a worker.

[78] The way the ECI is constructed makes it less susceptible to swings induced by changes in the composition of employment. In contrast, other aggregate estimates like the P&C measure simply divide total compensation by total hours, which means that if a disproportionate number of lower-wage workers lose their jobs it can cause the P&C measure (or a measure like average hourly earnings) to increase.

[79] The ECI omits employees with substantial discretion over their pay, and excludes stock options from compensation. The P&C measure captures stock options, but only when exercised (this can lead to large quarterly movements in the series).

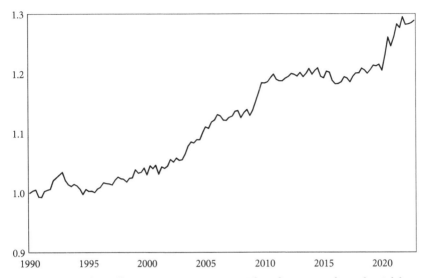

Figure 6.14 Markup of business prices over an ECI-based measure of actual unit labor costs (1990:Q1=1.0).

If we also think that firms set prices on the basis of a "normal" or smoothed level of productivity (since actual productivity fluctuates so much), we might want to use an estimate of trend productivity as a proxy. (This is what was done for the labor cost series used in the VAR from Section 6.1.) For the purposes of constructing a markup measure, we might prefer to use business-sector prices since they provide a better gauge of the prices that US firms are setting than do PCE prices (which include a nonmarket component and prices for goods that might be produced abroad, and which also omit prices for investment goods) and the GDP price index (which includes things like government compensation).[80] Business-sector prices also cover the same sector as business-sector productivity and roughly correspond to the scope of the private-industry ECI.

Figures 6.14 and 6.15 plot the markup of business prices over ECI-based and P&C-based actual unit labor costs (the series are smoother but have similar overall contours if trend productivity growth is used instead).[81]

---

[80] The VAR models used a PCE price measure because we were interested in assessing how the passthrough of prices to wages had changed over time, which makes a consumer price concept more relevant. (The models also included a control for import price changes and omitted the nonmarket component of PCE, which helps deal with the first two issues.)

[81] Because the ECI is an index, this markup measure has no "natural units" (for example, a value of "1.10" does not mean that the markup is 10 percent). The measure shown in the figure is arbitrarily indexed to equal 1.0 in 1990:Q1.

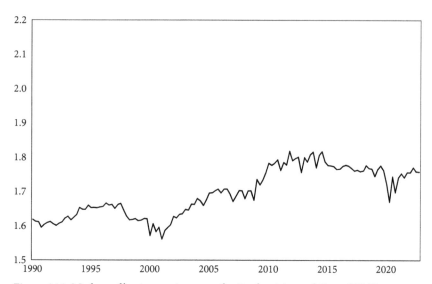

Figure 6.15 Markup of business prices over the Productivity and Costs (P&C) measure of actual unit labor costs (natural units). Inverse of this series gives labor's share of income for this sector.

The ECI and P&C series don't track each other especially closely, with a larger upward trend evident for the ECI-based measure.[82]

Although they are often used and discussed in connection with inflation and businesses' price-setting behavior, these sorts of aggregate markup measures aren't especially helpful for that purpose. For one thing, the series trend over time, so it is hard to know what (if anything) represents a normal or benchmark level.[83] Conceptually, the notion of an "economywide" markup is difficult to relate to the types of margins that firms actually face because the aggregate experience can mask what is happening across or within sectors: In many cases, one firm's price is another firm's input cost, while economywide margin measures like these – which only involve final demand and value-added – will largely net out the production and purchase of intermediate inputs. And, as we discussed in Chapter 4, it doesn't make sense to think of the overall economy in terms of a single producer using capital and labor to produce output – so it is also not very helpful to think of that output as being priced with reference to an aggregate markup.[84]

---

[82] The scales of the two figures have been calibrated such that the vertical distance of each corresponds to the same percent change.

[83] There's also no evidence that the components are cointegrated.

[84] Note that the markup of prices over unit labor costs is equal to the reciprocal of labor's share of income, so long as actual labor productivity is used, hourly compensation equals the compensation bill divided by hours, and all measures cover the same sector.

There are two other measures that are also sometimes used to think about price–cost margins. One is the profit share, though here too the profit share can be defined in different ways depending on whether the entire corporate sector is considered (as opposed to just nonfinancial corporations); whether "book" or "economic" profits are used in the calculation; and whether profits are defined pre- or post-tax. The national accounts define economic profits to be the portion of capital income that is not paid in the form of interest or rents, or absorbed by depreciation of capital. As a result, the profit share can rise even if capital's share of income stays fixed in situations where other components of the capital share (such as net interest) are declining; likewise, if labor costs go up but capital-related costs go down by a sufficient amount, the profit share could stay constant or rise.

Another measure of margins is the ratio of revenues to the acquisition cost of goods sold. The Bureau of Labor Statistics (BLS) produce measures like these for the retail and wholesale trade sectors; however, the earliest they are available is December 1999. These margin measures are also difficult to interpret without additional analysis, since they do not account for other types of costs that retailers face (like wages or inventory carrying costs).

6.9 Data Appendix for Chapter 6

National Income and Product Accounts (NIPA) data are produced by the Bureau of Economic Analysis (BEA); data on unemployment, productivity, and compensation come from the Bureau of Labor Statistics (BLS); the CBO series comes from *The Budget and Economic Outlook: 2023 to 2033*, released on February 15, 2023. All series except the ECI were downloaded from the Haver Analytics database on April 4, 2023 (the ECI series is incorrectly spliced to its earlier history in that database and was instead constructed using BLS data).

Market-based PCE price index: Official data for the core market-based PCE price index are published from 1987 to the present. Prior to 1987, a market-based series can be constructed by using detailed PCE data and a Fisher aggregation procedure routine (that replicates the procedure followed by the BEA in constructing the NIPAs) to strip out the prices of core nonmarket PCE components from the published overall core PCE price index (the definition of "nonmarket" mimics the BEA's). The core inflation series used in the estimation also subtracts out Blinder and coauthor's (2013) estimates of the effects of the Nixon-era price controls.

Import price inflation is defined as the annualized log difference of the price index for imports of nonpetroleum goods excluding natural gas, computers, peripherals, and parts, which is computed using detailed NIPA series. (As the data required to construct this series only extend back to 1967:Q1, the annualized log difference of total goods imports is used prior to that date.) The relative import price inflation term used in the VAR model equals the difference between this series and the core PCE price inflation measure used for the estimation (lagged one period), and is weighted by the two-quarter moving average of the share of nominal imports (defined consistently with the import price measure) in nominal core PCE.[85]

Trend unit labor cost growth equals the difference between the rate of change of the Productivity and Costs (P&C) measure of nonfarm hourly compensation (expressed as a log difference), and a measure of trend productivity growth that is obtained by applying a lowpass filter to the log difference of P&C nonfarm output per hour. I use the same filter width and cutoffs that Staiger et al. (2001) employ to measure trend productivity growth and an ARIMA(4,1,0) model to pad the actual productivity growth series prior to its 1947:Q2 starting point. After its 2022:Q4 endpoint, the series is padded with CBO's forecast of average trend labor productivity growth over 2023–2032 (which equals 1.69 in log differences), and CBO's projected 2033 value of trend productivity growth (which equals 1.67 in log differences) thereafter.

---

[85] The relative import price term uses actual core PCE prices (that is, unadjusted for the effect of price controls), and the nominal import share is scaled by its sample mean.

7

What Does Monetary Policy Do?

It became necessary to destroy the town to save it.
    "Major Describes Move," *New York Times, February 8, 1968 (p. 14)*

If the economics profession's inability to say anything especially insightful about inflation dynamics was embarrassing, its inability to say anything very useful about monetary policy is mortifying. Given the effects that monetary policy actions can have on millions of people, one would hope that the academic literature would have come up with a reasonably clear idea of how monetary policy actions affect the economy, how large these effects are, and how long it takes them to be felt. (It would also be nice to know how those effects might differ under alternative economic and financial conditions.) In reality, we have practically useable answers to none of these questions; worse still, the answers that are out there often contradict each other and are ridiculously implausible in other ways.

Hence, the best we'll be able to do in this chapter – and it won't be much – is to present some vaguely intuitive, halfway sensible statements about likely monetary policy transmission mechanisms. Before that, let's start with a highly tendentious overview of some of the more popular approaches to thinking about the effects of monetary policy.

7.1 Monetary Policy Shocks: Who Cares?

Since at least the early 1990s, much of the focus of empirical work on monetary policy has involved trying to identify monetary policy "shocks," defined as *non-systematic* movements in the stance of policy.[1] For a number of reasons, this is a challenging econometric undertaking.

---

[1] In many cases, these amount conceptually to deviations from a (possibly unobserved) policy rule.

- Most central banks don't behave randomly – their decisions reflect the current and expected state of the economy – which means that any observed changes in the policy instrument tend not to be all that exogenous.
- The shocks the econometrician identifies will only represent innovations to the policy rule if the econometrician has specified that policy rule correctly; doing so also requires correctly conditioning on all of the information (economic data) that policymakers are using to make their decision.
- Relatedly, if the public view the central bank as having more information about the economy than they (the public) do, or if they think that the central bank is interpreting commonly available information differently, then part of the public's reaction to a policy "surprise" can reflect their reassessment of how the central bank are conducting the systematic portion of their policy.
- Many policy decisions are telegraphed in advance, or contain information about planned future decisions (deliberate attempts to do this are known in the trade as *forward guidance*). As a result, changes in the current value of the policy instrument might not fully reflect the true change in policy stance that has occurred.[2]

The earlier literature on estimating monetary policy shocks mostly concerned itself with the first two problems. Initially, this work used recursively identified VAR models with the policy instrument ordered last in the system, on the grounds that its structural innovation would thereby be purged of the influence of the other time-t variables in the VAR. Later extensions involved including other variables that were arguably part of the central bank's information set, along with more careful attempts to use institutional knowledge to measure the "lever" that was actually being used by the central bank to effect policy changes.[3] Other work used FOMC documents to

---

[2] For those of a technical bent: As Ramey (2016) points out, another problem that can arise in this situation in the context of VAR models is that anticipated policy changes can yield a moving-average representation that is nonfundamental – intuitively, the estimated innovations will incorporate current news about policy as well as news received in earlier periods.

[3] For example, the factor-augmented VAR (FAVAR) approach of Bernanke et al. (2005) used high-dimensional data techniques to extract common signals from large numbers of economic indicators, on the grounds that this would do a better job capturing the myriad of series that the Federal Reserve (and the public) consider when assessing the state of the economy. Prior to that, Sims (1992) had used the argument that policy endogeneity (in the form of a central bank's reaction to anticipated higher inflation) was responsible

identify policy changes along with the Federal Reserve's staff forecasts to control for the Fed's reaction to anticipated future economic developments (Romer and Romer, 2004).[4]

The simplest VAR models of this sort fell apart pretty dramatically once the financial crisis entered the sample. One reason was that the zero lower bound was reached, which implied large positive shocks to the federal funds rate under conventional identification schemes.[5] In addition, the use of alternative policy tools such as forward guidance and asset purchases were not well captured by standard methods. However, as Ramey (2016) documents, many of the results from the alternative approaches also turn out to be fragile in samples that end *prior* to 2008. So it's fair to conclude that none of the results or identifying approaches from that earlier literature has stood up well to the passage of time, or provides us with useful estimates of the magnitude and timing of the effects of monetary policy on the economy.[6]

Over the past decade or so, a new consensus approach for identifying monetary policy shocks has emerged. Under this alternative methodology, revisions to asset prices (federal funds futures) that occur in a short window around when a policy decision is announced are treated as plausibly exogenous surprises that can be used as instruments to identify the effects of monetary policy shocks in a structural VAR model.[7] Because changes in interest rate futures are used, it also becomes possible to capture the effects of forward guidance; additionally, using a short-maturity (one- or two-year) Treasury yield as the policy indicator handles the zero-lower-bound

for a counterintuitive *increase* in prices that occurred in VAR models following a positive interest-rate shock; he supported this claim by considering what happened if commodity prices and exchange rates were included in the VAR (and hence assumed to be present in policymakers' information sets). For examples of papers that involved careful modelling of the policy levers, see Strongin (1995) and Bernanke and Mihov (1998). For accessible overviews of where things stood at the turn of the century, see Christiano et al. (1999) and Stock and Watson (2001).

[4] The staff forecast document used to be known as the Greenbook; it is now called the Tealbook. Over history, it's questionable how much influence the staff forecast has had on policymakers' outlooks: Arthur Burns was described by one former high-level staffer (Donald Kohn) as "autocratic" and intolerant of staff views that dissented from his own, while Paul Volcker was well known for viewing economic forecasts as worthless.

[5] Note that the term of art here is "effective lower bound," because the federal funds rate is typically kept a few basis points above zero so that money market mutual funds stay in business.

[6] It's also a sobering exercise to go back and read these earlier contributions to see how many results were judged to be reasonable simply based on whether they aligned with "conventional wisdom" regarding the effects of monetary policy – see Sims (1992), for example.

[7] See Stock and Watson (2018) for a discussion of some of the econometric intricacies.

problem (Gertler and Karadi, 2015). Of course, some of the challenges that faced the older approaches are still relevant here. In particular, we might continue to believe that policy actions convey information about the Fed's view of the economy, so that needs to be accounted for in some way. Work by Jarociński and Karadi (2020) uses stock price movements around policy announcements to accomplish this, the logic being that (say) a policy tightening accompanied by an increase in stock prices can be attributed to the market's learning that the Fed are bullish on the economic outlook.[8] A related approach is taken by Miranda-Agrippino and Ricco (2021), who purge the policy shock of a systematic component by projecting it on a proxy for the Fed's information set (the staff's Greenbook forecast).[9]

What does this newer literature find? About as much confusion as before. Ramey (2016) demonstrates that the Gertler and Karadi results are sensitive to how the impulse responses are estimated, and also finds that their policy shock is serially correlated (which suggests it is not capturing unanticipated interest rate changes).[10] Similarly, Miranda-Agrippino and Ricco (2021) obtain results that are noticeably different from both Gertler and Karadi *and* Romer and Romer (2004). These papers also find implausibly large and immediate effects on inflation: A contractionary shock in the Jarociński and Karadi paper, for example, has a one-for-one effect on the price level with virtually all of the effect in place after a few months (despite no noticeable effect on real activity). The inflation response from the Miranda-Agrippino and Ricco paper is even larger; they find an immediate drop in the CPI of 0.3 percent that then reaches 0.6 percent after a year, with a one-year increase in the unemployment rate of 0.3 percentage point. (That's an order of magnitude larger than what a well-fitting inflation equation would imply.) The effect on industrial production that they find is large and immediate as well.[11]

---

[8] This needn't reflect the Fed's having a better forecast; simply knowing that they are anticipating strong economic conditions going forward communicates something about likely future policy moves.

[9] My reason for considering these particular papers isn't to pick on them specifically; rather, at the time of writing they were considered best-practice examples of this methodology.

[10] Furthermore, excluding the 2009–2012 period from their sample causes the sign of the price response to flip – see figure 9 in their paper. Note that Ramey's use of local-projections methods to recompute the Gertler–Karadi impulse response functions should be viewed in light of a couple of problems that attend the local-projections approach; specifically, small-sample bias (Herbst and Johannsen, 2020) and autocorrelation (Lusompa, 2021).

[11] A true believer in a simple forward-looking new Keynesian model would find an immediate jump in inflation and output to be reasonable. Since empirical versions of that model aren't able to explain inflation (or output), we can probably dismiss that interpretation. In addition, Gertler and Karadi argue that TIPS breakevens are little changed following

There are some other issues with these papers that makes their results difficult to interpret – though not necessarily wrong.

- The sample periods typically use data that span very different inflation (and policy) regimes. For example, Gertler and Karadi use residuals that are generated from a VAR fit to data from 1979 to 2012 (where inflation is concerned, even including the 1990–1991 recession in the sample can yield significantly greater inflation persistence than what prevailed from 1995 to 2019).
- The papers' choice of price index – the total CPI or GDP deflator – is puzzling. For sample periods that start before the early 1980s, the CPI contains mortgage interest rates. In addition, the Fed started emphasizing the PCE price index (instead of the CPI) in 2000, and started publicly using the core PCE price index as an indicator of inflation in 2004. (It was likely "looking through" the effects of food and energy shocks on headline inflation well before that.)[12] The GDP deflator also includes "prices" for government expenditures, which are not closely related to monetary policy actions or the state of demand in the economy.
- The papers use *levels* of prices and output, which are clearly nonstationary and assuredly not cointegrated. Using (log) levels appears to be a holdover from the earlier VAR literature, but it seems difficult to justify econometrically and makes it difficult to use the results to think about inflation (though that's a narrow parochial concern on my part).
- The interest rate changes that are being derived from these high-frequency surprises are typically quite small. For example, the average absolute value of the surprises that Miranda-Agrippino and Ricco (2021) consider appears to be on the order of 2–3 basis points; omitting months with zeroes raises the average to just under 4 basis points.[13]

This latter point takes us to what is probably the biggest conceptual problem with this literature: Implicitly, it assumes that we can use the effects that we find from these (typically small) high-frequency shocks to infer something about the effects of the (much larger) systematic changes in monetary

---

a policy shock, which also doesn't seem consistent with what a new-Keynesian inflation equation would predict.

[12] Today, the Fed's official longer-run policy goal for inflation is defined in terms of the headline PCE price index; because it's a longer-run goal, the short-run volatility of food and energy prices isn't material, and people do eat, heat, and drive.

[13] These statistics come from tabulations of the "MPI/Monetary Policy Instrument" series in the paper's replication file.

policy that we really care about. Even if the world were fully linear, there's no reason to think that financial markets' trimming away of tail risks or the reduction in other residual uncertainty about a monetary policy action (within half an hour of its announcement) would have an important effect on things that matter for the real economy or inflation.[14] And it seems doubly unlikely inasmuch as the size of a "normal" change in policy in response to economic conditions (a 25-basis-point hike, say) would represent a five-sigma event given the distribution of these policy surprises.[15]

Put differently, the argument underpinning this approach is that these particular sorts of shocks – assuming they're actually fully exogenous – provide a source of variation that allows us to estimate and extrapolate the economy's response to *any* monetary policy action. As Sims (1998) pointed out, using random variation to uncover structural parameters is a standard technique in systems of simultaneous equations; the analogy he invoked was the usual one of using weather shocks to identify a demand curve. But in this particular case, a better analogy seems to be that we are using the estimated effect of a cigarette excise tax in a particular US state in order to get an estimate of what the effect would be of introducing a nationwide consumption tax. It's also worth pointing out that if we *could* do this, then we could estimate the effect of the systematic portion of monetary policy by offsetting the endogenous response of the policy instrument with a sequence of innovations.[16] If you feel a little uncomfortable about the plausibility of such an exercise – for one thing, the resulting set of innovations would be so large and one-sided as to be unprecedented – it's probably because you think it's best not to push a linear model too far.

Leaving these considerations aside, the fact remains that the various entries in this literature fail to pin down useable empirical estimates for how long it takes for a relatively standard monetary policy action to have an effect on output and inflation, or the likely magnitude of its effects. *A fortiori*, we can't say much about the effects of large-scale asset purchases (LSAPs) or of other unconventional policy actions – including whether those effects

---

[14] For what it's worth (probably not much), it's common to hear market chatter on the day after an FOMC decision that explains equity price or interest rate movements in terms of participants' having taken time to fully "digest" the FOMC statement (or the press conference that follows nowadays).

[15] The standard deviation of the Miranda-Agrippino and Ricco (2021) MPI series is 5 basis points.

[16] This approach was taken by Bernanke et al. (1997) to estimate how much of the economic effect of an oil price shock was attributable to the Fed's response to it; it was first suggested in a 1995 working paper by Sims and Zha (2006b).

are even different from zero. Of course, we know monetary policy actions matter – at least I'm convinced (though maybe not about LSAPs) – and we also know that the Federal Reserve has the tools it needs to cause a large recession if it were so inclined (see the 1980–1982 period for a case study). But that's roughly where our understanding ends.

If we allow ourselves to venture into the realm of speculation riding on the back of common sense (and with the historical record alongside), we can say a little more. Specifically, the main channels through which the Federal Reserve appears to be able to influence aggregate demand are the following.

- It can facilitate asset price bubbles; when these are sufficiently large and broad-based, the contribution to aggregate demand can be significant.[17] The ability of the US economy to reach an unemployment rate below 4 percent in 2000 was helped along by the dot-com bubble; likewise, the 4.4 percent unemployment rate first reached in late 2006 came at the tail end of a large house price bubble.[18]
- Federal Reserve policy actions also appear to influence risk pricing. If we believe Bernanke and Kuttner (2005) – who seem not to fully believe it themselves – policy shocks affect equity prices by affecting risk premia rather than future real rates or dividends. Outside of equity prices, we would expect to see effects on spreads and term premia.[19]
- Although our examination of aggregate demand in Chapter 3 found little role for interest rates in determining business investment, residential investment is very responsive to mortgage rates. In addition, the rates charged on auto loans are often tied to interest rates a few years out along the yield curve.
- Even if interest rates per se are not very material for spending decisions, policy actions can lead to changes in the amount of credit rationing faced by bank-dependent borrowers.[20] So-called credit crunches are an extreme example of this phenomenon.
- Finally, monetary policy can affect the exchange rate. Over the first half of the 1980s, relatively tight monetary policy led to a large appreciation

---

[17] When a bubble bursts, the central bank can also work with other parts of the government to socialize the losses of the financial sector.

[18] There are always instances of mispricing in asset markets; however, given the inequities in wealth and income distribution in the United States and the size of wealth effects on spending, bubbles need to be broad-based and large to have much effect on aggregate demand.

[19] Over a longer span of time, the reduction and concomitant stability in inflation's long-run mean likely also contributed to a reduction in term premia.

[20] This includes small- and medium-sized businesses, who finance their operations with bank loans (and credit cards).

in the real dollar exchange rate, with predictable effects on US net exports.

The first and second channels are an unfortunate consequence of the fact that monetary policy operates through financial markets. But their importance is disconcerting nonetheless. Keynes once pointed out that when the capital development of a country becomes a by-product of the activities of a casino, the job is likely to be ill-done.[21] Likewise, if the way the central bank stabilizes output and inflation essentially involves manipulating the odds at that casino in favor of one set of gamblers or another, monetary policy isn't likely to cover itself in glory either.

For those few spending categories that are influenced by interest rates, it's unclear whether it's real or nominal rates that matter to first order. And even if we think real rates are more important, the inflation rate that's relevant won't be the same for every group. A household deciding whether to take out a mortgage (or a car loan) is likely more concerned with expected future wage increases than with future consumer price inflation – it's only in simple models that the two are (implicitly) assumed to run at the same pace. Similarly, the ability of a business to pay its creditors is more related to changes in its selling price than to changes in a measure of consumer prices. Nominal rates also affect debt servicing costs (and hence cashflow) for businesses and households, while increases in interest rates can *contribute* to cashflow by raising interest income for rentier households.

The way that monetary policy influences inflation follows from its effects on aggregate demand and the exchange rate. A rise in the exchange value of the dollar can put downward pressure on prices for imported goods, which (as we saw in Chapter 6) helps to restrain domestic consumer price inflation by reducing the growth of imported input costs and of imported consumer goods prices. Placing sufficient restraint on the growth of aggregate demand results in people's being thrown out of work or prevented from finding work, which raises the unemployment rate and lowers compensation growth and (to a lesser extent) price inflation.[22] In principle, the increase in product-market slack can also cause price–cost margins to narrow, though it's difficult to ascertain whether and to what degree this actually happens: In the three recessions the economy endured prior to 2020, the nonfinancial

---

[21] Keynes (1936, p. 159).

[22] If it strikes you as more than a little perverse that economic policy should sometimes actively seek to increase unemployment and reduce wage growth, that's because it is. (It also hints that something isn't quite right with how our society is organized.)

corporate profit share started declining at or before the date when the unemployment rate reached its low point for the cycle.[23]

7.2 Monetary Policy in Theory

The 2003 publication of Michael Woodford's magnum opus *Interest and Prices* represents the culmination of the attempt to integrate rational expectations into a description of monetary policy that seemed to comport reasonably well with reality.[24] Although each of the three main elements of Woodford's intertemporal equilibrium framework – the new-Keynesian Phillips curve, the expectational IS curve, and the Taylor rule – are analytically and empirically deficient, it's fair to say that some version of a three-equation new-Keynesian model permeates the thinking of many (not all) contemporary macroeconomists in the same way that the IS/LM model organized the thoughts of past generations. In addition, something like Woodford's framework lies at the core of most DSGE models, which assume nominal rigidities that allow monetary policy actions to have purchase on the real economy; optimizing behavior and rational expectations on the part of households and firms; and a policy rule that describes the monetary authority's reaction function.[25]

Ironically, the shortcomings of the first iteration of the new-Keynesian model of monetary policy were exposed by the biggest challenge to monetary policy since the Great Depression: the global financial crisis. Starting in 2009, the federal funds rate hit its zero lower bound, leaving conventional monetary policy impotent.[26] Although Eggertsson and Woodford (2003) had already used a new-Keynesian framework to analyze policy options in this situation (the catalyst was Japan's experience after its "bubble economy" ended), their policy recommendation – the use of a price *level* target to reduce expected real short rates – was viewed as a bit too model-dependent to be taken seriously. (At a minimum, it was seen as something that needed

---

[23] Nekarda and Ramey (2020) find that various aggregate proxies for the markup of prices over marginal costs decline following a negative aggregate demand shock. There's less evidence of such a pattern in gross margins for the wholesale and retail trade sectors (as measured by the PPI), but the history of those series is extremely short.

[24] Early drafts of Woodford's manuscript were circulating before the mid-1990s, so the book's influence well predates its 2003 publication. (Important technical way stations included Yun, 1996 and Kimball, 1995.)

[25] I am told that in Europe, the three-equation new-Keynesian model is called the "Galí model." (Go back and re-read footnote 24.)

[26] Those IS/LM folks I mentioned used to call this a *liquidity trap* (look it up).

to be in place – and have an established track record – well before the zero lower bound was hit.) In addition, that same analysis predicted that the sorts of quantitative easing actions that the Fed eventually turned to would have no effect on spending: Unless quantitative easing involved a change in the Fed's policy rule (or the path of total government debt), households would have no reason to expect a different sequence of future short-term interest rates, which meant that their spending wouldn't change. Under these circumstances, then, neither the quantity or composition of asset purchases by the central bank would have (much) influence on real activity or inflation.[27] These impractical features of the model made it less appealing as a guide to policy.

Relatively simple versions of the new-Keynesian model also made predictions about the effects of forward guidance (announcements about future policy by the central bank) that were difficult to believe because they were exceptionally large. This "forward guidance puzzle," as Del Negro et al. (2012) labelled it, reflected the forward-looking nature of the model: Pegging the policy rate at a lower level for a specified period of time would immediately raise spending (given the expectational IS equation) and therefore inflation (given the new-Keynesian Phillips curve). That increase in inflation would further reduce real interest rates, leading to another increase in spending, more inflation, and so on. Under a standard calibration of the model, the result was a massive and nearly immediate rise in output that was far larger than any empirical estimates of the actual effect of forward guidance.[28]

The solutions to the forward-guidance puzzle that were initially proposed involved reducing the effective horizon of the agents in the economy (which made the future less relevant), or relaxing strict rational expectations.[29] However, the modification to the basic new-Keynesian model that seems to have gained the most traction at present involves the introduction of heterogeneity among households; the way that this is done reduces the

---

[27] A pure "helicopter drop" of money wouldn't work either, unless it implied a change in the policy rule. In addition, because the optimal rate of inflation is zero in these models, the central bank wouldn't be able to credibly commit to a positive inflation target.

[28] These results obtained even for a peg that implied a relatively small reduction in rates relative to what the regular policy rule would dictate (on the order of a dozen basis points), held over a relatively short period (a couple of years).

[29] When fully worked through, the latter proposal revealed that the canonical new-Keynesian model's results depended so crucially on the exact way in which expectations were formed that the model had essentially no predictive power (this is the basic message of García-Schmidt and Woodford, 2019).

importance of the intertemporal substitution channel (in the standard framework, this channel dominates because consumption is described by a permanent-income model), and increases the dependence of spending on income (similar to an old-Keynesian expenditure multiplier). Although the notion seems reasonable in the abstract, these "heterogeneous agent new-Keynesian" models also turn out to have various properties that make them useless as a guide for policy.

The first deficiency is one that was discussed in Chapter 3: At the heart of these models is an extremely complex intertemporal consumption problem that is intractable for a real-world individual to solve, and that also can't be solved well approximately or with a rule of thumb.[30] The models also use the theoretically and empirically questionable new-Keynesian Phillips curve to describe inflation (naturally). A more serious problem, however, is that the effect of a monetary expansion in these models hinges on what fiscal policy does – for example, if the government keeps its tax rates, transfers, and expenditures fixed following a monetary shock and just lets its debt adjust (which would seem to be a not-unrealistic case), the effect of the monetary policy action is sharply reduced (Kaplan, Moll, and Violante, 2018). Finally, the forward-guidance puzzle can't really be solved by the heterogeneous-agent framework unless one is willing to sacrifice the model's key element (the amplification of shocks through the heightened dependence of spending on income); to assume that the central bank follows a policy of price-level targeting; or to assume that the income distribution and a model-specific measure of risk co-move over the business cycle in a particular (and contrived) manner (Bilbiie, 2021).[31] None of these features makes one overly confident in the model's predictions.

The conclusion we're led to is that new-Keynesian models are not suitable for informing the conduct of monetary policy or for understanding its effects. Although the models meet the primary desideratum of a mainstream macroeconomic model – namely, they can generate precise predictions – those predictions depend on assumptions about economic behavior, expectations formation, and the nature of the monetary transmission mechanism that neither characterize reality nor receive strong empirical support.

---

[30] Specifically, household consumption is modelled using the sort of borrowing constraint-precautionary saving setup that yields a concave consumption function; this element is needed to obtain sufficiently large MPCs, which happens because a large share of consumers are on the consumption-equals-income part of the function.

[31] The exact way in which profits are distributed to households also affects the predictions of these models.

(The models also fail to deal seriously with the stability problem that any equilibrium model faces, though here that issue is even more of a problem because the models rely on rational expectations to select and characterize that equilibrium.) And while it is possible to incorporate additional elements that temper the models' more bizarre predictions, we should be extremely skeptical about a research project that involves adding more and more epicycles to a framework until we're satisfied that its conclusions are no longer silly – especially when those additions are themselves not very believable.

We should be equally wary of the estimated DSGE models that are derived from the new-Keynesian framework (or any other equilibrium approach). Imposing the restrictions implied by an incredible theory on a set of estimated difference equations is neither a test of the theory nor a guarantee that the resulting empirical model will be able to correctly predict the effects of a policy intervention. In particular, since empirical DSGE models allow for a sufficiently broad range of residuals and unobservables to allow them to fit the data (after a fashion), these models are no more structural – and possibly less reliable – than the large-scale macroeconometric models that they sought to replace. In fact, using these models is arguably worse than using nothing: Besides providing a false sense of precision, another detrimental side effect of the new-Keynesian framework has been to encourage monetary policymakers to focus on expectations management and credibility, which has in turn led them to place too much stock in how financial markets perceive their policy actions.

How, then, should monetary policy proceed in the absence of any sound empirical or theoretical guides? Very carefully. One of the best general lessons about economic policy was given by William Brainard in the 1960s: He pointed out that if you didn't know with certainty what effect a policy action will have, then you shouldn't set policy the same way you would if you did.[32] The practical implications are obvious, though often ignored.

7.3 Digression: Reasons to Be Skeptical about "R-Star"

Another downside of the new-Keynesian approach to monetary policy has been the emergence of yet another unobservable policy benchmark, this one known as "R-star." The idea is that R-star gives the level of the real policy rate that is consistent with zero monetary stimulus; typically, it is defined as the level of the real funds rate that would be consistent with a zero

---

[32] Brainard (1967).

output gap along with a stable rate of inflation (absent any other shocks).[33] In theory, R-star reflects real features of the economy, such as trend productivity growth and the amount of output that the government is preventing from entering household consumption. But, because it is unobservable, it is typically estimated using a statistical filter that tries to infer its value from a set of other macro time series.[34]

Simply thinking about the monetary transmission process reveals why the R-star concept has no practical relevance. Consider the various ways in which a change in the short-term policy rate feeds through to the asset prices that matter for real activity:

- *Equity prices*: The Fed appears to influence equity prices mainly by affecting risk premia (Bernanke and Kuttner, 2005); the effect it has on these premia, however, will depend on the current and prospective state of the economy.
- *Long rates*: Long-term Treasury yields will reflect the expected sequence of future short rates (not just the short rate's current level), plus a (time-varying) term premium. For mortgage rates, the MBS spread over Treasuries along with the primary–secondary spread will reflect market-specific conditions, resulting in a further (time-varying) disconnect between this rate and the Fed's policy rate.[35]
- *Exchange rates*: Once again, exchange rates will depend on expectations of future monetary policy, as well as what policy is doing (and expected to do) in *other* countries.

All of these factors drive wedges between the policy rate and the rates and asset prices that influence spending, production, and employment, and none of them is likely to have a well-defined "equilibrium" or long-run value that would emerge when the economy is at potential – not just because they can

---

[33] See Laubach and Williams (2003). Another definition of R-star that can be defined in the context of a macro model is the real policy rate that, if maintained, would achieve a zero output gap over some specified number of quarters.

[34] R-star can also be backed out from an empirical DSGE model. In the simple new-Keynesian framework, it is the rate of interest that is consistent with output's being at its "natural rate," defined as the level of output that would prevail under fully flexible prices. Hence, it can also be thought of as the equilibrium rate of return that would obtain if prices were fully flexible (Woodford, 2003, p. 248) – sticky prices being the only thing that prevents the output gap from always being closed in these models.

[35] MBS stands for mortgage-backed security; it is a claim to the income generated from a pool of mortgage loans. The primary–secondary spread is the difference between the mortgage rate that a borrower pays and the yield on new MBS issues (that is, the rate in the "primary" mortgage market – lenders to borrowers – and the yield that the securitized loans receive when they are bundled into an MBS and sold on the secondary market).

be path dependent, but also because they can depend on the expected future state of the domestic (and world) economy.[36] These factors also aren't tied down solely by real-side variables, but will depend on conditions in specific asset markets, including the state of market participants' expectations, as well as by the characteristics of inflation's long-run mean. Hence, the same value of the policy rate can be expansionary or contractionary under some circumstances, and neutral in others – again in ways that won't be captured simply by looking at the current level of output (or its rate of growth) relative to some estimate of potential. And in practical terms, expecting a statistical filter to correctly disentangle all of these channels – especially in real time, but even with the benefit of hindsight – is expecting way too much from a very blunt instrument.

---

[36] This is the same shoal on which the IS/LM model founders: We can't characterize the IS curve in terms of a single interest rate without making some very special assumptions. (We also can't derive the model rigorously without assuming the economy is in a state of excess supply, but that's a separate matter.)

8

What Does Fiscal Policy Do?

[P]olitics is the entertainment branch of industry, and government is what we need.
Frank Zappa

Just as the Volcker recessions of the early 1980s provided a convincing empirical demonstration that monetary policy could, in fact, affect economic activity, the actions taken to deal with the economic fallout of the COVID-19 pandemic showed that fiscal policy can too. Unfortunately – and as was also the case for monetary policy – the modern theoretical approaches that macroeconomists have used to think about fiscal policy aren't all that helpful, while the estimates from the empirical literature imply a range of effects that is uncomfortably large. (By now, though, we're used to that sort of thing.)

A basic question about fiscal policy is what sort of private-sector response it calls forth. For concreteness, let's consider the effect of an increase in government purchases. On the one hand, neoclassical theory argues that under most circumstances such a policy action will result in an increase in output that is much less than one-for-one; canonical new-Keynesian models are similar (though in those models the central bank also helps to curtail the output response). Old-Keynesian theories, by contrast, claim that an expansionary fiscal policy action will typically induce a private-sector reaction that *amplifies* the effect that the original impulse has on output. This amplification mechanism is known as an expenditure (or demand) multiplier; it is a concept that continues to be used within policy institutions for forecasting and modelling, though without much explicit theoretical grounding. Nevertheless, there is a useful but unfashionable way to think about the multiplier that takes the neoclassical model as a point of departure, and that can help us speculate as to when an expenditure multiplier is more or less likely to be present; it is worth spending some time on because it is relatively well grounded in a conventional macroeconomic framework and shows how minimal deviations from the Walrasian market-clearing paradigm can quickly land us in recognizably Keynesian territory. In addition to the propagation mechanism for changes in fiscal policy, we'll also look at how we might measure fiscal policy's *stance* – that is, the direct contribution of a policy action to aggregate demand – though here it will be necessary to apply some judgment regarding likely private-sector responses.

Over the longer run, other questions about fiscal policy become relevant, including fiscal sustainability, fiscal dominance, and the effects of government debt on capital formation. Additionally, an important practical question is how to manage government debt; in other words, what is the "best" mix of short-, medium-, and long-term debt to issue. We won't have anything to say about the first three questions, which aren't (yet) especially relevant for the United States. The last question has generated a reasonably large amount of research (which we'll review briefly), but almost none of it turns out to be useful.

Finally, a caveat is appropriate before we begin. Among economists, how one views the effects and efficacy of fiscal policy tends to be shaped by one's position on the proper role of government in society. In the interest of full disclosure, my own position is that there is far more truth than error in traditional Keynesian analyses of this topic, and that Kalecki (1943) was mostly right too. Consider yourself warned.

8.1 The Multiplier Perplex

In a standard market-clearing macro model, the decisions of producers and consumers are perfectly coordinated by spot and intertemporal prices. In older models of this type, the way this occurs is through the effect that the price level has on real wealth (and hence on consumption demand and labor supply), and the effect that the real wage has on production and labor demand. Let's look at a relatively transparent example of such a model, and see whether and how it can be made to yield a Keynesian-style expenditure multiplier.[1]

We assume a high level of aggregation with only two private markets: one for labor, and one for goods; the model also assumes continuous time.[2]

---

[1] The following discussion draws heavily from chapters 1 and 2 of Barro and Grossman (1976).
[2] This is essentially a simplified version of the model worked out by Patinkin (1965). More complicated versions allow for saving through capital formation and government debt that

The aggregate supply and demand schedules for labor and goods take the following form:

Labor market:
$$l^s\left(\frac{M}{p},\frac{w}{p}\right)=l^d\left(\frac{w}{p}\right) \qquad (8.1)$$
$$\underset{(-)\ (+)}{} \qquad \underset{(-)}{}$$

Goods market:
$$y^s\left(\frac{w}{p}\right)=c^d\left(\frac{M}{p},\frac{w}{p}\right)+g,$$
$$\underset{(-)}{} \qquad \underset{(+)\ (+)}{}$$

where the signs of the partials are indicated below each argument. (These can be explicitly derived from a continuous-time intertemporal optimization problem.) Here, $\frac{w}{p}$ denotes the real wage (so the money wage rate is w and the price level is p); assuming other factors are in fixed supply, then the usual profit-maximizing behavior of firms makes the supply of output y^s and demand for labor l^d decreasing functions of the real wage. Labor supply l^s and consumption demand c^d are increasing functions of the real wage (where labor supply and the real wage are concerned, we assume substitution effects dominate). They are also affected by real money balances (the only asset in the model), with an increase in $\frac{M}{p}$ reducing labor supply – leisure is a normal good – and raising consumption demand. Finally, g denotes real government purchases, which we assume are financed by increases in the real money stock.[3]

Figure 8.1 plots the market-clearing conditions with real money balances on the x-axis and the real wage on the y-axis. The labor-market-clearing locus slopes up: If we are on the locus and real wages rise, labor demand falls while labor supply increases. In order to restore labor market clearing, we need to reduce labor supply, which will occur if real money balances increase. Likewise, the goods-market-clearing locus slopes down: If we are on the locus and real wages go up, consumption demand rises while output supply declines; goods market clearing is then restored by a reduction in real money balances that is sufficient to bring consumption demand back into line with output. Both markets clear at the point where the two curves intersect; at this intersection, the price level is such that real money balances imply a level of real wealth $\frac{M}{p^*}$ and the nominal wage w (given this price level) yields the real wage $(\frac{w}{p})^*$.

---

receives a positive interest rate (Sargent, 1987, chapter 1), but the results are basically the same.

[3] The model can be easily extended to include taxes and profit income, but those extensions aren't needed to illustrate its key features.

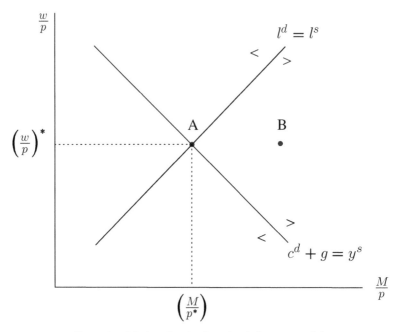

Figure 8.1 Market clearing in a classical macromodel.

The inequality signs give the state of excess demand or supply that obtains for a given market when the price level and the real wage are not equal to their market-clearing values. For example, at point B there would be excess demand in the labor market: At this level of real money balances, the real wage is below what would be needed to place us on the $l^d = l^s$ locus, so desired labor demand is higher than desired labor supply. There would also be excess demand in the goods market at point B: At this level of the real wage, real money balances (real household wealth holdings) are above the level that would leave us on the $c^d + g = y^s$ locus, so desired consumption demand is higher than current production. In the classical model, the way this situation is rectified is for the price level to jump, with a proportional increase in the nominal wage that keeps the real wage fixed. The resulting reduction in real wealth raises labor supply (reduces leisure) and reduces consumption until the market-clearing point A is restored.[4]

Now let's say that the government increase their flow of real purchases g, financing the increase by raising the rate of increase of the (real) money

---

[4] As we saw in Chapter 2, the real balance or real wealth effect might not be strong enough to restore market clearing even if prices are completely flexible.

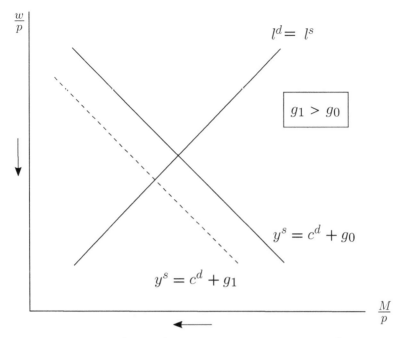

Figure 8.2 Crowding out from an increase in government purchases.

stock.[5] The effect of this would be to shift the $c^d + g = y^s$ locus inward, as shown in Figure 8.2. In order to meet the government's increased demand for goods, we need to reduce consumption demand and increase labor supply; for a given real wage, this can be achieved by reducing real money balances (the reduction in real household wealth holdings reduces consumption and leisure). The new point at which both markets clear involves a lower real wage and lower real money balances, with the latter occurring through a higher price level; the lower real wage increases production and labor demand and lowers consumption, and the reduction in real wealth from the higher price level increases labor supply and further lowers consumption. The effect of the increase in government purchases is therefore to raise the price level; in addition, because only part of the increase in g is met with higher production (the rest is met by crowding out private spending), the total rise in output is less than the increase in g and the "multiplier" is less than one. This last point is easy to see directly if utility is separable in consumption and leisure (that is, in hours worked h):

[5] That is, the government raise $\dot{M}/p$; in this continuous-time setup, M is initially unchanged.

$$U = u(c) - v(h), \tag{8.2}$$

where $u(\cdot)$ is concave and $v(\cdot)$ is convex. Under these assumptions, the household's first-order condition is:

$$\frac{w}{p} = \frac{v'(h)}{u'(c)}. \tag{8.3}$$

We therefore can't have an increase in output that is large enough to fully meet the rise in g and keep c fixed: Diminishing returns in production require the real wage to fall, while hours worked (and hence v') increase, so the only way to maintain the equality is to lower c (and raise u'). Essentially the same mechanism is at work in other variants of the (neo)classical model: The government's claim on private-sector resources makes workers poorer and induces them to work more and consume less, so some crowding out of private spending occurs. Things get even worse when distortionary taxes are used to finance the spending; in this case, the multiplier can even be *negative*.[6]

However, as Clower (1965) first pointed out, things change in an important way when markets fail to clear. If households and firms face constraints on what they can buy and sell in one market, it will affect how much they demand or supply in other markets. In particular, if workers can't find as much employment as they would like (so there is "excess supply" in the labor market), it will influence what they demand in the goods market. Likewise, if current levels of wages and prices imply that a given quantity of output can be sold at a profit, firms might nevertheless decide to produce less than that amount if they don't think they would be able to sell it all. And that constraint on sales in the goods market ends up being felt in the labor market, as firms will need fewer workers as a result.

The idea here is that when markets don't clear, agents' *effective* demands and supplies – the amounts they are actually willing to transact – need not be the same as their *notional* or Walrasian demands and supplies, as the latter are only relevant under full market clearing. Formally, when markets clear and agents are able to make whatever transactions they would like at going prices, demands and supplies only depend on market prices because quantity variables (like labor supply or output) are "optimized out." But when markets don't clear and transactions are restricted, the constraints imposed

---

[6] See Ramey (2011) for a useful overview of the literature. Ramey also cites results from models with capital in which the long-run multiplier can be (slightly) greater than one for a permanent increase in g financed by lump-sum taxes, though the short-run multiplier is still less than one.

on those transactions reappear as quantity terms in the effective demand and supply functions.

In particular, when there is excess supply in the labor and goods markets – conditions that typically emerge in a recession – firms and households will need to take into account that they might not be able to sell all of their output or work as much as they want, and this will affect their labor and consumption demand. For example, say that firms would find it profitable to produce an amount y^s at the going real wage rate *if* they were in fact able to sell it. If they don't think they will be able to sell the full amount – for example, if they think that demand for their output has fallen to a level $y < y^s$, then they will produce only this much and adjust their labor demand accordingly. Put differently, the sales constraint firms face on the goods market affects their behavior on the labor market, leading to an "effective" labor demand schedule $\widetilde{l^d}$:

$$\widetilde{l^d} = \widetilde{l^d}(y) = l, \tag{8.4}$$
$$\underset{(+)}{}$$

where l is the amount actually transacted (recall that we have excess supply in the labor market, so employment is demand-determined). It is this labor demand schedule, not the Walrasian labor demand function $l^d(\frac{w}{p})$, that firms bring to the labor market. And so long as the real wage doesn't rise to the point where the Walrasian output supply would be *less* than y, changes in the real wage have no effect on firms' labor demand.

With excess supply on the labor market, households view $l < l^s(\frac{w}{p})$ as a constraint on the amount they can work, and therefore on their labor income. Their effective consumption demand will then be:

$$\widetilde{c^d} = \widetilde{c^d}\left(\frac{M}{p}, \ l \ , \ \frac{w}{p} \right), \tag{8.5}$$
$$\quad\quad\underset{(+)}{} \ \underset{(+)}{} \ \underset{(+)}{}$$

where we can replace l with y because labor demand is tied to actual production.[7] Under conditions of excess supply, then, output is determined as

$$y = \widetilde{c^d}\left(\frac{M}{p}, \ y \ , \ \frac{w}{p} \right) + g. \tag{8.6}$$
$$\quad\quad\underset{(+)}{} \ \underset{(+)}{} \ \underset{(+)}{}$$

Totally differentiating Equation (8.6) and combining terms so that dy is on the left-hand side gives us

---

[7] For an alternative derivation using the standard tools of intertemporal consumer choice theory, see Deaton and Muellbauer (1980), sections 4.2 and 12.1.

$$dy = \frac{1}{1 - \tilde{c}'_y} \left(\tilde{c}'_1 \, d\left(\frac{M}{p}\right) + \tilde{c}'_3 \, d\left(\frac{w}{p}\right) + dg \right), \qquad (8.7)$$

where $1/(1 - \tilde{c}'_y)$ is the usual Keynesian expenditure (demand) multiplier.[8] In a situation of general excess supply, an increase in the effective demand for goods – induced in this particular model by an increase in real money balances, the real wage, or government purchases – relaxes the sales constraint faced by firms.[9] This leads firms to produce and hire more, which in turn relaxes the constraint households face on the labor market and results in an additional increment to effective demand, a further easing of the sales constraint, and so on until the process converges.[10]

The non-market-clearing approach can be used to analyze other situations, such as one where there is excess supply in one market but the other market clears; or when both markets are in a state of excess *demand*. That former case corresponds to the traditional AS/AD model, in which the goods market is assumed to clear but a fixed (and too high) nominal wage results in excess supply in the labor market.[11]

In the *latter* case – excess demand in *both* markets – rationing on the goods market leads households to supply less labor as they make up for their inability to satisfy their demand for goods by reducing their labor supply (consuming more leisure) and saving more (consuming more future consumption). Correspondingly, firms' production is constrained by the amount of labor they can hire, rather than the amount they think they can sell. Under these circumstances, a *supply* multiplier can emerge: If (say) the government reduces its purchases and frees up output for use by households, they will reduce their consumption of leisure and work more, thereby kicking off a cumulative process in which additional labor supply results in additional production that yields more consumption goods, resulting in a further increase in labor supply, another increase in production, and so on.[12]

---

[8] Using consistent notation, $\tilde{c}'_y = \tilde{c}'_2$.

[9] More generally, it would occur following any change in "autonomous" spending, defined as a change in aggregate spending that is unrelated to changes in income.

[10] It's worth noting that general excess supply can be present in this model even if the real wage is at the level that would be consistent with general market clearing. All that is needed is for the price level (and *nominal* wage rate) to be "too high," which depresses demand for goods and leaves firms off of their Walrasian labor demand curves.

[11] The model can also be extended to include capital investment and additional financial assets besides money, in which case something very much like an IS/LM framework emerges under conditions of general excess supply.

[12] It is tempting to interpret the period that followed the pandemic-induced recession in these terms; however, the shortfall in labor supply over that period likely instead reflected a desire

Despite being reasonably well grounded in choice-theoretic microeconomics, the non-market-clearing approach never really caught on in the United States (it had slightly better luck in Europe – see Bénassy, 1982, 1993 and the collection of papers in Drèze, 1991). One major reason was that two of its American proponents repudiated their own work in the same decade that it appeared, largely because they were uneasy that the theory did not explain *why* markets would fail to clear, but instead simply assumed that wages and prices were "stuck" at non-market-clearing levels.[13] Traditional and post-Keynesians also found little to like about the approach, as they saw it as either saying little that was new (relative to the *General Theory*) or as being too grounded in the Walrasian paradigm to be useful.[14] And serious general-equilibrium types found the whole thing kind of sloppy.[15] Finally, the rise of new-Keynesian economics – which simply assumed rational expectations and optimization subject to particular assumptions about price and wage setting – gave reasonable people an alternative to equilibrium business cycle theory (that is, real business cycle models), and the non-market-clearing approach was left behind.

There are good reasons to be skeptical about how the non-market-clearing approach is formalized. First, it's the usual representative-agent-with-a-production-function folderol. Second, by using the Walrasian model as a point of departure, it immediately runs into Fisher's stability critique – specifically, neither the Walrasian or the non-Walrasian equilibria in the model are shown to be stable, and there's also no discussion of what would tie down the process that would take us to them and keep us at them.[16] That said, the presence of perceived constraints on employment and sales in labor and product markets is certainly something that we would expect

---

for self-preservation rather than an inability to acquire market goods (the latter might explain a portion of the rise in saving over that period, though). In addition, Malinvaud (1977) tried to explain the 1970s stagflation in these terms; as we saw in Chapter 6, though, there are simpler explanations (at least where the US experience is concerned). Probably the only place we might actually find evidence of general excess *demand* would be in command economies such as the former Soviet Union; for two attempts to do so, see Howard (1976) and Portes and Winter (1980).

[13] See Barro (1979) and Grossman (1979). The reason for the change of heart was that neither author found it a priori plausible that agents would fail to realize potential gains from trade (preferring an alternative explanation of unemployment as the result of optimal risk sharing); Barro also viewed the approach as making government policy activism "too easy to justify."

[14] See Tobin (1993) and Rogers (1983).

[15] Grandmont (1977).

[16] See Hahn (1978), who points out that things are even worse for the standard general equilibrium model; also Hahn (1982).

to be present when the economy is in a recession. The obvious fact is that these markets don't always clear, so we need a way of thinking about how households and firms will behave under those circumstances. And as we saw in Chapter 2, there are a number of reasons *besides* the presence of sticky prices and wages in spot markets that could cause the economy to coordinate activity at a lower-than-feasible level.

So if the formalization is questionable, why bother with it – or with any of this history-of-thought stuff? Because the non-market-clearing approach to thinking about the multiplier seems to capture an important insight that's completely absent from today's more modern models. In order for a Keynesian demand multiplier to exist, two elements have to be present: Aggregate spending needs to change in response to changes in current income, and producers need to be willing (and able) to increase production and hiring when additional spending shows up at their doors. As we discussed in earlier chapters, both elements appear to be evident in the data, but received theory does a rather poor job modelling them convincingly.

In particular, we saw in Chapter 3 that part of the inability to capture the first element comes from forcing households to be permanent-income consumers, which mostly kills off the dependence of consumption spending on current income. As we also saw, attempts to remedy this flaw usually involve figuring out a way to introduce "hand-to-mouth" consumers and have them be responsible for a nontrivial fraction of consumer spending (those heterogenous agent new-Keynesian models), or by simply assuming the existence of a group of "rule-of-thumb" consumers for whom spending depends on income (which begs the question of why a Keynesian consumption function wasn't just assumed in the first place). Alternatively, we could take a different approach and structure the model so that households are able to be duped into thinking that a transitory productivity shock represents an innovation to their permanent income.[17] If one insists on using a permanent-income framework, a mechanism like this one is no doubt useful – though it probably isn't the reason why a worker who loses their job (or expects they might) would tend to respond by curtailing their current spending. On the production side, the assumed nature of contracts in new-Keynesian models requires individuals to supply as much labor as is demanded at the contracted wage, and for businesses to supply as much output at the contracted price; neither assumption seems terribly realistic or consistent with the principle of voluntary exchange. Finally, because it is

---

[17] Recall Angeletos and Lian (2022).

basically an RBC model with sticky prices and wages, the canonical new-Keynesian model delivers something like a standard expenditure multiplier only in very special circumstances.[18]

The non-market-clearing approach also suggests how the size of the multiplier might change as economic conditions do. To the extent that it reflects perceived sales and employment constraints, the multiplier should start to attenuate as the economy returns to a state of high employment, especially when the economy is expected to remain in that state for the foreseeable future. Under those conditions, most households will expect to find work (or remain employed) and most firms will expect to sell their output, implying that the multiplier mechanism will no longer be a feature of the economic landscape. That probably happens infrequently enough that some sort of multiplier mechanism is present "on average." Of course, whether the multiplier would drop below one if the economy were held at high employment for a prolonged period is anyone's guess: The neoclassical macro framework has so many dubious elements that it might remain a poor predictor of economic behavior even when the economy starts to resemble the idealized world it was designed to explain.

8.2 Empirical Evidence on the Multiplier

So far, we have been proceeding in the worst way possible – namely, without any reference to the empirical evidence. Just as for monetary policy shocks, there is a large literature on identifying and measuring the effects of government spending shocks. What does it say about the existence and likely magnitude of an expenditure multiplier?

As always, the results are all over the place and difficult to interpret, partly because researchers have measured the multiplier in different ways that are often incompatible. In addition, some of the same problems that arise in measuring the effects of monetary policy shocks (such as anticipation effects and issues related to exogeneity) also hamper attempts to measure the effect of a fiscal policy shock, especially in VAR-based studies. Finally, the endogenous response of monetary policy to output and inflation presents a further

---

[18] As Woodford (2011) details, a multiplier greater than one can occur when the economy is persistently at the zero lower bound, or if highly artificial assumptions are made about household preferences. In addition, the increase in government purchases needs to be temporary: In the new-Keynesian model, consumer spending is a forward-looking function of expected real rates and a long-run consumption level; persistent increases in government purchases imply a lower long-run consumption level that therefore reduces today's consumption.

confounding factor: Ideally, we would like to have an estimate of the expenditure multiplier holding the stance of monetary policy fixed; in practice there's no way to do this – even in a fully specified model – for the same reason that we couldn't believably shut down the response of monetary policy to other sorts of shocks.

In a comprehensive survey of the empirical literature, Ramey (2011) concludes that "… the range of plausible estimates for the multiplier in the case of a temporary increase in government spending that is deficit financed is probably 0.8 to 1.5," and that "[r]easonable people could argue that the multiplier is 0.5 or 2.0 without being contradicted by the data." Both this paper and Ramey (2016) also discuss evidence for state dependence of the multiplier. Here, things are murkier: Auerbach and Gorodnichenko (2012) find that the multiplier for government purchases is larger in recessions than in expansions, while Ramey and Zubairy (2018) argue that those results are not robust to changes in the methodology used to estimate the multipliers.

The simple multiplier estimate of 1.4 that we came up with in Section 3.8 falls within the "plausible" range (though near its upper bound); if we don't mind straining credulity a little, we can probably view this figure as being closer to an estimate of the multiplier holding the response of monetary policy fixed. In addition, comparing estimates from Ramey and Zubairy (2018) – which likely do reflect endogenous monetary policy responses in most periods – to those obtained from runs of the Federal Reserve's large macroeconometric model (FRB/US) under a Taylor-type rule reveals a surprising (and likely coincidental) similarity between the two; see Table 8.1.[19] That doesn't prove a multiplier is present, but it does indicate that a model that explicitly incorporates a multiplier mechanism is consistent with the empirical evidence; it also provides a rough idea of the order of magnitude of the likely monetary policy offset.[20]

---

[19] The Ramey and Zubairy (2018) estimates are taken from table 2 of the paper's supplemental appendix, which allows a direct comparison with the shock used for the FRB/US simulation (an increase in government purchases equal to one percent of GDP). The three-year integral shown for the Ramey–Zubairy estimates is the average of the two- and four-year values (the FRB/US runs only extend out three years).

[20] Spending depends on income or output through several channels in the FRB/US model, including an estimated portion of households who consume out of current income, but the model's main spending components error-correct reasonably quickly toward long-run targets. Absent a monetary policy response, the expenditure multiplier in the FRB/US model is about 1.2; under the assumed Taylor-type rule, the increase in government purchases induces a rise in the federal funds rate equal to 65 basis points after two years. (The model's documentation and code are publicly available on the Federal Reserve's website; I used the 2018 vintage of the model for these results.)

Table 8.1 *Comparing government spending multipliers*

	Ramey–Zubairy (2018)		
	News shock	Blanchard–Perotti	FRB/US
Two-year integral	0.76	0.54	0.88
Three-year integral	0.80	0.66	0.85

Note: Three-year integral multipliers imputed from table 2 of the supplemental appendix to Ramey and Zubairy (2018).

Estimates of tax multipliers are harder to compare, since the experiment often involves a shock to the tax *rate* (for example, a one percentage point increase in the personal tax rate) rather than to the value of tax *payments*. A meta-analysis by Gechert (2015) finds that for the sample of models that are fully estimated (not calibrated), the tax and transfer multipliers are smaller than spending multipliers, but the difference is only statistically significant for the subsample of VAR models (in addition, the studies used for the analysis involve various countries). For studies that use US data, Ramey (2016, p. 135) concludes that existing estimation methods are too lacking in precision and robustness to make such a comparison.

We're therefore left with a few bits of evidence that an expenditure multiplier is present in the US economy, and that its value is probably not too different to the value that was implied by the simple spending equations of Chapter 3. We have little evidence as to whether the multiplier is state dependent, though the estimates from time-series studies are likely not representative of sustained high-employment periods (those being a relatively small portion of the sample), and it is in these periods that we might expect to find an attenuated multiplier. The endogenous response of monetary policy probably also attenuates the expenditure multiplier and pushes it below one under most circumstances. Finally, tax and transfer multipliers might or might not be smaller than expenditure multipliers; if they *were* smaller, it would comport with the estimated spending equations since a change in disposable income receives a coefficient in the consumption equation that is much smaller than one. (Regarding transfers, it's still possible that the actual propensity to consume out of transfer income might be higher, since under normal circumstances transfers only represent about 15–20 percent of total disposable income.)

8.3 Measuring Fiscal Stance

Can we come up with an indicator of the overall stance of fiscal policy (ideally from both federal as well as state and local governments) that could serve as a measure of the direct *impulse* that is currently being imparted to the economy by government expenditures, transfers, and taxes? One candidate that is sometimes suggested is a measure of the high-employment budget deficit; in other words, what the government's deficit would be if the economy were at full employment. The purpose of such a measure is to control for the sensitivity of the deficit to economic conditions; this sensitivity largely arises from so-called automatic stabilizers that act to offset income losses during an economic downturn without requiring a change in discretionary fiscal policy (for example, unemployment insurance payments and other transfers go up when the economy weakens, while tax revenues go down).

However, the problem with using the high-employment deficit (or the actual deficit) as a measure of fiscal stance is that it treats a dollar of tax revenues the same as a dollar of government purchases; a preferable measure of fiscal impulse would be one that accounted for any differential effects of various fiscal actions on aggregate demand.[21] For example, we might think that an additional dollar used for an expansion of food stamps or an extension of unemployment insurance benefits would affect aggregate demand nearly one-for-one (a dollar of government purchases also enters the economy on a one-for-one basis), but that a one-dollar reduction in capital-gains taxes would have a smaller effect to the extent it mainly goes to low-MPC households. Note, however, that the discussion in the previous section suggests that the different weights that we give to different fiscal actions will need to be informed by studies that use *micro*economic data rather than VAR models (or, more likely, by educated guesses), and this is in fact what is done.

There are two available measures of fiscal stance that attempt to control for the differential effects on aggregate demand of different types of policy actions. One is an historical measure – it ends in 2019 – that uses estimated tax, transfer, and spending effects from various sources to compute the contributions of discretionary or legislated policy changes to aggregate demand. The resulting measure is called discretionary FE, for "fiscal effect."[22] Another closely related indicator is the "fiscal impact measure" (FIM) maintained by the Brookings Institution. The FIM differs from the

---

[21] An early measure along these lines was developed by Blinder and Goldfeld (1976) using a large-scale econometric model (the MIT–Penn–SSRC, or "MPS" model).

[22] Cashin et al. (2017).

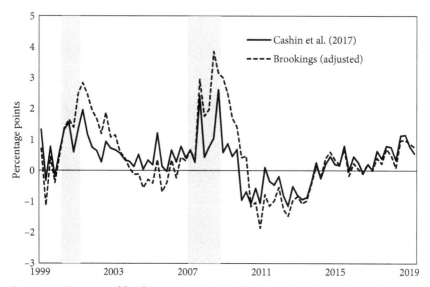

Figure 8.3 Measures of fiscal stance, 1999–2019. Each line gives the total contribution of fiscal policy measures to quarterly real GDP growth at an annual rate. Shaded bars denote recessions as defined by the NBER.

Cashin et al. measure in a couple of ways; first, the FIM measure includes the contributions of automatic stabilizers and of trend growth in entitlement spending; and second, it is expressed relative to a counterfactual neutral level in which taxes and spending rise with the CBO's estimate of potential output. Both measures are defined to include federal, state, and local fiscal policy actions; again, neither includes a contribution from the expenditure multiplier.[23]

Figure 8.3 plots the two measures together starting in 1999 (the first date that the Brookings measure is available). Both are quarterly and represent the percentage-point contribution to real GDP expressed at an annual rate.[24] The two series have broadly similar contours; the divergence between the two is largest during and immediately after recessions, when the contribution of the automatic stabilizers boosts the Brookings measure relative to the Cashin et al. (2017) fiscal stance measure. (We can therefore get a very rough

---

[23] That said, the automatic stabilizers will themselves be part of the multiplier mechanism, since they contribute to the propagation of autonomous shocks to aggregate expenditure.

[24] To make the Brookings series more comparable to the discretionary FE measure, I add in the CBO's rate of annualized quarterly potential output growth times the two-quarter moving average of the nominal share of government expenditures in GDP.

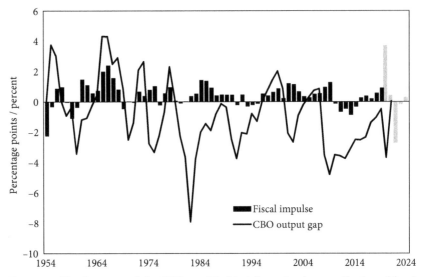

Figure 8.4 Fiscal stance and the GDP gap. The black bars give the contribution of fiscal policy actions to Q4-over-Q4 real GDP growth as measured by Cashin et al. (2017); the gray bars are the adjusted Brookings measure, which includes forecasts for 2023 and 2024. The line is the CBO's estimate of the output gap.

idea of the importance of the automatic stabilizers in these two periods from the difference between the two measures.)

Figure 8.4 plots a longer history of the Cashin et al. (2017) fiscal stance series (after 2019, I use the adjusted Brookings measure). Each bar represents the percentage-point contribution of the discretionary fiscal impetus to the Q4-over-Q4 change in real GDP; the line gives the CBO's estimate of the output gap in the fourth quarter of each year.[25] Several periods are worth highlighting. First, the large increase in discretionary spending over the second half of the 1960s is noteworthy both for its magnitude as well as its timing. A rough calculation suggests that including the expenditure multiplier would boost fiscal policy's total contribution to aggregate demand growth by a percentage point or more in each year, while estimates from a simple Okun's law relation imply that the unemployment rate would have been two percentage points higher at the end of 1969 – so around 5½ percent – had fiscal policy's contribution over 1965–1969 instead simply been in line with CBO's estimate of potential growth over that period.

---

[25] The CBO data come from the February 15, 2023 release of *The Budget and Economic Outlook: 2023–2033*.

The figure also reveals the utter inadequacy of the fiscal stimulus that was put in place to counter the 2007–2009 recession. Not only was the stimulus small relative to the total shortfall in aggregate demand – compare it with what was put in place during the less-severe 2001 downturn – but it was also removed quickly. Both features likely contributed to the slow and grinding recovery that followed. By contrast, the pandemic-related fiscal actions seem in retrospect to have been remarkably well timed and calibrated, helping output to return to the CBO's estimate of potential by the end of 2021. After that, the fiscal *drag* that emerged as the level of spending and transfers moved back to more-normal levels unwound the bulk of the direct effect of the stimulus, making a negative contribution to aggregate demand growth in 2022.[26]

Unfortunately, measures like these can't be used to estimate the effects of fiscal policy shocks. First, the stance measures capture changes in spending and tax revenues when they are realized, which means that they will be a mix of anticipated changes and actual surprises.[27] Second, the stance measures are explicitly intended to capture discretionary fiscal policy actions that are exogenous *or* endogenous to current economic conditions – spending is spending and taxes are taxes, no matter why they were put into place. Finally, the impact effects of the various policy actions that occur in a given period are *assumed* based on ancillary estimates from a variety of sources – so they are, in a sense, generated regressors.

8.4 Government Debt Management

Besides implementing policies that can be used to stabilize the economy, debt management is an important practical consideration for the fiscal authority. What does the academic literature say about the maturity structure of government debt that the Treasury should aim for?

As Treasury's Office of Debt Management indicate on their official website, the objective of the US Treasury is to "fund the government at the least cost to the taxpayer over time." The Treasury's strategies involve "regular and predictable issuance" of Treasury securities together with support for

---

[26] Note that the chart understates the size of the pandemic-related decline in GDP because it uses the fourth-quarter value of the output gap: At its 2020:Q2 trough, the CBO estimate that output was 11 percent below potential.

[27] For example, an increase in tax revenue will be a surprise to the extent people have underestimated their tax liability and only find out when their tax payment comes due, but it could also be a fully anticipated liability that has already affected their behavior in earlier periods.

market liquidity and functioning; they recognize that they are "too large an issuer to behave opportunistically in debt markets," and so they don't time the market and don't react to current interest rate levels. Finally, they seek to maintain a flexible response to the exigencies of government finance by issuing a sufficient amount of short-maturity debt. Every one of these precepts is eminently sound from a practical standpoint, as evidenced by the fact that the Treasury debt managers successfully conduct their business – financing government operations by issuing nominal and indexed debt across a wide range of maturities – in what is arguably the most important government debt market in the world.

By contrast, most theoretical papers on optimal government debt management either suggest actions that ignore (or violate) these precepts, or make normative recommendations that are completely at odds with what the Treasury actually do.[28] Starting from the unobjectionable (but not fully convincing) premise that distortionary taxes should be kept as smooth as possible over time, these models conclude that:

- Only long-term indexed (real) debt should be issued (Barro, 1995, 2003).
- The government should only issue long-term debt, but should also *invest* in a short-term asset (Angeletos, 2002, Nosbusch, 2008).
- The government should repurchase and reissue its entire stock of debt each period in order to take advantage of changes in bond prices and how they are correlated with fiscal shocks (pretty much every paper assumes this – see Faraglia et al., 2019).
- The maturity structure of US Treasury debt overweights shorter maturities and underweights longer maturities relative to an optimal portfolio (Aparisi de Lannoy et al., 2022).[29]

A very rough intuition for why many of these models emphasize issuing long-term debt (and require the government to be continually repurchasing and reissuing its debt stock) is as follows. The government's present-value budget constraint is given as

---

[28] I don't consider predictions from studies that assume that the government can trade state-contingent debt in complete (Arrow–Debreu) markets; for obvious reasons, that doesn't affect my basic point regarding the practical usefulness of this literature.

[29] In particular, the observed duration is about 5 years, while the "optimal" duration is about 14 years (p. 26). Note that the Aparisi de Lannoy et al. (2022) paper is distinct from other entries in this literature because it tries to match observed asset return co-movements rather than using the return co-movements implied by a standard (calibrated) neoclassical model.

$$qB = PV(T) - PV(G), \tag{8.8}$$

where qB is the market value of (long-term) government debt and the right-hand-side of the equation is the present value of taxes T less the present value of government spending G. Under the presumption that positive shocks to G are associated with increases in interest rates – and hence reductions in bond prices q – the reduction in the market value of debt can offset the increase in the present value of government spending, reducing the increase in taxes that is needed to keep the government's budget constraint balanced. Of course, in order for the government to realize what is in effect a capital gain on its debt, it needs to repurchase the outstanding stock of bonds (and replace it with new issues).

Several papers have pointed out various problems with this result. First, because interest rates don't move around too much, implementing this policy would require issuing a massive quantity of long-term bonds (Buera and Nicolini, 2004). Second, under such a policy the consequences of being wrong about certain features of the economy are so dire that the government would probably just decide to always run a balanced budget and forget about tax smoothing completely; likewise, even small transactions costs would be enough to induce the balanced-budget outcome (Faraglia et al., 2010). Finally, Faraglia et al. (2019) argue that the presence of small market frictions is sufficient to keep the government from repurchasing and reissuing its debt, and results in optimal outcomes that more closely match what the Treasury actually do (such as maintaining a large and relatively stable share of outstanding short-term debt, and financing an increase in the deficit with a mix of short- and long-term debt).[30]

It is difficult to find much of value after surveying this (considerable) literature, which is unfortunate given the importance of the topic. Even the way that optimal policy is defined – as something that ensures as much tax smoothing as possible – is somewhat artificial (and mostly adopted uncritically); it is also unlikely to be the objective of a real-world debt manager, or even to be an objective that they are charged with by the fiscal authority. It seems that the primary reason this literature has proven attractive to some is that it provides an interesting technical challenge, not because a serious set of policy-relevant results are desired.

---

[30] Plans announced by the Treasury in 2023 to buy back and reissue certain outstanding debt issues have been described as a way to improve market liquidity and Treasury cash management, not as a way to smooth taxes.

If the goal *were* to make a useful policy contribution, it seems as though the first thing to do would be to go and have meaningful conversations with Treasury and Federal Reserve staff and primary dealers so as to try to understand their collective motivations, the institutional environment in which they operate, and the concerns that they themselves identify as relevant and important.[31] Doing so might reveal a much more interesting – and very different – set of analytical problems than the ones that have been considered to date.

The bottom line is that there doesn't seem to be too much practical advice that the literature on optimal debt management can actually offer to the Treasury, except perhaps to keep on doing what they're doing. (Fortunately, Treasury staff seem to have been able to figure things out pretty well on their own.)

---

[31] To their credit, Faraglia et al. (2019) take a modest step in this direction.

9

Conclusion: Is (Macro)economics Useful?

The gulfs between doctrine and observation, between theory and practice, are chronic sources of malaise in our discipline.

James Tobin (1993)

Imagine that you are an analyst at an unnamed central bank, and one of your principals asks you to answer the following questions.

1. *The FOMC have raised their policy rate by x basis points. When should we expect to see an effect on output and inflation?*
2. *How do monetary policy actions affect real activity and inflation in the first place?*
3. *Should the Federal Reserve raise its longer-run inflation goal (currently 2 percent) to reduce the size and duration of future business cycles? If so, by how much?*
4. *Do changes in inflation expectations matter for actual inflation?*
5. *What caused the inflation process to change in the 1990s, and what might cause it to return to how it was in the 1970s?*
6. *What causes business cycles?*

Would the mainstream macroeconomics literature provide any useful or sensible guidance? Well, consider some of the answers it would give.[1]

1. Our best empirical estimates based on well-identified monetary policy shocks imply that large effects on real activity and inflation should appear immediately, with virtually all of the response occurring within six months.[2]

---

[1] Readers can judge for themselves whether these are fair representations of what a mainstream macroeconomist would say.
[2] Miranda-Agrippino and Ricco (2021), figures 4 and 7.

2. An increase in the real interest rate, which is possible because of sticky prices, causes consumers to postpone consumption. Investment is also affected through a higher cost of capital. These responses are amplified by some rule-of-thumb or hand-to-mouth consumers (so that we actually get a noticeable response) – but by how much depends critically on the fiscal response.[3]

3. The Fed should *lower* its longer-run inflation goal, as 2 percent is well above optimal according to a number of studies.[4] In fact, an all-singing, all-dancing DSGE model implies that relative to zero, a 2 percent inflation target costs the economy roughly $385 billion every year. And going from 2 percent to 4 percent would cost an additional $745 billion.[5]

4. Inflation expectations are extremely important. Why? Well, they're in the new-Keynesian Phillips curve. Also, when some businesses in Italy were treated with information about inflation, their short-run inflation expectations rose – and it had a "small and relatively transitory" effect on their prices. Plus, the empirical Phillips curve shifted out in the 1970s. And don't forget, *unanchored* short-run expectations propped up inflation during the 2007–2009 recession.[6]

5. The inflation process changed in the 1990s because the Fed's improved inflation-fighting credibility caused long-run inflation expectations to become anchored. The inflation process could revert back to the 1970s if inflation expectations become unanchored, or if the Fed lose their inflation-fighting credibility.[7]

6. The business cycle is mostly driven by shocks to the marginal efficiency of investment. (What's that? Well, it's better not to try to pin it down precisely, but one definition is that it's "a source of exogenous variation

---

[3] See any new-Keynesian model; also Kaplan, Moll, and Violante (2018).

[4] Using the updated dataset described in Diercks (2019), the average optimal inflation target found by research papers published after the financial crisis (that is, over the 2010–2020 period) is 0.55 percent. To be fair, though, you can pretty much pick whatever value you want: The bulk of the studies from this period imply optimal inflation targets that range from negative 4 percent to positive 6 percent.

[5] Ascari, Phaneuf, and Sims (2018) use a relatively sophisticated DSGE model to compute that the welfare cost of a 2 percent trend inflation rate (relative to zero) is 2.22 percent of consumption; the welfare cost of going from 2 to 4 percent is another 4.3 percent in consumption terms (table 3). Using the value of consumption in 2022 ($17.4 trillion) implies the values in the text.

[6] For the second and fourth claims, see Coibion et al. (2020), Coibion and Gorodnichenko (2015).

[7] Hazell et al. (2022).

in the efficiency with which the final good can be transformed into physical capital.")[8] But if you don't like that answer, how about neutral technology shocks? Shocks to the representative household's discount factor? Maybe shocks to the wedge between the policy rate and the interest rate that matters for spending? Well, anyway, it's some kind of shock – that's for sure.

Anyone bringing such answers to an actual policymaker should (rightly) fear being sacked and should at best expect to be ignored.[9] And yet, answers like these are exactly what mainstream macroeconomics professors teach their graduate students, and what they claim over and over again in their research. So how did academic macroeconomics become utterly incapable of giving sensible answers to important questions? To give an evolutionary biologist's answer, the problem is natural selection. Translated into an economist's terms, the problem starts with incentives.

9.1 Selection Pressures that Engender a "Two-Cultures" Problem in Economics

I suspect many people decide to study economics because they find the phenomena that economics analyzes to be inherently fascinating and socially vital. But by the time they finish graduate school, what they're mostly concerned with is producing research that conforms to current academic fashions and that can therefore get published in the so-called top journals. To best assist students in attaining this goal, the topics taught in graduate school (outside of history-of-thought classes) tend to be as trendy, modern, and narrowly focused as possible. (Relatedly, the fact that the research program in macroeconomics is so fad-driven provides a strong incentive to catch a wave before it crests.) Again, given the incentive structure of the US academic system, all of this is completely reasonable and understandable. But it's not something that encourages engagement with real problems, or with models that can deal with real problems.

Now, what this situation *also* doesn't encourage is a deep inspection of the implicit assumptions that underpin particular model elements or modelling techniques. Once a feature of a theoretical model becomes widely

---

[8] Justiniano et al. (2010).
[9] Actually, a monetary policymaker would probably be okay with the whole "improved credibility" megillah, since it flatters their self-image. But that's not quite the same thing as solid empirical evidence.

accepted – an aggregate production function, say, or a representative agent, or a new-Keynesian Phillips curve – there is no reason to deviate from it simply because that feature has deep theoretical or empirical failings. What that also means is that once things have gotten onto the wrong track, they're likely to stay there – how else can you explain why there continue to be so many papers written on DSGE models? (Or on *RBC models*?) Or why people continue to set themselves the challenge of teasing halfway sensible results out of a representative-agent permanent-income model? Or why no one gets laughed out of a seminar room when they scrawl a new-Keynesian Phillips curve on the chalkboard?

It also means that something like C. P. Snow's "two cultures" problem has come to pass – but within the *same* discipline, not across separate disciplines.[10] That's really remarkable, when you think about it: It's as though medical school professors continued to refine Hippocrates' theory of the four humors of the body, while practicing physicians decided to be guided by an imperfect but nonetheless serviceable understanding of the germ theory of disease. It's also a bit depressing, since it means that academics are just writing for themselves – which is hard to understand if you think that any research in economics should be done with an eye toward practical application. That doesn't mean that you shouldn't develop theoretical models or derive purely theoretical results, but if the way you build those models or get to those results requires using demonstrably false or silly constructs or assumptions that have no applicability to anything remotely related to the real world, then what's the point, really?

Where macroeconomics is concerned, I believe that the deeper reason why so much mainstream analysis is useless is that it's too narrow in its focus and too ignorant of its history. In the academic world, a high priority is given to "tractable" problems – questions whose answers can be precisely described in analytical or empirical terms using the tools of mainstream economics. Given the difficulties associated with thinking clearly about any sort of complicated system (which a modern economy certainly is), some amount of simplification or reductionism will always be needed. But in many situations, the resulting body of analysis proves to be almost useless for anyone who needs to describe or interpret real-world phenomena in a policy setting. Why might that be?

---

[10] C. P. Snow was a British scientist who, in the late 1950s, gave a famous lecture in which he lamented that there was a growing separation between the sciences and the humanities (the "two cultures"); he argued that the problem stemmed from structural features of the British educational system. (If you've never heard of any of this before, it's okay – though you should probably read more.)

First, the prioritization of analytical tractability combined with the preferred analytical approach that mainstream economics takes in trying to think about economic phenomena often yields theoretical contributions whose logic is airtight, but which have little or no ability to "explain the world." One collateral result of this mindset is that key elements of these models often come to be treated as features of reality simply because they are present in the theory, and even though the theory itself receives minimal to no empirical support.

Second, by only analyzing questions that can be answered with tractable theoretical models of a particular sort, a broad range of important phenomena end up being treated as out of bounds for study. The result is a sort of "lamppost logic" in which many of the topics deemed worthy of consideration by academic macroeconomists simply aren't relevant for practical policy decisions or useful to policy analysts. Relatedly, this approach ends up excluding fruitful and obvious ways of explaining the world that are perceived as lacking sufficient rigor. And it leads to a lot of people focusing their energy on adding additional epicycles to existing models that weren't all that persuasive to begin with.

Finally, the existing state of affairs is reinforced and propagated by the lack of any natural selection in the world of (academic) economics – or, rather, by the *presence* of natural selection of a pernicious sort. I once came across an essay by a software engineer who argued that a particular academic discipline had reached the point where it could no longer tell good-quality work from bad. The reason was that academics in the field mainly communicated with their peers; published in journals edited by and written for their peers; and faced decisions about their career advancement that were also made by their peers. The result was "a cautionary lesson about the consequences of allowing a branch of academia that has been entrusted with the study of important problems to become isolated and inbred." The author wasn't writing about economics specifically – but they might as well have been.[11]

At last count, over 32,000 NBER working papers have been written. Say the span of interesting questions in economics (loosely defined) numbers about 300. If each subject attracts roughly the same amount of attention

---

[11] The essay is Morningstar (1993); the academic discipline being written about was literary criticism – which, based on what I've seen and read, bears a passing resemblance to academic economics (though economics has more math and omits the "literary" bit). Morningstar also noted that the quality of the academic work in that field was judged "primarily on the basis of politics and cleverness." In mainstream economics, the politics are sufficiently uniform that "quality" is mostly judged by cleverness and the ability to come up with a precise answer (no matter how silly).

(and with a judgmental adjustment to drop the most cutesy papers), that's roughly 100 papers per topic. If more important questions tend to get more attention, then these have had more than 100 papers written about them (and maybe a few books). And yet, after all this work, virtually nothing in the field is settled (though occasionally a useful econometrics paper is written that corrects previous bad practice), while the profession's answers to policy-relevant questions like the ones posed above remain pretty weak tea – that's only gotten more watered down over time.

One valid response to all this "you kids off my lawn" irascibility is that the questions involved in economics are hard – really, *really* hard. That's certainly true, but the actual problem is more basic: Many of these questions aren't being approached with any degree of seriousness anymore, but are instead being treated as excuses to demonstrate one's skill in manipulating theoretical models, one's mathematical facility, or one's ability to coax something out of a single ensemble of aggregate postwar time-series data that gets a *p*-value of 5 percent or better. So we get hundreds (thousands?) of papers adding epicycles to the new-Keynesian model. Or innumerable supposedly "empirical" DSGE exercises. Or papers that simply show the author's ability to temporarily slip the handcuffs of received theory and generate results that aren't completely witless by adding additional layers of unrealistic and baroque assumptions. Meanwhile, existing empirical work routinely over-fits outliers; rarely actually turns up robust findings (despite numerous – and highly selective – "robustness checks"); often mistakes correlation for causation; and is so all-over-the-place that something exists somewhere that can support pretty much any conclusion you like.

A disturbing side effect is that the two-cultures problem is now starting to permeate policy institutions, where willfully embracing fantasy tends to have a slightly more corrosive effect. That's largely a self-inflicted wound, though. Much of the work that's done by staff at a central bank doesn't really require a Ph.D. – just an ability to write and present, a deep familiarity with economic data, basic time-series skills, and a large amount of institutional knowledge.[12] However, in order to justify hiring Ph.D. economists you need to make the job requirements a bit more stringent: namely, by requiring staff to produce published research. Naturally, you can't get research published in "serious" journals if it deviates too far from existing (academic) norms, so there's a lot of pressure to churn out that sort of thing. But it leaves a lot

---

[12] In fact, central banks outside the United States seem to rely much less on Ph.D.-trained economists; if the United States had better undergraduate economics instruction, you could probably get by in this country mostly with college graduates.

of the research that *is* done rather orthogonal to the (policy) business at hand. It also leads to a situation where, on the one side, you have a group of people who are typically (but not always) young, who are extremely conversant with and invested in current macroeconomic theory, and who are only capable of discussing real-world phenomena in those terms. On the other side, you have people who have to interpret and explain real-world phenomena in ways that are actually plausible. Both sides often baffle each other, but each plays a part: The latter group are useful for writing talking points or speeches for policymakers, while the former group give a whiff of analytical respectability to the whole deal.

Of course, one way that having a Ph.D. *would* be useful in a policy setting would be if it gave you the confidence and ability to critically assess the academic literature. Unfortunately, in many cases the effect of a graduate education is instead to lead you to think in terms of mainstream theories and to take mainstream empirical research at face value. (After all, that's what you were taught.) Plus, even if you do have doubts there's still a strong incentive to fall back on results from the academic literature when briefing policymakers – not because academic work is reasonable or especially persuasive, but because it's a lot easier to simply summarize established research. (It's also faster, and time is often of the essence in policy circles: It's not like you're given a month or two to make a full-throated critical assessment or to try to replicate the results of some literature on your own.) And since many principals either don't really understand the stuff themselves (but think they should) or come from academic circles and are thus already accustomed to taking it seriously, there's no real filter anywhere up the line. The result as far as policymaking is concerned is either not very helpful or (sometimes) actively harmful.[13]

9.2 Economics as Apologetics

With mainstream macroeconomics, therefore, we have an example of a discipline whose theories have little to no predictive power, that are pretty much useless for forecasting, that cannot convincingly explain many real-world phenomena (even in hindsight), and that can't convincingly deal with basic questions at the foundation of its intellectual edifice. Worse still, important (actually crucial) theoretical issues are ignored if they're inconvenient; in

---

[13] The obsession with inflation expectations and inflation-fighting credibility among central bankers likely falls into the latter category. Time will tell.

spite of that, though, economists still feel confident enough to use the theory to dictate policy advice.[14]

And yet, in our society economics is a thriving enterprise. It's an extraordinarily popular undergraduate major, it attracts a lot of funding (including from government sources), and economists are seen as necessary window dressing for any sort of policy institution or social policy think tank. Some of the more esteemed economists even seem to shape popular and business opinion. How can this be if there's no real substance there?[15]

The explanation, I believe, for why economics is held in such esteem in our society is because of the role it plays in justifying what elite interests want to do anyway: Deregulate, pay fewer taxes, keep wages as low as possible, and portray the government as a roadblock to prosperity. Economists – macro as well as micro – provide the intellectual shill work for these projects, and many economists seem willing to serve as handmaidens in this way. After all, all of these things are seen as impediments to the free-market ideal, and all the purported benefits that would flow forth as a result. Even vaguely left-of-center economists will typically label themselves "macro Democrats but micro Republicans" – that's how deep this mindset runs. And the profession reaps a reward for that service.[16]

So the reason why mainstream economics continues to be held in regard in our society is that it provides a reliable source of justification for a social order that is inherently difficult to justify. And what's even better is that this justification is conveniently cloaked in the supposedly positive and value-neutral guise of securing "efficiency" and "optimality." In other words, the

---

[14] The reason for this, I suspect, is partly sociological. In my experience, economics often tends to attract a certain type of person. That person is one who enjoys explaining to others why seemingly counterintuitive propositions – like the notion that free trade benefits everyone, or that deficit-financed government spending can't stimulate the economy – are actually true, and that you'd realize this too if you only understood matters as deeply as they do. (Regarding that latter claim about deficit-financed spending, it seems to me that anyone who wants to claim that Ricardian equivalence holds should probably be asking themselves why there isn't a lot more action on climate change.)

[15] On the other hand, there's a reason why investment banks hire physicists, computer scientists, and engineers to do the real work; at best, Ph.D. economists are hired to do dog-and-pony shows for clients, or maybe to do some sloppy drive-by analysis of macro data.

[16] As an aside, I think that this is why the economics profession in the United States has such a serious diversity problem. If you're a member of a marginalized group, you probably aren't going to find much appeal in a worldview that tries to prove via ruthless mathematical argument that you're getting exactly what the market knows that you deserve, and that asking for anything more than that runs counter to society's best interests. (Put more bluntly, why would you want to take up economics unless you're already an elite, or at least feel a strong affinity for elites?)

thing that separates economics from a field like sociology or anthropology isn't that economics is more successful in explaining the world, but is rather that mainstream economics serves our society's elite interests far better than (most) sociology or anthropology does. Economics can be used to justify reducing the government's involvement in "free" markets (on the grounds of Pareto optimality and efficiency); the existence of grotesquely unfair distributions of wealth and income (it's all your marginal product, you see); and cutting taxes and transfers as much as possible (those things just create disincentives to work and invest). On top of that, deficits and government debt are bad because they crowd out "truly productive" uses of private savings.

How unfair is this characterization? Well, I suspect that if asked, many mainstream economists – micro *and* macro – would see nothing obviously wrong or illogical with Milton Friedman's dictum that:

[In a free society], there is one and only one social responsibility of business – to use its resources and engage in activities designed to increase its profits so long as it stays within the rules of the game, which is to say, engages in open and free competition without deception or fraud.[17]

Leaving aside how (literally) sociopathic that view is, it's also mediocre social science: How can something like that be justified once we take broader institutional considerations into account and recognize that most of the "rules of the game" are set by corporations and by people who have the money that's needed to buy political influence? It's also telling to see what Friedman thinks the rules of the game *should* be – open and free competition. Now even if you agreed, trying to move the world in that direction from its current less-than-ideal state is actually bad economics even by mainstream standards: If you were a good mainstream economist and not an ideologue, you'd know enough about the theory of the second best to be worried about trying to make this kind of change.[18] And yet, views like these seem so commonplace among economists as to barely merit comment, let alone serious introspection.[19]

---

[17] The quote appeared in an essay Friedman wrote that appeared the *New York Times* on September 3, 1970.

[18] If you *are* an ideologue, or an Austrian economist, or a libertarian, you escape by falling back on the "no true Scotsman" argument: Free markets *must* be good, so if an outcome is bad, it can't be because it involves free markets.

[19] There is a literature that uses mainstream techniques to analyze less antisocial ways of organizing production; for some representative examples see Dow (2003, 2018), Magill et al. (2015), and Fleurbaey and Ponthière (2023). But I doubt that this work influences too many mainstream economists' conception of their ideal economic order.

9.3 A Code of Conduct for Policy Analysts

To first order, the answer to any question in (macro)economics should be "we don't know." Existing macroeconomic models and theories permit all sorts of subtle theological disputations – being able to interpret how a model arrives at its particular set of results is an important skill when it comes to writing an academic paper – and these kinds of debates are even a source of entertainment for some. But macroeconomics in its current state does very little to help us explain, predict, and control economic outcomes. In many ways, we really don't know much more about how the economy works than we did sixty years ago: Reading the history of the Martin Fed, for example, reveals that monetary policymakers had the same basic set of concerns – keeping inflation in control without jeopardizing financial stability or resorting to a deep recession – that they arguably still have today. And looking over the pablum that is today's body of economic research, it's clear that we as economists have about as much useful advice to provide regarding how to reliably secure these outcomes as our 1960s predecessors did. That's a sobering and depressing thought, but one that we need to be honest about.[20]

However, our principals still have to make consequential decisions, and will do so notwithstanding our ignorance (or theirs). How, then, do we responsibly advise them?

This question actually has two parts, the first being the role that models, theory, or forecasts can or should play in informing policy (especially given the non-ergodic nature of the economy), and the second being what professional standard should be followed by those who would seek to give policy advice.

Regarding the first question, there probably *isn't* much hope for using economic models to guide the policy process, except in a relatively superficial fashion that essentially involves trying to interpret economic statistics by identifying likely or potential causal channels based on institutional knowledge. The research paradigm of mainstream economics is largely

---

[20] It's cheating (and wrong) to claim that we have a better understanding of what causes inflation to become a mean-reverting process; what policy actions are needed to keep it that way; and whether and how inflation expectations factor in. Ask yourself: If inflation were to ratchet up to 6 percent and stay there, would you be able to give better advice to a monetary policymaker than to squeeze the economy until the pips squeak? That was Volcker's answer – and what he's lionized for – but besides driving the economy to the brink of a depression, all it seemed to do was to persistently reduce inflation by a couple of percentage points.

confined to using a particular theoretical framework to interpret observed phenomena; or, in its more degenerative state, starting from an axiomatic approach and deriving logical conclusions that are then taken as descriptive. The problem with the former approach is that it uses the same data that were used to formulate the theory to implicitly validate the theory; the second approach inherits the problem that the axioms of economic analysis are generally unconvincing and the resulting theory is almost never tested in a serious fashion (instead, the quality of the logical derivation or internal consistency of the model is taken as the standard of proof). In addition, the degree of attention paid to mainstream economic theories in policy circles is largely determined by two elements, neither of which is related to the theory's ability to explain real-world phenomena: ideological considerations (including the intellectual cover the theory provides for doing what you want to do anyway), and whether the theory delivers unambiguous predictions (people don't want to take "it's complicated" or "no one really knows" for an answer).

The best we can probably do, therefore, is to try to get an idea of how robust certain empirical correlations or statistical relations appear to be ("stylized facts"), especially across different regimes or historical periods. We can also try to get an idea of the broad orders of magnitude involved in relations among key variables. Finally, it can be useful as well to catalogue cases where previous stylized facts have been overturned by later developments. If one does insist on using a model to inform policy, then knowing whether its predictions would obtain under alternative assumptions about economic behavior is critical; as a corollary, any policy action that relies on the specific conclusions of a particular model is unlikely to be well founded. Finally, there is probably no sensible basis for using economic forecasting as an input to economic policy. While an argument can be made that the main duty of a forecaster is simply to "get right" that portion of the outlook that policy can actually do anything about, in practice that's a pretty small sliver of whatever's going to happen. And beyond a couple of quarters, not only is an economic projection no better than Arrow's weather forecasts, but our ability to characterize the actual uncertainty that surrounds future economic events – or even to characterize the event space itself – isn't good enough to provide a useful input into a Bayesian decision-maker's subjective loss function.[21]

---

[21] A senior policy economist whom I respect once argued that if all you want is the lowest root-mean-square forecast error, there are ways to get that (at least for a while). Where an economic forecaster adds value, however, is in developing a coherent view about the

All that being the case, it is an open question whether policy can expect to be successful under most conditions, though I suppose the single best principle is to move away from a given policy as soon as obvious imbalances or problematic outcomes emerge. Unfortunately, that's more about tactics, not strategy – and "as soon as" might not be soon enough.

Regarding the second question, people who would seek to influence policy – either public intellectuals or analysts in policy institutions – have the duty to clearly explain exactly what framework they are using to generate their conclusions, whether the key elements of that framework are in line with basic stylized facts (as best as can be determined), and what the consequences of their advice would be if the key elements of their framework were wrong. Unfortunately, what we tend to see in practice is that many public intellectuals are often unaware of the most elemental empirical facts and simply make their case by appealing to weak analogies (or their reputations), while analysts within policy institutions are pressured to come up with point estimates and pithy answers that are stripped clean of any hint of nuance by the time they reach their principals.

My intention here is not to be a complete nihilist. I still believe that what economics claims as its purview is utterly fascinating. Every day millions upon millions of people wake up, go to work, and make and do things as part of an immensely complex social system. The result is partly good, in that many people are able to feed, clothe, shelter, heal, and enjoy themselves better. It's also got an obnoxious downside: The US system of state capitalism involves a lot of corruption, exploitation, meaningless waste, and human degradation (both at home and abroad), while industrial society as a whole has left such large-scale environmental destruction in its wake that the result might well be to drive humanity down the same road as the trilobites. Less dramatically, the fruit of all this effort is unfairly and inefficiently distributed (among industrialized countries, that seems to be especially true for the United States), and sometimes the machine that makes any of this possible breaks down in spectacular fashion in ways that we barely know how to fix, let alone prevent. So how things actually *do* work in this sphere, and how we might improve their workings (even if only at the margins), is something that's well worth thinking hard about. And thinking about in any number of ways. Just not in the ways that we've been doing it lately.

outlook – the stories that they tell about how the economy got to where it is now, and how it is likely to evolve. I don't really believe that argument anymore, because the stories that do get told are too close to fairy tales – or too redolent of the "just-so" genre.

Appendix A

Measuring Prices

[A cynic is] a man who knows the price of everything and the value of nothing. And a sentimentalist ... is a man who sees an absurd value in everything, and doesn't know the market price of any single thing.

Oscar Wilde, *Lady Windermere's Fan (Act 3)*

Constructing a price index involves making several decisions: what prices to include; how to measure them; and how to combine them into a single summary measure. Since there is no consensus about any of these questions – and since different answers will be correct depending on what we want to use the index for – there are a variety of price measures that are constructed by US statistical agencies and other institutions. This note provides an overview of some of these measures, and discusses some technical issues that anyone using them needs to be aware of.[1]

A.1 Consumption Price Indexes

The consumer price index (CPI), which is produced by the Bureau of Labor Statistics (BLS), is the oldest source of reasonably consistent price data in the United States (an annual version of the index dates back to 1913). The idea behind the CPI is to price a specified set of goods over time (a "basket"),

---

[1] This note only covers the barest minimum that a practitioner needs to know about these data. More comprehensive discussions of index number theory can be found in the *Consumer Price Index Manual* (2004) produced by the ILO (International Labour Office) and various other agencies; that book also includes detailed background on a number of practical issues related to computing a consumer price index. For information about the US CPI and PPI specifically, the BLS *Handbook of Methods* (available online) is useful; for the PCE and GDP price indexes, one can turn to various BEA methodology papers on the national income and product accounts.

where the basket is updated periodically to reflect changes in spending patterns; the Consumer Expenditure Survey (CEX) is used for this purpose. In 2023, the BLS started updating the basket annually, though the expenditure weights introduced in year t reflect expenditures in year $t - 2$ (roughly) because it takes a while to collect and process the CEX data. (In the following year, year $t + 1$, the weights will reflect year $t - 1$ expenditures.)[2]

The CPI is a type of modified Laspeyres index. (The modification is that the weights use quantities and prices from different periods; the technical name for this is a Lowe index.) However, the easiest way to think about CPI aggregation is in terms of *relative importance weights*. The relative importance weight (RIW) for item i in period t is given by

$$RIW_{i,t} = \frac{Q_{i,b}P_{i,t}}{\sum_{i=1}^{n} Q_{i,b}P_{i,t}}, \tag{A.1}$$

where $Q_{i,b}$ is the quantity purchased in the base year and $P_{i,t}$ is the time-t price. Note that in a given period, the relative importance weights sum to one (we assume there are a total of n items in the index).

If we define a *price relative* as the (gross) change in item-i's price in month t,

$$1 + m_{i,t} \equiv P_{i,t}/P_{i,t-1}, \tag{A.2}$$

then the monthly percent change in the CPI, m_t, can be written as:

$$1 + m_t = \sum_{i=1}^{n} RIW_{i,t-1}(1 + m_{i,t}), \tag{A.3}$$

which simplifies to $m_t = \sum RIW_{i,t-1}m_{i,t}$ (again because the relative importance weights sum to one).

The CPI report publishes relative importance weights for month $t - 1$ in the month-t release. In addition, the official CPI release contains "special aggregates," such as core CPI (CPI less food and energy), core services (services less energy services, where the latter are electricity and natural gas), and so on. It is also possible to construct your own special aggregates, either by combining individual series or "stripping out" specific series from an aggregate, so long as you have the necessary relative importance weights.[3] There is a trick to constructing a strip-out, however, that is worth noting.

---

[2] Previously, the weights covered two years' worth of expenditures and were updated every two years; before 2002, the weights were updated every ten years or so.

[3] Having a time series of the relative importance weights is best; it is possible to construct a time series from an initial period's weight since the time-t relative importance weight for

To take a concrete example, the percent change in the total CPI, T_t, equals the contributions of the food, energy, and core indexes:

$$T_t = RIW_{F,t-1}F_t + RIW_{E,t-1}E_t + RIW_{C,t-1}C_t, \qquad (A.4)$$

in obvious notation. From this, it's evident that to compute the core change, it is not enough to simply subtract the food and energy contributions from the total; once that's done, the result needs to be divided by the core's relative importance weight. (The idea is that within a subaggregate the weights need to sum to one – here, the components of the core need to be aggregated with weights that are divided by the weight of the core in the total index; using that scaling ensures that the "core weights" sum to one.)

Although the not seasonally adjusted (NSA) CPI is (essentially) never revised, the methodology used to construct the index has changed numerous times, resulting in breaks in the published series.[4] The most important of these involves the change made to the measurement of owner-occupied housing services. From 1953 to 1983, the CPI measured the price of these services using home prices and mortgage costs (among other things); the effect was that this component – and by extension the total CPI – included a nominal interest rate. (For obvious reasons, that's problematic for analyzing things like the effect of monetary policy on inflation.) The BLS publish a research series that corrects for this problem prior to 1983 (as well as for other methodological changes); in practice, though, using a PCE-based price measure (see below) is simpler because the PCE price index never included mortgage rates (or house prices), and its history is closer to being methodologically consistent (both for housing and for other components).[5]

The coverage of the headline CPI (the one everyone talks about) is the population of all urban consumers (for that reason, this measure is sometimes referred to as the CPI-U). There is also a CPI for households of urban wage earners and clerical workers (the CPI-W); the size of the population captured by the CPI-W is roughly a third of the CPI-U's population.

item i equals the $t-1$ relative importance weight times $(1 + m_{i,t})/(1 + m_t)$, but accuracy can be an issue.

[4] The BLS also started reporting the CPI to three decimal places in 2007. In earlier periods, the use of data with one decimal place has a noticeable effect on the monthly changes in the index (for example, from 1967 to 1972).

[5] Currently, the CPI use what is called a *rental equivalence* measure to capture the price of owner-occupied housing; the resulting measure is called owners' equivalent rent (OER). Loosely, the idea is to measure the opportunity cost of owning a home – that is, what the home could be rented out for. The way this is calculated is by reweighting the sample of tenants' rents such that areas with a relatively larger share of owner-occupied housing receive a relatively larger weight in OER.

Another important consumption price index is the price index for personal consumption expenditures (PCE) from the national income and product accounts (NIPAs). Many of the individual prices that are used in the PCE price index come from the CPI; however, the weights come from the national accounts' measure of consumption, which is both broader than the CPI and based on different data (for example, measures of retail sales and service producers' revenue rather than expenditures from the CEX). In some cases, the PCE weights are arguably more accurate than the CPI's CEX-based weights: There is evidence that spending on certain goods tends to be underreported in the CEX, in part because the household head (the respondent for the CEX) doesn't have a full idea of what other members of the household are consuming; by contrast, measures of retail sales can capture everyone's spending (in principle). In addition, PCE is intended to cover the entire United States (not just urban consumers). There is also a core PCE price index, though there are a few differences in how food is defined in PCE and the CPI.[6]

A major difference between the two indexes comes from the broader scope of the PCE price index. The CPI mainly tries to capture out-of-pocket expenditures (OER being a significant exception) and also omits things that BLS consider to be investments or assets, such as life insurance. By contrast, the PCE price index includes a number of "nonmarket" components that BEA consider to be consumption, but that are not priced in observable market transactions. For example, the BEA impute a flow of financial services from households' bank accounts; the idea is that households could purchase things like Treasury securities directly instead of holding a bank account that yields little to no interest. That opportunity cost is used to value the other services that a bank account provides, such as the ability to write checks.[7] Other examples of nonmarket items include services provided by nonprofit institutions serving households: Since these services aren't sold at a market price, the BEA value them according to their production costs; roughly, the difference between production costs and sales to households is treated as a separate component of PCE, while sales to households are allocated to specific PCE components (such as medical services or higher

---

[6] The main difference is that food away from home – restaurant meals, for example – is in the core PCE index (as "food services") but is not in the core CPI index. In addition, alcohol is in the CPI core but not the PCE core.

[7] One reason that this is necessary is that banks would make a negative contribution to GDP otherwise, because the net interest portion of their production costs (interest paid less interest received) tends to be much less than zero for a well-run bank.

education services).[8] However, even though owners' equivalent rent is also an imputed price, BEA consider it to be market-based.

Although including nonmarket components like these in total PCE makes sense from a national accounting perspective, because the prices of these items are imputed (and are in some cases based on wage data) it also makes sense to exclude them from an inflation measure that is being used to analyze inflation dynamics. The BEA publish market-based total and core PCE price indexes that extend from 1987 to the present (in rough terms, market-based prices account for about 85 percent of the overall index).

The PCE price index also uses other price measures besides individual CPIs; the most important of these is for medical services prices (both because the indexes that are used, which come from the PPI, can move very differently to the CPI measures, but also because the broader definition of consumer expenditures in PCE result in medical services' having a larger weight in PCE relative to the CPI). In contrast, while the PCE price index uses the CPIs for tenants' and owners' equivalent rent, the weights for these prices come from a different (non-CEX) source; in addition, the broader scope of PCE reduces the weight of housing in the PCE price index relative to the weight it receives in the CPI. (This can be a significant source of difference between the indexes – in late 2022, housing services accounted for 15 percent of the total PCE price index and 34 percent of the CPI.)

Finally, the formula used to compute the PCE price index differs from the one used for the CPI; we'll see how in the next section.

A.2 Chain Aggregation

The national accounts use Fisher ideal price and quantity indexes to compute aggregate price and output measures.[9] The Fisher price index is the geometric mean of a Laspeyres and a Paasche price index, where the Laspeyres price index between time 0 and time 1 is given as

$$P_L = \frac{\sum_{i=1}^{n} p_i^1 q_i^0}{\sum_{i=1}^{n} p_i^0 q_i^0},\tag{A.5}$$

and the Paasche price index is

---

[8] Using input cost measures causes compensation to enter the nonmarket component of PCE prices.
[9] The index is called "ideal" because the change in a nominal aggregate will be equal to the change in the Fisher price index times the change in the Fisher quantity index.

$$P_P = \frac{\sum_{i=1}^{n} p_i^1 q_i^1}{\sum_{i=1}^{n} p_i^0 q_i^1}. \qquad (A.6)$$

Note that the Laspeyres index uses time-0 quantities to weight prices in the two periods, while the Paasche uses time-1 quantities. The Fisher price index P_F between periods 0 and 1 is therefore:

$$P_F = \sqrt{P_L P_P}. \qquad (A.7)$$

The Fisher index can be computed for adjoining time periods, then "chained" together to yield a time series of index values.[10] This is how price (and quantity) indexes are computed in the US national accounts. It is straightforward to compute these aggregates, especially if you are working at a relatively high level of aggregation. If you don't have the patience to use the Fisher formulas to make aggregates (or to remove specified series from an aggregate), a reasonable approximation is provided by the Törnqvist index number formula.[11] Given a set of individual prices p (indexed by i), the Törnqvist measure of aggregate price change P between two periods t and $t-1$ can be written as

$$\ln P_{t,t-1} = \sum_i \tfrac{1}{2}(\omega_{i,t} + \omega_{i,t-1}) \ln \left(\frac{p_{i,t}}{p_{i,t-1}} \right), \qquad (A.8)$$

where $\omega_{i,t}$ is the *nominal* expenditure share for good i in period t. As for the Fisher index, the total price changes can be chained together to yield a time series of index values. In practice, the only reason to use the Fisher formula instead of the Törnqvist is if you need to exactly replicate what BEA are doing (or you prefer percent changes to log differences – see Appendix E).

Several issues can arise when chained indexes are used. The first is something called "chain drift." This refers to a situation where a chained index doesn't return to its initial value even if all of the individual prices and quantities do. Relatedly, if we want to measure price change over two periods t and $t+k$ that are reasonably separated in time, one way is to compute an index that just uses the data from these two periods; another is to chain together k

---

[10] Confusingly, the term "chain aggregation" or "chained data" is typically used to refer to the process of making a Fisher index or to a series that is a Fisher index, rather than to chaining per se. (Other indexes can be "chained" as well; for example, the CPI is technically a chained index because the expenditure weights are periodically updated, so each link in the chain involves a particular set of expenditure weights.)

[11] The BLS produce a chained version of the CPI-U, called C-CPI-U, that is a Törnqvist index in its final form.

individual price indexes. In general, the two answers will differ.[12] (Measures like the Fisher and Törnqvist indexes tend to be better behaved along this dimension.) There are also more-sophisticated tests to assess whether chain drift is present.

A related problem arises when using high-frequency data, such as scanner data at a grocery store. When a nonperishable good goes on sale (tins of tuna fish), individuals might stock up and then not need to buy any more for a while (including in the period when the good goes back to full price). The low price is therefore overweighted and the full price is underweighted, which puts downward pressure on the price index relative to one that just used fixed "average" weights throughout or that used weights from before the sale and from after expenditure patterns had returned to normal. Other forms of price and quantity behavior can result in chain indexes with poor properties; generally, problems arise when prices or quantities "bounce around" a lot (which can be the result of seasonality, temporary sales, or simple volatility).

A.3 Potential Sources of Bias

A commonly used theoretical benchmark for a measure of consumption prices is the *true cost-of-living-index* (TCOLI) of Konüs (1939). A TCOLI measures the cost of maintaining a particular level of utility over time; if $e(\cdot)$ denotes the expenditure function, then the Konüs TCOLI between t and $t + 1$ is defined as

$$P_K(p_t, p_{t+1}, u^*) \equiv \frac{e(p_{t+1}, u^*)}{e(p_t, u^*)}, \tag{A.9}$$

where u^* denotes a reference level of utility. It is possible to show that the t to $t + 1$ price change implied by a Laspeyres index using time-t quantity weights will be greater than or equal to the TCOLI computed using time-t utility as the reference level. Similarly, the Paasche index using time $t + 1$ quantity weights will be less than or equal to the TCOLI evaluated using time $t + 1$ utility as the reference.

None of this has much practical relevance for real-world price measurement. Although a cost-of-living index is the stated measurement goal of

---

[12] This comparison is known as a "circularity test." The only index number formula that passes the circularity test is a weighted geometric mean with constant aggregation weights; using constant (expenditure) weights for aggregation over long spans of time is undesirable, however.

the CPI, the definition of the TCOLI pertains to an individual, so it only has broader applicability if we are willing to assume a representative agent, or that everyone has the same preferences (and that those preferences are homothetic).[13] In addition, the reliance of the measure on a fictional unobservable (utility) makes it impossible to implement a TCOLI in practice, even for a single consumer. Finally, a true COLI would also account for changes in the consumer's environment that make it harder to attain the reference utility level, such as the emergence of a pandemic or of severe weather events as a result of climate change. Since those sorts of things (and certain goods) are out of scope for the CPI, the BLS refer to the CPI's goal as a "conditional COLI," where these other factors are held fixed.

BLS do use the concept of a TCOLI as a touchstone for assessing whether "bias" is present in the CPI, where bias is defined as things that cause the actual CPI to fall short of the TCOLI ideal. For example, the first Konüs inequality has been used to argue that a Laspeyres(-ish) index like the CPI yields a price change that is larger than the true cost of living, and so is biased upwards. This particular source of bias is often referred to as "upper-level substitution bias," because it reflects the effect of not allowing spending patterns to change when relative prices do (the basket is kept the same across periods). In the CPI, the basket is fixed at the "upper" level (that is, across the categories of items and areas that are used to compute the CPI).[14] In addition to upper-level substitution bias, _lower_-level substitution bias can also be present; this term refers to substitution _within_ an item-area category. (For example, a consumer might change the brand they buy if its price goes up.) The CPI attempts to correct for this by using a geometric mean to aggregate prices within most item-area strata.

Upper-level substitution bias doesn't really exist in this form. Realistically, there is close to no scope for substitution across the CPI's various item-area strata: When the price of ground beef goes up in Cincinnati, it is unlikely to induce substitution toward purchases of televisions in Honolulu. This point was made by Bradley (2001), who also observed that what passes for upper-level substitution bias – which is typically measured by comparing the

---

[13] It is possible to _define_ a "group COLI" and examine its properties. But because such a large amount of information would be needed to implement it – and because the assumptions needed to say anything useful about it are unlikely to hold in reality – it's no better than a theoretical curiosum. Moreover, such a concept is just a hair's breadth away from requiring interpersonal comparisons of utility, which used to be considered poor taste (Pollak, 1980, 1981).

[14] There are 243 item strata and 32 index areas in the CPI at present, so more than 7,700 upper-level series are combined.

published CPI to a CPI constructed using a formula that allows expenditure weights to change – is actually the result of how sampling error affects different types of aggregation procedures. Hence, while it is still a "bias" in the sense of being a form of measurement error, it doesn't have any behavioral interpretation (only a statistical one).

There are other types of bias that are claimed to be present in the CPI. Some of these are technical: For example, because the CEX might not measure all household expenditures accurately, it can result in measurement error if over- or under-measured categories of spending have above- or below-average rates of price change. Quantitatively, the largest source of bias is usually seen as resulting from inadequate adjustment for changes in quality, the idea being that the increase in utility that results from quality improvements to an item is similar to a price decline and should be captured as such. BLS deal with this problem in several ways (the problem also arises when a specific good can no longer be found and needs to be replaced with a not-quite-comparable item). First, the CPI tries to keep the quality of the products it prices constant by repricing the same good over time or by matching models or types of goods as closely as possible. Second, when a good disappears the CPI has several procedures, including the use of hedonic models, that try to adjust for any quality differential in the replacement item that enters the sample.

There is an argument, however, that the use of matched-model or hedonic techniques can *over*state the amount of quality improvement and cause downward bias in a price index.[15] The way this can happen is if price per unit quality is an upward-sloping function of quality (this appears to be the case for computers, and possibly other types of capital equipment and consumer durables). The first panel of Figure A.1 shows such a situation: The line represents the range of models that are available in a given period; it is upward sloping because price per unit quality, P/A, is an increasing function of quality, A. The line shifts down as price per unit quality in the overall market declines over time; the goal of a COLI should be to capture the average change in P/A that results. This is straightforward in the situation shown in the first panel: The same set of models exist in periods 1 and 2, so pricing a sample of them captures the average reduction in P/A. More problematic situations are shown in the other three panels. In the upper-right panel, the lower-quality models disappear as higher-quality models are introduced. As the figure is drawn, average P/A is unchanged in the two

---

[15] I believe I was first shown a variant of this argument by Bart Hobijn; please don't blame him if I get it wrong.

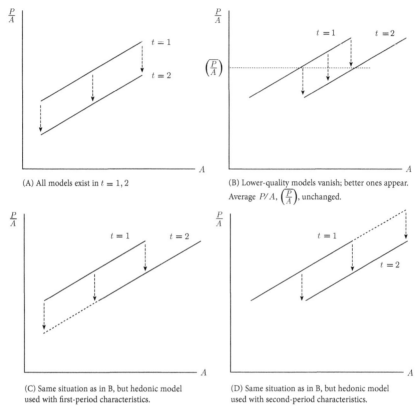

(A) All models exist in $t = 1, 2$

(B) Lower-quality models vanish; better ones appear. Average P/A, $\left(\frac{P}{A}\right)$, unchanged.

(C) Same situation as in B, but hedonic model used with first-period characteristics.

(D) Same situation as in B, but hedonic model used with second-period characteristics.

Figure A.1 Overstatement of price declines by matched-model or hedonic techniques.

periods, but the matched-model procedure finds a quality-adjusted price decline. In the bottom panels, hedonic techniques are used to impute P/A values for models that have disappeared (the dashed portions of the lines). The left panel shows what happens if initial-period characteristics are used for the imputation; the right panel shows what happens if second-period characteristics are used. In both cases, we measure a decline in P/A even when the average change in P/A given the models that are available in the market is zero.

This example also illustrates how certain types of measurement error can cause problems elsewhere in the statistical system. In most cases, real quantities in the national accounts are computed as nominal values divided by prices; any mismeasurement of price changes will therefore affect real values, along with anything based on a real value (like productivity). So how large is the total measurement error in the CPI and other price statistics likely to be? Most of the quantitative estimates are extremely subjective (and based on very little hard evidence); that said, a relatively recent accounting by Moulton (2018) calculates that the CPI rises 0.85 percentage point per year faster than it would have had the various identified sources of bias been absent. (Moulton also gives this point estimate a "plausible range" of 0.3–1.4 percentage points.) For the PCE price index, which uses different aggregation formulas and non-CPI prices for several key categories, Moulton's bias estimate works out to 0.47 percentage point per year.

A feature of the CPI and PCE price index that is *not* considered a source of bias (but probably should be) is that these measures are *plutocratic*: Because they use actual expenditures, people who spend the most (generally upper-income types) receive the largest effective weight in the index.[16] (An alternative would be to weight each household the same; this is known as a *democratic* price index.) In addition, the CPI doesn't capture representative price changes for various subgroups (such as poorer persons or the elderly), both because their expenditure patterns can be different from the average, and because they can face different prices. (Experimental CPIs produced by the BLS for demographic subgroups only capture the first source of difference; price data specific to a particular subgroup are not available from CPI price quotes.)

A.4 Other Price Measures

Several other price measures are also often used in empirical work. The producer price index (PPI) measures businesses' revenue per unit sold for *domestic* producers, and also measures gross margins for wholesale and retail trade as well as prices for a number of services.[17] The PPI also includes price data for intermediate inputs and raw materials, which can be useful for analyzing the passthrough of these prices to more-finished goods. The PPI uses a (modified-) Laspeyres formula for aggregation, and (in most cases) shipment values as weights. Individual PPIs are often used as deflators in the NIPAs to compute real investment quantities at a highly disaggregated level.

In addition, output-price indexes exist for major business sectors (such as nonfinancial corporations) and for the economy as a whole (the GDP price

---

[16] This is one reason why these indexes might be a poor gauge of the inflation rate that an average household is actually seeing. Another reason is that the measures implicitly assume that every household is purchasing every good in every period, which is unlikely in the case of infrequently purchased items like new motor vehicles or legal services.

[17] In contrast to the CPI, which nowadays measures prices throughout the month, the PPI measures the price on the Tuesday of the week containing the 13th of each month.

index). Because the GDP price index includes prices for the government sector, much of which represents compensation to government employees, it is typically less useful for analyzing inflation dynamics. These price indexes use chained Fisher aggregation formulas.

A.5 Alternative Measures of Core Inflation

The official measures of core inflation exclude food and energy prices (though, as noted previously, the definition of "food" differs for the CPI and PCE price indexes). The focus on food and energy reflects the oil and food price shocks of the 1970s, which were viewed as volatile, temporary, and largely unrelated to the state of aggregate demand. However, if the goal is to extract a signal from a noisy price index by excluding volatile categories then there are more scientific ways to proceed, and some variants of the CPI and PCE price index are computed with this goal in mind.[18] Two of the most common approaches involve computing median or trimmed-mean measures of CPI or PCE inflation; these measures are plotted in Figure A.2 for the CPI and in Figure A.3 for PCE prices, together with the standard core indexes for these series (the market-based index is used for core PCE prices).[19]

   In these cases, the median CPI or PCE price index is obtained for a given month by ordering the price changes of the index's components from smallest to largest. If we think of each component as lying on a line with the width of each component equal to its expenditure share, then the median CPI or PCE price change for that month is the price change of the component that straddles the line's halfway point. The trimmed-mean CPI is computed by removing the top and bottom 8 percent of the line (so 16 percent in total) and then combining the remaining components using their resulting expenditure weights (each of which will be $1/0.84 = 19$ percent larger as a result).[20] The computation of the trimmed-mean PCE price index is more

[18] The resulting inflation measures – core inflation included – are sometimes referred to as *underlying inflation*, with the idea being that these measures better reveal the signal or trend in overall inflation. An alternative (and unrelated) use of the term underlying inflation is as a label for inflation's long-run stochastic trend, the argument being that this is the rate of inflation that would eventually prevail absent any slack, supply shocks, or idiosyncratic relative price changes.

[19] The Cleveland Federal Reserve Bank maintain a series of median CPI and PCE price indexes, along with a trimmed-mean CPI. The Dallas Federal Reserve Bank maintain a trimmed-mean PCE price index.

[20] The 16 percent trim was originally chosen because it minimized the difference between the trimmed-mean index and a wide (36-month) centered moving average.

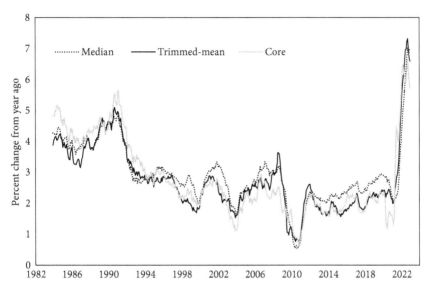

Figure A.2 Median, trimmed-mean, and core CPIs (12-month changes).

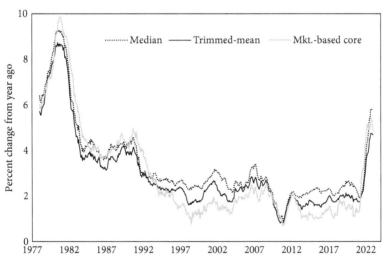

Figure A.3 Median and trimmed-mean PCE price indexes and core market-based PCE price index (12-month changes).

complicated. First, the trims are determined such that the resulting measure minimizes the root-mean-square difference between three separate benchmarks: a long moving average, a lowpass-filtered series whose filter cutoff is set to maximize its correlation with the federal funds rate, or a 25-month moving average of current and *future* inflation rates.

Indexes like these can't be justified as approximations to a cost-of-living measure, but what about their statistical justification? The usual motivation for using a trimmed-mean measure to provide an estimate of a location parameter comes from Crow and Siddiqui (1967), who found that trimmed means worked well ("robustly") in terms of their efficiency when used to estimate the location parameter of six candidate distributions.[21] However, that finding doesn't apply here. The problem that Crow and Siddiqui specified assumed a sample of i.i.d. random variables from a continuous symmetric unimodal distribution; there is no basis, therefore, for using (expenditure-)weighted data (so if this problem applies at all, it is to the individual *unweighted* price changes). In addition, the "optimal" trims are computed over a long period (for the trimmed-mean PCE price index, the sample starts in 1977), during which time the time-series process for inflation changed rather noticeably. So the fiction that we're dealing with a single invariant distribution is pretty hard to maintain.

In addition, the indexes have other undesirable properties that make them mostly useless for analyzing or discussing aggregate inflation behavior. First, the median series is often housing. For the median CPI, a measure of owners' equivalent rent (OER) was the median series more than 50 percent of the time (roughly twice its relative importance weight).[22] Likewise, for the trimmed-mean PCE price index, OER is almost never excluded (per Dolmas, 2005, it is included 95 percent of the time).[23] The reason this is an issue is that the change in housing services prices is one of the most cyclically sensitive components of CPI (and PCE) inflation; it therefore receives a larger slack coefficient than overall CPI or PCE price inflation, and also does a great job spuriously fitting inflation during the housing collapse that occurred during the 2007–2009 recession. (Housing services prices also have atypical persistence properties because of the way the BLS compute rent changes.) Second, the Dallas Fed's trimmed-mean index excludes 55 percent of PCE

---

[21] The location parameter is the value of μ in $F(x - \mu)$, where $F(\cdot)$ represents a distribution function. Crow and Siddiqui also found that the median worked well if it were combined with two other symmetric order statistics.

[22] The period used for this calculation is 1998–2007; the value comes from materials posted on the Cleveland Federal Reserve Bank's website. Before the median CPI started using the four regional subcomponents of OER (instead of total OER) in its computation, OER was the median series 64 percent of the time.

[23] Another series that is almost never excluded is casino gambling – note that BEA impute the price for this series with the total CPI.

from the total (24 percent from the lower tail and 31 percent from the upper tail), which roughly doubles housing's effective weight and also leaves the measure rather difficult to use for central bank communications or as a monetary policy goal. This latter point is underscored by the fact that median and trimmed-mean PCE price inflation don't run in line with the Fed's longer-run inflation measure (the total PCE price index): Over the relatively stable inflation regime that prevailed from 1997 to 2019, the trimmed-mean PCE measure rose 0.2 percentage point per year faster than the total PCE price index (for the median measure, the average gap was 0.6 percentage point).

A.6 Measures of Nominal and Real Wages

There are two principal macroeconomic indicators of hourly nominal compensation in the United States, and two main indicators of hourly wages. (Note that "compensation" typically refers to wages and salaries plus benefits, while "wages" usually refers to wages and salaries only.)

Productivity and Costs Compensation per Hour

The broadest hourly compensation measure is based on NIPA compensation data and BLS measures of hours; it is reported in the BLS's "Productivity and Costs" (P&C) data release. The source data for these measures are as close to full-universe as possible, as they are benchmarked to the Quarterly Census of Employment and Wages (QCEW), which covered 95 percent of US jobs as of 2022. For pay, the QCEW provides data on total wage and salary payments, including bonuses, stock options (when exercised), severance pay, and tips and gratuities. The P&C measures include all benefits as measured by the NIPA compensation data; however, some of these benefit components are themselves benchmarked much less frequently and come from a variety of source data.[24]

The P&C hourly compensation measure is the total compensation bill divided by total hours. Published data are given as indexes, though unpublished data are available in natural units for most series (which also allows a

---

[24] The BEA began using the QCEW to benchmark *quarterly* wages and salaries starting in 2002; prior to that date, annual data were used for the benchmark and quarterly estimates were interpolated using a quarterly proxy for the wage bill. Quarterly changes in the P&C hourly compensation series become visibly more volatile after around 2000, though results reported by Peneva and coauthor (2017) suggest that the rise in volatility actually began after 1990 or so.

labor share to be computed). Series are published for the total and nonfarm business sectors, the nonfinancial corporate sector, and manufacturing, and start in the late 1940s. In addition, an unpublished "total economy" series is produced. Except for nonfinancial corporate business, the "all persons" hourly compensation measures include imputed values for self-employed workers; separate unpublished data exist for "all employees." In addition, the various P&C series are frequently revised (including over history) to reflect revisions to the employment and NIPA data; in some cases, the P&C revision occurs several months after the revised source data are available.

The P&C report also includes a series for *real* compensation per hour, where the price measure used is the CPI for all urban consumers. (The CPI series used by the BLS for this calculation includes adjustments for past methodological changes.) For most purposes, a better measure is probably the PCE price index (total or market-based); in addition, real compensation per hour can be computed using the nominal series and the relevant output price index for the sector (though a comparable output price index is not available on a quarterly basis, only annually).[25]

Average Hourly Earnings (AHE)

Average hourly earnings (AHE) come from the monthly payroll or "establishment" survey (this is the same survey used to produce payroll employment estimates – see below).[26] These data are revised for two months after their initial release to capture late reporting, as well as annually (to reflect benchmark revisions to the payroll employment data). The measure is computed as aggregate weekly payrolls divided by aggregate weekly hours; the pay concept includes overtime pay, paid vacations, paid sick leave, and regular monthly commissions – but *not* benefits. (It is therefore technically a wage measure, not a compensation measure.) A series for production and nonsupervisory workers is available starting in 1964; the all-employees series only starts in 2006. Real versions of average hourly earnings are also reported after the CPI is released: For real production and nonsupervisory AHE the CPI-W is used; for real all-employee AHE the CPI-U is used.

---

[25] Note that hourly compensation adjusted for consumer prices is sometimes called the *consumption wage*; adjusting for the sector's output price yields what is known as a *product wage*. (Confusingly, in this particular context, "wage" usually refers to hourly *compensation*.)

[26] Like all establishment survey data, the reference period is the pay period that includes the 12th of the month.

The total AHE series covers the private nonfarm sector; detail is included for broad industry categories as well. Note that because of how the aggregate AHE measure is computed, the proper "weights" for aggregating industry-specific AHE values are the share of total private nonfarm hours accounted for by the industry. Specifically, for total payrolls P_i and total hours H_i in industry i, industry-specific AHE values P_i/H_i will aggregate to total AHE, P/H, as follows:

$$\frac{P}{H} = \frac{\sum_i P_i}{\sum_i H_i} = \frac{\sum_i (P_i/H_i) H_i}{\sum_i H_i} = \sum_i \frac{H_i}{H} \frac{P_i}{H_i}. \tag{A.10}$$

Since hours in natural units are not available by industry, industry employment shares are sometimes used when individual industries' contributions to the total need to be calculated.

One quirk about the AHE data is that the seasonally adjusted data should be used to compute 12-month changes, since the BLS include an adjustment in the seasonally adjusted data (but not in the NSA data) to account for whether four or five weeks are included in the relevant survey interval.

Employment Cost Index (ECI)

The employment cost index (ECI) attempts to measure the total cost of labor to an employer in a manner that controls for shifts in employment across different industries and occupations (sometimes called "composition effects"). For example, if employment in a low-wage industry declines, measures like P&C hourly compensation and average hourly earnings will increase, but the ECI shouldn't.[27]

The ECI measures total hourly compensation together with separate indexes for hourly wages and salaries and benefits paid by employers; in addition, health insurance benefits are broken out separately. (Stock options are excluded, as are tips; in addition, bonuses, paid leave, and overtime pay are classified as benefits by the ECI.) Indexes exist for private industry workers as well as for civilian workers, where the latter includes state and local (but not federal) employees. Subindexes broken out by industry and occupation are available, and the aggregate series can be extended as far back as 1979 with a ratio splice to an historical ECI series. Although the ECI is released quarterly it is actually reported for the third month of each

---

[27] An especially large swing of this sort occurred in the P&C and AHE data during the pandemic, when job losses were concentrated among lower-wage workers.

quarter, so quarterly changes in the index are three-month changes (not quarterly average changes).

A.7 Measures of Long-Run Inflation Expectations

Various measures of long-run expected inflation can be obtained from financial-market and survey data. For survey data, the median response is typically preferred to the mean response (this is especially true for the Michigan Survey, where using the median is recommended by the analysts who run the survey).

- The *Survey of Professional Forecasters* (SPF), which is maintained by the Philadelphia Federal Reserve Bank, reports expectations for average annual inflation over the next 10 years. CPI inflation expectations are available starting in 1979 and PCE inflation expectations start in 2007; for the CPI, the 1979–1991 data come from the Blue Chip survey of private forecasters (with two quarters taken from the Livingston survey). The 10-year average inflation rate can be affected by expected short-term inflation, so a better measure of a "long run" expectation is the six-to-ten-year-ahead projection. However, these data are probably not fully reliable until 2011: In January of that year, the survey started showing respondents what their implied six-to-ten-year-ahead forecast was based on their five-year and ten-year projections, so that they could ensure that it looked sensible. (Users of the survey had already been backing out the implied six-to-ten-year-ahead projections on their own, and they didn't always look reasonable.)
- The *Michigan Survey* asks respondents what they expect the average percent change in prices will be during the next 5–10 years. (The survey doesn't ask about a particular price index.) Statistically, there is some evidence that these long-run expectations move in response to current food and energy price inflation. The median measure is available sporadically starting in February 1975 (with some multi-year gaps); a little more regularly starting in 1981 (though still with gaps); and continuously starting in April 1990.
- The New York Federal Reserve Bank run a *Survey of Consumer Expectations* that asks respondents what they expect the 12-month rate of price inflation will be in three years and in five years. The three-year series starts in June of 2013; the five-year series starts in January of 2022.
- Finally, the Atlanta Federal Reserve Bank maintain a survey of businesses that ask about firms' expected change in *unit costs* (not prices)

over the next five to ten years. These data start in February of 2012, and only cover firms in the Atlanta Federal Reserve District.

Most of these surveys also ask questions about shorter-term (year-ahead) inflation expectations. In addition, the Conference Board report a year-ahead expected inflation measure as part of their consumer confidence survey. Over history, the Conference Board measure (which is an average) runs noticeably above the median measure from the Michigan Survey; the reason appears to be less related to the upper tail's pushing up the mean than to the Conference Board's survey instrument.[28]

The main source of longer-term expected inflation data from *financial markets* comes from comparisons of nominal and inflation-indexed Treasury yields (TIPS yields). One way to do this is to simply calculate the spread between nominal Treasury yields and real yields for TIPS with the same time to maturity; a more-refined calculation takes into account that the effective duration of a TIPS is longer than that of the same-maturity nominal Treasury because of the different timing of their cashflows (for TIPS, the inflation adjustment to the principal is paid out when the security matures). The spread between comparable-maturity nominal and TIPS yields is called inflation compensation, or the "implied breakeven." As TIPS are indexed to the not seasonally adjusted (NSA) CPI, the resulting expectation is for the change in the headline CPI.[29]

In practice, a problem with a TIPS-based expectations measure is that it is difficult to determine whether a change in inflation *compensation* reflects a change in inflation *expectations*, as movements in TIPS yields can also reflect the lower liquidity of these securities relative to nominal Treasuries as well as changes in perceptions of inflation *risk*.[30] In addition, because the inflation-adjusted principal payment can never go below the security's par value, there is an embedded option that needs to be accounted for too (this is only relevant in periods with low inflation, since that's when there's a realistic possibility that the average inflation rate from issue to maturity might be negative).[31] Generally, the TIPS-based longer-run inflation expectation

---

[28] The Conference Board ask respondents to indicate where their expectation falls in a range; it's possible this draws respondents to whatever value is in the middle. That would tend to prop up the measure in periods where actual inflation is low.

[29] And because it's the NSA CPI, there are predictable seasonal swings in TIPS returns that in theory should be arbitraged away, but in actuality don't seem to be. (True believers in the efficient markets hypothesis should ignore that last part.)

[30] The liquidity of TIPS issues varies along the yield curve, which appears to be why things like oil-price shocks can affect the long end of the curve.

[31] There's also an indexation lag.

that people focus on is the five-year five-year-forward rate, which can be obtained from the relevant yield curves; the idea is that this measure should be largely free of the effects of transitory near-term inflation shocks.

Another market-based indicator of expected inflation comes from *inflation swaps* (sometimes called CPI fixings). These tend to track TIPS inflation breakevens relatively closely up to a spread (known as the *inflation basis*); the spread reflects the fact that a swap is a derivative that is intermediated by a dealer, who incurs a funding risk because of the way that they hedge their position. Although overall trading volumes for swaps tend to be much lower than for TIPS, swaps are more liquid at the short end of the curve, which suggests that swaps might provide a better read on near-term expected inflation than TIPS with a short time to maturity.

Appendix B

Measuring Output

To say that net output to-day is greater, but the price-level lower, than ten years ago ... is a proposition of a similar character to the statement that Queen Victoria was a better queen but not a happier woman than Queen Elizabeth ...

Keynes, General Theory, p. 40

In terms of the index number formulas involved, quantity measurement in the National Income and Product Accounts (NIPAs) is very similar to how prices are measured. But before we get into that, it's worth thinking about the conceptual basis of GDP – otherwise, how will we know how well it represents the Y_t of our theories?[1]

B.1 The Logic of the NIPAs

For those of a certain bent, the NIPAs are an endless source of fascination. (For those who don't share such enthusiasms, please feel free to skip this section – but you're really missing out.)

Start with the income statement of a firm (panel A of Figure B.1) for a given period of time, such as a quarter. On the left-hand side are the receipts from goods sold and on the right-hand side are the expenses incurred in production. From an accounting standpoint, additions to inventories (of intermediate or final goods) do not count as a current expense because they

---

[1] One other measure of output that is commonly used for empirical work is the Federal Reserve's index of industrial production. This index covers the entire (private) industrial sector (manufacturing, mining, and utilities); part of the index is based on actual physical quantities (ingots of aluminium, numbers of autos, and so on). It has the advantage of being monthly, and is one of the indicators used by the NBER to date business cycles, but it only covers a subset of the economy. (There is a related measure called *industrial goods GDP* that is based on NIPA data; the two don't always match, though.)

(A) Income statement of a firm

Receipts	Expenses
Sales	Compensation of employees Rents Interest paid net of interest received Indirect taxes paid to government Purchases of intermediate goods minus Change in inventories of intermediate goods Depreciation of capital minus Change in inventories of final goods Profits

(B) Calculation of value added

Output	Costs
Sales plus Change in inventories of final goods minus Purchases of intermediate goods plus Change in inventories of intermediate goods	Compensation of employees Rents Interest paid net of interest received Indirect taxes paid to government Depreciation of capital Profits

Figure B.1 How to measure value added from an income statement.

represent acquisition of an asset (that's also why capital investment isn't considered an expense); reductions in inventories *do* count as an expense because – like the depreciation of the firm's physical capital – it represents a portion of the firms' assets that are used up in that period. In addition, indirect taxes represent a cost attached to goods sold, and so are considered an expense as well. Both sides of the ledger are equal because profits are defined that way (that is, as a residual).

We can measure GDP three ways; the income statement provides two of them. Since the ledger initially balances, we can maintain that balance if we add or subtract the same amount from each column. Panel B does just that, by subtracting purchases of intermediates and adding changes in intermediate and final inventories to both sides. Written like this, the left column represents the firm's value added – that is, total output less the intermediates it uses for that period's production.[2] Total output is what the firm sells in a given period with an adjustment to account for whether it sold the good from its existing inventory (which shouldn't count as current production), or whether it added to its inventory (which is unsold production but production nonetheless). The use of intermediates is deducted from gross output to yield value added; note that intermediate inputs used in production need to include those that are taken out of inventories, but not those that are added to inventories (as the latter aren't used in that period's production). The right-hand side, then, gives all of the costs incurred in that period's production. Summing across all firms in the economy yields total value added (GDP) on the left, and total incomes generated from producing that value added on the right, which is called gross domestic income (GDI).

The other way to measure GDP is to measure final expenditures on currently produced domestic output; the only complication is that we need to include three other things in our definition of "final expenditures." The first is inventory changes: If a firm makes a net addition to inventories during a period, the national accounts convention is that the firm is making a "purchase" of either its own output or of intermediate goods. The idea behind counting the net addition to inventories of final or intermediate goods is that for all we know, the firm meant to acquire these as an asset, just as they make purchases of capital goods (investment) to add to their plant and equipment. The change in inventories in a period is actually counted as business investment, though it is distinguished from "fixed" investment – buildings and equipment. In any case, goods that are produced this period – including intermediate goods not used up in production – represent *somebody's* output, and should count as such; if they weren't, then the expenditure side of the NIPAs wouldn't be able to capture total production.

The second thing that needs to be included is government purchases of final output. This comes in two forms, consumption (payment of compensation to government workers and depreciation of the government's capital stock), and the purchase of new capital goods (office buildings, fighter jets, and so on). The idea behind the consumption portion is that this represents the value of government services, which are measured in terms of their production cost.[3] Finally, we need to deduct imports, because these

---

[2] This is how the BEA measure value added for their industry accounts.
[3] When there is a government shutdown but government workers are (eventually) paid, it implies an increase in the price index for G: Real output (hours worked) declines, but compensation accrued during the shutdown (which goes into *nominal* output) remains the same.

aren't purchases of domestically produced output (exports, by contrast, are considered a final expenditure on US output by foreigners).

In reality, things aren't so straightforward as all this makes it sound. The NIPAs want changes in final goods inventories to be comparable to this period's sales, but accounting practices allow the firm to value what's taken out of inventories in different ways (the adjustment that the BEA make to rectify this is known as the inventory valuation adjustment – IVA). Similarly, the way depreciation is measured on a firm's balance sheet involves various accounting conventions (it's really depreciation as measured for tax purposes), so a "capital consumption adjustment" (CCAdj) is needed to convert accounting (or "book") depreciation into NIPA depreciation, where the latter is trying to measure what part of the capital stock is being used up in that period's production.[4] Yet another wrinkle is that we need to make sure to measure proprietors' income, which is basically a form of profits ("profits" in the NIPAs correspond to *corporate* profits). Finally, it turns out that the two measures – GDP and GDI – don't usually equal each other: There's some slippage because expenditures are measured from one set of data sources, while incomes are measured using another; the result is a *statistical discrepancy* between expenditure-based GDP and GDI.[5]

All of these measures are nominal. For GDI, the real measure is obtained by dividing the nominal measure by the price index for (expenditure-side) GDP.

B.2 Fisher Quantity Indexes

The Fisher quantity index is the geometric mean of a Laspeyres and a Paasche quantity index, where the Laspeyres quantity index between time 0 and time 1 is given as

---

[4] When profits are adjusted for the IVA and CCAdj, they are known as "economic" profits, since they represent profits generated by production (which is what BEA are trying to measure). Profits *without* this sort of adjustment are sometimes (loosely) referred to as "book" profits, since they are closer to an accounting measure – what's actually on firms' ledger books.

[5] Is one measure more accurate? It's hard to know. Even though it seems as though incomes would be relatively straightforward to measure, they aren't always reported accurately (or at all). The BEA therefore make adjustments as best as they can based on things like IRS studies of income underreporting, but ultimately there's only so much you can do (also, some of these studies aren't all that recent). One practice that avoids having to come down on one side or the other is to use the geometric mean of GDP and GDI (the BEA now report the arithmetic mean, but the geometric mean is more appropriate); another is to use both in a statistical filtering exercise.

$$Q_L = \frac{\sum_{i=1}^{n} p_i^0 q_i^1}{\sum_{i=1}^{n} p_i^0 q_i^0}, \qquad (B.1)$$

and the Paasche quantity index is

$$Q_P = \frac{\sum_{i=1}^{n} p_i^1 q_i^1}{\sum_{i=1}^{n} p_i^1 q_i^0}. \qquad (B.2)$$

We've just swapped the price and quantity variables relative to the corresponding price indexes; hence, the Laspeyres index uses time-0 prices to weight quantities in the two periods, while the Paasche uses time-1 prices.[6] Likewise, the Fisher quantity index Q_F between periods 0 and 1 is:

$$Q_F = \sqrt{Q_L Q_P}. \qquad (B.3)$$

Just as for prices, the Fisher quantity index can be computed for adjoining time periods, then "chained" together to yield a time series of index values. Once again, if you don't have the patience to use the Fisher formulas to make aggregates (or to remove a component from an aggregate), a reasonable approximation is provided by the Törnqvist *quantity* index number formula:

$$\ln Q_{t,t-1} = \sum_i \tfrac{1}{2}(\omega_{i,t} + \omega_{i,t-1}) \ln \left(\frac{q_{i,t}}{q_{i,t-1}} \right), \qquad (B.4)$$

where, as before, $\omega_{i,t}$ is the *nominal* expenditure share for good i in period t. These total quantity changes can then be chained together to yield a time series of index values.

B.3 Practical Considerations When Using the NIPAs

That's a Cook's tour of the national accounts. What are some things to watch out for when using these data?

The most important thing to know about chained quantity data is that they are not additive – in other words, real $C + I + G + NX$ is *not* equal to real GDP.[7] The reason this can be a source of confusion is that the BEA report real series both as an index number and in what is called "chained dollars." However, the way that the chained-dollar quantity is computed simply involves multiplying the nominal value of the series in the year for which

---

[6] In most cases, these $q_{i,t}$ terms come from deflating detailed (that is, highly disaggregated) nominal components by suitable price indexes.

[7] One very minor caveat is that the BEA do try to get the arithmetic average of the quarterly indexes in a given year to equal the annual index (and make some adjustments to do so).

the index equals 100 by the index in each period (divided by 100). Just as one cannot simply add together index numbers for subaggregates to obtain an aggregate real index, the chained dollar series are not generally additive.[8] Similarly, just as the ratio of two quantity indexes is meaningless, "real shares" computed from the ratios of chained-dollar aggregates are meaningless as well. If you want to make your own aggregates, you need to use the Fisher (or Törnqvist) formulas. And if you want to compute shares, using nominal data is (almost) always best.

Second, the national accounts data are subject to revision at various times. For a given quarter, there are initially three different estimates that are reported (for the first quarter, say, the BEA put out estimates in April, May, and June); each one incorporates more-complete source data (for the first release in a quarter not all months of data are available for the quarter, so the BEA make assumptions about their values). In addition, when the BEA receive the QCEW data (with a one-quarter lag), they revise the income side of the accounts for the previous and current quarters. After that, BEA revise the accounts annually (because they get better source data, including tax data, on a yearly basis), as well as every five years (when they get the most-comprehensive data from the quinquennial industrial censuses). The BEA can also change their methodology, which means that a lot of history can revise: For example, the BEA didn't always use chained Fisher indexes to measure output, but when they moved to that (in two stages), all of history was eventually revised. Similarly, the idea of counting intellectual property as a form of investment is a relatively new one, and was done retroactively after it was introduced. What that means is that many results won't look exactly the same (or even vaguely the same) after the data have been revised.[9] If you want to make sure that your own results stay reasonably robust for more than a few months, it's not a bad idea to use data that have already been through an annual revision (especially if they involve income-side variables). It's also good to check other peoples' results using current data if they are more than a few years old.[10]

---

[8] Except, of course, in the year for which the underlying index equals 100 (which gives you nominal GDP in that year).

[9] The BEA will also occasionally change the year that's used to compute the "chained-dollar" estimates. By itself that won't change the growth rates, because the underlying quantity indexes are the same.

[10] For example, some of the original empirical findings for the new-Keynesian Phillips curve change noticeably when revised data are used, even when the estimation period is the same as that used for the original results (Mavroeidis et al., 2014).

Appendix C

Measuring Employment

It's a recession when your neighbor loses his job; it's a depression when you lose yours.
Harry S Truman

Although measuring employment *seems* as though it should be easier than trying to make summary statistics for prices and output, it turns out to be more complicated – and more interesting – than you'd expect.

The Bureau of Labor Statistics (BLS) draw on two sources of data to compute employment: the Current Establishment Survey (CES), which surveys businesses about employment, hours worked by their employees, and employee earnings; and the Current Population Survey (CPS), which is a detailed survey of households that is used to compute the unemployment and labor force participation rates (among many other things). The establishment survey breaks down employment by industry, and has separate subaggregates for the private sector and government. The household survey has demographic detail (including age, gender, educational attainment, and race or ethnicity) and BLS break out some of their principal statistics along these lines. Data from both surveys are summarized together in a BLS release that usually comes out on the first Friday of the month following the survey period (sometimes it comes out a week later). In this part of the appendix, we'll go through a very high-level overview of each set of estimates, with a focus on some first-order problems that analysts can face when using these data.

C.1 The Establishment Survey (CES)

When people talk about "the number of jobs created in the economy last month," they are talking about the change in the nonfarm payroll employment measure from the CES, which is also known as the *establishment survey.* (Recall that the average hourly earnings data also come from the CES.) There are several things worth knowing about these data.

- First, the CES counts someone as employed if they are on the payroll and receive pay during the pay period that contains the 12th of the month. The period that contains the 12th is sometimes called the reference period; occasionally, how an analyst interprets the published data for a given month will be influenced by whether strange events occurred around the 12th of that month.
- Second, because the CES is a sample its estimates reflect sampling variability. As of early 2023, the standard error for the change in nonfarm payroll employment in a given month was about 81,000, implying a 90 percent confidence interval of plus or minus 130,000.
- Third, the CES sample misses employment at two types of firms: those that have newly opened, and those that have recently gone out of business. (The BLS can eventually sort this out, but it takes about a year for the necessary data to become available.) BLS therefore compute what is known as a *births–deaths model* and use its results to make projections of the requisite adjustments in real time. They do this by first excluding establishments that report zero employment (naturally, those that don't report at all are also excluded). The rationale for this is that BLS find that births and deaths in a given month tend to roughly offset each other, so excluding apparent deaths does most of the work. The BLS then use an ARIMA model to fit and forecast the portion of net births over deaths that isn't captured by the first calculation (they use QCEW data for this).

In a particular month, the CES data are open for revision in the preceding two months to incorporate late reporting by respondents. Because BLS use concurrent seasonal adjustment (which means that seasonal factors are computed using all data up to the current month), the seasonal factors for the preceding two months can also revise. In addition, once a year (when the January data are released) the data are benchmarked to the QCEW from March of the preceding year.[1] (BLS provide a preliminary estimate of the benchmark revision in late summer.) Unlike how the household survey's population controls are handled, the benchmarking procedure "wedges in"

---

[1] As was noted in the discussion of compensation, the QCEW is close to a full-universe sample (it covers something like 97 percent of in-scope CES employment). For the other 3 percent (called "noncovered employment"), the BLS use other data sources to come up with the full benchmark adjustment.

the revisions for the year preceding the March benchmark; it also revises the data going forward (that is, in April and later) by using the same growth rates but applying them to the new benchmarked level. As part of the benchmark revision, BLS reestimate their births–deaths model, and apply newly computed seasonal factors to the preceding five years' worth of data. The Productivity and Costs (P&C) data also incorporate the benchmarked CES estimates on their own revision schedule.

C.2 The Household Survey (CPS)

The CPS is also known as the *household survey*. We have already looked at a number of series from the household survey in Chapter 5 and discussed one of the issues associated with using these data (the periodic introduction of *population controls* – see note 35 in that chapter). Some other things to be aware of include the following.

- In the CPS, a given household is assigned to a *rotation group* (there are eight, and each is supposed to be representative of the population); the household is sampled for a total of eight months (they are in the sample for four months, out for the next eight, and back again for four more months). The rotation groups are staggered such that 75 percent of the sample are the same across two months and 50 percent are from a year earlier. The typical survey reference week (that is, the week that is used to define a respondent's employment or unemployment status) is the week (Sunday to Saturday) that contains the 12th of the month. The sample that the CPS is trying to capture is the civilian noninstitutional population of the 50 states plus the District of Columbia; it therefore excludes active-duty military and people in nursing homes (or in jail).
- The household survey also reports employment data, but they tend to be much noisier than the CES payroll estimates and so aren't used as much. An important difference between the two is that the CPS counts someone as "employed" only once even if they have two or more jobs; by contrast, the CES would (in principle) pick up each job in its employment total.[2]
- Once again, since the CPS is a sample the statistics that are based on it are affected by sampling variability: The BLS report that at an unemployment rate of 6 percent, the 90 percent confidence interval

---

[2] There can also be problems with misclassification of employment or labor-force status in the CPS; see Ahn and Hamilton (2022) for a discussion.

for a monthly change in the unemployment rate would be plus-or-minus 0.2 percentage point.

The rotation of the CPS sample means that it is possible to make an algorithm that allows one to roughly follow the same respondent over the four months they are interviewed (the Atlanta Federal Reserve Bank exploit this feature of the CPS sample to compute a wage change measure for continuously employed workers). The microdata from the CPS are also made available with a lag, and have been used in countless empirical labor papers.

Appendix D

Seasonal Adjustment in a (Very Small) Nutshell

The poet says that April is the cruelest month, but seasonally adjusted, January is the cruelest month.

Herbert Stein

No, seasonally adjusted, January is the warmest month.

Arthur Burns[1]

We saw in Chapter 2 that real GDP was subject to a pronounced seasonal cycle. This is true of many indicators of real activity and inflation; the reason we don't see them in the published data is that statistical agencies *seasonally adjust* any series for which seasonality appears to be present.

There are two rationales for seasonal adjustment: one practical, and one economic. The practical reason is that seasonal swings can account for so much of the observed variation in a series that important lower-frequency movements – such as the start of a recession – can be obscured, especially in real time. (Similarly, correlations between unadjusted series can be overstated if both contain a seasonal cycle.) The economic reason is that the predictability of seasonal movements suggests that individuals and firms mostly expect and look through them, so seasonally adjusted data provide a better indicator of what people are basing their actions and decisions on. That last point is debatable, though. Say we are thinking about adjustment costs – why shouldn't we use not seasonally adjusted (NSA) data to try to ascertain how important such costs are? The NSA data are what firms and individuals actually see and react to; using smoothed (seasonally adjusted) data would seem to remove a large amount of salient variation. These questions and others

---

[1] Both are wrong: If the seasonal adjustment is done properly, every month is equally mediocre.

were hotly contested back in the day; they seem to receive less attention now, with much of the concern among practitioners being standardization of procedures and what constitutes best practice.[2]

If seasonal patterns are stable, then one simple way to correct for them is to compare current data with data from a year ago. A common convention for monthly series, therefore, is to calculate their "official" 12-month percent change with NSA data (this is done for the CPI, for example). Most of the time the difference between using SA or NSA data to compute a 12-month change is pretty small (as was noted earlier, average hourly earnings is an exception in that the SA data should always be used to calculate a 12-month change).

For better or worse, most US data series are seasonally adjusted (the only ones that aren't are those that don't have a statistically discernable seasonal, or those for which not enough history is yet available to perform seasonal adjustment). The main seasonal adjustment procedure used in the United States is the Census Bureau's X-13 ARIMA routine, which can be used for monthly or quarterly data; "13" denotes the 13th iteration of the program (the filter itself is called "X-11" because it's in its 11th iteration), while "ARIMA" refers to the use of ARIMA models to extend ("pad") a series past its final observation, which keeps the filter from becoming one-sided as it approaches the series' endpoint.[3] The intuition behind the algorithm itself (when used on monthly data) is that it involves successive applications of weighted moving averages (filters), with the first being a two-month moving average of a 12-month moving average: The 12-month average takes care of seasonality, and the two-month moving average centers the moving average window on a month (instead of between two adjacent months).

[2] The implicit assumption among users of seasonally adjusted data seems to be that applying the same seasonal adjustment filter to each series minimizes the chance that nonseasonal relationships across series will be distorted (or spurious). To appreciate some of the deeper economic and econometric questions that are involved, Hylleberg (1992) is a good (though somewhat dated) single source; Eurostat's 2015 guidelines provide a recent example of the practical concerns that vex statistical agencies; and Eurostat's 2018 *Handbook on Seasonal Adjustment* is a comprehensive and accessible technical guide. Macaulay (1931) remains worth reading both because it is one of the first studies to focus on the topic in the context of economic data and because its basic approach to seasonal adjustment is the ancestor of the seasonal adjustment algorithm used by US statistical agencies; the book also gives an idea of how difficult and labor-intensive such procedures were when a "computer" referred to a person who could do sums. (This Macaulay is the same person who came up with the concept of duration for a coupon-bearing bond; apparently he had a real knack for weighted averages.)

[3] A common alternative is SEATS (Signal Extraction in ARIMA Time Series), which starts from an ARIMA representation of the series.

The various other filters that are applied are ones that, based on experience, seem to do well with most time series.[4] The conceptual underpinning for all this is the idea that a time series Y_t can be decomposed into a trend and cycle component TC_t, a seasonal component S_t, and other irregular (unexplained) movements I_t; in multiplicative form this implies

$$Y_t = TC_t \times S_t \times I_t. \tag{D.1}$$

We can also express the decomposition in additive form, which is typically used for the seasonal adjustment of growth rates (taking the log difference of Y_t in equation D.1 suggests why this is sensible.)

In many cases, statistical agencies will also perform what is known as "intervention analysis." This is basically a way of judgmentally removing particular outliers in order to ensure that the estimated seasonal factors are not distorted; for example, when computing the seasonal factors for the CPI for fuel oil an analyst might dummy out a winter month that was especially cold in New England so that it doesn't influence seasonals in later years. (Seasonal adjustment routines can also screen for outliers generally.) In addition, the data are corrected for things like trading-day effects (not all months have the same number of business days, and some days of the week are more important than others) and holiday effects (for example, Easter can appear in March or April). Some other practical considerations involve whether to compute seasonal factors concurrently (using all available data) or currently (using last year's estimated seasonals for this year), and how far back to allow seasonals to revise before they are considered final. Another question that arises is whether to use direct or indirect seasonal adjustment for a series that is an aggregate of other series: Direct seasonal adjustment seasonally adjusts the aggregate itself, while indirect seasonal adjustment seasonally adjusts each component and then aggregates them up to obtain a series that is (hopefully) free of seasonality. GDP, for example, is indirectly seasonally adjusted because it is an aggregate of seasonally adjusted subcomponents (we would say that residual seasonality is present if seasonal cycles remain in the aggregated series).

To make all of this a little more concrete, Figure D.1 performs a seasonal adjustment exercise on not seasonally adjusted monthly growth in industrial production (IP) for the manufacturing sector (the sample runs from 1957 to 2007). The first panel plots the spectrum of the raw (NSA) series; in the figure, the x-axis scale is expressed as a fraction of π (call it f), so the period

---

[4] One of them, the Henderson moving average, first appeared more than a hundred years ago (in 1916).

(A) Spectrum of raw series

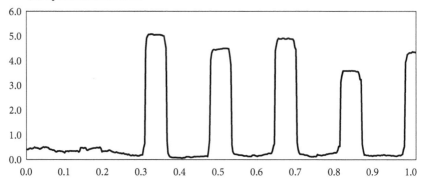

(B) Spectrum of series after X-11 seasonal adjustment

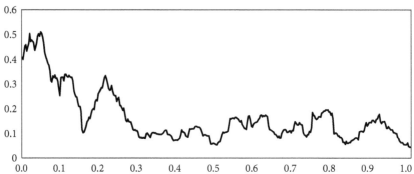

(C) Spectrum of published seasonally adjusted series

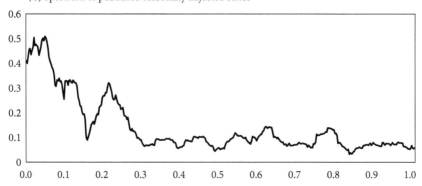

Figure D.1 Effects of seasonal adjustment. Panel A plots the spectrum of the monthly log difference of NSA manufacturing IP (the x-axis is expressed as fractions of π). Panel B plots the spectrum that results after applying the X-11 filter; panel C plots the spectrum of the published seasonally adjusted series. Sample used for the figures runs from 1957 to 2007.

(in months) is given as $2/f$. The five large peaks correspond to periods of 6, 4, 3, 2.4, and 2 months, which definitely points to the presence of seasonality; in fact, so much of the variability of the series is accounted for by seasonal swings that the very small blip indicating an annual cycle (at 0.17π, or 11.8 months) is barely visible, as are the minor wiggles that show up at business-cycle frequencies.

Panel B plots the spectrum of the series that is obtained by simply applying the default version of the X-11 seasonal filter under the assumption of additive seasonals (recall that the data are monthly growth rates). The series is now mostly free of any seasonality (the small dips in the spectrum around 0.5 and 0.85 suggest that, if anything, the filter has worked too well). With the effects of seasonality removed, the contribution at business-cycle frequencies is much more apparent (note that the range of the y-axis in this panel is a tenth as large as in the top panel). Finally, panel C plots the spectrum of the *published* seasonally adjusted series, which does an even better job flattening out the spectrum at higher frequencies. (A large amount of skilled labor is applied to the seasonal adjustment of the published IP data.)

Appendix E

Other Odds and Ends

In instruction there is no separation into categories.

Lun Yü, XV:39

There are several statistical conventions and results that are worth knowing about, especially when using data from the NIPAs or other government
sources.

E.1 Growth Rates

Most US statistical agencies report growth rates in one of three ways: as
a percent change, as a percent change at an annual rate, or as a percent
change from the same period a year ago. How a percent change is annualized
depends on the fraction of the year that the original change is computed
over – specifically, the gross growth rate $(1 + g_t)$ over a period is raised to
the power p, where p is the number of periods that span a year. For example,
if x_t is a quarterly series, then a quarterly percent change at an annual rate
is given by

$$100 \times \left(\left[\frac{x_t}{x_{t-1}} \right]^4 - 1 \right), \tag{E.1}$$

while a five-month percent change at an annual rate would be given as

$$100 \times \left(\left[\frac{y_t}{y_{t-5}} \right]^{\frac{12}{5}} - 1 \right), \tag{E.2}$$

where here y_t represents a monthly observation. Likewise, a two-year percent change at an annual rate would be given by

274

$$100 \times \left(\left[\frac{z_t}{z_{t-2}} \right]^{\frac{1}{2}} - 1 \right), \tag{E.3}$$

because half of a two-year period equals a year (here, z_t is an annual observation).

Most data in the NIPAs are annual or quarterly averages; the growth rate for the former is just a simple percent change, while growth rates for the latter are reported either as a four-quarter change or as a quarterly change at an annual rate. Growth rates for monthly series tend to be reported either as a 12-month change or a three-month change at an annual rate. (The monthly levels can also be averaged into a quarterly value, in which case the quarterly formulas can be used.)

By contrast, most empirical work uses suitably scaled log-differences instead of annualized percent changes.[1] One reason is that an exponentially growing series will be linear in logs; by contrast, annualized percent changes involve a nonlinear transformation. Economists prefer linear models, especially when regressions are involved. (Also, a log difference of -0.2 is exactly offset by a log difference of 0.2; by contrast, a 20 percent decline requires a 25 percent increase to return to the initial value.) A growth rate computed as a log-difference will be smaller than the corresponding percent change; the easiest way to see this – short of typing a few examples into a calculator – is to note that a first-order Taylor expansion of $\ln x$ around $x_0 = 1$ equals $x - 1$. If x is defined as a gross growth rate (for example, if $x = \frac{y_t}{y_{t-1}}$), then $x - 1$ yields the percent change in y_t divided by 100, while $\ln x$ yields the log difference of y_t. But $x - 1$ is a line that is everywhere higher than $\ln x$ (except for a single point of tangency at $x = 1$). Hence, the log difference (times 100) of a series that is rising or falling will always be smaller than the percent change in the series.

Note that a 12-month log difference of a variable x in period t equals the 12-month moving sum of the monthly log differences; if each monthly is expressed at an annual rate, then you need to take the average. (This is why regressing the 12-month change in month t on the 12-month change in month $t - 1$ is in questionable taste: Eleven of the monthly changes will be the same across the two series; also, the month-to-month variability

---

[1] "Suitably scaled" means 400 times the log difference for a quarterly "percent" change at an annual rate, or 1,200 for a monthly "percent" change at an annual rate. If the reason why log-differences are used in the first place is unintuitive, recall from calculus that $d \ln(x) = dx/x$; the right-hand side is the continuous-time equivalent of the usual formula for a growth rate, $\Delta x_t / x_{t-1}$.

of the 12-month change can be larger than the variability of a monthly change.)

E.2 Quarterly Arithmetic

A useful approximation that also demonstrates a potential pitfall associated with using quarterly average or annual average data is the following.

Say that we have quarterly data for Q_T and Q_{T-1} that represent averages of the relevant months. Assume that the three months in a quarter T are denoted as M_1^T, M_2^T, M_3^T, so that

$$Q_T = \frac{1}{3} \times \left(M_1^T + M_2^T + M_3^T \right). \tag{E.4}$$

If the annualized percent change of Q_T is denoted as q_T, so that

$$q_T = 100 \times \left(\left[\frac{Q_T}{Q_{T-1}} \right]^4 - 1 \right), \tag{E.5}$$

and if the one-month percent change for a given month i in quarter T, *not* expressed at an annual rate, is written as m_i^T, then it's straightforward to show that

$$q_T \approx \frac{1}{3} \left(4 \cdot m_2^{T-1} + 8 \cdot m_3^{T-1} + 12 \cdot m_1^T + 8 \cdot m_2^T + 4 \cdot m_3^T \right) \tag{E.6}$$

will be a reasonable approximation so long as none of the m values is too large in absolute terms.[2] Note in particular that the growth rate for the first month of the $T-1$ quarter doesn't enter the approximation.

The intuition for this result can be seen from Figure E.1 (it can also be derived explicitly if we use the approximation $\ln(1+g) \approx g$ for small g). The chart plots the Q_{T-1} and Q_T levels implied by the monthly growth rates m; for this example, all of the monthly growth rates are initially zero except for a positive growth rate in m_1^T. In the first panel of Figure E.1, the level for the first month of the first quarter will be increased if the first monthly growth rate increases; since both quarters rise by the same amount, the *quarterly* average change is the same. (That's why the m_1^{T-1} term doesn't enter the

---

[2] This is a useful result when dealing with monthly data from the national accounts, as the NIPAs typically report quarterly average growth rates; using this formula lets you quickly compute the effects of a revision to the monthlies. (The approximation is sometimes called *quarterly arithmetic*; analysts who work with both types of growth rates can recite these weights in their sleep.)

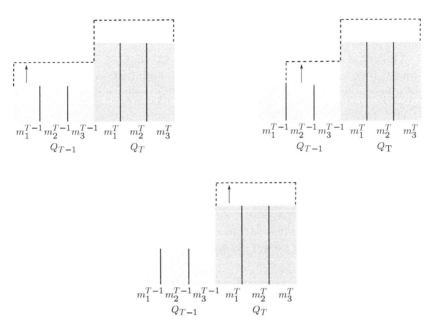

Figure E.1 Intuition behind quarterly arithmetic. Figure shows effects of an increase in a given month on Q_T and Q_{T-1} levels.

approximation.) Panel 2 shows a case when the monthly growth rate in the second month of the first quarter becomes positive; the level of Q_T is boosted fully while the average level of Q_{T-1} rises by a little less; the result is a modest increase in the Q_T growth rate. The final panel shows a case where only the growth rate for the first month of the second quarter increases; this has no effect on Q_{T-1} but boosts the level in every month of Q_T, which yields the largest increase in the quarterly growth rate. (This is why the m_1^T term receives the biggest weight in the approximation.)

Why is this important? Well, say that the monthly values are just uncorrelated draws from a mean-zero distribution. If we regress the resulting quarterly series on its lag, we would expect to find an AR parameter of around 0.2105 – in other words, even though the underlying monthlies are just noise, the process of quarterly averaging will induce a positive autocorrelation between two adjacent quarters.[3] That has implications for how we should interpret an observed autocorrelation in time-aggregated data, and

---

[3] This is straightforward to show – just compute $cov(Q_T, Q_{T-1})$ and $var(Q_T)$ under the assumption that the approximation (E.6) holds with equality.

also demonstrates why using the quarterly average growth rate q_{T-1} as an instrument for q_T is a bad idea.[4]

This result is a specific application of a general result by Working (1960), who also showed that in the continuous-time limit (that is, as the number of subperiods n becomes very large), the AR parameter approaches 0.25. Working's general formula is

$$\frac{n^2 - 1}{2(2n^2 + 1)}, \tag{E.7}$$

which for our monthly example ($n = 3$) evaluates to $8/38 = 0.2105$ (what we would find by direct computation).[5]

Finally, a similar formula exists for the contribution of quarterly percent changes x_t (not at an annual rate) to an annual-average over annual-average growth rate. If A_T is an annual-average level, and a_T is its percent change:

$$a_T = 100 \times \left(\frac{A_T}{A_{T-1}} - 1\right), \tag{E.8}$$

then

$$a_T \approx \frac{1}{4}\left(1 \cdot x_2^{T-1} + 2 \cdot x_3^{T-1} + 3 \cdot x_4^{T-1} + 4 \cdot x_1^T + 3 \cdot x_2^T + 2 \cdot x_3^T + 1 \cdot x_4^T\right). \tag{E.9}$$

From Working's formula (E.7) with $n = 4$, we would expect these annual average growth rates to have an AR parameter of 0.2273 if the x values are uncorrelated with each other.

E.3 Flows and Stocks

A flow variable is a quantity expressed "per unit time," for example, dollars spent on consumer goods per quarter, or output per year. When dealing with periods shorter than a year, a common convention is to express a flow at an annual rate; this is done by multiplying the flow by p, where p is the number of periods that would span a year. (Note that this will have no effect on the growth rate.)

---

[4] One way to (mostly) get around the problem is to use the three-month change over a quarter, except that these are usually noisier.

[5] A related question is how tests of a model would be affected by observing the data at (say) a quarterly frequency even though decisions are made at a higher frequency, and also whether spurious statistical relationships might result from time aggregation. This problem periodically vexes people; see Christiano and Eichenbaum (1987) for one of the earlier attempts to ponder it.

What this also means is that the flow over a year can be computed as the average of the flows over contiguous subannual periods, so long as the subannual periods are each expressed at an annual rate. For example, if four quarterly flows in a year are expressed at annual rates, averaging them cancels out the annualization factor (here, four), which is the same thing as summing the four quarterly flows if those flows are *not* at an annual rate. Note that the denominator will still be "per unit time," except that the time period will be increased as the flows are cumulated. For example, if we have four quarterly flows a, b, c, d, each one expressed at a quarterly rate (so "flow per quarter"), the units for $a + b$ are "$(a + b)$ per two quarters," the units for $a + b + c$ are "$(a + b + c)$ per three quarters," and the full year is given as "$(a + b + c + d)$ per four quarters" (that is, "per year").

Stocks are cumulated flows. The usual convention is to report stocks as of the end of a specified period, which means that the December value of a stock reported at a monthly frequency will also be its fourth-quarter and annual values. In empirical work, it's important to keep track of the timing: For example, if you want the start-of-year t value of a stock variable, it will equal the value reported in period $t - 1$. Similarly, multiplying the stock by a rate (for instance, multiplying a $t - 1$ stock of wealth by a time-t interest rate) will yield a flow (asset income) over period t.[6]

E.4 Dimensional Analysis in Economics

The dimension of a variable in this context refers to the units in which it is measured. For example, the units of a nominal flow y_t would be "dollars per quarter" [$\$/t$], while those of a real flow x_t would be "goods per quarter" [O/t] – the "O" here stands for "output," the "t" stands for "time," and the square brackets refer to the variable's dimensions. We get a real from a nominal by dividing the nominal by a price P_t, whose dimensions are "dollars per good" (that is, "dollars per unit of real output") [$\$/O$], so:

$$[x_t] = \left[\frac{y_t}{P_t} \right] = \frac{[\$/t]}{[\$/O]} = [O/t]. \tag{E.10}$$

Here are some slightly less trivial examples.

- *An interest rate:* Percent per unit time (for example, percent per year).
- *Unit labor costs:* Unit labor costs are measured as the nominal wage (dollars per hour, [$\$/h$]) divided by average labor productivity (real

---

[6] Of course, this calculation ignores the effects of any changes in the stock over period t.

output per hour of labor input, $[O/h]$). The resulting units are "dollars (spent on labor) per unit output," or $[\$/O]$, which is what we would expect to find as the dimensions of an average (or marginal) cost. Similarly, some people like to call labor's share of output "real unit labor costs" – if you divide $[\$/O]$ by P ("dollars per unit output", also $[\$/O]$), you get a dimensionless scalar [1] (a number).

- *The real exchange rate:* From the vantage of the United States, the exchange rate e is dollars per unit foreign currency, or $[\$/f]$. The US price level P is $[\$/O]$, dollars per unit of US output, while the foreign country price level P^* is $[f/O^*]$. The real exchange rate, eP^*/P, therefore has units $[O/O^*]$, or number of US goods per unit of foreign goods – a very sensible way to express a real exchange rate (at least its relative values over time, given that the output and price measures are index numbers).
- *"Velocity" in the quantity theory of money*: If we take the quantity theory to be $Mv = Py$, where y is real output, then velocity equals Py/M. This is a nominal flow (dollars per unit time) divided by a nominal stock (total number of dollars), which gives the dimension of v as "per unit time," or $[1/t]$. That makes sense, as Mv is supposed to be "dollars (circulating) per period."[7]

A slightly more subtle example is total factor productivity (TFP) growth, which is defined as "the growth in flow output minus the growth in flow total factor input." The latter is the growth of a suitably weighted index of total inputs; for example, if you were unconvinced by Chapter 4 and still believe in production functions, the growth in the total factor input index for a (not necessarily CRS) Cobb–Douglas production technology would be $\Delta \ln(K^\alpha L^\beta)$. Here, α and β are elasticities, so "percent change in flow output per percent change in flow input."[8]

As the preceding suggests, this sort of thing gets a little strained when we are dealing with index numbers like a Fisher aggregate for real GDP (the dimensions of which can be thought of loosely – though not completely correctly – as "units of real output per quarter," or $[O/t]$). Even so, it's still

[7] The fact that the dimensions are sensible doesn't mean that the quantity theory is all that useful – if money is created through the banking system, then $M = M(y)$, and is not an exogenously determined stock. (This is a very crude variant of an argument by Tobin, 1970.)
[8] Not everyone would agree with this characterization of an elasticity – they are supposed to be dimensionless, after all – but since the two main protagonists of this debate are deceased, we can do what we want. Also, pursuing the question in any depth seems like a poor use of time.

useful in terms of thinking about whether our expressions make sense (if you get that a nominal flow equals a real flow, you've gone awry somewhere), and what the units of our model parameters are (if they have any besides "it's a number").[9] Note that converting a flow to an annual rate involves multiplying the subannual flow – say, GDP per quarter, x_t – by the constant "4 quarters per year" to obtain $4 \times x_t$ with dimensions [output per year], which is an unnecessarily complicated way of putting it.[10]

---

[9] It's also the only way that people like me can remember the formula for a real exchange rate.

[10] Dimensional analysis is a serious business in the natural sciences, where what you're measuring actually exists (Einstein supposedly made use of it a lot when thinking about his physics); and it even has a theorem that goes with it (Buckingham's π theorem, which like any good mathematical theorem with a name attached, apparently antedates Buckingham). In economics, there is an entire book devoted to the subject (De Jong, 1967), which is kind of neat (or a little weird, depending). For a remarkably humorless paper on this topic that gets pretty much everything wrong (and that also doesn't seem to realize that De Jong, 1967 exists), see Barnett (2004).

Bibliography

Abel, Andrew B. and Olivier J. Blanchard. The present value of profits and cyclical movements in investment. *Econometrica*, 54(2):249–273, 1986.

Abraham, Katharine G. Structural/frictional vs. deficient demand unemployment: Some new evidence. *American Economic Review*, 73(4):708–724, 1983.

Help-wanted advertising, job vacancies, and unemployment. *Brookings Papers on Economic Activity*, 1987 (1):207–248, 1987.

Ahn, Hie-Joo. A modified Bayesian sign-restricted structural VAR. Mimeo, 2023.

Ahn, Hie-Joo and James D. Hamilton. Measuring labor-force participation and the incidence and duration of unemployment. *Review of Economic Dynamics*, 44:1–32, 2022.

Ahn, Hie-Joo and Jeremy B. Rudd. (Re)-connecting inflation and the labor market: A tale of two curves. Mimeo, 2023.

Allen, Todd W. and Christopher D. Carroll. Individual learning about consumption. *Macroeconomic Dynamics*, 5(2):255–271, 2001.

Angeletos, George-Marios. Fiscal policy with noncontingent debt and the optimal maturity structure. *The Quarterly Journal of Economics*, 117(3):1105–1131, 2002.

Angeletos, George-Marios and Chen Lian. Confidence and the propagation of demand shocks. *The Review of Economic Studies*, 89(3):1085–1119, 2022.

Aoki, Masanao. *New Approaches to Macroeconomic Modeling*. Cambridge University Press, Cambridge, 1996.

Modeling Aggregate Behavior and Fluctuations in Economics. Cambridge University Press, Cambridge, 2002.

Aoki, Masanao and Hiroshi Yoshikawa. *Reconstructing Macroeconomics*. Cambridge University Press, Cambridge, 2007.

Non-self-averaging in macroeconomic models: A criticism of modern micro-founded macroeconomics. *Journal of Economic Interaction and Coordination*, 7(1):1–22, 2012.

Aparisi de Lannoy, Leo R., Anmol Bhandari, David Evans, Mikhail Golosov, and Thomas J. Sargent. Managing public portfolios. Working Paper 30501, National Bureau of Economic Research, September 2022.

Ascari, Guido and Argia M. Sbordone. The macroeconomics of trend inflation. *Journal of Economic Literature*, 52(3):679–739, 2014.

282

Ascari, Guido, Louis Phaneuf, and Eric R. Sims. On the welfare and cyclical implications of moderate trend inflation. *Journal of Monetary Economics*, 99:56–71, 2018.

Ascari, Guido, Leandro M. Magnusson, and Sophocles Mavroeidis. Empirical evidence on the Euler equation for consumption in the US. *Journal of Monetary Economics*, 117:129–152, 2021.

Asimov, Issac. *Foundation*. Doubleday, New York, 1951.

Auerbach, Alan J. and Yuriy Gorodnichenko. Measuring the output responses to fiscal policy. *American Economic Journal: Economic Policy*, 4 (2):1–27, 2012.

Azar, José, Emiliano Huet-Vaughn, Ioana Marinescu, Bledi Taska, and Till von Wachter. Minimum wage employment effects and labor market concentration. Working Paper 26101, National Bureau of Economic Research, 2019.

Bak, Per, Kan Chen, José Scheinkman, and Michael Woodford. Aggregate fluctuations from independent sectoral shocks: Self-organized criticality in a model of production and inventory dynamics. *Ricerche Economiche*, 47(1):3–30, 1993.

Ball, Laurence M. Has globalization changed inflation? Working Paper 12687, National Bureau of Economic Research, November 2006.

Ball, Laurence M. and N. Gregory Mankiw. A sticky-price manifesto. *Carnegie-Rochester Conference Series on Public Policy*, 41:127–151, 1994.

Ball, Laurence M., Daniel Leigh, and Prachi Mishra. Understanding U.S. inflation during the COVID era. Working Paper 30613, National Bureau of Economic Research, October 2022.

Baqaee, David Rezza and Emmanuel Farhi. Macroeconomics with heterogeneous agents and input-output networks. Working Paper 24684, National Bureau of Economic Research, 2018.

JEEA-FBBVA Lecture 2018: The Microeconomic Foundations of Aggregate Production Functions. *Journal of the European Economic Association*, 17 (5):1337–1392, 2019.

Supply and demand in disaggregated Keynesian economies with an application to the COVID-19 crisis. *American Economic Review*, 112(5):1397–1436, 2022.

Barnett, William. Dimensions and economics: Some problems. *The Quarterly Journal of Austrian Economics*, 7 (1):95–104, 2004.

Barnichon, Regis. Building a composite Help-Wanted Index. *Economics Letters*, 109(3):175–178, 2010.

Barnichon, Regis and Andrew Figura. Labor market heterogeneity and the aggregate matching function. *American Economic Journal: Macroeconomics*, 7 (4):222–249, 2015.

Barro, Robert J. Second thoughts on Keynesian economics. *American Economic Review: Papers and Proceedings*, 69 (2):54–59, 1979.

Optimal debt management. Working Paper 5327, National Bureau of Economic Research, October 1995.

Optimal management of indexed and nominal debt. *Annals of Economics and Finance*, 4(1):1–15, 2003.

Barro, Robert J. and Herschel I. Grossman. *Money, Employment and Inflation*. Cambridge University Press, Cambridge, 1976.

Barsky, Robert B. and Lutz Kilian. Do we really know that oil caused the Great Stagflation? A monetary alternative. *NBER Macroeconomics Annual*, 16:137–198, 2002.

Basu, Susanto and John Fernald. Why is productivity procyclical? Why do we care? In Hulten, Charles R., Edwin R. Dean, and Michael J. Harper, editors, *New Developments in Productivity Analysis*, pages 225–302. University of Chicago Press, Chicago, 2001.

Basu, Susanto, John G. Fernald, and Miles S. Kimball. Are technology improvements contractionary? *American Economic Review*, 96(5):1418–1448, 2006.

Baumeister, Christiane and James D. Hamilton. Sign restrictions, structural vector autoregressions, and useful prior information. *Econometrica*, 83(5):1963–1999, 2015.

Baxter, Marianne and Robert G. King. Measuring business cycles: Approximate band-pass filters for economic time series. *The Review of Economics and Statistics*, 81 (4):575–593, 1999.

Bénassy, Jean-Pascal. *The Economics of Market Disequilibrium*. Academic Press, New York, 1982.

Nonclearing markets: Microeconomic concepts and macroeconomic applications. *Journal of Economic Literature*, 31(2):732–761, 1993.

Berman, Yonatan, Ole Peters, and Alexander Adamou. Wealth inequality and the ergodic hypothesis: Evidence from the United States. *Journal of Income Distribution*, 2021. https://doi.org/10.25071/1874-6322.40455

Bernanke, Ben S. and Kenneth N. Kuttner. What explains the stock market's reaction to Federal Reserve policy? *The Journal of Finance*, 60(3):1221–1257, 2005.

Bernanke, Ben S. and Ilian Mihov. Measuring monetary policy. *The Quarterly Journal of Economics*, 113(3):869–902, 1998.

Bernanke, Ben S., Mark Gertler, and Mark Watson. Systematic monetary policy and the effects of oil price shocks. *Brookings Papers on Economic Activity*, 1997 (1):91–142, 1997.

Bernanke, Ben S., Jean Boivin, and Piotr Eliasz. Measuring the effects of monetary policy: A factor-augmented vector autoregressive (FAVAR) approach. *The Quarterly Journal of Economics*, 120(1):387–422, 2005.

Bernstein, Michael A. *A Perilous Progress: Economists and Public Purpose in Twentieth-Century America*. Princeton University Press, Princeton, 2001.

Beveridge, Stephen and Charles R. Nelson. A new approach to decomposition of economic time series into permanent and transitory components with particular attention to measurement of the 'business cycle'. *Journal of Monetary Economics*, 7(2):151–174, 1981.

Beveridge, William H. *Full Employment in a Free Society*. George Allen & Unwin Ltd, London, 1944.

Bewley, Truman F. *Why Wages Don't Fall in a Recession*. Harvard University Press, Cambridge, MA, 1999.

Bilbiie, Florin O. Monetary policy and heterogeneity: An analytical framework. Working Paper, 2021.

Blanchard, Olivier Jean and Peter Diamond. The Beveridge curve. *Brookings Papers on Economic Activity*, 1989 (1):1–76, 1989.

Blinder, Alan S. and Stephen M. Goldfeld. New measures of fiscal and monetary policy, 1958–73. *American Economic Review*, 66(5):780–796, 1976.

Blinder, Alan S. and Jeremy B. Rudd. The supply-shock explanation of the Great Stagflation revisited. In Bordo, Michael D. and Athanasios Orphanides, editors, *The Great*

Inflation: The Rebirth of Modern Central Banking, pages 119–175. University of Chicago Press, Chicago, 2013.

Blinder, Alan S., Elie R. D. Canetti, David E. Lebow, and Jeremy B. Rudd. *Asking About Prices: A New Approach to Understanding Price Stickiness*. Russell Sage Foundation, New York, 1998.

Blundell, Richard and Thomas M. Stoker. Models of aggregate economic relationships that account for heterogeneity. In Heckman, James J. and Edward E. Leamer, editors, *Handbook of Econometrics*, volume 6A, chapter 68, pages 4609–4666. Elsevier, New York, 2007.

Bradley, Ralph. Finite sample effects in the estimation of substitution bias in the consumer price index. *Journal of Official Statistics*, 17(3):369–390, 2001.

Brainard, William C. Uncertainty and the effectiveness of policy. *American Economic Review*, 57(2):411–425, 1967.

Brockie, Melvin D. and Arthur L. Grey. The marginal efficiency of capital and investment programming. *The Economic Journal*, 66(264):662–675, 1956.

Brown, Donald J. and Rosa L. Matzkin. Testable restrictions on the equilibrium manifold. *Econometrica*, 64(6):1249–1262, 1996.

Brown, Donald J. and Chris Shannon. Uniqueness, stability, and comparative statics in rationalizable Walrasian markets. *Econometrica*, 68(6):1529–1539, 2000.

Browning, Martin, Lars Peter Hansen, and James J. Heckman. Micro data and general equilibrium models. In Taylor, John B. and Michael Woodford, editors, *Handbook of Macroeconomics*, volume 1, chapter 8, pages 543–633. Elsevier, New York, 1999.

Bryan, Michael F., Brent H. Meyer, and Nicholas B. Parker. The inflation expectations of firms: What do they look like, are they accurate, and do they matter? Working Paper 2014-27a, Federal Reserve Bank of Atlanta, January 2015.

Buera, Francisco and Juan Pablo Nicolini. Optimal maturity of government debt without state contingent bonds. *Journal of Monetary Economics*, 51(3):531–554, 2004.

Bureau of Economic Analysis. *Fixed Assets and Consumer Durable Goods in the United States, 1925–1999*. U.S. Department of Commerce, Washington, DC, 2003.

Burns, Arthur F. and Wesley C. Mitchell. *Measuring Business Cycles*. Number 2 in Studies in Business Cycles. National Bureau of Economic Research, New York, 1946.

Caballero, Ricardo J. Aggregate investment. In Taylor, John B. and Michael Woodford, editors, *Handbook of Macroeconomics*, volume 1A, chapter 12, pages 813–862. Elsevier, New York, 1999.

Cajner, Tomaz, Tyler Radler, David Ratner, and Ivan Vidangos. Racial gaps in labor market outcomes in the last four decades and over the business cycle. Working Paper 2017-071, Federal Reserve Board of Governors, 2017.

Carroll, Christopher D. A theory of the consumption function, with and without liquidity constraints. *Journal of Economic Perspectives*, 15(3):23–45, 2001.

Carroll, Christopher D. and Miles S. Kimball. On the concavity of the consumption function. *Econometrica*, 64(4):981–992, 1996.

Carroll, Christopher D., Misuzu Otsuka, and Jiri Slacalek. How large are housing and financial wealth effects? A new approach. *Journal of Money, Credit and Banking*, 43 (1):55–79, 2011.

Carroll, Christopher D., Martin B. Holm, and Miles S. Kimball. Liquidity constraints and precautionary saving. *Journal of Economic Theory*, 195, 2021.

Carter, Susan B., Scott Sigmund Gartner, Michael R. Haines, Alan L. Olmstead, Richard Sutch, and Gavin Wright, editors. *Historical Statistics of the United States, Earliest Times to the Present: Millenial Edition.* Cambridge University Press, New York, 2006.

Cashin, David, Jamie Lenney, Byron Lutz, and William Peterman. Fiscal policy and aggregate demand in the U.S. before, during and following the Great Recession. Working Paper 2017-061, Federal Reserve Board of Governors, 2017.

Christiano, Lawrence J. and Martin Eichenbaum. Temporal aggregation and structural inference in macroeconomics. *Carnegie-Rochester Conference Series on Public Policy*, 26:63–130, 1987.

Christiano, Lawrence J. and Terry J. Fitzgerald. The band pass filter. *International Economic Review*, 44(2):435–465, 2003.

Christiano, Lawrence J., Martin Eichenbaum, and Charles L. Evans. Monetary policy shocks: What have we learned and to what end? In *Handbook of Macroeconomics*, volume 1, pages 65–148. Elsevier, New York, 1999.

Clarida, Richard, Jordi Galí, and Mark Gertler. Monetary policy rules and macroeconomic stability: Evidence and some theory. *The Quarterly Journal of Economics*, 115(1):147–180, 2000.

Clark, Peter K. Okun's law and potential GNP. Mimeo, Federal Reserve Board of Governors, June 1983.

Clark, Todd E. and Stephen J. Terry. Time variation in the inflation passthrough of energy prices. *Journal of Money, Credit and Banking*, 42:1419–1433, 2010.

Clower, Robert. The Keynesian counterrevolution: A theoretical appraisal. In Hahn, F. H. and F. P. R. Brechling, editors, *The Theory of Interest Rates*, pages 103–125. Macmillan & Company, London, 1965.

Cogley, Timothy and Thomas J. Sargent. Drifts and volatilities: Monetary policies and outcomes in the post WWII US. *Review of Economic Dynamics*, 8:262–302, 2005.

Cogley, Timothy, Giorgio E. Primiceri, and Thomas J. Sargent. Inflation-gap persistence in the US. *American Economic Journal: Macroeconomics*, 2 (1):43–69, 2010.

Coibion, Olivier and Yuriy Gorodnichenko. Is the Phillips curve alive and well after all? Inflation expectations and the missing disinflation. *American Economic Journal: Macroeconomics*, 7 (1):197–232, 2015.

Coibion, Olivier, Yuriy Gorodnichenko, and Rupal Kamdar. The formation of expectations, inflation, and the Phillips curve. *Journal of Economic Literature*, 56(4):1447–1491, 2018a.

How do firms form their expectations? New survey evidence. *American Economic Review*, 108(9):2671–2713, 2018b.

Coibion, Olivier, Yuriy Gorodnichenko, and Tiziano Ropele. Inflation expectations and firm decisions: New causal evidence. *The Quarterly Journal of Economics*, 135(1):165–219, 2020.

Crow, Edwin L. and M. M. Siddiqui. Robust estimation of location. *Journal of the American Statistical Association*, 62 (318):353–389, 1967.

D'Acunto, Francesco, Ulrike Malmendier, and Michael Weber. What do the data tell us about inflation expectations? Working Paper 29825, National Bureau of Economic Research, March 2022.

Dawid, Herbert and Domenico Delli Gatti. Agent-based macroeconomics. In Hommes, Cars and Blake LeBaron, editors, *Handbook of Computational Economics*, volume 4, chapter 2, pages 63–156. Elsevier, New York, 2018.

de Chazeau, Melvin G. *Regularization of Fixed Capital Investment by the Individual Firm*, pages 75–116. Princeton University Press, Princeton, 1954.

De Jong, Frits J. *Dimensional Analysis for Economists: With a Mathematical Appendix on the Algebraic Structure of Dimensional Analysis by Wilhelm Quade*. North-Holland, Amsterdam, 1967.

Deaton, Angus. Saving and liquidity constraints. *Econometrica*, 59(5):1221–1248, 1991. *Understanding Consumption*. Clarendon Press, Oxford, 1992.

Deaton, Angus and John Muellbauer. *Economics and Consumer Behavior*. Cambridge University Press, Cambridge, 1980.

Debreu, Gerard. Excess demand functions. *Journal of Mathematical Economics*, 1:15–21, 1974.

Del Negro, Marco, Marc Giannoni, and Christina Patterson. The forward guidance puzzle. Technical Report 574, Federal Reserve Bank of New York, October 2012. Revised December 2015.

Diamond, Peter A. Aggregate demand management in search equilibrium. *Journal of Political Economy*, 90(5):881–894, 1982.

Dickens, Charles. *David Copperfield*. Chapman & Hall, London, 1867.

Diercks, Anthony M. The reader's guide to optimal monetary policy. Mimeo, August 2019.

Dolmas, Jim. Trimmed mean PCE inflation. Working Paper 0506, Federal Reserve Bank of Dallas, July 2005.

Dow, Gregory K. *Governing the Firm: Workers' Control in Theory and Practice*. Cambridge University Press, Cambridge, 2003. *The Labor-Managed Firm: Theory and Practice*. Cambridge University Press, Cambridge, 2018.

Drandakis, E. M. and E. S. Phelps. A model of induced invention, growth and distribution. *The Economic Journal*, 76(304):823–840, 1966.

Drèze, Jacques H. *Underemployment Equilibria: Essays in Theory, Econometrics and Policy*. Cambridge University Press, Cambridge, 1991.

Ebersole, J. Franklin. The influence of interest rates upon entrepreneurial decisions in business – a case study. *Harvard Business Review*, 17(1):35–39, 1938.

Eggertsson, Gauti B. and Michael Woodford. The zero bound on interest rates and optimal monetary policy. *Brookings Papers on Economic Activity*, 2003 (1):139–211, 2003.

Elsby, Michael W. L., Bart Hobijn, and Ayşegül Şahin. The decline of the U.S. labor share. *Brookings Papers on Economic Activity*, 2013:1–52, 2013.

Elsby, Michael W. L., Ryan Michaels, and David Ratner. The Beveridge curve: A survey. *Journal of Economic Literature*, 53(3):571–630, 2015.

ESS Guidelines on Seasonal Adjustment. Eurostat, 2015.

Handbook on Seasonal Adjustment. Eurostat, 2018.

Evans, George and Lucrezia Reichlin. Information, forecasts, and measurement of the business cycle. *Journal of Monetary Economics*, 33:233–254, 1994.

Faraglia, Elisa, Albert Marcet, and Andrew Scott. In search of a theory of debt management. *Journal of Monetary Economics*, 57(7):821–836, 2010.

Faraglia, Elisa, Albert Marcet, Rigas Oikonomou, and Andrew Scott. Government debt management: The long and the short of it. *The Review of Economic Studies*, 86(6):2554–2604, 2019.

Farmer, Roger E. A. *Expectations, Employment, and Prices.* Oxford University Press, Oxford, 2010.

Felipe, Jesus and Franklin M. Fisher. Aggregation in production functions: What applied economists should know. *Metroeconomica*, 54:208–262, 2003.

Felipe, Jesus and J. S. L. McCombie. Some methodological problems with the neoclassical analysis of the East Asian miracle. *Cambridge Journal of Economics*, 27(5):695–721, 2003.

Fernald, John G. A quarterly, utilization-adjusted series on total factor productivity. Working Paper 2012–19, Federal Reserve Bank of San Francisco, 2012. Updated March 2014.

Fisher, Franklin M. *Disequilibrium Foundations of Equilibrium Economics.* Number 6 in Econometric Society Monographs. Cambridge University Press, Cambridge, 1983.

Aggregation: Aggregate Production Functions and Related Topics. MIT Press, Cambridge, MA, 1993.

Models of aggregate economic relationships that account for heterogeneity. In Bridel, Pascal, editor, *General Equilibrium Analysis a Century after Walras*, chapter 5, pages 34–45. Routledge, London, 2011.

Fisher, Irving. *The Rate of Interest: Its Nature, Determination and Relation to Economic Phenomena.* The Macmillan Company, New York, 1907.

Fleurbaey, Marc and Grégory Ponthière. The stakeholder corporation and social welfare. *Journal of Political Economy*, 131(9):2556–2594, 2023.

Forni, Mario and Marco Lippi. *Aggregation and the Microfoundations of Dynamic Macroeconomics.* Oxford University Press, Oxford, 1997.

Frank, Murray Z. and Tao Shen. Investment and the weighted average cost of capital. *Journal of Financial Economics*, 119(2):300–315, 2016.

Friedman, Milton. *A Theory of the Consumption Function.* Princeton University Press, Princeton, 1957.

Windfalls, the "horizon," and related concepts in the permanent-income hypothesis. In *Measurement in Economics: Studies in Mathematical Economics and Econometrics in Memory of Yehuda Grunfeld*, chapter 1, pages 3–28. Stanford University Press, Stanford, 1963.

The role of monetary policy. *American Economic Review*, 58(1):1–17, 1968.

Perspective on inflation. In *There's No Such Thing as a Free Lunch*, pages 113–115. Open Court, La Salle, IL, 1975. Reprint of June 24, 1974 *Newsweek* article.

Frisch, Ragnar. Propagation problems and impulse problems in dynamic economics. Technical Report 3, Universitetets Økonomiske Institutt, Oslo, 1933.

Gabaix, Xavier. The granular origins of aggregate fluctuations. *Econometrica*, 79(3):733–772, 2011.

Gabaix, Xavier and Augustin Landier. Why has CEO pay increased so much? *The Quarterly Journal of Economics*, 123(1):49–100, 2008.

Ganong, Peter, Damon Jones, Pascal Noel, Diana Farrell, Fiona Greig, and Chris Wheat. Wealth, race, and consumption smoothing of typical income shocks. Working Paper, June 10, 2020.

García-Schmidt, Mariana and Michael Woodford. Are low interest rates deflationary? A paradox of perfect-foresight analysis. *American Economic Review*, 109(1):86–120, 2019.

Gechert, Sebastian. What fiscal policy is most effective? A meta-regression analysis. *Oxford Economic Papers*, 67(3):553–580, 2015.

Gertler, Mark and Peter Karadi. Monetary policy surprises, credit costs, and economic activity. *American Economic Journal: Macroeconomics*, 7 (1):44–76, 2015.

Giandrea, Michael D. and Shawn Sprague. Estimating the U.S. labor share. *Monthly Labor Review*, February 2017.

Gilchrist, Simon and Egon Zakrajšek. Investment and the cost of capital: New evidence from the corporate bond market. Working Paper 13174, National Bureau of Economic Research, 2007.

Credit spreads and business cycle fluctuations. *American Economic Review*, 102(4):1692–1720, 2012.

Goldin, Claudia. The quiet revolution that transformed women's employment, education, and family. *American Economic Review*, 96(2):1–21, 2006.

Goodwin, Richard M. Secular and cyclical aspects of the multiplier and the accelerator. In *Income, Employment and Public Policy: Essays in Honor of Alvin H. Hansen*, chapter 5, pages 108–132. W. W. Norton & Company, New York, 1948.

Gordon, Robert J. Recent developments in the theory of inflation and unemployment. *Journal of Monetary Economics*, 2(2):185–219, 1976.

The Phillips curve is alive and well: Inflation and the NAIRU during the slow recovery. Working Paper 19390, National Bureau of Economic Research, 2013.

Grandmont, Jean-Michel. The logic of the fix-price method. *Scandinavian Journal of Economics*, 79(2):169–186, 1977.

Money and Value: A Reconsideration of Classical and Neoclassical Monetary Theories. Number 5 in Econometric Society Monographs. Cambridge University Press, Cambridge, 1983.

Grossman, Gene M. and Ezra Oberfield. The elusive explanation for the declining labor share. *Annual Review of Economics*, 14:93–124, 2022.

Grossman, Herschel I. Why does aggregate employment fluctuate? *American Economic Review: Papers and Proceedings*, 69 (2):64–69, 1979.

Hahn, Frank. On non-Walrasian equilibria. *The Review of Economic Studies*, 45(1):1–17, 1978.

Hahn, Frank. Stability. In Arrow, Kenneth J. and Michael D. Intriligator, editors, *Handbook of Mathematical Economics*, volume 2, chapter 16, pages 745–793. Elsevier, New York, 1982.

Hamilton, James D. A new approach to the economic analysis of nonstationary time series and the business cycle. *Econometrica*, 57(2):357–384, 1989.

Why you should never use the Hodrick–Prescott filter. *The Review of Economics and Statistics*, 100 (5):831–843, 2018.

Hansen, Bent. Excess demand, unemployment, vacancies, and wages. *The Quarterly Journal of Economics*, 84(1):1–23, 1970.

Havranek, Tomas and Anna Sokolova. Do consumers really follow a rule of thumb? Three thousand estimates from 144 studies say "probably not". *Review of Economic Dynamics*, 35:97 122, 2020.

Hazell, Jonathon, Juan Herreño, Emi Nakamura, and Jón Steinsson. The slope of the Phillips curve: Evidence from U.S. states. *The Quarterly Journal of Economics*, 137(3):1299–1344, 2022.

Herbst, Edward P. and Benjamin K. Johannsen. Bias in local projections. Working Paper 2020-010, Federal Reserve Board of Governors, 2020.

Hicks, J. R. *The Theory of Wages*. Macmillan & Company, London, 1932.

Hicks, J. R. *Value and Capital: An Inquiry into Some Fundamental Principles of Economic Theory*. Oxford University Press, Oxford, 2nd edition, 1946.

Hicks, J. R. *A Revision of Demand Theory*. Oxford University Press, Oxford, 1956.

Hildenbrand, Werner. *Market Demand: Theory and Empirical Evidence*. Princeton University Press, Princeton, 1993.

Hodrick, Robert J. An exploration of trend-cycle decomposition methodologies in simulated data. Working Paper 26750, National Bureau of Economic Research, 2020.

Hodrick, Robert J. and Edward C. Prescott. Postwar U.S. business cycles: An empirical investigation. *Journal of Money, Credit and Banking*, 29 (1):1–16, 1997.

Holt, Charles and Martin David. *The Concept of Job Vacancies in a Dynamic Theory of the Labor Market*, pages 73–110. National Bureau of Economic Research, 1966.

House, Christopher L. and Matthew D. Shapiro. Temporary investment tax incentives: Theory with evidence from bonus depreciation. *American Economic Review*, 98(3):737–768, 2008.

Howard, David H. The disequilibrium model in a controlled economy: An empirical test of the Barro–Grossman model. *American Economic Review*, 66(5):871–879, 1976.

Hulten, Charles R. Growth accounting with intermediate inputs. *The Review of Economic Studies*, 45(3):511–518, 1978.

Huo, Zhen and José-Víctor Ríos-Rull. Sticky wage models and labor supply constraints. *American Economic Journal: Macroeconomics*, 12:284–318, 2020.

Hylleberg, Svend. *Modelling Seasonality*. Oxford University Press, Oxford, 1992. Edited volume.

ILO, and others. *Consumer Price Index Manual*. International Labor Office, Geneva, 2004.

Jaeger, H. M., Chu-heng Liu, and Sidney R. Nagel. Relaxation at the angle of repose. *Physical Review Letters*, 62(1):40–43, 1989.

Jagannathan, Ravi, David A. Matsa, Iwan Meier, and Vefa Tarhan. Why do firms use high discount rates? *Journal of Financial Economics*, 120(3):445–463, 2016.

Jarociński, Marek and Peter Karadi. Deconstructing monetary policy surprises – the role of information shocks. *American Economic Journal: Macroeconomics*, 12 (2):1–43, 2020.

Jump, Gregory V. Interest rates, inflation expectations, and spurious elements in measured real income and saving. *American Economic Review*, 70(5):990–1004, 1980.

Justiniano, Alejandro, Giorgio E. Primiceri, and Andrea Tambalotti. Investment shocks and business cycles. *Journal of Monetary Economics*, 57(2):132–145, 2010.

Kalecki, Michal. Professor Pigou on "The classical stationary state," a comment. *The Economic Journal*, 54(213):131–132, 1944.

Kalecki, Michal. Political aspects of full employment. *The Political Quarterly*, 14(4):322–330, 1943.

Kamber, Güneş, James Morley, and Benjamin Wong. Intuitive and reliable estimates of the output gap from a Beveridge–Nelson filter. *The Review of Economics and Statistics*, 100 (3):550–556, 2018.

Kaplan, Greg and Giovanni L. Violante. Microeconomic heterogeneity and macroeconomic shocks. *Journal of Economic Perspectives*, 32(3):167–194, 2018.

Kaplan, Greg and Giovanni L. Violante. The marginal propensity to consume in heterogeneous agent models. Working Paper 30013, National Bureau of Economic Research, 2022.

Kaplan, Greg, Benjamin Moll, and Giovanni L. Violante. Monetary policy according to HANK. *American Economic Review*, 108(3):697–743, 2018.

Karabarbounis, Loukas and Brent Neiman. The global decline of the labor share. *The Quarterly Journal of Economics*, 129(1):61–104, 2014.

Kaufman, Roger T. and Geoffrey Woglom. The effects of expectations on union wages. *American Economic Review*, 74(3):418–432, 1984.

Kennedy, Charles. Samuelson on induced innovation. *The Review of Economics and Statistics*, 48 (4):442–444, 1966.

Keynes, John Maynard. *The General Theory of Employment Interest and Money*. Macmillan & Company, London, 1936.

Khan, Aubhik and Julia K. Thomas. Inventories and the business cycle: An equilibrium analysis of (S,s) policies. *American Economic Review*, 97(4):1165–1188, 2007.

Kim, Chang-Jin and Charles R. Nelson. *State-Space Models with Regime Switching: Classical and Gibbs-Sampling Approaches with Applications*. MIT Press, Cambridge, MA, 1999.

Kimball, Miles S. The quantitative analytics of the basic neomonetarist model. *Journal of Money, Credit and Banking*, 27 (4):1241–1277, 1995.

Kirman, Alan P. Whom or what does the representative agent represent? *Journal of Economic Perspectives*, 6(2):117–136, 1992.

Kitchen, John and Matthew Knittel. Business use of special provisions for accelerated depreciation: Section 179 expensing and bonus depreciation, 2002–2009. Mimeo, November 2011.

Kiyotaki, Nobuhiro and Kenneth D. West. Business fixed investment and the recent business cycle in Japan. *NBER Macroeconomics Annual*, 11:277–323, 1996.

Knittel, Matthew. Small business utilization of accelerated tax depreciation: Section 179 expensing and bonus depreciation. *Proceedings. Annual Conference on Taxation and Minutes of the Annual Meeting of the National Tax Association*, 98:273–286, 2005.

Corporate response to accelerated tax depreciation: Bonus depreciation for tax years 2002–2004. Working Paper 98, U.S. Department of the Treasury, Office of Tax Analysis, 2007.

Knowles, James W. The potential economic growth in the United States. Study Paper 20, Joint Economic Committee of the 86th U.S. Congress, 1960.

Konüs, A. A. The problem of the true index of the cost of living. *Econometrica*, 7(1):10–29, 1939. Translation of 1924 article.

Kothari, S. P., Jonathan Lewellen, and Jerold B. Warner. The behavior of aggregate corporate investment. Working Paper 5112-14, MIT Sloan School of Management, September 12, 2014.

Lai, Kon S. Aggregation and testing of the production smoothing hypothesis. *International Economic Review*, 32(2):391–403, 1991.

Laibson, David. Golden eggs and hyperbolic discounting. *The Quarterly Journal of Economics*, 112(2):443–477, 1997.

Laubach, Thomas and John C. Williams. Measuring the natural rate of interest. *The Review of Economics and Statistics*, 85 (4):1063–1070, 2003.

Lewbel, Arthur. An examination of Werner Hildenbrand's *Market Demand*. *Journal of Economic Literature*, 32:1832–1841, 1994.

Lucas, Robert E. Expectations and the neutrality of money. *Journal of Economic Theory*, 4(2):103–124, 1972.

Understanding business cycles. *Carnegie-Rochester Conference Series on Public Policy*, 5:7–29, 1977.

Comments on Ball and Mankiw. *Carnegie-Rochester Conference Series on Public Policy*, 41:153–155, 1994.

Lucas, Robert E. and Thomas J. Sargent. After Keynesian macroeconomics. Federal Reserve Bank of Minneapolis *Quarterly Review*, Spring: 1–16, 1979.

Luo, Yulei, Jun Nie, Xiaowen Wang, and Eric Young. Production and inventory dynamics under ambiguity aversion. Working Paper RWP 21-05, Federal Reserve Bank of Kansas City, 2021.

Lusompa, Amaze. Local projections, autocorrelation, and efficiency. Working Paper RWP 21-01, Federal Reserve Bank of Kansas City, 2021.

Macaulay, Frederick R. *The Smoothing of Time Series*. National Bureau of Economic Research, New York, 1931.

Magill, Michael, Martine Quinzii, and Jean-Charles Rochet. A theory of the stakeholder corporation. *Econometrica*, 83(5):1685–1725, 2015.

Malinvaud, Edmond. *The Theory of Unemployment Reconsidered*. Yrjö Jahnsson lectures. Basil Blackwell, Oxford, 1977.

Mantel, Rolf R. On the characterization of aggregate excess demand. *Journal of Economic Theory*, 7:348–353, 1974.

Mantel, Rolf R. Homothetic preferences and community excess demand functions. *Journal of Economic Theory*, 12(2):197–201, 1976.

Marglin, Stephen A. *The Dismal Science: How Thinking Like an Economist Undermines Community*. Harvard University Press, Cambridge, MA, 2008.

Mas-Colell, Andreu, Michael D. Whinston, and Jerry R. Green. *Microeconomic Theory*. Oxford University Press, Oxford, 1995.

Mavroeidis, Sophocles, Mikkel Plagborg-Møller, and James H. Stock. Empirical evidence on inflation expectations in the new Keynesian Phillips curve. *Journal of Economic Literature*, 52(1):124–188, 2014.

McLeay, Michael and Silvana Tenreyro. Optimal inflation and the identification of the Phillips curve. *NBER Macroeconomics Annual 2019*, 34:199–255, 2020.

Meade, J. E. and P. W. S. Andrews. Summary to replies to questions on effects of interest rates. *Oxford Economic Papers*, (1):14–31, 1938.

Medawar, Peter. *Advice to a Young Scientist*. Basic Books, New York, 1979.

Miranda-Agrippino, Silvia and Giovanni Ricco. The transmission of monetary policy shocks. *American Economic Journal: Macroeconomics*, 13 (3):74–107, 2021.

Miron, Jeffrey A. *The Economics of Seasonal Cycles*. MIT Press, Cambridge, MA, 1996.

Miron, Jeffrey A. and J. Joseph Beaulieu. What have macroeconomists learned about business cycles from the study of seasonal cycles? *The Review of Economics and Statistics*, 78 (1):54–66, 1996.

Mitchell, Wesley C. *Business Cycles: The Problem and Its Setting*. Number 1 in Studies in Business Cycles. National Bureau of Economic Research, New York, 1927.

Montiel Olea, José Luis, and Carolin Pflueger. A robust test for weak instruments. *Journal of Business and Economic Statistics*, 31 (3):358–369, 2013.

Morley, James C., Charles R. Nelson, and Eric Zivot. Why are the Beveridge–Nelson and unobserved-components decompositions of GDP so different? *The Review of Economics and Statistics*, 85 (2):235–243, 2003.

Morningstar, Chip. How to deconstruct almost anything: My postmodern adventure, June 1993. Mimeo.

Moulton, Brent R. The measurement of output, prices, and productivity: What's changed since the Boskin commission? Report, Hutchins Center, Brookings Institution, July 2018.

Murray, Christian J. Cyclical properties of Baxter-King filtered time series. *The Review of Economics and Statistics*, 85 (2):472–476, 2003.

Nachbar, John H. General equilibrium comparative statics. *Econometrica*, 70(5):2065–2074, 2002.

Nekarda, Christopher J. and Valerie A. Ramey. The cyclical behavior of the price–cost markup. *Journal of Money, Credit and Banking*, 52 (S2):319–353, 2020.

Nelson, Richard R. and Sidney G. Winter. *An Evolutionary Theory of Economic Change*. Harvard University Press, Cambridge, MA, 1982.

Nordhaus, William D. The recent productivity slowdown. *Brookings Papers on Economic Activity*, 1972 (3):493–536, 1972.

Nosbusch, Yves. Interest costs and the optimal maturity structure of government debt. *The Economic Journal*, 118(527):477–498, 2008.

Okun, Arthur M. Potential GNP: Its measurement and significance. *Proceedings of the Business and Economic Statistics Section of the American Statistical Association*, pages 89–104, 1962.

Orphanides, Athanasios. Monetary policy rules, macroeconomic stability, and inflation: A view from the trenches. *Journal of Money, Credit and Banking*, 36 (2):151–175, 2004.

Palumbo, Michael, Jeremy Rudd, and Karl Whelan. On the relationships between real consumption, income, and wealth. *Journal of Business and Economic Statistics*, 24 (1):1–11, 2006.

Patinkin, Don. *Money, Interest, and Prices: An Integration of Money and Value Theory*. Harper and Row, New York, 2nd edition, 1965.

Peneva, Ekaterina V. and Jeremy B. Rudd. The passthrough of labor costs to price inflation. *Journal of Money, Credit and Banking*, 49 (8):1777–1802, 2017.

Perry, George L. Labor force structure, potential output, and productivity. *Brookings Papers on Economic Activity*, 1971 (3):533–565, 1971.

Petrongolo, Barbara and Christopher A. Pissarides. Looking into the black box: A survey of the matching function. *Journal of Economic Literature*, 39(2):390–431, 2001.

Pissarides. The ins and outs of European unemployment. *American Economic Review: Papers and Proceedings*, 98 (2):256–262, 2008.

Phelps, Edmund S. Phillips curves, expectations of inflation and optimal unemployment over time. *Economica*, 34(135):254–281, 1967.

Philippon, Thomas. *The Great Reversal: How America Gave Up on Free Markets*. Harvard University Press, Cambridge, MA, 2019.

Additive growth. Working Paper 29950, National Bureau of Economic Research, 2022.

Phillips, A. W. The relation between unemployment and the rate of change of money wage rates in the United Kingdom, 1861–1957. *Economica*, 25(100):283–299, 1958.

Pigou, A. C. The classical stationary state. *The Economic Journal*, 53(212):343–351, 1943.

Piketty, Thomas. *Capital in the Twenty-First Century*. Harvard University Press, Cambridge, MA, 2014.

Plosser, Charles I. and G. William Schwert. Potential GNP: Its measurement and significance: A dissenting opinion. *Carnegie-Rochester Conference Series on Public Policy*, 10:179–186, 1979.

Pluchino, Alessandro, Alessio Emanuele Biondo, and Andrea Rapisarda. Talent versus luck: The role of randomness in success and failure. *Advances in Complex Systems*, 21, 2018.

Pollak, Robert A. Group cost-of-living indexes. *American Economic Review*, 70(2):273–278, 1980.

The social cost of living index. *Journal of Public Economics*, 15(3):311–336, 1981.

Portes, Richard and David Winter. Disequilibrium estimates for consumption goods markets in centrally planned economies. *The Review of Economic Studies*, 47(1):137–159, 1980.

Poterba, James M. and Lawrence H. Summers. A CEO survey of U.S. companies' time horizons and hurdle rates. *Sloan Management Review*, 37(1):43, 1995.

Ramey, Valerie A. Can government purchases stimulate the economy? *Journal of Economic Literature*, 49(3):673–685, 2011.

Macroeconomic shocks and their propagation. In Taylor, John B. and Harald Uhlig, editors, *Handbook of Macroeconomics*, volume 2, pages 71–162. Elsevier, New York, 2016.

Ramey, Valerie A. and Sarah Zubairy. Government spending multipliers in good times and in bad: Evidence from US historical data. *Journal of Political Economy*, 126(2):850–901, 2018.

Rhode, Paul W. and Richard Sutch. Estimates of national product before 1929. In Carter, Susan B., Scott Sigmund Gartner, Michael R. Haines, Alan L. Olmstead, Richard Sutch, and Gavin Wright, editors, *Historical Statistics of the United States, Earliest Times to the Present: Millenial Edition*, chapter Ca, pages 3-12–3-20. Cambridge University Press, New York, 2006.

Robertson, D. H. The non-econometrician's lament. In Lundberg, Erik, editor, *The Business Cycle in the Post-War World: Proceedings of a Conference Held by the International Economic Association*, page 313. Macmillan, London, 1955.

Rogers, Colin. Neo-Walrasian macroeconomics, microfoundations and pseudo-production models. *Australian Economic Papers*, 22(4):201–220, 1983.

Romer, Christina D. The prewar business cycle reconsidered: New estimates of Gross National Product, 1869–1908. *Journal of Political Economy*, 97(1):1–37, 1989.

Romer, Christina D. and David H. Romer. A new measure of monetary shocks: Derivation and implications. *The American Economic Review*, 94(4):1055–1084, 2004.

Romer, Paul M. Crazy explanations for the productivity slowdown. *NBER Macroeconomics Annual*, 2:163–202, 1987.

Rotemberg, Julio J. and Michael Woodford. The cyclical behavior of prices and costs. In *Handbook of Macroeconomics*, volume 1, chapter 16, pages 1051–1135. Elsevier, New York, 1999.

Samuelson, Paul A. A theory of induced innovation along Kennedy–Weisäcker lines. *The Review of Economics and Statistics*, 47 (4):343–356, 1965.

The fundamental singularity theorem for non-joint production. *International Economic Review*, 7(1):34–41, 1966a.

Rejoinder: Agreements, disagreements, doubts, and the case of induced Harrod-neutral technical change. *The Review of Economics and Statistics*, 48 (4):444–448, 1966b.

Sargent, Thomas J. *Macroeconomic Theory*. Academic Press, Boston, 2nd edition, 1987.

Scheinkman, José A. and Michael Woodford. Self-organized criticality and economic fluctuations. *American Economic Review (AEA Papers and Proceedings)*, 84(2):417–421, 1994.

Shackleton, Robert. Estimating and projecting potential output using CBO's forecasting growth model. Working Paper 2018-03, Congressional Budget Office, 2018.

Shaikh, Anwar. Laws of production and laws of algebra: The humbug production function. *The Review of Economics and Statistics*, 56 (1):115–120, 1974.

Sharpe, Steven A. and Gustavo A. Suarez. Why isn't business investment more sensitive to interest rates? Evidence from surveys. *Management Science*, 67(2):720–741, 2021.

Simon, Herbert A. On parsimonious explanations of production relations. *The Scandinavian Journal of Economics*, 81 (4):459–474, 1979.

Sims, Christopher A. Theoretical basis for a double deflated index of real value added. *The Review of Economics and Statistics*, 51 (4):470–471, 1969.

Interpreting the macroeconomic time series facts: The effects of monetary policy. *European Economic Review*, 36(5):975–1000, 1992.

Comment on Glenn Rudebusch's "Do measures of monetary policy in a VAR make sense?". *International Economic Review*, 39(4):933–941, 1998.

Sims, Christopher A. and Tao Zha. Were there regime switches in U.S. monetary policy? *American Economic Review*, 96(1):54–81, 2006a.

Does monetary policy generate recessions? *Macroeconomic Dynamics*, 10(2):231–272, 2006b.

Slutzky, Eugen. The summation of random causes as the source of cyclic processes. *Econometrica*, 5(2):105–146, 1937.

Smets, Frank and Rafael Wouters. Shocks and frictions in US business cycles: A Bayesian DSGE approach. *American Economic Review*, 97(3):586–606, 2007.

Solow, Robert M. A skeptical note on the constancy of relative shares. *American Economic Review*, 48(4):618–631, 1958.

Where have all the flowers gone? Economic growth in the 1960s. In Pechman, Joseph A. and N. J. Simler, editors, *Economics in the Public Service: Papers in Honor of Walter W. Heller*, pages 46–83. W. W. Norton, New York, 1982.

Comment. In Tobin, James, editor, *Macroeconomics, Prices, and Quantities: Essays in Memory of Arthur M. Okun*, pages 279–284. Brookings Institution, Washington, DC, 1983.

Sonnenschein, Hugo. Market excess demand functions. *Econometrica*, 40(3):549–563, 1972.

Do Walras' identity and continuity characterize the class of community excess demand functions? *Journal of Economic Theory*, 6(3):345–354, 1973.

Staiger, Douglas and James H. Stock. Instrumental variables regression with weak instruments. *Econometrica*, 65(3):557–586, 1997.

Staiger, Douglas, James H. Stock, and Mark W. Watson. Prices, wages, and the U.S. NAIRU in the 1990s. In Krueger, Alan and Robert Solow, editors, *The Roaring Nineties: Can Full Employment Be Sustained?*, pages 3–60. Russell Sage Foundation and Century Foundation Press, New York, 2001.

Staiger, Douglas O., James H. Stock, and Mark W. Watson. How precise are estimates of the natural rate of unemployment? In Romer, Christina D. and David H. Romer, editors, *Reducing Inflation: Motivation and Strategy*, pages 195–246. University of Chicago Press, Chicago, 1997.

Stiglitz, Joseph E. and Bruce Greenwald. *Towards a New Paradigm in Monetary Economics*. Cambridge University Press, Cambridge, 2003.

Stock, James H. and Mark W. Watson. Vector autoregressions. *Journal of Economic Perspectives*, 15(4):101–115, 2001.

Stock, James H. and Mark W. Watson. Identification and estimation of dynamic causal effects in macroeconomics using external instruments. *Economic Journal*, 128(610):917–948, 2018.

Stock, James H. and Motohiro Yogo. Testing for weak instruments in linear IV regression. In Andrews, Donald W. K., editor, *Identification and Inference for Econometric Models*, pages 80–108. Cambridge University Press, New York, 2005.

Stoker, Thomas M. Empirical approaches to the problem of aggregation over individuals. *Journal of Economic Literature*, 31:1827–1874, 1993.

Strassner, Erich H., Gabriel W. Medeiros, and George M. Smith. Annual industry accounts: Introducing KLEMS input estimates for 1997–2003. *Survey of Current Business*, pages 31–65, September 2005.

Strongin, Steven. The identification of monetary policy disturbances: Explaining the liquidity puzzle. *Journal of Monetary Economics*, 35(3):463–497, 1995.

Summers, Lawrence H. *Investment Incentives and the Discounting of Depreciation Allowances*, pages 295–304. University of Chicago Press, Chicago, 1987.

Temin, Peter. *Lessons from the Great Depression*. MIT Press, Cambridge, MA, 1989.

Tobin, James. Money and income: Post hoc ergo propter hoc? *The Quarterly Journal of Economics*, 84(2):301–317, 1970.

Inflation and unemployment. *American Economic Review*, 62(1/2):1–18, 1972.

Price flexibility and output stability: An old Keynesian view. *Journal of Economic Perspectives*, 7(1):45–65, 1993.

Trimbur, Thomas M. and Tucker S. McElroy. Modelled approximations to the ideal filter with application to GDP and its components. *The Annals of Applied Statistics*, 16(2):627–651, 2022.

Veracierto, Marcelo. Worker flows and matching efficiency. *Federal Reserve Bank of Chicago Economic Perspectives*, 35(4):147–169, 2011.

Wang, Pengfei, Yi Wen, and Zhiwei Xu. What inventories tell us about aggregate fluctuations – a tractable approach to (S,s) policies. *Journal of Economic Dynamics and Control*, 44:196–217, 2014.

Watson, Mark W. Univariate detrending methods with stochastic trends. *Journal of Monetary Economics*, 18:49–75, 1986.

Inflation persistence, the NAIRU, and the Great Recession. *American Economic Review*, 104(5):31–36, 2014.

Wen, Yi. Understanding the inventory cycle. *Journal of Monetary Economics*, 52(8):1533–1555, 2005.

Woodford, Michael. *Interest and Prices: Foundations of a Theory of Monetary Policy.* Princeton University Press, Princeton, 2003.

Simple analytics of the government expenditure multiplier. *American Economic Journal: Macroeconomics*, 3 (1):1–35, 2011.

Working, Holbrook. Note on the correlation of first differences of averages in a random chain. *Econometrica*, 28(4):916–918, 1960.

Yun, Tack. Nominal price rigidity, money supply endogeneity, and business cycles. *Journal of Monetary Economics*, 37(2):345–370, 1996.

Zambelli, Stefano. A rocking horse that never rocked: Frisch's "Propagation problems and impulse problems". *History of Political Economy*, 39(1):145–166, 2007.

Zwick, Eric and James Mahon. Tax policy and heterogeneous investment behavior. *American Economic Review*, 107(1):217–48, 2017.

Index

www.ingramcontent.com/pod-product-compliance
Ingram Content Group UK Ltd.
Pitfield, Milton Keynes, MK11 3LW, UK
UKHW022222190125
453804UK00008B/223